THE GEOGRAPHY OF IDENTITY

Edited by Patricia Yaeger

Ann Arbor

THE UNIVERSITY OF MICHIGAN PRESS

Copyright © by the University of Michigan 1996
All rights reserved
Published in the United States of America by
The University of Michigan Press
Manufactured in the United States of America
⊗ Printed on acid-free paper

2001 2000 1999 1998   6 5 4 3

A CIP catalog record for this book is available from the British Library.

Library of Congress Cataloging-in-Publication Data

The geography of identity / edited by Patricia Yaeger.
        p.   cm. — (Ratio)
    ISBN 0-472-10672-4 (hardcover : alk. paper). — ISBN 0-472-08350-3
(pbk. : alk. paper)
    1. Identity. 2. Human geography. I. Yaeger, Patricia.
II. Series.
HM291.G398 1996-
304.2—dc20   96-3233
                                                        CIP

The Geography of Identity

RATIO
INSTITUTE FOR THE HUMANITIES
Edited by Tobin Siebers

EDITORIAL COMMITTEE:
Elaine K. Gazda
Mette Hjört
Michael D. Kennedy (interim)
Kendall L. Walton

> To take the measure of things and their
> mismeasure, to reason unto unreason, to
> suffer to count and to be accountable—such
> is the ratio of that form of life called the
> human.

Discourses of Sexuality: From Aristotle to AIDS
    Edited by Domna C. Stanton

Religion and the Authority of the Past
    Edited by Tobin Siebers

*Envisioning Eastern Europe: Postcommunist
    Cultural Studies*
    Edited by Michael D. Kennedy

Heterotopia: Postmodern Utopia and the Body Politic
    Edited by Tobin Siebers

The Geography of Identity
    Edited by Patricia Yaeger

In Memory of Marilyn Sibley Fries

Acknowledgments

It has been said that every story is a travel story, and the making of *The Geography of Identity* is no exception. This narrative began with the generous work of its sixteen authors, whose essays have brought unexpected pleasures and taught me a great deal about the delights and perils of rethinking the relationship between place and identity. This journey continued within the heady intellectual atmosphere provided by the University of Michigan's Institute for the Humanities, under the inspirational leadership of James Winn, with ample help from Mary Beecher Price and Eliza Woodford. Eliza became a fellow adventurer who offered much-appreciated support and advice in the playing fields of the new geography; she must be singled out for her extraordinary assistance on behalf of this volume. Thanks as well to the Office of the Vice President for Research and to the Office of Faculty Programs, Rackham Graduate School for their financial support of this volume and to Peg Lourie for her thoughtful and creative copyediting.

As this journey comes to an end, I would like to note a special debt of thanks to Tobin Siebers, the editor of the Ratio series, whose meticulous, patient suggestions for revision gave the introductory essay more weight and point. Finally, I want to thank Michael Awkward, Linda Gregerson, Marjorie Levinson, Anita Norich, Yopie Prins, and P. A. Skantze for a year of incredible conversations about the facticity and philosophy of social space. Their insights have made the work of editing this volume both more edifying and a great deal of fun.

—Patricia Yaeger

Contents

INTRODUCTION:
Narrating Space

Patricia Yaeger

The Strange Effects of Ordinary Space

The inspiration for this essay comes from a recent trip to Disney World—a trip marking my own changed relationship to geography, to social space. Introducing my three-year-old to one of the large cartoon characters who roam the edges of the park, I foolishly reached out to stroke its fake fur, hoping to demonstrate that these creatures are safe, that they invite interaction. Suddenly, a woman reached over and slapped my hand. Registering my confusion, she exclaimed, "Can't you see that my husband is taking a picture?" Teetering on the edge of obscenity, filled with vertigo in this dizzy space where adults behaved like three-year-olds and my daughter's three-year-old fears turned out to be quite grown up, I trudged into wonderland, into a play space so disciplined that its pathways had already been carved out by the leering sight-lines of a thousand camera eyes.

Having absorbed this new territorial imperative, we crossed the line dividing the Magic Kingdom from Epcot Center. Since I had read Baudrillard's critique of Disney and the simulacrum, I was inoculated against an enthusiast's obsession with Disney World as commodity paradise, immune to the bizarre effects of a postmodern Elysium constructed as the copy of a copy, a world in which imitative space can seem more palpable, more desirable and real than its origins, than "reality" itself. And so I strode into Epcot's multinationed "World Showcase" and courageously purchased nothing; I braved that "wonderland of 11 nations surrounding a beautiful lagoon ... the nighttime setting for the breathtaking 'Illumi-Nations,' presented by G.E."

And then we reached the Chinese Pavilion, the replica of an ancient place of worship in Beijing, the Hall of Prayer for Good Harvest. This temple-clone was breathtaking; its inner sanctum had been hollowed out to simulcast a movie whose optical unconscious might have wooed Benjamin himself. The political and topographical complexities of each of China's territories were instantly revealed in 360 degrees of celluloid transcendence: the movie swept through the time and space of Chinese history in ten minutes flat. Driven by this extraordinary space-time compression, the audience was attacked from all sides by Mongol hordes, awed by crowd-crushing mountains, hungered by the populous beauty of Beijing's busy streets. This film was not simply designed to celebrate human monumentality but to give the Disney audience a colonizer's vacation in a cloud-country other than its own.

Trying hard to maintain an attitude of critique, I experienced rush after rush of phantom pleasure, until the projector paused, and across the screen floated a single, still photograph of the temple itself—the original Chinese structure built during the Ming dynasty. Stung by its beauty, I turned to my sister, pointed to the image hovering on the screen, and asked, "Nancy, isn't that a copy of the building we're standing in now?"

My sister gave me a puzzled look, while I felt a bizarre combination of shame and elation. Despite my best efforts, I had begun to embody the very postmodern practices I had planned to critique. What is it about space that invites self-forgetting, that solicits these delicious misprisions about boundaries, origins, solidarity, and the politics of community? Why did I find the "themed" space of Disney World so seductive, so persuasive?

In an effort to catalogue the deceptive fullness of empty space, Baudrillard describes a fable of Borges in which "the cartographers of the Empire" draw a map so complete in every detail that it becomes a substitute for the territory it was meant to describe: even the map's edges begin to decay in just those places where empire gives way to desert or alienated colony. For Baudrillard this strange act of mimesis in which "the real" disappears and an imitation takes its place is not a tall tale but a description of ordinary space: an encomium or memento mori for a world flooded with simulation.

> Simulation is no longer [the imitation of] a territory, a referential being or a substance. It is the generation by models of a real without origin or reality: a hyperreal.... If we were to revive the fable today, it would be the territory whose shreds are slowly rotting across the map. It is the real, and not the map, whose vestiges subsist here and there, in the deserts

which are no longer those of the Empire, but our own. *The desert of the real itself.*[1]

According to Baudrillard's theorem I had entered this desert of forgetting by finding the copy more persuasive, more real than the imagined plenitude of the Chinese original—which was only a floating photograph anyway, a de-realized image of a thing that in its copied state was already punctured with duplicity, de-created in this hollow duet with its American double.

There are other paths into this desert. In *The Archaeology of Knowledge* Foucault echoes Baudrillard's dismal geography when he spatializes the historian's journey "beyond familiar territory" in search of a method transcending Enlightenment categories. Letting go of the maps of the past, Foucault hopes to discover "a full, tightly packed, continuous, geographically well-defined field of objects," but finds only the cartography of forgetting: an empty space "full of gaps, intertwined with one another," a new and despairing intellectual terrain.[2] For Foucault the danger of this new epistemology is the possibility that the West's "ground of thinking"—the spatial basis for thought itself—will be lost:

> Instead of providing a basis for what already exists ... instead of finding reassurances ... that all is saved, one is forced to advance beyond familiar territory, far from the certainties to which one is accustomed, towards an as yet uncharted land and unforeseeable conclusion. Is there not a danger that everything that has so far protected the historian in his daily journey and accompanied him until nightfall ... may disappear, leaving for analysis a blank, indifferent space, lacking in both interiority and promise? (38–39)

Is it any wonder that we cling to the simulacrum?

In search of an antidote, we need to consider other ways of characterizing the communal spaces of late capitalism. First,

---

[1] Jean Baudrillard, *Selected Writings*, ed. Mark Poster (Stanford: Stanford University Press, 1988) 166.

[2] Michel Foucault, *The Archaeology of Knowledge*, trans. A. M. Sheridan Smith (New York: Pantheon, 1972) 37. Subsequent page numbers are incorporated in the text.

we must recognize that Foucault and Baudrillard are partially right in their despair; in its copious physicality, ordinary space resists traditional patterns of narrative. Space is a fragmentary field of action, a jurisdiction scattered and deranged, which appears to be negotiable or continuous but is actually peppered with chasms of economic and cultural disjunctions. In contrast, time has seemed, until recently, consolingly linear. While temporal narratives (like histories or chronologies) offer a comforting seriality that initiates the queuelike patterns of traditional narrative, space moves out in all directions at once, and it is difficult to imagine a narrative structure capable of capturing this multiplicity.[3] We know, of course, from the work of historians like Hayden White, that temporal or historical narration is much more problematic than it appears, since the orderliness of time relies on its own supreme fictions. When the historian plunges into the historical record, the resulting story depends on inherited plots, for the narratives told by historians build on received cultural myths. Since historians begin to assimilate these conventions from the earliest moments of childhood and since representations of historical events depend upon communal myths, White concludes that "there are ... 'rules' if not 'laws' of historical narration."[4]

Are there "rules" if not "laws" driving the narration of space? If ordinary space can be scripted as heterogeneous and multidimensional, refusing the simplicity of linear narrative, if local politics can be concealed or immersed in tropes of tragedy and romance or in the figures of void and simulacrum, space has an additional political-psychological dimension. The physical world is also a site where unrequited desires, bizarre ideologies, and hidden productivities are encrypted, so that any narration of space must confront the dilemma of geographic enigmas head on, including the enigma of what gets forgotten, or hidden, or lost in the comforts of ordinary space.[5]

---

[3] Doreen Massey produces a wonderful overview of these issues in "Politics and Space/Time" in *Place and the Politics of Identity*, ed. Michael Keith and Steve Pile (New York: Routledge, 1993) 141–61.

[4] Hayden White, *Tropics of Discourse: Essays in Cultural Criticism* (Baltimore: Johns Hopkins University Press, 1978) 59. Subsequent page numbers are incorporated in the text.

[5] There is now a rich and diverse literature distinguishing space from place. For example, in "Creating Places or Designing Spaces?" *Journal of Envi-*

This vision of lost or encrypted space suggests two directions for analysis. First, to get an overview of contemporary thinking about space, we need to explore the insights and methods of the new cultural geography: its recognition that the dominant modes of talking about space conceal its social basis. But we also need to risk a more personal or phenomenological approach to representations of the local. Although the minimal outline for a cultural geography suggests that space must be recognized as a social product that relentlessly reproduces the social, the pressure to recover what is repressed or forgotten in space demands more than a new sociology. The omnipresence of political encryption requires a new self-consciousness about the relation of place and narration: it demands the invention of a poetics of geography: a site for investigating the metaphors and narrative strategies that we use to talk about space. The invention of such a poetics will require, above all, a rhetoric that can unearth the strange effects of ordinary space: place-centered narration not only refocuses our attention on the ways in which place is political; it necessitates the geographic

---

ronmental Psychology 6 (1986) Jonathan D. Sime argues that "place" is a term that "implies a strong emotional tie ... between a person and a particular physical location," while space is associated with an abstract or geometric vision of the built environment (50). But while place is associated with the heimlich work of self-construction versus the unheimlich anonymity of "space," theorists like David Harvey turn these terms on end: "The capacity of most social movements to command place better than space puts a strong emphasis upon the potential connection between places and social identity" but also creates a new kind of pressure on social movements. "The consequent dilemmas of socialist or working-class movements in the face of a universalizing capitalism are shared by other oppositional groups—racial minorities, colonized peoples, women, etc.—who are relatively empowered to organize in place but disempowered when it comes to organizing over space." Regional resistance (a passion for place) can become part of the fragmenting drive that transnational capitalism and flexible accumulation feed upon. David Harvey, The Condition of Postmodernity (Cambridge, MA: Blackwell, 1990) 302–3. Hence the slippage between space and place in my own essay. In a global economy where multiple places converge in a single space, where the space/place binary becomes porous and provisional, we need to destabilize the organicism and integrity that place-centered analysis sometimes assumes, to recognize within a transnational economy the strange effects that happen in the margins between "space" and "place."

equivalent of the ghost story—an awareness of the irreducible strangeness of space and a narrative capable of addressing its encryption.[6]

Virginia Woolf captures this irreducible strangeness in her parable of Judith Shakespeare from *A Room of One's Own.* Here Woolf imagines that William Shakespeare had an equally talented sister who was refused access to the stage because of her gender. Denied the power to use her great gift for poetry, she finds herself alone in London, where "Nick Greene the actor-manager took pity on her; she found herself with child by that gentleman and so—who shall measure the heat and violence of the poet's heart when caught and tangled in a woman's body?—killed herself one winter's night and lies buried at some cross-roads where the omnibuses now stop outside the Elephant and Castle."[7] By inserting Judith Shakespeare's pregnant body into the space of the present, Woolf achieves two concurrent goals. First, by making Shakespeare's sister a ghost haunting the local omnibus, Woolf invents an analogue for the geographical crypt: Judith Shakespeare becomes an exemplum of the stories hidden in normative space. Second, within her hypothetical grave Woolf creates a ghostly inspiration for a communal politics. She invents an emblem of feminist collectivity: the feminist equivalent of the Tomb of the Unknown Soldier. Benedict Anderson invokes the nameless emptiness of this civic tomb as a state-sponsored echo chamber "saturated with ghostly *national* imaginings."[8] In Woolf's text empty space (the absence of women from poetic or commercial history) is also filled with ghostly *gendered* imaginings, with forgotten relationships. Her point is not only that subjects who are absent from history must be granted temporality and ex-

---

[6] This ghost story is wonderfully dramatized in Yi-Fu Tuan's redefinition of place in "Place and Culture: Analeptic for Individuality and the World's Indifference" in *Mapping American Culture*, ed. Wayne Franklin and Michael Steiner (Iowa City: University of Iowa Press, 1992). Tuan complicates the notion of encrypted space by reminding us that the materiality of place can provide a blessed forgetting. "Place helps us forget our separateness and the world's indifference. More generally speaking, culture makes this amnesia possible" by integrating us into a world of shared language and custom (44).

[7] Virginia Woolf, *A Room of One's Own* (New York: Harcourt Brace Jovanovich, 1929) 48.

[8] Benedict Anderson, *Imagined Communities* (London: Verso, 1983) 17.

tension in space but that we can use these crypts to reconstruct a radical politics.

After Woolf, Foucault may be the "master" narrator of
spatial cryptography; he offers a springboard from which to
leap into a description of the ghostly effects of ordinary places.
Confirming Woolf's description of the geographical crypt, Foucault argues that we still entertain delusional notions about
what happens when bodies converge in everyday space. Although world-historical events seem to take place on a pro-
scenium where contending forces "leap from the wings to center stage each in its youthful strength," the place where these
encounters happen should not be imagined as a closed field
"offering the spectacle of a struggle among equals." The stage
of history is much stranger; it is a "void, a space that di-
vides"—a place of nonencounter, then, or even worse, "a 'non-
place,' a pure distance which indicates that adversaries do not
belong to a common space."[9]

Foucault's refusal of the physical continuities of place
evacuates the trope of the level playing field, resulting in the
startling suggestion that there may be no field at all, and Baudrillard seconds this suggestion in his analysis of the simulacrum as hollow, imitative space. But in *The Production of Space*
Lefebvre supplements these theories with a third approach to
the problem of narrating space. Like Woolf, he suggests that
the dominant ways of talking about space legislate acts of forgetting: space simulates or "appears as 'reality' inasmuch as it
is the milieu of accumulation" or growth, of commodity exchange or capital; but "this 'reality' loses its substantial and
autonomous aspect," its veneer of naturalization once its development or its production is traced.[10] For Lefebvre, modern
places must be reinterpreted within the complex thematics of
"abstract space"—that homogeneous realm manufactured by
an immense network of banking systems, business conglom-
erates, and information lattices that produce state and com-

---

[9] Michel Foucault, "Nietzsche, Genealogy, History," in *Language,
Counter-Memory, Practice: Selected Essays and Interviews*, ed. Donald F.
Bouchard (Ithaca: Cornell University Press, 1977) 150. Subsequent page
numbers are incorporated in the text.

[10] Henri Lefebvre, *The Production of Space*, trans. Donald Nicholson-
Smith (Oxford: Blackwell, 1991) 129. Subsequent page numbers are incorporated in the text.

mercial power. In this dense spatial grid, the nation-state not only functions as a horizon of power in which decisions are made to safeguard the interests of select minorities; these interests are imposed so effectively that they become "indistinguishable from the general interest" (218). If this description of a docile, well-disciplined world sounds familiar, Lefebvre gives his thesis an unexpected twist. He argues that the disciplinary framework of state power is neither discursive nor discourse-driven. Rather, "sovereignty implies space": that is, space can be defined as that necessary zone where power achieves its concreteness (280). With its naturalized hierarchies and economic asymmetries, politicized space operates as a field of opportunity for the exercise of hegemony, but it also functions as a scrim or veil concealing the relentless push of sovereign power.

If sovereignty requires space to survive, its politicized places—those everyday sites where power is promulgated—become the very domain where the politics of space is forgotten. Each new form of political power partitions space in its own way, constructing a set of classifications that "makes it possible for a certain type of non-critical thought simply to register the resultant 'reality' and accept it at face value" (280). Lefebvre, then, outlines the psychological difficulty that a new poetics of geography will encounter—the inevitability of spatial amnesia. He refuses to view space as a neutral, isometric grid, observing that each place is a social product that laboriously masks the contradictions of the social.[11]

Baudrillard, Foucault, and Lefebvre create a grotesque threshold for the new geography's social themes. They not only emplot the epistemology of ordinary space as tragedy; they invent figures of the counterfeit, the void, and forgotten space because these images mobilize communal archetypes of calamity or catastrophe that seem to capture the geographic dysphoria of the postmodern world. What are the repercus-

---

[11] While conceding that the state is a framework of epistemic power, Lefebvre adds that "we must not forget that the framework in question is a spatial one. If no account is taken of this spatial framework, and of its strength, we are left with a state that is simply a rational unity—in other words we revert to Hegelianism. Without the concepts of space and of its production, the framework of power (whether as reality or concept) simply cannot achieve concreteness" (281).

sions of these generic choices for the analysis of social space? Why is the postmodern object world perpetually arrayed in metaphors of emptiness, vacuity, or amnesia? Is this an adequate response to the crisis in translocality, globalization, deterritorialization, and postcolonization that has changed the face of the earth? Do these metaphors describe the emptying out of space, or are they really ciphers for the evacuation of old spatial categories? Finally, why are these metaphors so enthralling?[12] To understand the power of these and other spatial metaphors, we will need to rethink the narrative dimensions of the strange effects of ordinary space, to fathom the idea of place as forgetting, and to appreciate the lexical/indexical powers that geographical figures have to reinvent spatial memory.

The Table Vanishes

Empty space not only haunts Foucault, Baudrillard, and Lefebvre; it haunts a passel of other postmodern theorists. We have to ask why the trope of abandonment, blankness, vacancy, or void appears willy-nilly, whether we are contemplating the archival provinces of poststructuralist history, the hyperreal world of commodity fetishism, or the uncivil world of political action. We find a provisional answer in Hannah Arendt's description of the public realm as a place that has ceased to hold its citizens together. For Arendt, we possess an intimate, ever-changing relation to habitable space: "Whatever touches or enters into a sustained relationship with human life immediately assumes the character of a condition of human existence."[13] While common objects condition us, we also rely

---

[12] These questions are not meant to deny the accuracy of Foucault's description of phantom space—the world's unreality as a "non-place" of seismic interaction. The alienation effect inherent in these figures is poignant and frightening; Baudrillard, Foucault, and Lefebvre invent a radical topography that alerts us to what is sleeping in space. But my suggestion is that we also need to analyze the rhetorical power that these new spatial metaphors possess.

[13] Hannah Arendt, *The Human Condition* (Chicago: University of Chicago Press, 1958) 9. Subsequent page numbers are incorporated in the text.

on communal intimacy—on "the presence of others who see what we see and hear what we hear" to reassure us about "the reality of the world and ourselves" (50).

If Arendt describes a world of shared interests and objects that sets the conditions for collective identity, she also insists on the radical undoing of this common world: "To live together in the world means essentially that a world of things is between those who have it in common as a table is located between those who sit around it; the world, like every in-between, relates and separates at the same time." The world of shared things has a magical velocity that gathers people in a nonepic way and "prevents our falling over each other" (52). In contrast, life within mass society legislates vertigo not only because of its vast numbers of people but because "the world between them has lost its power to gather them together, to relate and to separate them" (53). When the world ceases to offer the comforting illusion of dwelling in common, it changes meaning-filled places into the derangements of anonymous space—a crisis that Arendt typifies through the conceit of the vanishing table:

> The weirdness of this situation resembles a spiritualistic seance where a number of people gathered around a table might suddenly, through some magic trick, see the table vanish from their midst, so that two persons sitting opposite each other were no longer separated but also would be entirely unrelated to each other by anything tangible. (53)

The table and its rhetoric have disappeared from our midst, and we confront a new revolution in social space. This revolution is partly physical, reflecting cataclysmic changes in the corporeal world. But it is also conceptual. Why has the spatial world—the dislocated realm of the table and its dissociated denizens—become such an indispensable category of social and cultural analysis? Why space now?

1. *Deterritorialization.* First and most obviously, the boundaries of the physical world have shifted drastically—enforcing the need for new ways to talk about space. Endless examples come to mind, including a recent "Name-That-Era" contest sponsored by *The New York Times Week in Review*:

Which of the disparate threads of this time will be woven together by future historians in defining the era? The technologies or the hatreds? The holy wars? The markets? *The
Week in Review* invites suggestions for a name for the post
post-cold war era. Send them in by March 24 to Era, Box
957, *The New York Times*.[14]

Confronted by the quick metamorphosis of localities into translocalities, by the rapid unmooring of nations and peoples in
real time and space, why does *The Times* adopt a cereal-box
rhetoric? In *The Condition of Postmodernity*, David Harvey explains the narrative crisis brought about by modern deterritorialization. He argues that the apocalyptics of postmodern
space will only become more acute as the asymmetrical distribution of wealth exacerbated by Fordism is heightened by the
scattershot effects of global assembly lines and flexible accumulation. The result is a labor-intensive, union-free society
hooked on the instant: instant commodities, instant values,
instant lifestyles. When the panic of space-time compression is
coupled with a new nirvana—with the floating disposability of
the commodity world and the purgatorial deprivations of a migratory global work-force—the result is a sensory overload of
"acute geopolitical" proportions in which consciousness cannot
catch up with swift transformations in space and time. Under
such rapidly changing conditions "there is an omni-present
danger that our mental maps will not match current realities,"
and the result is an increased hystericization of space.[15]

The quest for a public language that will make simple the
complex connections between space and time, between holog-
raphy and holy wars, seems entirely symptomatic of this overwhelming need to invent a new space-time imaginary. As *The
Times*'s reporter hieratically intones: "With the increased pace
of change, the need to impose a narrative on events becomes

---

[14] "Pinpointing a Moment on the Map of History," *The New York Times,
Week in Review*, 24 March 1995, 5. Subsequent page numbers are incorporated in the text.

[15] Harvey, *The Condition of Postmodernity* 306. Subsequent page numbers are incorporated in the text. Harvey details this hysteria quite exactly. He
argues that "localism and nationalism have become stronger precisely because
of the quest for the security that place always offers in the midst of all the
shifting that flexible accumulation implies" (306).

more urgent than ever. To name an era is to classify what otherwise feels random, to give what is still indistinct a clear identity" (1). In search of such an identity, the rhetoric of the "Name-That-Era" contest is obsessed with turning time into space: "What about the era we find ourselves in now?" "Isn't this obsession ... another way of acknowledging that we don't know where we are?" (1).

2. *Losing the Temporal.* If the experience of everyday time has shifted beneath the siege of space-time compression, the experience of scholarly time has shifted as well. In demolishing the comforts of end-directed time or teleology, a number of philosophers (Arendt and Foucault among them) have also demolished the narrative salvation of history. In order to destroy generic history once and for all Foucault disparages the consolation of births, beginnings, and lost origins, while Arendt refuses finales—the consolation of deaths and endings.[16] As Foucault suggests, "the purpose of history, guided by genealogy, is not to discover the roots of our identity but to commit itself to its dissipation" (162). Have scholars turned to space in pursuit of an ever-receding prospect: the need for a stable home, an undissipated ground of being that might secure their analysis? As time's reliable design fades from view and its linear pleasures (winged with their dreams of cradles and closures) become less certain, suddenly space—time's earthy twin and Enlightenment double—heaves into view as a potential site of physical continuity and analytic constancy.

3. *Losing the Local.* The object world also looms large when the local seems in need of protection. A workman who visited

---

16 In "Nietzsche, Genealogy, History" Foucault dissolves the conceptual apparatus that attaches to the concept of beginning. Instead of the "Wunderursprung," the miraculous origin sought by historical excavations, origin becomes plurality, a simultaneity of "myriad events" that simply grow out of "the exteriority of accidents" (146). In contrast, Arendt critiques the violence of endings. If history is "the object of a process of fabrication or making, there must come a moment when this 'object' is completed, and ... if one imagines that one can 'make history,' one cannot escape the consequence that there will be an end to history. Whenever we hear of grandiose aims in politics, such as establishing a new society in which justice will be guaranteed forever, or fighting a war to end all wars ... we are moving in the realm of this kind of thinking." Hannah Arendt, "The Concept of History: Ancient and Modern," *Between Past and Future* (New York: Penguin, 1977) 79.

my home on the day of the bombing of the Oklahoma City Federal building insisted that the bombing was initiated to prove a
point by some gruesome and anonymous "they": "The idea," he
said, "is that they can get to the middle. Just think, Oklahoma
is 1,000 miles from either coast." As we talked, the terror of
this event triggered a need in both of us to transform our most
basic spatial vocabularies. Margins have long been the conventional sites of plurality and vulnerability, while middles
have seemed solid, rooted, nonplural. As the parameters that
we use to evaluate space fall apart, the complexity of reproducing the local seems especially precarious: an obsession with
space and its objects becomes paramount.

   4. *The Hermeneutics of Suspicion.* In his book on Freud,
Paul Ricoeur describes Marx, Nietzsche, and Freud as three
masters of the school of suspicion, "great destroyers" who have
taught us the art of interpreting. Well versed in the business of
unmasking error, illusion, false-consciousness, and political
mythology, the scholar must take on the new task of negation:
of reversing the relation hidden/shown.[17]

   In this vale of suspicion, space remains one of the last
great "frontiers." After demystifying religion, economics, consciousness, and language, after refuting the naturalization of
the body and the suppositions of the natural sciences, after
unmasking the norms of race, gender, sexuality, and nationality, where can we turn but to space itself, to that named and
unnamable anchor that seems to moor both nations and bodies in place?

   But while the hermeneutics of suspicion turns practi-
tioners away from essentialism, universalism, and other forms
of metadiscourse, the metanarrative turn has not vanished altogether in contemporary spatial cartographies—nor should it
vanish.[18] New local conditions and the pressures of globaliza-

---

[17] This characterization of the hermeneutics of suspicion is described in
more detail by Paul Ricoeur in *Freud and Philosophy: An Essay on Interpretation*, trans. Denis Savage (New Haven: Yale University Press, 1970) 32ff.

[18] In other words, there is room in the new geography for both
"macrotheory" and the work of deconstruction. Best and Kellner summarize
the need to synthesize these conflicting trends. Since "postmodern theory
tends to map in fragments and to ignore the more systemic features and relations of social structure that were the focus of modern social theory," as remedy they suggest an admixture of theoretical positions capable of mapping

tion require both skepticism and inclusive social theorems capable of exploring the place-centeredness of social being. For example, Saskia Sassen's *The Global City* sets out to redefine the nature of urban life even as it deconstructs current truisms about nationalism.

Sassen argues that cities as historically diverse as New York, London, and Tokyo have experienced similar economic transformations in a very brief period of time, placing them at the very axis of economic power.[19] "Constituting a system rather than merely competing with each other" (8–9), these cities share an intriguing career path; each has become an administrative hub that manages the wealth produced by global assembly lines. This rapid massing of power has produced dire results for individual wage-laborers and for the political alliances of city governments, especially their economic coupling with the imagined space of the nation-state, since "what contributes to growth in the network of global cities may well not contribute to growth in nations" (8–9). Global cities

---

"the broader features of social organization and conflicts" while preserving the poststructuralist "features of fragmentation and various micro-domains." Steven Best and Douglas Kellner, *Postmodern Theory: Critical Interrogations* (New York: Guilford Press, 1991) 259.

[19] Sassen describes three disturbing new trends: 1) Urban growth has resulted in the need for a "vast supply of low-wage jobs required by high-income gentrification." Paradoxically, this expansion of low-wage work has occurred as a function of growth and suggests the de-invention of progressive relations between capital and labor. 2) The global city also represents a nexus of paranational power. Major cities like Detroit, Manchester, and Osaka have lost their vigor as "leading export centers for industrial manufacturing" while financial centers capable of managing global production and markets are thriving. This creates new urban triangulations in which a city like New York plays a more pronounced role in the fortunes of Detroit (as a mere cog in the worldwide assembly line) than before. 3) Global telecommunication has not created a dispersal of population and resources (the anticipated dissemination of the good life) because it demands a new logic of concentration in which the assembly of products in shops and depots around the world requires the consolidation of wealth in global cities. The dispersal of production results not only in lower wages for labor but in an increasing need for "centralization and complexity of management" (10). Saskia Sassen, *The Global City: New York, London, Tokyo* (Princeton: Princeton University Press, 1991). Subsequent page numbers are incorporated in the text.

contain, then, an "agglomeration" of service industries resulting in a staggering concentration of power: a concentration
that demands new theorems about urban space even as it invites new forms of geographical skepticism—a hermeneutics of
spatial suspicion.

5. *An Escape Route from Binary Thinking.* Social geography's insistence on the interstitial, hybrid nature of place—its
refusal to conceptualize location as either ethnically or ideologically bounded—also offers an important antidote to some of
the dead-end binarisms within cultural studies. In *The Rhetoric
of English India* Sara Suleri includes these binaries among the
narratives of anxiety that emerge from the colonial system.
Here Hayden White's suggestion that historians rely upon
common topoi or cultural archetypes to obtain an "explanatory
affect" lending their narratives recognizable social meaning
may be extended to cultural critics. Although cultural studies
has a strong social history of unmasking cultural-academic
norms, it shares with Anglo-Indian fiction the topos of romance—a genre that reorganizes "the materiality of colonialism
into a narrative of perpetual longing and perpetual loss."[20]
Thus colonizing narratives divide themselves along binary lines
describing either the colonizer's terrified encounter with otherness (a terror that translates into the frightening "unreadability of the colonized subcontinent") or the antithetical "will to
cultural description" (insisting that colonized peoples are
completely "interpretable within the language of the colonizer").
But Suleri argues that cultural studies is also captivated by
romance; it is a discipline enthralled with its own tales of otherness (6–7). Held captive by alterity, cultural studies reinvents
the story it sets out to critique and may reproduce "a theoretical repetitiveness that finally entrenches rather than displaces
the rigidity of the self/other binarism already governing traditional colonial discourses" (11).

The new social geography offers a useful antidote to this
agonistic cultural thinking.[21] As Henri Lefebvre asks, "How

---

[20] Sara Suleri, *The Rhetoric of English India* (Chicago: University of Chicago Press, 1992) 10. Subsequent page numbers are incorporated in the text.

[21] For Suleri the "emptiness of geography" in Forster's description of the
Marabar caves in *A Passage to India* forces "cultural description into a recognition of its own vacuity" (145). I would add that the turn to social geography need not end in a void; it can also mimic Forster's invention of a geogra-

many maps, in the descriptive or geographical sense, might be needed to deal exhaustively with a given space, to code and decode all its meanings and contents? It is doubtful whether a finite number can ever be given in answer to this sort of question." Presented with an "instant infinity" or "an unlimited multiplicity," geography not only has to contend with the law of uneven development, but "the intertwinement of social spaces is also a law" (86).

Insofar as location represents a concatenation of social spaces, insofar as it represents a physical site that is continuous, contradictory, convoluted, splintered, layered, and inconsistent, insofar as the borderland displaces traditional descriptions of normative, nuclear space, social geography creates a site for studying social identity more intricate than the discourse of alterity, with its rigid self/other dichotomies, can suggest.

6. *Reterritorialization.* Finally, if the new obsession with social space heals an old fascination with alterity, it also remobilizes dreams of a transnational, translocal habitus. If locality is especially beleaguered in a deterritorialized world, this does not imply a cosmos in which the local is lost, a cosmos without neighborhoods, beyond consolation. Although there was once an unproblematic link between identity and place, this link has been healthily severed by our growing recognition of the hybrid nature of all localities and the arduous cultural work required to maintain local customs.[22]

---

phy that recognizes the hollowness of traditional cartography: a mobile antidote to binary explanations.

[22] For a description of the hybridity of the local see Akhil Gupta and James Fergusson, "Beyond 'Culture': Space, Identity, and the Politics of Difference," *Cultural Anthropology* 7 (1992): 7. Subsequent page numbers are incorporated in the text. For a discussion of the complexity of reproducing the local see also Arjun Appadurai's "The Production of Locality" in *Counterwork,* ed. Richard Fardon (London: Routledge, 1995) 204–25. Appadurai proposes that reterritorialization is an ongoing process, since "all locality-building" refers to an initiating moment of colonization that demands repetition if a new culture is to survive (208). Since locality is "an inherently fragile social achievement" (205), he asks anthropologists to reexamine daily activities like house-building or garden cultivation as social techniques for reproducing the material world and those structures of feeling that support the reinvention of the local. Although we inhabit an increasingly conflictual world in which

This is to suggest that the turn to geography, place studies, or an obsession with social terrain can also represent an
act of progressive political intervention. If the invention of a
transnational public sphere makes the concept of bounded
communities or localities obsolete, this invention also challenges any symptomatic nostalgia for a world of lost objects
and alterities. As Akhil Gupta and James Fergusson have argued, obsolescence does not mean utter loss, since the translocal world sanctions new forms of solidarity and identity independent of those familiar, ideologically bound habitats "where
contiguity and face-to-face contact are paramount" (9). In the
pulverized space of postmodernity, locality has not "become
irrelevant: it has been reterritorialized in a way that does not
conform to the experience of space that characterized the era
of high modernity." This lack of conformity "forces us to recon-
ceptualize fundamentally the politics of community, solidarity,
identity, and cultural difference" (9).

Suddenly, a life lived within one set of conceptual parameters confronts a terrain in need of new concepts. At best, these
fresh markers of spatial community become the site for renewed political action. At worst, they become melancholy
place-markers for the absence of an older world. We return,
then, to Arendt's concern for the vanishing table. If the dream
of a world of common things or shared materiality has vanished, what has taken its place? I want to suggest that one
strategy of reterritorialization, as well as one of the most
strenuous and omnipresent place-markers of postmodern locality, is the hypersaturated, hypergratifying, hypercommodi-
fied presence of "themed" or prenarrated space.

---

reterritorialization is particularly challenging, Appadurai also argues that localities have begun to fracture and regroup along a new set of fault lines.
These are characterized by 1) an intensification of the struggle between localities and the homogenizing influence of the nation-state, 2) the recent growth of
exorbitant patterns of migration and deterritorialization, and 3) the explosion
of technologies into new forms of electronic telepathy that create complex an-
tagonisms between "spatial and virtual neighborhoods" (231). These contesta-
tions of the local require the invention of increasingly complex theoretical tools
for analyzing social space.

Themed Space

Why do people want to visit, to dwell within, a space that is extrinsically storied or narrated? What is the lure of themed space? As space that is precolonized and prefabricated around an idea or point of view, a themed land suggests a subject of representation that is blatant, repetitious, and blandly revelatory. For example, the brochures inviting client-earthlings to Disney World are filled with the promise of "theming," the pledge of space endowed with a motif, thesis, topic, or argument. The Magic Kingdom not only duplicates the solace of home and community where "you can see Mickey and his 'Disney Afternoon' TV friends in person," "where Mickey Mouse keeps house," but this space is deliberately hyperarticulated: there are seven "themed 'lands' of delightful attractions filled with ... that delightful Disney charm that remains unmatched!"[23] Clever theming guarantees coherence and readability and, as an ecstatic bonus, has the capacity to be embodied or expanded; themes promise communal plenitude and coherent extension in space, as if Arendt's common table might magically reappear.

We have been considering two related questions. First, why space now? Why are scholars from a range of disciplines suddenly reinvested in the energetic pursuit of geography? Second, how should we go about inventing a new poetics of geography: a set of narrative strategies that capture the strange effects of ordinary space as well as the political dimensions of place as a praxis? With these questions in mind, I want to turn to a geographical site that embodies the narrative problem at the heart of the postmodern commodity world: the prevalence—and the preposterousness—of inhabiting "themed" space.

Themed space is not only coherent and analyzable: it tries to be convincing. Themes express concepts or doctrines that are "persuasive" to their audience. But theming gratifies much more than a whimsical desire for homogenized, coherent space; it suggests a longing for incorporation, a longing to inhabit credible space. What does it take for space to be convincing? In

---

[23] Advertisement, "Walt Disney World Resort Has It All," *Florida Roadmap: A Gousha Travel Publication*, n.d.

the absence of the support systems provided by communal life, costumes, props, and crowded stage settings help, and thus a whirl of costume dramas and artificial backdrops have invaded our lives. Consider the bogus effects of the real in these program notes written by fashion designer Marina Spadafora to promote her new collection:

> It's the ancient beating of Africa, the inspiration of the new collection: urban Africa ... downtown Dakar or maybe Nairobi. Odd characters in multicolored atmosphere: mercenary soldiers on secret mission, schoolgirls in school uniforms, prostitutes in colored dresses.[24]

Dan Rather and Morley Safer try to create another version of costume drama as spatial certitude by showing up in safari jackets to interview ghetto toughs and federal prisoners—as if to emphasize their ability to brave the urban jungle with only a microphone in hand. The prison stripes that have just been adopted in Alabama's state prisons represent an even more frightening example of the "reality effects" that politicians manufacture to connect with their constituencies. Wearing prison stripes and leg irons, Alabama's prisoners are now forced to withstand the horror of the chain gang; they participate in a hellish tableau designed to convince Alabama's white citizens that law and order prevails. Each of these dehumanizing citations creates a mirage of credibility, but these citations also have the effect of reminding us that locality is invented—an effect of semiplausible quotation and reiteration.

The advent of incredibility—the loss of "persuasive" space that can guarantee solidity and solidarity or produce comforting "reality effects"—is one of the many casualties of the 1995 bombing of the Federal building in Oklahoma City. Why did so many Oklahomans react to this tragedy by expressing an obsessive concern not only with geography but with whether the space that they inhabited was real? "One by one they said the same thing: this does not happen here. It happens in countries so far away, so different, they might as well be on the dark side of the moon. It happens in New York. It happens in Europe." Even the *New York Times* reporter played to the drama of dismayed credibility, insisting that terrorism could not happen "in

---

a city that has a sign just outside the city limits 'Oklahoma City, home of Vince Gill,' a country singer."[25]

The *Philadelphia Inquirer* expanded the scope of the tragedy in an ironic cartoon showing a map of the U.S. with a dozen coastal and midsection cities all labeled "Oklahoma City," thereby displacing the much-reproduced *New Yorker* cover where New York as global city takes up the majority of national space.[26] "It just all came apart," said a woman living in an apartment building next to the bomb site. Her words suggest a double precariousness: first, a sense that place is too brittle—that neither her apartment nor the surrounding city can be reproduced in real time or space; and second, an intimation that materiality is not just solid but also imaginary—that place only persuades us because it is made out of reiterated stories and objects that produce a constant, pervasive sense of locatability.

In this fragile climate Disney has become a premier site of cultural analysis; its motifs reiterate the spatial longings played out in the media after the Oklahoma bombing. In Disney World space not only attempts to be persuasive; it is also *designed* to be brittle, to shatter on contact. Thus, "Disney's newest resort," Port Orleans, is a place blending "the exquisite charm of the French Quarter with Disney magic.... It has a cleverly-themed food court, family restaurant, close proximity to all three Theme Parks." The dream of a Bourbon Street that is family-friendly pales beside this colonizing fantasy of immediacy, presence, proximity, nearness (a consumer's short-cut to reterritorialization).[27] In these spaces that

---

[25] "In Shock, Loathing, Denial: 'This Doesn't Happen Here'," *The New York Times*, 20 April 1995, 1.

[26] *The Philadelphia Inquirer*, 29 April 1995. The cartoon suggests that Henri Lefebvre's vision of interchangeable space in the reign of capitalism has been brought to a grisly conclusion. Within abstract, commodified space "the entirety of space must be endowed with exchange value. And exchange implies interchangeability.... The commodity world and its characteristics, which formerly encompassed only goods and things produced in space, now govern space as a whole" (336–37).

[27] This dream of painless intimacy is the mirror image of the narcissistic fantasies driving American politics today. As the United States representative to the United Nations Madeleine Albright said of Republican attempts to cut U.N. funding: "Maybe their problem with the U.N. is that there are just too

open onto one another and self-destruct at a touch, Bourbon Street becomes a scrim that gives way to Epcot's "IllumiNations" or Mickey's playhouse. In this phantasm of intimacy everything alien and far away becomes self-referential, close up, and local, while everything local seems to submit to the alien.

This is phantasmatic space that makes use of its hollowness to create the dream of closeness or proximity: it is a simulacrum with a vengeance. But are there other ways to describe the experience of inhabiting the brittle, all-too-breakable space of the postmodern façade? I want to argue that our enjoyment of themed space depends on a series of strange effects, most notably on the sublimation of catastrophe. Michel de Certeau illuminates this sublimation capturing the intense migratory spaces of Disney in his suggestion that urban walking is both transient and unreal:

> To walk is to lack a place. It is the indefinite process of being absent and in search of a proper. The moving about that the city multiplies and concentrates makes the city itself an immense social experience of lacking a place—an experience, that is, to be sure, broken up into countless tiny deportations (displacements and walks).[28]

Can we transpose this narrative onto the act of photographing or strolling through Disney World? To imagine these perambulations "as an immense social experience of lacking a place" runs counter to popular hype about theme parks as pleasure principles. But de Certeau gives us a snapshot of the burden of credibility that Disney's themed work of persuasion takes on and soothes. If our pleasure in themed space relies on the sublimation of tragedy, if it happens "in search of a proper," then we need to envision the theme park as ghost story—as a tale of migration, deportation, nomadism, displacement: a veritable festival of ostracism and banishment. The need for "themed 'lands'," or for the imperial magnetism of G. E.'s "IllumiNations," suggests not only the easy gratification of

---

many foreigners there, but that really can't be helped." Thomas L. Friedman, "Dissing the World," *The New York Times*, 19 February 1995, E 13.

[28] Michel de Certeau, *The Practice of Everyday Life*, trans. Michel de Certeau (Berkeley: University of California Press, 1984) 103.

colonizing fantasies but a quest romance not unlike Baudrillard's or Foucault's or the Oklahoma apartment dweller's—an unfulfilled romance plot in which Disney World offers tourists a disciplinary site for exploring their own undisciplined vagrancy, for expressing and repressing the "countless tiny deportations" that drive the transitory spaces of an increasingly expatriated modern world.

In widening the description of the multiple sources driving the need for themed space, I want to suggest that theming may also be gratifying (and dangerous) for postmodern scholars. Clearly, the simulacrum as explanatory principle tells us only a little about the American desire for spectacles like "the breathtaking 'IllumiNations" or the exorbitant dramas of safari-jacketed anchormen, and yet the dream of the simulacrum (or any other ravishing spatial metaphor) may also be appealing precisely *because* of its theatrical persuasiveness: it can offer consumer-academics the equivalent of themed space.[29]

In its readability and imagined abundance themed space is cousin to the museum collection—its pop-up equivalent. Susan Stewart suggests that adding motifs or concepts to the world of things is the primary activity of the museum's bureaucratically assembled space, where an Ibo mask promises a covenant with all Ibo culture, while a ten-minute movie of China pretends to survey the vast differentiations of all Chinese history.[30] This parable applies to monographs as well as museums. If the simulacrum exerts a powerful but limited ap-

---

[29] To summarize Disney World by invoking the emptied-out places of the Disney map ignores, for example, the complex desires of the girl-groups and female flaneurs that a cultural critic like Susan Willis discovers in Disney's margins or the underground lives of those Disney workers who swelter in animal costumes or labor deep in the bowels of Epcot, ferrying fireworks and garbage among the themed lands. See Willis, "Disney World: Public Use/Private State," in *The World According to Disney*, ed. Susan Willis, *South Atlantic Quarterly* 92 (1993): 119–38.

[30] Susan Stewart, *On Longing: Narratives of the Miniature, the Gigantic, the Souvenir, the Collection* (Baltimore: Johns Hopkins University Press, 1984). Although the theming of the museum evacuates fellowship to such a degree that the "illusion of a relation between things takes the place of a social relation" (162–65), in the "themed" space of Disney social relations (as long as they remain heterosexual and familial) are allowed to flood in; perhaps because these relations have been so thoroughly anaesthetized or disciplined.

peal as an exegetic model of the intricate hungers that "themed" parks try to channel, is it fair to add that scholars in search of new geographies or new spatial narratives also need to beware of themed space?

In "Theory in Anthropology: Center and Periphery," Arjun Appadurai asks scholars to think about the omnipresence of academic themes or "gate-keeping metaphors"—a potentially restrictive set of scholarly codes for thinking about place.[31] In reinscribing the habitual rubrics that link place and ethnic identity, the academic essay comes to resemble the museum collection in which "a few simple theoretical handles become metonyms and surrogates for the civilization or society as a whole; hierarchy in India, honor-and-shame in the circum-Mediterranean, filial piety in China are all examples of what one might call gate-keeping concepts in anthropological theory." These signposts not only limit theorizing about "the place in question" but can have the disastrous effect of defining the "dominant questions of interest in the region" (357).

Appadurai's list of themed academic spaces is sobering:

> Thus it is that Africa becomes the locus of many classical social forms, such as the lineage or the segment; tropical South America the arch representative of dual organizations and structured mythological discourse; Melanesia the principal exhibit of the manipulation of bodily substances in the management of society and the cosmos ... Polynesia the central place for the mechanics of reciprocity, and so forth. (357–58)

These places become "showcases" that restrict our understanding of the local and create a narrative dilemma. Do these metonyms offer significant descriptions of localities, or do they simply reveal an unlettered fetishism that reflects "the whims of anthropological fashion" (358)? How do we work through this crisis in representation?[32]

---

[31] Arjun Appadurai, "Theory in Anthropology: Center and Periphery," *Comparative Studies in Society and History* 28 (1986): 356–61.

[32] Any poetics of geography would have to consider, as well, a second narratological crisis, namely the convention that space is infinitely mappable and thus unrepresentable. For a summary of this narrative impasse see Massey, "Politics and Space/Time." For a complicating analogue that might

Inventing a Lexicon: The Geographical Crypt

First, we need to recognize that there are strains of desire and resistance inherent in all our discussions of space, making it easy to fetishize places and difficult to attend to their hyper-complexity. Michael Taussig captures the shape of this resistance quite eloquently:

> we act and have to act as if mischief were not afoot in the kingdom of the real and that all around the ground lay firm. That is what the public secret, the facticity of the social fact, being a social being, is all about. No matter how sophisticated we may be as to the constructed and arbitrary character of our practices ... our practice of practices is one of actively forgetting such mischief each time we open our mouths to ask for something or to make a statement.[33]

We return to this essay's central enigma, to the search for a narrative commensurable with the strange effects of space and the need to invent a poetics of geography that will take on, as one of its subcategories, the archaeology of forgetting. In many respects this archaeology is well under way. Biddy Martin and Chandra Talpade Mohanty have argued that the comforts of space invite political acts of forgetting. Not only are the architecture and "the layouts of buildings ... complicitous in making us feel safe in the world," but particular "buildings and streets witnessed and [then] obscured particular race, class and gender struggles."[34] Describing Minnie Bruce Pratt's courageous journey from the white, heterosexual enclaves of North Carolina to life as an uncloseted lesbian in the African-American neighborhoods of Washington, D.C., Martin and Mohanty suggest the need for new forms of cultural and geographical critique.

---

provide a potential solution, see Lefebvre's discussion of the hydrodynamics of space in *The Production of Space*, 87.

[33] Michael Taussig, *Mimesis and Alterity: A Particular History of the Senses* (New York: Routledge, 1993) xvii-xviii.

[34] Biddy Martin and Chandra Talpade Mohanty, "What's Home Got to Do with It?," in *Feminist Studies, Critical Studies*, ed. Teresa de Lauretis (Bloomington: Indiana University Press, 1986) 196.

But Taussig sounds a more ominous note. Our immersion in the persuasiveness of space has serious consequences for the work of cultural critique. Living in the world invites an acceptance of space's comforts: its ability to uphold the body, even in a range of terrible positions. One criterion of social space is its attempt to be thematic or real, to convince us of its solidity or authenticity even when we are skeptics or disbelievers: to treat something as real is to endorse it. How do we deal with the devilish impenetrability of social space, with our bodies' temptation to misremember the categorical struggles that have founded our world? In answer, I want to return to geography as ghost story and suggest two concluding arguments.

First, we need to invent a lexicon or dictionary of the strange effects of space—a lexicon that is compendious, regional, historical and that addresses the ways in which the physical world first elicits desires, then disappoints or reapportions these desires, and finally masks the ache of this disappointment and asymmetry. It is my hypothesis that what is unrepresentable about space is not only the pressure of diverse social maps multiplying space toward infinity but the additional pressure of what is hidden, encrypted, repressed, or unspoken in global and local histories. And this repression is exacerbated by the quiddity and seeming impenetrability of created social space.

Second, I want to argue that the essays gathered in *The Geography of Identity* offer a powerful cartography of these strange effects. This volume is extraordinary and persistent in puncturing spatial norms, altering geographic truisms, and exploring the bizarre omnium-gatherum that constitutes the hypercomplexity of lived social space.

1. Lost in Space. A repertoire or lexicon of the strange effects of space would have to recognize that, although space seems to work horizontally, stretching out in all directions at once, it also possesses a history: not as a vertical dimension but as a series of folds and pockets, as the dimensional incorporation and exhalation of time. We could argue that, just as time enfolds and produces space, space also enfolds and tries to consume time—a consumption that is always vertiginous since, as Marx maintains, the timebound work of productive labor can be alienated or reified in commodified objects: not just lost but hidden in space.

This encryptment is powerfully illustrated in the interpretation of the Parthenon recently proposed by Joan Connelly. If this new hypothesis is correct, the relief does not celebrate Athena's birth or a joyful celebration of the city of Athens; instead, it shows the frightening tale of Erectheus, king of Athens, on the verge of sacrificing his youngest daughter to save Athens from siege. Helping to unfold her shroud, he has decided that "she will be the first to die."[35] A lexicon of the strange effects of space would have to recognize the persistent effect of this spatial shrouding. As de Certeau has argued: "there is no place that is not haunted by many different spirits…. Haunted places are the only ones people can live in" (108). But the repression of these local spirits seems just as pervasive. The discovery of Erectheus's bloody story at the very portals of Western culture astounds the *New York Times*'s reporter: "To think that this iconic structure of grace and just proportion could turn out to have been dedicated to the glorification of a practice as primitive, cruel and irrational as the sacrifice of children! And worse, that it dated from the time the Greeks were boldly experimenting with democracy and rationalism, from that age whose creative spirit the renaissance sought to emulate" (19). Characteristically, what has been displaced is the blasphemous notion that urban foundations might be porous, discontinuous, "fragmented strata" built violently upon the subordinations and the secrets of others.[36]

2. *Luminous Space, or Why Geographers Need Literature.* In *The Production of Space,* Lefebvre argues that literary texts are useless for exploring the secrets of everyday space: "the problem is that any search for space in literary texts will find it everywhere and in every guise…. What texts can be considered

---

[35] John Noble Wilford, "New Analysis of the Parthenon's Frieze Finds It Depicts a Horrifying Legend," *The New York Times*, 4 July 1995, 19.

[36] As de Certeau adds: "the places people live in are like the presences of diverse absences. What can be seen designates what is no longer there: 'you see, here there used to be …' but it can no longer be seen…. It is the very definition of a place, in fact, that it is composed by these series of displacements and effects among the fragmented strata that form it and that it plays on these moving layers" (108). The spatial is filled with lost sociality, with still influential penumbras of power and domination. A lexicon of the strange effects of space must supplement the ideological fullness of space with an investigation of this spatial amnesia.

special enough to provide the basis for a 'textual' analysis?" (15). But Lefebvre also elicits flights of literary fantasy when he describes a series of utopian spaces in which a community's idealized needs and desires might reappear:

> There still exist—and there may exist in the future—spaces for play, spaces for enjoyment, architectures of wisdom or pleasure. In and by means of space, *the work may shine through the product*, use value may gain the upper hand over exchange value ... as the imaginary and the utopian incorporate (or are incorporated into) the real. (348)

Without endorsing such hopefulness (in this conservative, nonluminous era) I want to suggest that literary texts are especially canny in providing a portrait of this negative shining; they provide a place where productivity—in its most radiant, as well as its most tragic and imbecilic forms—visibly irradiates the things it has made. Think, for example, of Thoreau's description in *Walden* of each railroad tie as a "sleeper" whose dreams have bound America together. These sleepers are, of course, the bodies of the dead or mangled Irish workers who labored to install the iron path in conditions of incredible suffering and peril. Thoreau describes the forgotten effects of spatial melancholia—the unmourned phantoms that still hover, dreaming and cursing, in geography's thoroughfares.[37]

Labor also has an uncanny power to shine through its products in Charles Chesnutt's *The Conjure Woman*, in a magical tale called "Po' Sandy" in which a slave who has been changed into a tree to prevent being sold off the plantation is sawed down for lumber to make a kitchen for his master's wife.[38] The haunted kitchen made from Sandy's bones stutters and sighs in the wind—creating a hollow space that his companions refuse to enter. The body's time and labor blend with the physical landscape to create a commentary on the horrors inhabiting the built environment of Southern history. I want to add that even though literature may not be valuable for its straightforward geography, it is extraordinarily useful in its

---

[37] Henry Thoreau, *Walden & Civil Disobedience* (New York: Viking Penguin, 1983).

[38] Charles W. Chesnutt, *The Conjure Woman* (Ann Arbor: University of Michigan Press, 1969) 36–63.

constant, uncanny rendering of laborious space—a crucial concept within any compendium of geographical encrypting or the strange effects of space.

3. *Impossible Space.* Geographers are developing theories that capture these strange effects. Doreen Massey's theory of four-dimensional space recovers temporality as physicality, as a forgotten component of the local. If we add time to every analysis of space, then: 1) space cannot be separated from time since neither can be conceptualized "as the absence of the other."[39] 2) Since space and time are coterminous, space is constructed out of interrelationships, out of the simultaneous coexistence of everything. 3) In addition, space will have to be analyzed as both order and chaos, linear and haphazard: as a place that is continually resutured and disaggregated.[40] 4) Finally, the central problem of geographical description is, for Massey, "the difficulty of dealing with a world which is 4–D" (159). If space can be envisioned as both the terminus and inception of time, the point "is to try to think in all the dimensions of space-time. It is a lot more difficult than at first sight it might seem" (155).

In contrast, Sue Golding's theory of chimeric or "impossible spatiality" investigates the ghostly dimensions of the local. But rather than focusing on melancholic space, Golding insists that we experiment with a "radical geography" capable of acknowledging the ways in which space both "exists and does not exist exactly at the same time."[41] While Massey confronts the temporal dimensions of invisible space, Golding explores its ethics; she insists that geography is haunted by phantasms constituted from "the memory of an un-dead trace operating 'as if' it were always-already still there, disfiguring the homo-

---

[39] Doreen Massey, "Politics and Space/Time" 155. Subsequent page numbers are incorporated in the text.

[40] Massey explains that causality is an attribute of space because all phenomena have causes and can therefore be explained. But chaos is an attribute as well because the juxtaposition of different objects in space may not be planned, purposeful, or structurally connected.

[41] Sue Golding, "Quantum Philosphy, Impossible Geographies and a Few Small Points about Life, Liberty and the Pursuit of Sex (All in the Name of Democracy)," in *Place and the Politics of Identity*, ed. Michael Keith and Steve Pile (New York: Routledge, 1993) 206. Subsequent page numbers are incorporated in the text.

geneity of a totalized body" (207–8). The "mischief" that is afoot in the kingdom of the real is already plagued by the counter-reality that it excludes.

4. *Desire, Woman-as-landscape, and Geographic Scopophilia.* Together, Massey and Golding begin to define space as a cycle of strange effects; they demand that geographers develop the powers of the evil eye or second sight. But we need to go even farther in inventing a lexicon that will help us decipher the bizarre effects of inhabiting the very medium we are trying to decipher. We have already explored the halo or psychological penumbra of a series of spatial disturbances, among them the "illusory clarity" that makes space the site of forgetting. Space also plays tricks with desire, so that even Lefebvre becomes a spatial allegorist and poet of melancholy when he attempts to explain what happens when desire drifts into space:

> Our space has strange effects. For one thing, it unleashes desire. It presents desire with a 'transparency' which encourages it to surge forth in an attempt to lay claim to an apparently clear field.... Searching in vain for plenitude, desire must make do with words, with the rhetoric of desire. Disillusion leaves space empty—an emptiness that words convey. Spaces are devastated—and devastating. (97)

Why does desire bring us back to the image of devastation or ruin, to space as emptiness or void? In inventing this delirious lexicon, we need to explore our own class and gender positions. Is Lefebvre's analysis of the seeming "transparency" of space also a bourgeois fantasy? Is this imagined devastation of space a class-based nightmare about democratic acts of leveling or "massification"? In assessing the phantom effects of space, the disasters bred by the tombs of others, we need to assess the depth of our own tombs as well.

To explore another set of spatial fantasies we could also look at Roland Barthes's theory of the punctum as well as his notion of landscape as eros—an eroticism bound up with gendered melancholy, with his unresolved yearning for his mother's body.[42] Or we could examine Michael Keith and Steve Pile's dramatization of a persistent geographic scopophilia in

---

[42] Roland Barthes, *Camera Lucida: Reflections on Photography*, trans. Richard Howard (New York: Hill and Wang, 1981) 25–40.

which landscapes turn into "Woman," and "the power of geographers to gaze on the beauty of the world is unquestioned because it is associated with the power of men to stare at women, who are thus objectified."[43]

As we leap from the fetishism of themed space—where everything seems extrinsic, premasticated, prenarrated—to the fecklessness of these strange effects of space, we tumble into a great abyss. This abyss is not empty, however. It is animated by a local politics that gives the places we inhabit (however violently or tenuously), the quality of permanence, of luminous "there-ness." A lexicon of spatial delirium—a trip to geography's crypt—may not help to dissolve this quiddity, but it will provide a partial map for relocating the hiding places of power. David Harvey suggests that spatial and temporal practices "express some kind of class or other social content" and are always the subject of "intense social struggle." Under capitalism this struggle intensifies in unpredictable ways. Not only does society redefine its space-time coordinates for the sake of commodity production, "but the dynamic force of capital accumulation (and overaccumulation), together with conditions of social struggle, renders the relations unstable" (239). The empty magic of capital may create the strangest spatial effects of all, and it behooves us to name these effects wherever we can find them.

The Geography of Identity

Although this lexicon of strange effects is far from complete, the essays in this collection provide a dazzling and encyclopedic vision of how this lexicon might become more comprehensive. In reappropriating overlooked or analytically neglected space, these essays also redefine the cartographies of globalization, nationalism, and the urban grid, as well as the spatial bases of identity politics and the psychological determinants of homeland. The writing itself becomes a minor form of reterritorialization in which the unsettled precepts of a new

---

[43] Keith and Pile, "Conclusion: Towards New Radical Geographies," in *Place and the Politics of Identity*, ed. Michael Keith and Steve Pile (New York: Routledge, 1993) 221.

spatial order create new forums for social/intellectual inquiry. Finally, each of these essays provides an incisive new way of approaching spatial narratology.[44] In reinventing old strategies for narrating space, the essayists who have contributed to *The Geography of Identity* construct a series of improbable maps with the power to apprehend the strange effects of ordinary space and to remedy the geometry of forgetting.

Part one, "Globalization and the Transformation of the Local," challenges the place-absorbing power of globalization. Arjun Appadurai's opening essay describes a world in which national narratives are beginning to fray. Without the stability provided by these narratives, space begins to play strange tricks indeed. In an increasingly mobile world, minorities and migrating workers are funneled into national arenas and instantly disrupt the mythos of "ethnic coherence and citizenship rights" (56), so that the host state is constantly combating the omnipresence of undesired "ethnic noises" even as the state itself is forced to bestow a second- or third-class version of entitlements upon imported workers and refugees. In this new world order (defined less by a territorial imperative than by the cacophony of translocalities) there is increasing pressure on the narratives supporting the nation-state. Appadurai questions the dominant status of the nation as imagined community and traces the postmodern disintegration of the nation as political entity; "since states, territories, and ideas of national ethnic singularity are always complicated historical coproductions," the mix of translocalities, guest workers, and diasporic communities has the startling effect of embarrassing "all nar-

---

[44] For example, Rashid Khalidi and Mark Liechty refuse monochromatic cartographies that might become metonyms for the societies they examine. Since place is both contagious and discontinuous, they argue that geographical narratives have to reflect this incongruity by exploring the lack of common ground within overlapping social spaces. From another perspective Saskia Sassen suggests our mode of narration creates the destructive categories of center and margin that disenfranchise corporate workers. If, as Harvey has argued, the central task of the "capitalist state is to locate power in the spaces which the bourgeoisie controls, and disempower those spaces which oppositional movements have the greatest potentiality to command" (236), Sassen takes this analysis one step farther; it is not just narratives of resistance that the bourgeoisie repress but narratives of the value and contributions of a whole range of peoples and classes.

ratives that attempt to naturalize" state or national histories
(57).

While Appadurai challenges the dominance of the nation-
state, Michael Watts takes on another set of postmodern my-
thologies insisting that globalization inevitably leads to the
erasure of the local. In "Mapping Identities: Place, Space, and
Community in the African City," he argues that the new elas-
ticity of place resulting from the transnationalization of capital
and technology can also contribute to local revitalization—to
new modes of resistance. Watts not only synthesizes the latest
theories of spatiality but provides a complex picture of the interactions of residual, emergent, and dominant discourses of
capitalism and Islam in petroleum-rich Nigeria. As these narratives tangle together, we come to understand how Nigerian
commodity fetishism differs from the fetishisms of the West. In
contrast, Mark Liechty's "Kathmundu as Translocality: Multiple Places in a Nepali Space" suggests that globalization de-
ranges the stability of place, but in unexpected ways. Rather
than the emptying out of place that Arendt and Baudrillard
find so devastating, Liechty argues that "certain spaces" become "overpopulated with places" (98). The touristic centers of
Kathmundu become home to "a host of places" that overlap
and yet claim the same ground for different configurations of
meaning. Finally, in "Identity in the Global City: Economic and
Cultural Encasements" Saskia Sassen demonstrates that we
need to rethink the economic underpinnings of the terms *center* and *margin*. Contemporary narratives of a city's corporate
and economic core tend to overvalorize highly educated workers while expelling "marginal" actors whose services underwrite
this elite's rise to power. Sassen argues that the results of this
economic and narratological ostracism are not only debilitating
for workers but also falsify the sources of corporate wealth.
She urges the recovery of devalorized subjects in any account
of the advanced economy of the global city.

The second group of essays, "The Crisis in the Nation-
State," defines a double crisis in the material and ideological
structures supporting nations and aspiring nation-states and
in academic constructs of nationality. In "Figures of the Subject in Times of Crisis," Achille Mbembe and Janet Roitman
describe what has happened when postcolonial aspirations
confront severe economic contraction in Cameroon, where a
once-thriving commercial economy is now immobilized. They

follow the imbrications of this crisis within Cameroon's fiscal networks, in the hard surfaces of buildings and streets caught in the bizarre flux of national decay but also in the decomposition of Cameroon's psychic economy. Since the atrophy of homes and workplaces has happened so quickly, without landmarks or historical referents, Cameroon's citizens have exiled this crisis "to the domain of the inexplicable" (155). But Mbembe and Roitman refuse both this local trope of unreadability and the academic demand for gate-keeping metaphors that will Westernize this crisis or hold it at bay. They argue for a new narratological perspective in which these events register as a "prosaic" or "routinization" of daily improvisations rather than as a structure or system; they reimagine Cameroon's cities as a vast and disrupted internet of postcolonial nation-building and local customs met by the upheavals of capitalism: an internet that is transformed (and must be retheorized) as it encounters the coping mechanisms and workaday strategies of a national crisis.

Rashid Khalidi's essay on "Contrasting Narratives of Palestinian Identity" describes the equally strange and violent effects of ethnically shared space in Palestinian and Israeli chronicles of time and place. Khalidi takes on two different projects. First, he redefines the imagined cartographies of Israel and Palestine (two peoples who cohabit yet dwell in dissimilar symbolic space). The oppositional construction of Jerusalem/al-Quds al-Sharif casts light on Foucault's description of the heteroclite in which "things are 'laid,' 'placed,' 'arranged,' in sites so very different from one another that it is impossible" to find a common ground beneath them all (xvii-xviii). As Khalidi explains, "in much of what it does, each side chooses to be oblivious to the existence of the other. In a sense, each party to this conflict ... operates in a different dimension from the other, looking back to a different era of the past and living in a different present, albeit in the very same place" (197). In addition to exploring the costs of this nonconvergence, Khalidi renegotiates the Palestinian drive toward nationalism. Rather than inventing a narrative of villification in which external forces absorb the blame for the loss of Palestinian nationhood, Khalidi reopens the question of lost nationality as an external and internal affair, as a multistoried exchange of injury and identity.

If Mbembe and Roitman and Khalidi define aspiring nation-states as interpenetrating stories, Herman Lebovics defines a national strategy of censorship; he zeroes in on postwar
efforts to restrain the leakage of American words and Muslim
customs into the lofty altitudes of French culture. Stripped of
its colonies and international power, modern France deployed
the ideas of an aesthetic elite "to give it a comparative advantage in the new international competition" (225). In describing
the ways that André Malraux marketed Parisian culture to ad-
vance the bureaucratization of a new national unity, Lebovics
describes the invention of a "top-down regionalism" in which
the spacious provinces of France were reconstructed as the
simulacrum and hinterland of Paris. These bureaucratized
modes of local forgetting suggest that we have yet to fathom
the ways that nations interact with "texts and images ... to
make and to change cultures" (238).

Part three, "The Urban Heteroclite," explores the queer
communities, underground economies, and architectural
anomalies encouraged by urban sprawl. In "Queer Sites in
Modernism: Harlem/The Left Bank/Greenwich Village" Joseph
Boone notes that the geography of gay identity expands into
urban spaces in the twentieth century. Exploring the city as a
place of autonomy/anonymity for gay women and men, Boone
revolutionizes the topography of queer modernism. How did the
"desiring queer body" interact with urban space? While the
Village and Left Bank become pockets within the urban grid
escaping its homogenizing influence, the queering of the urban
promenade also heightens the city's "ceaseless mobility": any
walk could become a cruise, an escape from carcereal space.
Boone defines a litany of queer spatial effects: while the city's
permeable boundaries provide access to queer dramas "from
which no city-dweller is immune," the city also provides a
space in which homosexual flaneurs can appropriate public
space. Boone also discusses a series of modernist narratives
that mimic the city's spaces, inviting drag queens and straight
plebeians to immerse themselves in the heterogeneous pleas-
ure-spaces of homoeroticism.

The city streets that Boone finds so liberating for gay modernists become a complex site of crisis and mobility for the African-Americans who participated in the Great Migration. In
her essay on "Mediums, Messages, and Lucky Numbers: African-American Female Spiritualists and Numbers Runners in

Interwar Detroit," Victoria Wolcott suggests that while the African-American elite in Detroit tried to distance itself from rural Southern immigrants to create a new rhetoric of black respectability, these new arrivals invented a strange geography of urban empowerment and an underground economy that brought together numbers runners and sanctified women from spiritualist churches. In this disruptive mix of respectable and disreputable economies new subject positions emerged for African-American women who refused to conform to top-down notions of community identity.

This permeability contaminated the canons of modernist architecture as well. In "Modernism and the Specifics of Place" Gwendolyn Wright argues that the strengths of modern American architecture have been neglected because scholars lack a narrative that foregrounds its regional peculiarities as a response to the pragmatic contexts of American life and an ongoing project for American architects determined to carry out their own vernacular reading of place. American architects affirmed collectivity and experience over European theory and abstract aesthetics, and Wright describes their invention of an accommodating style that could also be celebrated as a canny form of modernist parochialism.

If these reevaluations of transnational, national, and urban places construct social space as a field of force where politics behaves unpredictably, in the next section on "Remapping Identity Politics" we see the ways in which identity politics exerts a terrifying pressure on the local. In "Landscapes of Terror: A Reading of Tuskegee's Historic Campus" Kenrick Ian Grandison argues that the physical plant of Tuskegee was shaped by domestic terrorism. Amidst the racial hostility and economic deprivations of post-Reconstruction Alabama, Southern geography was literally encrypted by the secret activities of the Ku Klux Klan and Knights of the White Camellia. Grandison traces the progress of Tuskegee's built environment and describes Booker T. Washington's architectural strategies for dealing with white supremacy, including the stockadelike avoidance of public thoroughfares and the privatization of Tuskegee's public façades. In addition, Grandison contributes an important chapter to the annals of landscape architecture by explicating its refusal to record "the stories of poor, marginalized, and oppressed people" (266)—a refusal that can only distort the histories of shared civic space.

The politics of African-American identity created Tuskegee as an actual site of African-American learning but as a phantasmatic site for white fantasies about black degradation. In "The Politics of Trust" Bernard Williams argues that these phantasms of duplicity also play a central role in the construction of individual identity politics. If authenticity and self-transparency cannot become the basis for a viable identity politics, how can we chart a geography of identity; how do we recapture identity for political projects based on common interests or the desire to reform public space? First, Williams describes sincerity as a form of self-steadying, as the attempt to invent a stable ground that will allow the self to discover and internalize the tenets of a shared political identity. Noting that it is difficult to stabilize the self into a form that "will fit with shared political or social roles" but also represent "a life that is worth living" (378), he argues that identity politics offers a modern solution to this dilemma; in our split subjectivity and collective mutability, we try to appropriate a series of physical and emotional structures that establish the necessary illusion of common ground. An "identity," Williams explains, "is something that each of us individually has, but it is also something that is essentially shared" (378) by those with whom we live, where we live. The idea of sincerity as a model of self-expression rather than self-discovery speaks to the double nature of identity, to its individual and group aspects. Williams redefines sincerity as a logical structure mediating between the one and the many. Such identities may not last a lifetime; they represent only the short-term project of stabilizing selfhood under the pressure of the conflicting demands made on people by individual and ethnic or personal and political notions of what identity is. Williams's analysis of trust and sincerity as negotiated rather than transparent "truths" describes the project of self-steadying that shared landscapes require, while his model of authenticity as praxis, as created identity, sheds light on the complex psychological strategies often used to find public acceptance for subversive forms of identity.

Finally, in "Frontiers, Islands, Forests, Stones: Mapping the Geography of a German Identity in the Habsburg Monarchy, 1848–1900" Pieter Judson describes the advent of a new spatial hermeneutic among postliberal German nationalists. By historicizing a German nostalgia for place, Judson discovers a revolution in nationalist metaphors involving a mystification of the "German-ness" of frontiers, islands, forests, and stones. This spatial chauvinism—newly minted in the 1880s—reflects a new territorial chauvinism that lent spatial and temporal depth to a floating ideology of nationalist fervor. By linking nationalism and the pressure to invent a new spatial episteme, Judson also provides a strategy for understanding the peculiar politics of the spatial fetish as well as the ways in which our investments in nationalist symbols change over time.

The Geography of Identity ends with "Phantasmatic Homelands," where fantasy and politics compete in the construction of place. In the modern age, Hannah Arendt argues, the private home is no longer regarded as a space of privation but a place that "shelters the intimate" (38). But in "Dinnsheanchas: The Naming of High or Holy Places," Nuala Ní Dhomhnaill discovers this intimacy in the vast natural spaces carved out by Irish placenames. She asks why the mysteries sustaining these placenames persist in Ireland when most modern cultures have lost them (or have converted the "numinosity of place" into the bloody tenets of nationalism) (408). If the "killing sense of place" that characterizes nationalist debacles like Bosnia needs to be separated from Ireland's peculiar brand of spatial mysticism, this is because the naming of holy places fulfills a "mythopoeic function ... that we deny at our peril" (429). Ní Dhomhnaill argues that the collective pleasures called forth by the idea of homeland should be viewed as essential to our well-being but that this need can and should be satisfied by local narratives that eschew a national ethos of blood and soil. Instead, Irish storytellers can "possess the land emotionally and imaginatively without any particular sense of ... titular ownership" (431).

While Ní Dhomhnaill resurrects the satisfactions of luminous space, her essay also raises the question of how this progressive mythopoiesis might be preserved among expatriates, refugees, and immigrant workers who must negotiate alien placenames within a translocal, postnational world. In response, Billie Melman explores the politics of dispossession among the European women who helped deterritorialize the East. She argues that Western women invented their own geography of colonization involving unexpected forms of gender solidarity. Within Western women's fantasies of the colonized "other" Melman describes the veil as a transcultural symbol system that operates "as a moving contact zone between spaces: interior and exterior, personal and political, Eastern and Western" (465). In this setting Western women used their encounters with Eastern women to deconstruct the gender asymmetries of their own households and to reveal the very real consequences of phantasmatic constructions of homeland.

In the concluding essay, "Autocartography: The Case of Palestine, Michigan," Anton Shammas initiates a captivating conversation about that no-place called home. As Shammas's wishes for Palestine half migrate to Michigan, geography becomes a ghost story riddled with pleasure and loss. His wry definitions of homeland also irradiate this book's central themes, from the traumas of globalization and national crisis to the delirium of the urban simulacrum and forgotten space.

The essays in this volume not only provide new descriptions of locality under the aegis of the new geography but suggest the changing status of geographical representation under the pressures of globalization. If globalization can be defined 1) as the unexpected ability of labor and capital to range freely around the globe—a capacity to move rapidly or erratically across political, economic, and social borders, and 2) as a new temporal and spatial volatility in which events happening in one part of the globe have an instantaneous impact elsewhere, locality seems not only to disappear, but locals (i.e., neighbors, bystanders, migrant workers, secretaries, CEOs, or refugees) feel the need to invent a new geographic imaginary. Accounting for no less than everything becomes the global task of the new poetics of geography. *The Geography of Identity* contributes to this new poetics by embarking on many operations at once— not only rethinking spatial binaries (urban/rural, global/local, colony/postcolony, nation-state/borderland, citizen/refugee, tourist/guest worker, diasporic fellowship/nativist paranoia), not only analyzing places that are simultaneously borders and origins, entrances and exits, centers and peripheries, not only deciphering (within global internets and local neighborhoods) the effects of chimeric space, but tinkering with the remains of a territorial imaginary, with an old phenomenology that ignores the strange effects of ordinary space.

PART ONE: GLOBALIZATION AND THE TRANSFORMATION OF THE LOCAL

SOVEREIGNTY WITHOUT TERRITORIALITY:
Notes for a Postnational Geography

Arjun Appadurai

Introduction

I have elsewhere argued that we need to think ourselves beyond the nation.[1] In this essay, I seek to deepen that argu-

This paper was first presented as a forum lecture at the Institute for the Humanities, University of Michigan, in April 1994. It was subsequently revised for presentations at the universities of Oslo, Stockholm, and Copenhagen during September 1994, and at Northwestern University (Chicago) in February 1995. It was the basis for the Ecumene Lecture delivered at the annual meetings of the Association of American Geographers in Chicago in April 1995. I am grateful for criticisms and queries raised on all these occasions. An earlier version of this paper was delivered (on my behalf) at a conference sponsored by the Wenner-Gren Foundation in Mijas, Spain on 14–22 June 1994. I am especially grateful for the feedback I received from the organizers of that conference. I would like to make special mention of the critical contributions, in various of these contexts, of Fredrik Barth, Fred Cooper, Gudrun Dahl, Micaela di Leonardo, Ulf Hannerz, and Jane Jacobs. Special thanks to the editor of this volume, Patricia Yaeger, for her patience, her probing questions, and her enthusiasm.

This text reflects a moment of transition between two extended research projects, one focused on the cultural dynamics of global cultural flow and another, just beginning, on the relationship between liberal social theory and the modern idea of the nation-state. It is in many ways preliminary and does not take up many important and related problems. Two large areas that are relevant to this argument are not taken up in the current essay. The first is the relation between the crisis of territorial sovereignty that I have described and the workings of colonial capitalism in the ex-colonies of Africa, the Middle East, and Asia. There is also the wider historical issue of the extent to which the crisis I have described has always been part of the history of the nation-state in the West, both in the domain of political theory and in the actual material workings of national formations on the ground. These are matters that I consider to be very important and will be taking up in future work on this subject.

ment by paying close attention to one dimension of the modern nation form—territoriality. Recognizing with Anderson[2] that the nation is an imagined thing, I also recognize the critical reciprocal of his insight, that it is the imagination that will have to carry us beyond the nation. Thus what follows is a critical work of the imagination, which recognizes the difficulty, sharply articulated by Shapiro, of constructing "post-sovereign" moral geographies. [3]

After the agreements associated with the Westphalian peace settlements of 1648, the embryonic principle of territorial sovereignty becomes the foundational concept of the nation-state,[4] though many other ideas affect its subsequent cultural self-imaging and self-narrativizing. These include ideas about language, common origin, blood, and various other conceptions of ethnos. Still, the fundamental political and juridical rationale and basis of the system of nation-states is territorial sovereignty, however complexly understood and delicately managed in particular postimperial settings.[5]

Nationality and Locality

While nationalism (whatever that might exactly mean) is showing many signs of recrudescence, the modern nation-state

---

[1] Arjun Appadurai, "Patriotism and Its Futures," *Public Culture* 5, 3 (1993): 411–29.

[2] Benedict Anderson, *Imagined Communities: Reflections on the Origin and Spread of Nationalism* (London: Verso 1983).

[3] Michael J. Shapiro, "Moral Geographies and the Ethics of Post-Sovereignty," *Public Culture* 6, 3 (1994): 479–502.

[4] The importance of this moment is discussed in many sources. One interesting discussion is to be found in Hans Gross, *Empire and Sovereignty: A History of the Public Law Literature in the Holy Roman Empire, 1599–1804* (Chicago: University of Chicago Press, 1973), who places the Westphalian treaties in the context of a wider discussion of the evolution of public law in the Holy Roman Empire in the seventeenth and eighteenth centuries.

[5] For an interesting discussion of the principle of territorial sovereignty in the framework of international law, and its vagaries during and after colonial rule in Africa, see Malcolm Shaw, *Title to Territory in Africa: International Legal Issues* (Oxford: Clarendon Press, 1986).

as a compact and isomorphic organization of territory, ethnos, and governmental apparatus is in a serious crisis. I have elsewhere laid out the argument for the transnational conditions for this crisis,[6] my evidence for the emergence of major nonnational and indeed postnational social formations,[7] and a perspective on the globalized production of locality in the contemporary world.[8] I shall not review these prior observations but shall paraphrase them in the following paragraphs, since they constitute the background for the arguments put forward here.

The production of locality,[9] as a dimension of social life, as a structure of feeling, and in its material expression in lived "copresence,"[10] faces two challenges in a postnational order. On the one hand, the production of locality challenges the order and orderliness of the nation-state. On the other hand, human motion in the context of the crisis of the nation-state encourages the emergence of *translocalities*. This double challenge is addressed below.

The work of producing localities, in the sense that localities are life-worlds constituted by relatively stable associations, relatively known and shared histories, and collectively traversed and legible spaces and places, is often at odds with the projects of the nation-state. This is partly because the commitments and attachments that characterize local subjectivities (sometimes mislabeled "primordial") are more pressing, more continuous, and sometimes more distracting than the nation-state can afford. It is also because the memories and attachments that local subjects have to their neighborhoods and street names, to their favorite walkways and streetscapes, to their times and places for congregating and escaping are often at odds with the needs of the nation-state for regulated

---

[6] Arjun Appadurai, "Disjuncture and Difference in the Global Cultural Economy," *Public Culture* 2,2 (1990): 1–24.

[7] Appadurai, "Patriotism and Its Futures."

[8] Arjun Appadurai, *Modernity at Large: Cultural Dimensions of Globalization* (Minneapolis: University of Minnesota Press, forthcoming 1996).

[9] Appadurai, *Modernity at Large*.

[10] Deidre Boden and Harvey L. Molotch, "The Compulsion of Proximity," in *NowHere: Space, Time and Modernity*, ed. R. Friedland and D. Boden (Berkeley: University of California Press, 1994).

public life. Further, it is the nature of local life to develop partly by contrast to other localities by producing its own contexts of alterity (spatial, social, and technical), contexts that may not meet the needs for spatial and social standardization prerequisite for the modern subject-citizen.

Paradoxically, the human movements characteristic of the contemporary world are as much a threat to the nation-state as are the attachments of local subjects to local life. The isomorphism of people, territory, and legitimate sovereignty that constitutes the normative charter of the modern nation-state is under threat from the forms of circulation of people characteristic of the contemporary world. It is now widely conceded that the world we live in is one in which human motion is more often definitive of social life than it is exceptional. Work, both of the most sophisticated intellectual sort and the most humble proletarian sort, drives people to migrate, often more than once. The policies of nation-states, particularly toward populations regarded as potentially subversive, create a perpetual motion machine, where refugees from one nation move to another, creating new instabilities there, which cause further social unrest and thus more social exits.[11] Hence the "people" production[12] needs of one nation-state can mean ethnic and social unrest for its neighbors, creating open-ended cycles of ethnic cleansing, forced migration, xenophobia, state paranoia, and thus further ethnic cleansing. Eastern Europe in general, and Bosnia-Herzegovina in particular, are perhaps the most tragic and complex examples of such state/refugee domino processes. In many such cases, people and whole communities are turned into ghettos, refugee camps, concentration camps, or reservations, sometimes without anyone moving at all.

Other forms of human movement are created by the reality or lure of economic opportunity (this is true of much Asian migration to the oil-rich parts of the Middle East). Yet other forms of movement are created by permanently mobile groups of specialized workers (United Nations soldiers, oil technologists,

---

[11] A. Zolberg, A. Sahrke, and S. Aguayo, *Escape from Violence: Conflict and the Refugee Crisis in the Developing World* (Oxford: Oxford University Press, 1989).

[12] Etienne Balibar, "The Nation Form: History and Ideology," in *Race, Nation, Class: Ambiguous Identities*, ed. E. Balibar and I. Wallerstein (London: Verso, 1991).

development specialists, agricultural laborers, etc.) Still other forms of movement, particularly in sub-Saharan Africa, involve major droughts and famines, often tied to disastrous alliances between corrupt states and opportunistic international and global agencies. In yet other communities, the logic of movement is provided by the leisure industries, which create tourist sites and locations around the world. The ethnography of these tourist locations is just beginning to be written in detail,[13] but what little we do know suggests that many such locations create complex conditions for the production and reproduction of locality, in which ties of marriage, work, business, and leisure weave together various circulating populations with various kinds of "locals" to create localities that belong in one sense to particular nation-states but are, from another point of view, what we might call *translocalities*.

Translocalities come in many forms and, as an emergent category of human organization, require serious attention. Border zones are now becoming spaces of complex quasi-legal circulation of persons and goods. The border between the United States and Mexico is an excellent example of one kind of translocality. Similarly, many tourist zones may be described as translocalities, even where they may lie nominally within the jurisdiction of particular nation-states. All Free Trade Zones (FTZs) are to some extent translocalities. Finally, every major refugee camp, migrant hostel, or neighborhood of exiles and guest workers is a translocality.

Many cities are becoming translocalities, substantially divorced from their national contexts. These cities fall into two types: those major economic centers that are so deeply involved in foreign trade, finance, diplomacy, and media that they have become cultural islands with very weak national referents: Hongkong, Vancouver, and Brussels are examples of this type of city. Whether because of global economic processes that tie these cities together more than they tie them to their hinterlands or because of implosive, transnationally driven civil wars, other cities are becoming translocalities, weakly tied

---

[13] I have been stimulated to think about the complexities of cultural reproduction in tourist translocalities by the work-in-progress of Jacqueline McGibbon, of the Department of Anthropology at the University of Chicago, who is engaged in a study of the village of St. Anton in the Tirolean Alps.

to their national hinterlands: Sarajevo, Beirut, Belfast, and Mogadishu are examples of this second type. I shall return to the relevance of translocalities at a subsequent point in the argument.

In this paper, I propose some ways to examine how the foundational principle of the modern nation-state—the principle of territorial sovereignty—is faring in the sort of world I have described, not as a narrow legal or jurisdictional issue but as a broader cultural and affiliational one.

Mobile Sovereignties

Throughout the world, the problem of immigrants, cultural rights, and state protection of refugees is growing, since very few states have effective ways of defining the relationship of citizenship, birth, ethnic affiliation, and national identity. The crisis is nowhere clearer than in France today, where the struggle to distinguish the Algerian population within France is threatening to unravel the very foundation of French ideas of full citizenship and to expose the deeply racialized foundation of French thinking about cultural markers of national belonging. But in many countries race, birth, and residence are becoming problems of one or other kind.

One source of this problem is that modern conceptions of citizenship, tied up with various forms of democratic universalism, tend to demand a homogenous people with standardized packages of rights. Yet the realities of ethnoterritorial thinking in the cultural ideologies of the nation-state demand discrimination among different categories of citizens even when they all occupy the same territory. The civil status (or nonstatus) of Palestinians in respect to the Israeli state is only the extreme example of this contradiction. Resolving these conflicting principles is increasingly a violent and uncivil process.

With economic liberalization in many parts of the world, there is also a cultural form of liberalization that invites citizens who have moved abroad to reinvest in their nations of origin, especially if they have not switched passports. India, for example, has the category Non-Resident Indian (NRI). At the present moment, in the continued euphoria over the end of communism and the command economy, as well as the wave of

enthusiasm over marketization and free trade, NRIs have special rights, driven by national and regional forces seeking expatriate money and expertise in India. Thus Indian banks, states,
and private entrepreneurs, in their desire for this expertise and
wealth, are committed to special deals for NRIs, especially in
regard to taxation, property rights, and freedom of movement
in and out of India. At the same time, in their lives in the
United States, many diasporic Indian communities are deeply
involved in reproducing "Hindu" identity for themselves and
their children and have thus become active supporters of
Hindu right-wing movements and organizations in India. This
is a complex story, which needs detailed engagement elsewhere, but it is worth noting the link between the cultural
politics of NRIs, which draws them into communal politics in
India, and the willingness of state and capitalist interests in
India to extend them extraterritorial economic rights.

This sort of territorial paradox (special rights for citizens
who are outside the national territory) is part of a broader set
of postnational geographic processes. There is growing tension
between issues of territorial sovereignty and issues of military
security and defense, as with the current campaigns through
the United Nations to demand on-site inspections in Iraq and
North Korea. Likewise, as with Haiti, Somalia, and Bosnia, the
distinction between "civil" and international war is becoming
increasingly blurred. Finally, debates in North America, Japan,
and Europe about NAFTA and GATT indicate that "commodity
conquests" are increasingly viewed as threats to national sovereignty and integrity: an excellent example is the French
panic about Americanization through Hollywood products.
Dangers to sovereignty are thus not always tied up with warfare, conquest, and defense of borders. Territorial integrity and
national integrity are themselves not always consistent or coe-
val issues.

National space can come to be differently valorized for the
state and for its citizen-subjects. The state is typically concerned with taxation, order, generally stability and fixity,
whereas from the point of view of subjects, territory typically
involves rights to movement, rights to shelter, and rights to
subsist. Thus "soil" needs to be distinguished from territory
("sons of the soil"). While soil is a matter of a spatialized and
originary discourse of belonging, territory is concerned with
integrity, surveyability, policing, and subsistence.

As fissures emerge among local, translocal, and national space, territory as the ground of loyalty and national affect (what we should mean when we speak of national "soil") is increasingly divorced from territory as the site of sovereignty and state control of civil society. The problem of jurisdiction and the problem of loyalty are increasingly disjunct. This does not bode well for the future of the nation-state in its classic form, in which the two are imaged as coextensive and mutually supportive.

Not all state apparatuses are concerned about territorial integrity in the same way and for the same reasons. In some cases, state panic has to do with major, and restive, populations of refugees: the presence of large numbers of Afghans is this sort of concern for the government of Pakistan. Other states are worried about borders, which they may see as imperfect membranes, letting in undesirable aliens and commodities, while deterring legitimate tourists and workers. The U.S.–Mexico border is clearly of this kind, with osmotic capabilities (to filter out the wrong kinds of goods and services) now seen as highly imperfect. Yet other states, for example in Africa, care less about policing borders but focus their energies on policing and sanctifying important cities, monuments, and resources at the urban centers of the regime. Some states worry about commodity violations of territory; others worry more about people or diseases or political pollution. In the new South Africa, concerns about territory are tied up with the question of the reclamation of valuable agricultural lands previously monopolized by the white minority and with the rehabilitation of the vast squatter communities previously meant to be minimal containers for blacks and now seen as the living space of the enfranchised majority. These variations in state anxiety about territory have much to do with other aspects of state security and viability and varying resources for civil society, which cannot be discussed here.

For many national citizens, the practicalities of residence and the ideologies of home, soil, and roots are often disjunct, so that the territorial referents of civic loyalty are increasingly divided for many persons among different spatial horizons: work loyalties, residential loyalties, and religious loyalties may create disjunct registers of affiliation. This is true whether migration of populations is across small or large distances and whether or not these movements traverse international boundaries.

From the point of view of the nation, there is a rapidly growing distance between the promiscuous spaces of free trade and tourism, where national disciplines are often relaxed, and the spaces of national security and ideological reproduction, which may be increasingly nativized, authenticated, and culturally marked. Thus the Sri Lankan state encourages a remarkable cultural promiscuity and "inauthenticity" in its beach resorts (which are now explicitly pushed into a translocal Caribbean-style aesthetic) while intensively nationalizing other spaces, which are carefully marked for enacting "Sinhala" national development and "Buddhist" national memory.[14]

These disjunctures in the links among space, place, citizenship, and nationhood have several far-reaching implications. One of these is that territory and territoriality are increasingly the critical rationale of state legitimacy and state power, while ideas of nation seem increasingly driven by other discourses of loyalty and affiliation—sometimes linguistic, sometimes racial, sometimes religious, but *very rarely territorial.*

The question of why state and nation seem to be developing different relationships to territory is critical to the main argument of this essay and requires some elaboration, especially because not all nation-states are equally wealthy, ethnically coherent, internally contested, or globally recognized. Given that all state apparatuses are faced, in one or other way, with the reality of moving populations, legal and illegal commodity flows, and massive movements of arms across state borders, there is very little that they can realistically monopolize except the idea of territory as the crucial diacritic of sovereignty. Yet what Monroe Price has called the global "market for loyalties"[15] is not one in which states are set up to compete very well: the global competition for allegiances now involves all sorts of nonstate actors and organizations and various

---

[14] Valentine Daniel, oral communication.

[15] Monroe Price, "The Market for Loyalties: Electronic Media and the Global Competition for Allegiances," *The Yale Law Journal* 104, 3 (1994): 667–705.

forms of diasporic or multilocal allegiance. The result is a historically peculiar development. Where states could once be seen as legitimate guarantors of the territorial organization of markets, livelihoods, identities, and histories, they are now to a very large extent arbiters (among other arbiters) of various forms of global flow. So territorial integrity becomes crucial to state-sponsored ideas of sovereignty, which, on close inspection, may be in the interest of no other organization than the state apparatus itself. In short, states are the only major players in the global scene that really need the idea of territorially based sovereignty. All sorts of other global competitors for popular allegiance (artists and writers, refugees and guest workers, scientists and scholars, health workers and development specialists, feminists and fundamentalists, transnational corporations and United Nations bureaucracies) are already evolving nonstate forms of macropolitical organization: interest groups, social movements, and actually existing transnational loyalties. Transnational religious formations (often associated with Islam but equally salient with respect to Christianity, Hinduism, and Judaism) are the richest examples of such loyalties.[16]

Postnational Cartographies

Where does this perspective leave the hyphen between the nation and the state, a hyphen that I have elsewhere argued is the true site of crisis?[17] There is no doubting that the national imaginary has not given in readily to the emergence of nonnational, transnational, or postnational markets for loyalty. Indeed, many observers have noted that new nationalisms, often tied up with ethnic separatism and state-level turbulence, are on the rise. Can we make sense of these emergent nationalisms in relation to the problematic of territory and sovereignty? Let us consider some concrete examples of the extent to which

---

[16] Suzanne H. Rudolph, "Religion, the State and Transnational Civil Society," unpublished paper prepared for Program in International Peace and Security (SSRC).

[17] Appadurai, "Disjuncture and Difference."

discourses of nationalism remain vessels for the ideology of territorial nationalism.

The search for homelands and autonomous states by groups as different as the Palestinians, the Kurds, the Sikhs, and others seems to suggest that territory is still vital to the national imaginary of diasporic populations and stateless peoples of many sorts. It is this impulse that was cynically manipulated by the white South African government in earlier times to create the idea of "homelands" for various South African populations. In fact, in all these cases, territory is not so much the driving force behind these movements as a response to the pressure of already sovereign states, which couch their opposition to these groups in territorial terms. The case of Khalistan is particularly interesting. Khalistan is the name of the imagined nation that some Sikhs in India (and throughout the world) have given to the place that they would like to think of as their own national space, outside of the territorial control of the Indian state. Khalistan is not simply a separatist, diasporic nationalism in the classic post-Westphalian mode of the modern nation-state. Rather, Sikhs who imagine Khalistan are using spatial discourses and practices to construct a new, postnational cartography in which ethnos and demos are unevenly spread across the world and the map of nationalities cross-cuts existing national boundaries and intersects with other translocal formations.[18] This topos of Sikh "national" identity is in fact a topos of "community" (*qom*), which contests many national maps (including those of India, Pakistan, England, and Canada) and contains one model of a post-Westphalian cartography.

This emergent postnational cartography will probably issue from a variety of translocal affiliations: some global or globalizing, as in the case of Islamic, Christian, and Hindu fundamentalisms; some continental, such as the emerging European Union; and some racial and diasporic, for example the discourses of "Afro-diasporic" consciousness in Latin

---

[18] I owe my awareness of emergent Sikh cartographies to the important ongoing research of Brian Axel of the Department of Anthropology at the University of Chicago.

America, the Caribbean, Britain, and Africa,[19] and others involving counterhegemonic conceptions of race and space.[20] None of these relies on the idea of separate and bounded territorial entities on which our current nation-state cartography relies. Rather, in these new cartographies, counterhistories and counteridentities are used to organize maps of allegiance and affiliation that are built around historical labor flows, emergent racial solidarities, and counternational cartographies. In several cases, such as those of the Sikhs and the Kurds, counternational movements are sedimenting into permanent transnational forms. This process is one example of the general challenge of identifying the emergent morphologies (and cartographies) of a postnational order. The most important feature of these emergent cartographies is that they do not appear to require horizontally arranged, contiguous, and mutually exclusive claims to territory. They frequently involve transecting maps of allegiance and a politics of nonexclusive, territorial copresence. Kurds, Sri Lankan Tamils, and Sikhs may have their various problems as citizens in the new Germany, but they appear to have no difficulty with the territorial overlapping, in Frankfurt, Berlin, or Hamburg, of their diasporic maps. When violence does occur in these diasporic contexts, it usually involves factional issues within exile communities or extraterritorial warfare between diasporic communities and their states of origin,[21] as in the recent episodes of violence between Kurds and Turks in contemporary Germany.

The "capitals" of this emergent postnational cartography, as I have already suggested, are likely to be found in a variety of spatial formations that may not have much to do with the self-representation of sovereign states. Some of these postnational capitals will be found in the different sorts of translocalities to which I alluded earlier. These translocalities might be formed by refugee dynamics, by permanent efforts to organize social life around tourism, or by the structural effects of the

---

[19] Michael Hanchard, "Black Cinderella?: Race and Public Sphere in Brazil," *Public Culture* 7, 1 (1994): 165–85.

[20] Paul Gilroy, *The Black Atlantic: Modernity and Double Consciousness* (Cambridge, MA: Harvard University Press, 1993).

[21] Yossi Shain, *The Frontier of Loyalty: Political Exiles in the Age of the Nation-State* (Middletown, CT: Wesleyan University Press, 1989).

emergent global networks of labor and capital.[22] Such places, usually cities, tend to be weakly associated with their national environments and are, rather, integrally involved with transnational allegiances and interests. Of course, nation-states often try to exercise strong control over these cities and their civic life (as with China in respect to the anticipated acquisition of Hongkong). But such efforts will no longer be able to rely on the commonsense that there is a national territory to which these cities and their inhabitants naturally belong. The relationship of such "translocal" places to the quotidian production of locality as a feature of human life[23] and to the changing cartographies of diasporic groups will require serious rethinking of our existing images of cities, space, and territorial affiliation.

The United Nations, which continues to operate as a powerful validator of the territorial nation-state, might also seem to contradict my suggestion that the territorial basis of the nation-state is rapidly eroding. Yet, if we look at the moral and material role of the United Nations in peacekeeping and humanitarian operations throughout the world, it seems clear that it is itself emerging as a major transnational force in Africa, the Middle East, Cambodia, Eastern Europe, and elsewhere. Of course, its troops are few, its funds are limited, and it often seems incapable of decisive action. But until we have more careful studies of the composition, commitment, and politics of United Nations forces, their national sources and their ideological practices, it would not be wise to dismiss the possibility that the U.N. is helping to erode the idea of the territorial integrity of existing nation-states. In this sense, whether in Korea or Cambodia, Somalia or Palestine, the United Nations is in the process of exemplifying the transmutation of national resources into transnational interests of a new and puzzling sort. What is puzzling about this example is that national resources given over to an organization intended to be a vehicle of international wishes are subsidizing activities that might actually reduce national control over a growing number of "trouble spots." Thus the United Nations, particu-

---

[22] Saskia Sassen, *Global City: New York, London, Tokyo* (Princeton: Princeton University Press, 1991), and *Cities in a World Economy* (Thousand Oaks, CA: Pine Forge Press, 1994).

[23] Appadurai, *Modernity at Large.*

larly after the Cold War, looms as a serious player in its own right in the global market for loyalty.

Territorial Habits

Territorial tropes for the idea of the nation persist in part because our very ideas of cultural coherence have become imbricated with the commonsense of the nation. In the history of culture theory, of course, territory and territoriality have played an important role: in a general way the idea that cultures are coherent, bounded, contiguous, and persistent has always been underwritten by a sense that human sociality is naturally localized and even locality-bound. The concern of anthropologists with rules of residence and their relation to descent groups and other social formations, for example, is based on a continuing sense that territorial realities of one or other sort both bound and determine social arrangements. Despite some vigorous efforts to counter such varieties of territorial determinism,[24] the image of spatial resources and practices as both constituting and determining forms of sociality is remarkably resilient. This idea is utterly explicit in those branches of ecology, archaeology, and material culture studies that take spatial practices as their main source of evidence and analysis. Though books like Robert Ardrey's *The Territorial Imperative* are no longer in vogue, there is still a widespread sense that human beings are conditioned to demand spaces of allegiance that are extensions of their bodies. Variations of this assumption not only characterize anthropology but are also deeply entwined with the discipline of geography as a component of various national and imperial projects.[25]

The tenacity of the primordialist thesis reminds us that such thinking is very much with us, and in one or other form the primordialist hypothesis underwrites otherwise different

---

[24] Marshall Sahlins, *Stone Age Economics* (Chicago: Aldine-Atherton, 1972), and *Culture and Practical Reason* (Chicago: University of Chicago Press, 1976).

[25] Anne Godlewska and Neil Smith, eds., *Geography and Empire* (Oxford: Blackwell Publishers, 1994).

theories of nationalism. In spite of the heavy inroads of historical and historicizing critiques of the primordialist thesis,[26] it
frequently reappears in both popular and academic thinking
about nationalism. It is nowhere more apparent than in recent
popular and media opinion about Eastern Europe, in which it
is assumed that the ethnocide and terror of Bosnia-
Herzegovina is part of a long history of primordial ethnic conflict only briefly interrupted by communist rule. Weak and un-
scholarly as this thesis is, it is particularly weak on the issue
of territory as part of what nationalism is about.

In contemporary Europe, in fact, the divorce of ethnona-
tionalism from territory takes the form of a disturbing reversal
that increasingly informs the neo-fascist movements of Germany, Hungary, and elsewhere; the argument simply is: wherever there are Germans, there is Germany. Here—far from the
classical Romanticist argument that blood, soil, language, and
perhaps race are the isomorphic foundations of the sentiments
of nationhood—is the peculiar inverse argument that ethnic
affiliation generates territory. Thus Germanness creates German soil rather than being produced by it. This inversion is a
possible, though not necessary, pathology of diaspora, because
it involves a process of reterritorialization, antecedent to processes of deterritorialization. It is, more exactly, a pathology of
territorial nationalism, provoked by the historical specificities
of German national socialist ideology, the particular history of
state formation in Europe after the Hapsburg Empire, and the
tempting contiguity of "ethnic" Germans, separated by relatively recently created state borders.

In general, though the world we live in has been referred
to by me and others as "deterritorialized,"[27] it needs to be
pointed out that "deterritorialization" generates various forms
of "reterritorializaton." Not all reterritorialization is counterna-
tionalist or nativist. Reterritorialization can involve the effort to
create new localized residential communities (slums, refugee
camps, hostels) that rest not on a national imaginary but only

---

[26] Appadurai, *Modernity at Large*; J. Comaroff and J. L. Comaroff, "Of
Totemism and Ethnicity," in *Ethnography and the Historical Imagination*
(Boulder, CO: Westview Press, 1992).

[27] G. Deleuze and F. Guattari, *A Thousand Plateaus: Capitalism and
Schizophrenia*, trans. B. Massumi (Minneapolis: University of Minnesota Press,
1987); Appadurai, "Disjuncture and Difference."

on an imaginary of local autonomy or of resource sovereignty. In such "transit communities," there is frequently an effort to create and defend various forms of rights (formal and informal; legal and illegal) that allow the displaced community to continue its reproduction under unstable conditions by assuring reliable access to the material needs of reproduction: water, electricity, public safety, bank loans. Such resources are frequently siphoned off from "legitimate" civic structures by large communities of "slum" dwellers, refugee camps, and other quasi-legitimate built communities. It is often under these conditions that discourses of exile and homeland emerge, and only rarely (as in Germany) do these reterritorializing efforts involve direct attempts to extend national maps outward to follow diasporic communities. Most often, as in the case of the "civics" of the new South Africa, these efforts are exercises in the creation of new local imaginaries, relatively free of the discourses of patriotism and nationality but rich in the discourses of citizenship, democracy, and local rights.

There is a vital difference between such imagined cartographies as those of the Sikhs in respect to Khalistan and those of the German neo-fascists about Sudetenland. In the first case there is an effort to create a diasporic ethnos by carving out a homeland from existing national territories (in the Sikh case with respect to India). In the German neo-fascist case, there is an effort to extend and expand a majority ethnos already in command of a territorial nation-state into the territories of other, existing nation-states. This extension of official nationalism through linkage with emigrants needs to be sharply distinguished from the construction of a breakaway nationalism on the basis of a global diaspora.

Yet these different efforts to extend the territorial imaginary to situations of political change and diaspora do have something in common, which is a tendency to use the territorial imaginary of the nation-state to grasp and mobilize the large-scale and dispersed populations of the contemporary world into transnational ethnic formations. This effort often creates tension with one or more nation-states, since the logics of deterritorialization and reterritorialization often generate various sorts of local, regional, and global domino relations. As I suggested earlier, the ethnic cleansing exercises of many nation-states (especially those committed to some sort of "son of the soil" ideology) inevitably create refugee problems for neighboring or distant societies, thus exacerbating local problems in the always delicate relationship among residence, race, and rights in modern societies.

Territory thus can be seen as the crucial problem in the contemporary crisis of the nation-state, or, more precisely, the crisis in the relationship between nation and state. Insofar as actually existing nation-states rest on some implicit idea of ethnic coherence as the basis of state sovereignty, they are bound to minoritize, degrade, penalize, murder, or expel those seen to be ethnically minor. Insofar as these minorities (as guest workers, refugees, or illegal aliens) enter into new polities, they require reterritorialization within a new civic order, whose ideology of ethnic coherence and citizenship rights they are bound to disturb, since all modern ideologies of rights depend, ultimately, on the *closed* (enumerated, stable, and immobile) group of appropriate recipients of state protection and patronage. Thus second-classness and third-classness are conditions of citizenship that are inevitable entailments of migration, however plural the ethnic ideology of the host state and however flexible its accommodation of refugees and other weakly documented visitors.

None of this would be a problem except that the conditions of global economic, labor, and technological organization create dramatic new pushes and pulls in favor of uprooting individuals and groups and moving them into new national settings. Since these individuals and groups have to be cognized within some sort of vocabulary of rights and entitlements, however limited and harsh, they pose a threat to the ethnic and moral coherence of all host nation-states, which is at bottom predicated on both a singular and an immobile ethnos. In these conditions, the state as a push factor in ethnic diasporas is constantly obliged to pump out the sources of ethnic noise that threaten or violate its integrity as an ethnically singular territorial entity. But, in its other guise, virtually every modern nation-state is either forced or seduced to accept into its territory a whole array of nonnationals, who demand and create a wide variety of territorially ambiguous claims on civic and national rights and resources.

Here we are at the heart of the crisis of the contemporary nation-state. It looks at first glance as if the crisis is the mere fact of ethnic plurality, which is the inevitable result of the flow of populations in the contemporary world. But on closer in-spection, the problem is not ethnic or cultural pluralism as such but the tension between diasporic pluralism and territo-rial stability in the project of the modern nation-state. What ethnic plurality does (especially when it is the product of population movements within recent memory) is to violate the sense of isomorphism between territory and national identity on which the modern nation-state relies. What diasporic plu-ralisms particularly expose and intensify is the gap between the powers of the state to regulate borders, monitor dissent, distribute entitlements within a finite territory *and* the fiction of ethnic singularity on which most nations ultimately rely. In other words, the territorial integrity that justifies states and the ethnic singularity that validates nations are increasingly hard to see as seamless aspects of each other. Put another way, since states, territories, and ideas of national ethnic sin-gularity are always complicated historical coproductions, dias-poric pluralism tends to embarrass all narratives that attempt to naturalize such histories.

Conclusion

I suggested that a series of paired ideas that we have taken to be closely connected are gradually coming apart. In my title, I implied that sovereignty and territoriality, once twin ideas, live increasingly separate lives. This split is related to other disjunctures that are becoming apparent. Territorial in-tegrity is increasingly not a simple expression of national in-tegrity, as the privileges of overseas Indians make clear. Dis-courses of the soil tend to flourish in all sorts of populist movements, both local and transnational, while discourses of territory tend to characterize border conflicts and international law. Loyalty often leads individuals to identify with transna-tional cartographies, while the appeals of citizenship attach them to territorial states. These disjunctures indicate that territory, once a commonsense justification for the legitimacy of the nation-state, has become the key site of the crisis of sov-ereignty in a transnational world.

Yet a postnational geography will not emerge from our researches in the academy, even from the newest of our geographies and the most technically inventive of our cartographic technologies. It will emerge—indeed, it is emerging—from the actual spatializing contests between diasporic groups and the efforts of various states to accommodate them without giving up on the principle of territorial integrity. That principle is hardly likely to survive, in the long run, but it would be foolhardy to look to some simple new organizational principle for the large-scale political organization of human societies. It may well be that the greatest peculiarity of the modern nation-state was the idea that territorial boundaries could indefinitely sustain fictions of national ethnic singularity. This utopian idea might be our most lasting memory of the modern nation-state.

MAPPING IDENTITIES:
Place, Space, and Community in an African City

Michael Watts

> Territorial place-based identity, particularly when conflated with race, gender, religious and class differentiation, is one of the most pervasive bases for both progressive political mobilization and reactionary exclusionary politics.
>
> —David Harvey[1]

> Emergent modernism has tended to take the specific form of ... a "reshuffling of the self." Here historical change not only forces upon the individual a search for a new identity but also imposes upon whole social groups the task of revising or replacing defunct beliefs.
>
> —Carl Schorske[2]

Writing in the Quarterly News in 1839, an English commentator speculated on the rather extraordinary prospect of railroads linking all points of England, permitting, as he put it, the whole population of the country to "place their chairs nearer to the fireside of the metropolis by two thirds of the time which now separates them from it." To the extent that the railway annihilated distance, so would the surface of the country "shrivel in size until it became ... one immense city."[3] In view of the new White House plan currently on offer to us, namely to make use of the "global information superhighway," talk of railways, chairs, and fireplaces all sounds rather quaint, if not pedestrian. According to Vice President Al Gore, and I suppose he should know, we will all be soon speeding down the global telecommunications highway in search of knowledge, adventure, profit, and, I have no doubt, traffic jams

---

[1] "From Space to Place and Back Again," in *Mapping the Futures: Local Culture, Global Change*, ed. J. Bird et al. (London: Routledge, 1993) 4.

[2] *Fin de Siecle Vienna: Politics and Culture* (New York: Vintage, 1981) xviii.

[3] Cited in Nigel Thrift, "Hyperactive World," in *Geographies of Global Change*, ed. R. Johnson, P. Taylor, and M. Watts (Oxford: Blackwell, 1995) 7.

Nigeria

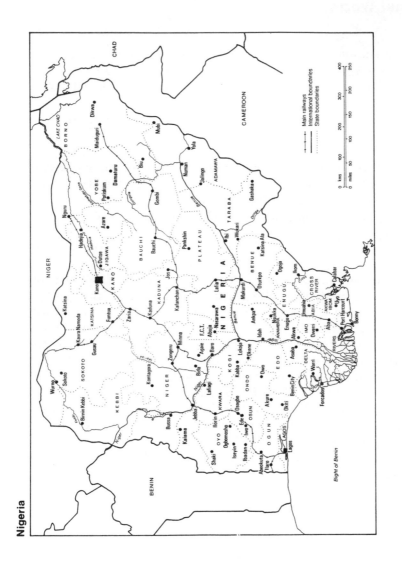

Figure 1. Nigeria

and roadkills. But the processes by which the English, more than one and a half centuries ago, moved their chairs a little closer to the metropolis and Americans of the next millennium will travel through cyberspace care of Internet are in at least one respect woven from the same cloth. Both the railroad and superhighway speak to the ways in which lived experience has been projected outward beyond the confines of the local. The friction of space has been, if not exactly annihilated, then markedly reduced. Our understanding and experience of space and time, in other words, are framed by the larger transformations by which, to quote Jean and John Comaroff, "markets, money and mechanical media extend across the planet."[4]

As a gloss for this stretching of social relations over space, globalization represents a sort of touchstone for the new millennium. The General Agreement on Trade and Tariffs (GATT) of the Uruguay round signed early in December 1993—and the new World Trade Organization (WTO) to appear early in 1995— marks a radical deepening of what appears to be the inexorable shift from shallow trade-based linkages to what the United Nations calls "deep international economic integration."[5] While it is all too easy to exaggerate the consequences of trade liberalization and regional agreements such as the North American Free Trade Agreement (NAFTA), the transnationalization of capital—underwritten by the new technologies of communication, image processing, and transmission—has clearly been a propulsive force in the transformation of the postwar economy. According to the United Nations *World Investment Report*, there are now almost 40,000 transnational corporations with 170,000 affiliates accounting for $5.5 trillion in worldwide sales. Finance and banking capital, stimulated by electronic transfers, governmental deregulation, and the genesis of twenty-four-hour trading, have been in the vanguard of the globalization process. Foreign exchange trading across the world's leading financial centers, for example, currently averages $650 billion a day: that is $500 million a *minute* or, put differently, forty times the value of world trade in a day! The invention of the truly global commodities such as the World

---

[4] "Introduction," in *Modernity and Its Malcontents*, ed. Jean and John Comaroff (Chicago: University of Chicago Press, 1993) xi.

[5] United Nations, *World Investment Report* (New York: United Nations, 1993) 161.

Car—designed, manufactured, and assembled through integrated global production systems—and of global outsourcing systems employing the model of the Mexican maquiladoras or the Asian off-shore export platforms all suggest a final push toward the internationalization of everything from construction to cleaning, from toy production to tourism. In short, the complex reconfigurations of industrial capitalism during the last two decades, whether characterized in terms of flexible accumulation or of postfordist economics, reveal the distinctively global ambitions of capital flows and the unprecedented extensions of the world market. As a consequence, space has been restructured, altering "the relative locations of places within the global patterning of capital accumulation," while diminished transport costs have made capitals of all sorts "much more geographically mobile than heretofore."[6]

At the very moment that globalization as a set of real-world practices has occupied the center stage, so has space been rehabilitated as a category worthy of scrutiny within social and cultural theory. It was Henri Lefebvre who tersely observed that "inasmuch as space is the locus of all such chronologies [of history], might it not constitute a principle of explanation at least as acceptable as any other."[7] Since geography is a discipline which speaks to the broad proposition that the social and the spatial are inseparable and that the spatial form of the social has causal powers, the geographic community should be delighted that Anthony Giddens, Fredric Jameson, Edward Said, Homi Babha—indeed many figures within the cultural studies pantheon—talk the language of space and spatiality.[8] It is therefore somewhat ironic that at the very moment of its rehabilitation, space has been practically erased from the real world of markets, media, and money, a product of the fact that under capitalism space apparently is

---

[6] Harvey, "From Space to Place" 7.

[7] Cited in Doreen Massey, "Politics and Space-Time," *New Left Review* 196 (1992): 70.

[8] The key works are: Doreen Massey, *Spatial Divisions of Labour* (London: Macmillan, 1984); Derek Gregory, *Geographical Imaginations* (Oxford: Blackwell, 1993); Ed Soja, *Postmoden Geographies* (London: Verso, 1989); David Harvey, *The Condition of Postmodernity* (Oxford: Blackwell, 1989); Michael Watts and Allan Pred, *Reworking Modernity* (New Brunswick: Rutgers University Press, 1992).

"annihilated by time."[9] There are a number of ways in which this erasure is effected by a profoundly globalized system of capitalist production, consumption, and distribution. For Fredric Jameson, late capitalism undermines any sense of space and distance—"the truth of the experience no longer coincides with the place in which it takes place"—thereby manufacturing a sort of illegibility, a depthless world of confusion and dislocation in which "people are unable to map ... either their own positions or the urban totality in which they find themselves."[10] For Manuel Castells—like Deleuze and Guattari[11] — globalization produces a sort of "deterritorialization"; the space of flows dominates the space of places:

> The space of flows dominates the historically constructed space of places, as the dominant organization detaches itself from the social constraints of cultural identities and local societies.[12]

Places are powerless, and power is placeless. In short, a world of frictionless, hypermobile capital, of speed, illegibility, confusion, and erasure.

In this view, the global space of electronic information flows and the globalization of culture produce a Frankfurt School nightmare: a sort of hollowing out and homogenization as the link between culture and place is ruptured. The whole world watches Oprah and drinks Coca Cola. Whether this radical view—that the singularity of space is disappearing—is tenable is perhaps less significant than the general recognition that a major reshaping of the spatial organization of social relations is occurring at every level of social reality and across all cultures. The mobility of capital, commodities, and people, coupled with the restlessness of cultural products and practices, makes for "an erosion of the cultural distinctiveness of

---

[9] See Harvey, *Condition of Postmodernity*.

[10] Fredric Jameson, "Cognitive Mapping," in *Marxism and the Interpretation of Culture*, ed. C. Nelson and L. Grossberg (Urbana: University of Illinois Press, 1988) 349, and *Postmodernism or the Logic of Late Capitalism* (Durham, NC: Duke University Press, 1991) 51.

[11] G. Deleuze and F. Guattari, *The Anti-Oedipus* (New York: Viking, 1977).

[12] M. Castells, *The Informational City* (Oxford: Blackwell, 1989) 6.

places."[13] And with the crisis of place comes the crisis of the border:

> Not only has the border [between the West and the rest] been punctured porous by the global market [and capital and migration] ... but the border has dissolved and expanded to cover the lands it once separated such that all land is borderland.[14]

To put the matter starkly, globalization, as the historic form in which space is currently being reconstructed, threatens the particularity of places, borders, and territoriality in a way that necessarily challenges local identities rooted precisely in the particularities of space and place. Corresponding to the erasure of place is the extinction of some identities and the emergence of others that are in some sense placeless, liminal (the hybrid, the expatriate, the refugee), or at the very least no longer subject to the discipline of definite and distinctive local borders and boundaries. It all seems to bid a fond farewell to what Raymond Williams called militant particularism.[15]

I want to take issue with some aspects of this picture, not by contesting a distinctive sense of *fin de siècle* globalization but by challenging the notion of frictionless mobility and a relentless annihilation of space (a simple puncturing of borders, as Taussig puts it). In so doing, I want to argue that globalization does not so much mark the erasure of place but in a curious way contributes to its revitalization, or more properly to a *new* sort of valorization. If space is socially constructed, so too is place, which implies that places are rarely stable, or simply bounded, or indeed singular identities. The fact that places are now global sites—we need in other words a "global sense of place," as Doreen Massey says[16]—means that they will be unstable, contested, and reconstructed in new ways as a product

---

[13] A. Gupta and J. Ferguson, "Beyond 'Culture'," *Cultural Anthropology* 7 (1992): 9.

[14] Michael Taussig, *Mimesis and Alterity: A Particular History of the Senses* (London: Routledge, 1993) 248–49.

[15] Raymond Williams, *Marxism and Literature* (Oxford: Oxford University Press, 1977).

[16] Doreen Massey, *Space, Place and Gender* (Minneapolis: University of Minnesota Press, 1994) 146.

of the concrete connections—what I shall call networks—
linking the local to global spaces. Globalization here implies
less the erosion of place than a sensitivity to how location,
identity, and community are refashioned in incompletely
globalized sites.

To illustrate a quite specific global sense of place and the
construction of a rather particular identity and community in
such a globalized site, I shall describe the case of a Muslim
fundamentalist[17] movement in Kano, northern Nigeria (fig. 1).
This story reveals how a distinctive Muslim community was
built, as it were, *within* a Muslim community, and to tell it I
shall have to trace the dialectical relations between a local social structure of Islam and a local social structure of capitalist
accumulation driven by the boom in the world oil market during the 1970s. I have employed the metaphor of mapping to
inform the ways in which these two locally constituted global
force fields—Islam and capitalism—informed each other and
thereby challenged, reconfigured, and reconstituted place and
place-based identifications. To return to the words of David
Harvey and Carl Schorske with which I opened this essay, I
want first to interrogate a particular Muslim territorial, place-
based communal identity and second to examine the reshuffling of the self associated with an emergent Muslim modernism rooted in the long engagement of Islam with capitalist
modernity. In this instance as in so many others within the
contemporary Muslim world, this engagement takes the form
of a struggle over Muslim orthodoxy—what Talal Asad calls "a
reordering of knowledge that governs the 'correct' form of Islamic practices"[18]—in the context of radical social and economic change in a big, sprawling urban metropolis in northern
Nigeria.

---

[17] By fundamentalism I refer to a scripturalist form of religious piety affirming the centrality of the Qur'an for all aspects of life and practice. See Y.
Haddad, "Islam, Women and Social Revolution in Twentieth Century Arab
Thought," in *Women, Religion and Social Change*, ed. Y. Haddad and E. Find-
lay (Albany: SUNY Press, 1985) 275–306.

[18] *Genealogies of Religion* (Baltimore: Johns Hopkins University Press,
1993) 210.

Changing Places

A bustling, kinetic city forged in the crucible of seven-teenth- and eighteenth-century trans-Saharan trade, Kano is the economic fulcrum of Nigeria's most populous state, a densely settled agricultural landscape of well over ten million people. An ancient city whose iron workings date back to the seventh century, Kano was by the mid-sixteenth century com-parable in size and significance to Cairo and Fez and by the eighteenth century an Islamic city of international repute. In the course of sixty years of British colonial rule (1902–60), Kano emerged as West Africa's preeminent entrepôt, a self-consciously Muslim city whose prospects were wrapped up with the fortunes of one world commodity—the peanut—used in the manufacture of vegetable oil. But it was oil of an alto-gether different sort—petroleum—and its successful carteliza-tion in the form of the Organization of Petroleum Exporting Countries (OPEC) that ushered in a new, and in some respects a more radical, integration of the Nigerian polity and economy into the world market in the wake of the first oil boom in 1973.

Awash in petro-dollars, urban Kano was transformed during the 1970s from a traditional Muslim mercantile center of some 400,000 at the end of the civil war (ca. 1970) into a sprawling, anarchic metropolis of over 1.7 million by 1980 (fig. 2). Seemingly overnight, Kano emerged as a fully fledged in-dustrial periphery. The heart of Kano, the old walled city (*birni*), was engulfed by the new suburbs sprouting up outside the walls (*waje*), a process that suggested an important erosion in the autonomy and stature of the traditional Hausa core of the city.[19] At the zenith of the petroleum boom, new industrial estates sprung up at Challawa and Sharada in the city periph-

---

[19] For Kano citizens (*Kanawa*), the classical Muslim heart of the city is the *birni*. But from 1902 onwards, the suburbs outside the *birni* grew rapidly, populated in the first instance by Westerners and Nigerians from the south of the country. As such, *waje* was associated with Christianity, permissiveness, and evil. As Barkindo notes, *waje* was an evil to be tolerated, but "this view radically changed from about 1970 onwards." B. Barkindo, "Growing Islamism in Kano since 1970," in *Muslim Identity and Social Change in Sub-Saharan Africa*, ed. L. Brenner (Bloomington: Indiana University Press, 1993) 94.

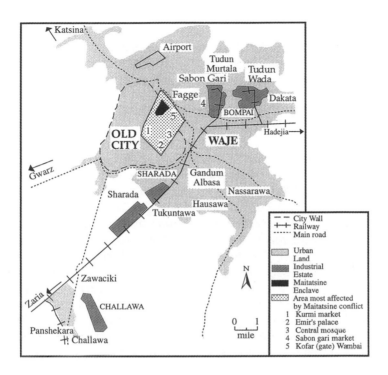

Figure 2. The geography of the
Matatsine movement, December 18–
28, 1980, Kano City

ery, armies of migrants poured into the city, and the icons of modernity—the massive state-sponsored building and infra-structural projects—dotted the city skyline. Kano was, on the one hand, a huge construction site and, on the other, a theater of wildly unregulated consumption. Murray Last has captured this ethos perfectly: Kano had become, he says, a modern city in which "dishes for satellite television dominate the com-pounds of the rich whose wealth is growing ever more dispro-portionate as austerity ... hits the poor. A watch for $17,000; a house for $2 million; private jets to London or the Friday prayer at Mecca—this is the style to which Kano's guilded youth are the heirs."[20]

---

[20] "Adolescents in a Muslim City," *Kano Studies*, special issue (1991): 4.

The reconfigurations of urban life, community relations, and styles of consumption in urban Kano were naturally part and parcel of an overarching transformation of Nigerian society initiated by an ambitious state-led modernization program and lubricated—care of OPEC—by swollen petroleum revenues. The Nigerian state banked a staggering $140 billion between 1970 and 1983 from its federally controlled petroleum industry, and government revenues exploded, growing at close to 40 percent *per annum* during the 1970s. Oil price hikes in 1973/74 and in 1978/79 permitted the Nigerian federal state to unleash a torrent of expenditure, particularly industrial investment: the Nigerian national index of manufacturing output, for example, almost tripled between 1972 and 1980. The absolute number of manufacturing establishments and of industrial wage workers, the scale of direct investment by multinationals, and the shares of federal and regional state capital in industrial output all witnessed positive growth rates throughout a boom period presided over by a succession of military governments (1972–79). Black gold promised, for the chosen few at any rate, the "dawn of prosperity and progress for the petroleum rich."[21]

Fifteen years later the luster of the oil boom had tarnished, and Nigeria's economic future appeared by contrast to be quite bleak, if not altogether austere. Spiraling debt fueled by a seemingly infinite appetite for imports, the collapse of oil prices in the early 1980s, and the onslaught of Draconian retrenchment programs imposed by the World Bank and the International Monetary Fund produced a stunning recession. The "oil fortress" had, as *Le Monde* put it (2 October 1994, 15), been rocked. This roller-coaster economy, whose volatility was apparent even by the mid-1970s, had fundamentally shaped the everyday life of all sectors of Nigerian society. Kano's experience of a rather spectacular commodity boom was felt, to borrow from Walter Benjamin, as a "shock" of modernity, and it was from within this world awash with money, commodities, and corruption that the very idea of local Muslim identity, and of correct Muslim practice, came to be challenged and contested.

---

[21] J. Amuzegar, "Oil Wealth: A Very Mixed Blessing," *Foreign Affairs*, Spring 1982, 814.

Changing Identities

> Eternal religious truths, like other beliefs, are perceived, un-
> derstood and transmitted by persons historically situated in
> "imagined" communities, who knowingly or inadvertently
> contribute to the reconfiguration or interpretation of those
> verities, even as their fixed and unchanging natures are af-
> firmed.
>
> —Dale Eickelman and James Piscatori[22]

Born into rural poverty in 1927 in northern Cameroon, Mohammedu Marwa (alias Mallam Maitatsine alias Muhammedu Marwa alias Muhammedu Mai tabsiri) left his birthplace when he was about sixteen years old. He attached himself to a local Muslim cleric and apparently displayed exceptional brilliance in the Qur'anic science of exegesis (*tafsir*). His exegetical skills were acquired as a student (*almajirai*) in local Muslim networks and informal schools (*makarantar allo*). Settling in Kano City around 1945, he was a regular visitor at the preaching sessions around Shahauci and Fagge grounds in the old quarters of the city *(birni)*, providing unorthodox interpretations of Qur'anic verses read by an associate, Mallam Aminu Umar or Limanu, who had returned from learning "in the East." Marwa insisted that the Qur'an was the *only* valid guide to behavior and belief and thus rejected both the Sunnah and the Shari'ah.[23] According to the official tribunal on the causes of the Kano riots, Maitatsine preached that "any Muslim who reads any book besides the Koran is a pagan."[24] His inflamma-

---

[22] "Social Theory in the Study of Muslim Societies," in *Muslims Travellers*, ed. D. Eickelman and J. Piscatori (Berkeley: University of California Press, 1990) 20.

[23] Shari'ah (the path of God) is Islamic law in the form of a set of divinely revealed principles derived from the Qur'an, from the example of the Prophet, and from tradition and applied by judges in Shari'ah courts. Sunnah refers to good conduct or highly desirable acts based on the example of the Prophet, custom, and reason. Maitatsine denounced the Sunnah as being made "only for Arabs."

[24] Federal Government, *Report of Tribunal of Inquiry on Kano Disturbances* (Lagos: Federal Government Press, 1981) 26.

tory reading of the Qur'an rested on a stripping away of the hidden meanings in the sacred text by rooting his analyses of verse in local, that is to say West African, conditions. In particular, by playing on the meanings and phonetic associations of certain Arabic and Hausa words, Marwa—or Maitatsine, as he became known locally—provided a powerful literalist and on occasion antimaterialist thrust to the Qur'an.[25] His vehement denunciation of bicycles, apparels, cigarettes, buttons, cars, and so on brought him his name, Maitatsine, derived from the Hausa adage "Allah ta tsine" ("God will curse"). By 1962, Marwa had gained some local notoriety as a troublesome, charismatic, and unorthodox preacher, and Emir Sanusi of Kano actually brought him to trial. He was imprisoned for three months and promptly deported. Marwa's local stature grew substantially, however, following his prediction that Emir Sanusi would fall from power; he was ousted several years later in the wake of the military coup.

Marwa returned to Kano shortly after his deportation—sustaining the popular belief that reactionary forces in high places supported his variety of militant political Islam—and continued to live and preach in the city. He was arrested and imprisoned again in 1966–67 and also in 1973–75 but was not deported. In the period following Marwa's return to Kano City, the open spaces of 'Yan Awaki and Kofar Wombai provided a sort of beachhead, a sanctuary in which his students could be housed in makeshift dwellings and which by the late 1970s included urban gardens to sustain the growing numbers of followers. By 1979 something like a community (*tsangaya*) had been built, and Maitatsine's compound in 'Yan Awaki housed at least 3,000 persons.[26] Witness #49 to the official government tribunal, one Uzairu Abdullahi, was one such Hausa disciple recruited from Niger eleven months prior to the insurrection.[27] At the suggestion of Maitatsine, the followers carried little or no money—to sleep with more than one naira ($0.75) was to exhibit a lack of trust in Allah—and dressed simply,

---

[25] A. Yusuf, *Maitatsine: Peddler of Epidemics* (Syneco: Kano, 1988).

[26] Maitatsine's diaspora extended across much of northern Nigeria and into southern Niger Republic, a region sharing a cultural kinship with the Hausa heartland in Nigeria. These networks provided fertile recruiting grounds for *almajirai* and *gardawa*.

[27] Federal Government, *Report of Tribunal* 58.

characteristically begging for alms or working as transient laborers in occupations typically reserved for dry-season migrants ('yan cin-rani), such as cart pushing, tea selling, and petty trade.

Maitatsine's followers ('yantatsine) became increasingly visible around the old city, operating in small groups of three to five people, preaching at major junctions near the Sabon Gari mosque, around Koki, and at Kofar Wombai. Through recitations and unorthodox interpretations of the Qur'an, the students vigorously attacked materialism, unjust leaders, corrupt ulema, and all followers of the powerful Sufi brotherhoods[28] (darikat) who were deemed to be non-Muslim. Unorthodox behavior fueled rumor on a grand scale. Kano's wealthiest contractors and some of the most powerful voices of the northern oligarchy, popular opinion had it, energetically supported the Maitatsine movement. Hearsay had it that Maitatsine was lent support, and financial sustenance, from luminaries within both the ruling Nigerian federal party, the conservative and northern Muslim dominated National Party of Nigeria (NPN), and perhaps from the incumbent Kano state administration (the populist Peoples' Redemption Party, PRP). Local rumor fed the mystique of Maitatsine's magical powers. The tribunal reported grotesque (but largely unsubstantiated) tales of cannibalism, human slaughter (a "human spare parts department," as the local northern press referred to it), mass graves, drugged students, and brainwashed women. At the same time, there were reports of extraordinary bravery (Marwa certainly felt himself to be invulnerable) and impressive self-discipline by the 'yantatsine; indeed, there was something like a moral economy within the tsangaya. Sometime in 1979, according to testimony by one of his wives, Marwa apparently declared his own prophethood.

On 26 November 1979, the governor of Kano State wrote to Marwa demanding a vacation of the quarter within two weeks. Originally intending to vacate 'Yan Awaki, Marwa apparently changed his mind and promptly sent out a letter to diaspora

---

[28] Rooted in Muslim mysticism, a Sufi master (shaykh) typically associated himself with a founding saint and a brotherhood distinguished by initiation and other rituals. In northern Nigeria the two main brotherhoods are founded by Abd al-Qadir Jilani of Baghdad (Qadiriyya) and Ahmad al-Tijani of North Africa (Tijaniyya).

communities calling in reinforcements to fight the "infidels." The 'yantatsine planned to overrun and take control of the Friday mosque in Kano, NEPA (the national electricity utility company), and the emir's palace. In their denunciation of the government and appropriation of "all land in the name of Allah," there was an allusion at least to some sort of seizure of power. On 18 December 1980, four police units were sent to Shahauci playground near the emir's palace to arrest some of Maitatsine's preachers. Disorganized police forces were ambushed by "fanatics"—the language is taken from the influential northern newspapers the *New Nigerian* and *Gaskiya ta fi Kwabo*—armed with bows and arrows, daggers, and machetes. According to the official tribunal:

> The fanatics in procession and many more emerging from the cover provided by onlookers ... launched an attack on the Police ... using matchets, bows and arrows, swords and clubs, dane guns, daggers and other similar weapons ... while attacking they kept shouting "Kefri, Kefri" meaning infidels.[29]

Arms were seized by the 'yantatsine and police vehicles burned. By late afternoon a huge plume of smoke hung over the city. Over the next few days, in a climate of growing chaos and popular fear, fighting spread and casualties mounted. By 21 December, with the police effectively unable to control the situation, vigilante groups ('yan tauri) entered the scene, and complex negotiations ensued between the Kano State governor Abubakar Rimi, who feared the imposition of martial law by the federal government and hence his own political survival, and local authorities. On 22 December 'yantatsine were reportedly entering Kano to join the insurrection (six busloads of supporters from Sokoto were intercepted en route to Kano), while trucks full of corpses were seen leaving the city.

After five days of stalemate, confusion, and escalating violence, the army intervened on 29 December with ten hours of mortar barrage, supported by air force bombardment. Incurring major losses, the 'yantatsine escaped and marched out of the city into the western districts along the Gwarzo road. Maitatsine led the exit from 'Yan Awaki quarter following the fero-

---

[29] Federal Government, *Report of Tribunal* 28.

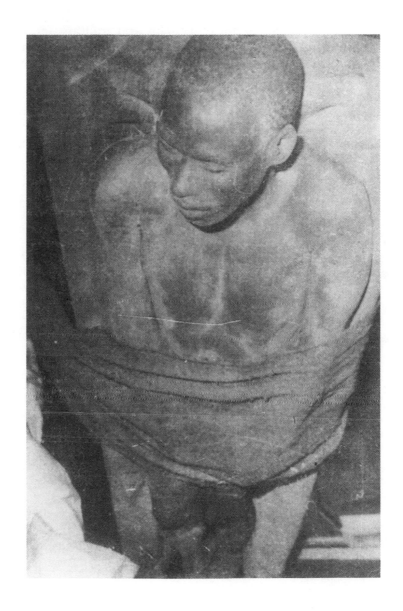

Figure 3. The corpse of Maitatsine.
Photographed at the Kano police
station

cious bombardment by state security and military forces but was injured and died in the western districts outside the city walls. His body was removed from a shallow grave and kept at a local mortuary for several days before it was cremated at the request of local authorities to obviate possible martyrdom among his converts and followers. Photographs of Maitatsine's body were hot-selling items in the aftermath of the insurrection, pedaled by young boys at busy intersections in the city (fig. 3).[30]

Reconfiguring National Space

> Oil creates the illusion of a completely changed life, life without work, life for free.... Oil is a resource that anesthetizes thought, blurs vision, corrupts.... Look at the ministers from oil countries, how high they hold their heads, what a sense of power.
>
> —Ryszard Kapuchinski[31]

The 1970s was the decade of oil and of bristling petrolic nationalism. Twenty-eight third world states were exporters of petroleum; each experienced, in varying measure, a substantial influx of oil rents leveraged from a petroleum-dependent world by OPEC's successful cartelization. Among OPEC members petroleum became the linchpin of the national economy, representing on average at least three-quarters of national export earnings in 1980. Oil producers are, however, a heteroge-

---

[30] According to the official tribunal figures, 4,177 people died (excluding police and military), but the human toll was clearly much greater. Some quite reliable estimates range as high as 10,000; 15,000 were injured and 100,000 rendered homeless. The physical damage was enormous: in Fagge 82 houses and 249 shops were destroyed; in 'Yan Awaki 165 houses were destroyed and heavily scarred; 917 people were arrested (12 percent juveniles), of which 185 were non-Nigerian. Many thousands more of Maitatsine's supporters avoided arrest and scattered to various states in the north. Between 1981 and 1985 four more incidents occurred between Maitatsine's followers and state authorities in urban and quasi-urban locations across northern Nigeria; perhaps 4,000–5,000 persons died in these conflagrations.

[31] *Shah of Shahs* (New York: Harcourt, 1982) 35.

neous lot, and Lilliputian city-states like Qatar with limited capacity to absorb the revenues locally stand in sharp contrast to populous so-called "high absorbers" like Indonesia, Venezuela, and Mexico. Nigeria stands, in this regard, as an archetypical high absorber since domestic petroleum output in the 1970s—roughly 1.3 million barrels per day—was sufficient to sustain unprecedented growth rates in domestic state expenditures. By 1980 Nigeria had become a monocultural economy, more so than it had ever been in the colonial era; 95.3 percent of total export revenues derived from oil, and almost two-thirds of government revenue was dependent upon the petroleum sector. Average annual growth rates for credit, money supply, and state expenditures were stunning: respectively, 45 percent, 66 percent, and 91 percent between 1973 and 1980!

How, then, can we begin to grasp the social and geographic character of Nigeria's petrolic modernization? Two rather obvious points at the outset. The first is that oil is a, in some respects *the*, archetypical global commodity. It necessarily projects its producers fully into the vortex of international circuits of capital and global finance. To this extent one might talk of an internationalization, or globalization, of the Nigerian economy and polity. The second is that the enclave character of the oil industry, combined with the fact that oil revenues typically flow directly into national treasuries, has profound implications for state centralization and autonomy, for what are sometimes called fiscal linkages. In this sense, the disposition of oil acts as a powerful centralizing force at the level of the state, which is, at it were, projected into civil society (i.e., "domesticated") via expanded forms of public ownership, investment, and service provision (i.e., fiscal linkages). In other words, Nigeria's oil boom transformed its national space in three ways: through an ostensibly new relationship with the world economy, through a new strategy of capital accumulation as oil earnings overwhelmed previous sources of state surplus, and through a process of state centralization, growth, and enhanced autonomy from civil society.

The genesis of an enlarged state as the mediator of the oil boom appears with particular clarity in Nigeria in the aftermath of the first oil shock. State centralization had commenced during the civil war, but the creation of new regional states (nineteen states from four autonomous regions) deepened the fiscal dependency on a federal purse through statutory revenue allocation procedures. At the same time, the multiplication of states in the wake of the first oil boom vastly expanded, in a simple quantitative sense, bureaucratic strata at all levels of government. Creeping state bureaucratization, or *etatization*, is seen in a variety of guises: capital expenditures at the federal levels increased by 800 percent in real terms between 1973 and 1980, the number of parastatals mushroomed from almost nothing in 1970 to over 800 in 1980, and the number of federal employees leapt to 280,000. The period after 1975 under the Murtala and Obasanjo military administrations (1975–79) represents the high-water mark of state-bureaucratic growth and the consolidation of a state-capitalist sector. The federal government encouraged auto assembly and initiated an ambitious capital and intermediate goods program, including an iron and steel sector, petrochemicals, and light engineering. In the same way that oil promised for the shah of Iran a Great Civilization, so effortless money produced boundless ambition in Nigeria. El Dorado had been located, and it was an oil well.

Naturally, the rise of a centralized, bureaucratic petro-state with earnings in 1980 in excess of U.S.$25 billion had serious implications for politics and class rule in Nigeria. The regional elites no longer depended on access to surpluses generated by peasant producers but on oil rents redistributed through the state apparatuses. Indeed, while the military–civil servant alliance maintained its precarious northern political hegemony, the vastly expanded oil revenues bankrolled a huge rent-seeking edifice, a "flabby and heterogeneous dominant coalition preoccupied with a grabbing of public resources ...through an elaborate network of patronage and subsidies."[32] Not only did the state embark upon a massive program of infrastructural and industrial modernization—attempting to lay the groundwork for systematic capitalist accumulation—but these expenditures became the means by which petro-dollars created pacts and coalitions within a national polity sharply divided along regional, ethnic, and religious lines. Patronage, contracting, and subsidies were part and parcel of the desperate political struggle to win control of the state. Indeed, the

---

[32] Pranab Bardhan, "Dominant Proprietary Classes in India's Democracy," in *India's Democracy*, ed. A. Kohli (Princeton: Princeton University Press, 1988) 82.

state was privatized in the sense that public office became, to employ Max Weber's language, a prebend, a public position to be used for personal gain. Corruption flourished on a gargantuan scale; in fact, the bureaucratic environment was characterized by astonishing indiscipline, chaos, and venality. In the wake of the return to civilian rule in 1979 these pathologies of the state reached new levels of venality. Government became more than ever, as Chinua Achebe observed in his novel *Anthills of the Savannas*, a "crummy family business."[33]

There were, in other words, several key ways that oil-driven globalization fundamentally reconfigured the Nigerian national space in which Maitatsine operated. The first was the extraordinary commodity boom. Nigerian merchandise imports increased from N1.1 billion in 1973 to N14.6 billion in 1981. Fueled by the explosion of federal and state bureaucracies and the infusion of money ushered in by official government-mandated (Udoji Commission) salary increases in 1975, the oil boom unleashed a consumer spending spree. The proliferation of everything from stallions to stereos produced a commodity fetishism that approximated what one commentator aptly described as a Nigerian "cargo cult." The second was a state-financed urban construction boom of gargantuan, one might say Stalinist, proportions. The construction industry (roads, office construction, industrial plant) grew at 20 percent in the 1970s, sucking rural labor into dynamic but hopelessly unplanned cities. Third, the boom in oil produced distortions in the non-oil sectors, what economists refer to as the Dutch disease. Labor drawn from the rural sector, combined with escalating input costs, created a profit squeeze for many peasant producers, which was reflected in the collapse of the traditional export sector (cocoa, groundnuts, palm oil). Food imports such as wheat increased sharply, prompting a series of expensive state irrigation schemes to produce wheat for the local bread industry. Expensive, corrupt, and socially disruptive, these state agricultural schemes contributed less to national food self-sufficiency than to the growth of land speculation and quite dramatic social differentiation in some rural communities associated with the rise of so-called overnight farmers and farmer-trader speculators. Agriculture's Dutch

---

[33] Chinua Achebe, *Anthills of the Savannas* (New York: Vintage, 1988) 46.

disease contributed to rural-urban drift, social dislocation in the countryside, and a profound sense of state corruption and violence.

Experiencing Modernization

> This letter is from the Prophet Mohammed. It came from Medina to Mecca ... to Wadi ... to Kukawa ... to Bornoland ... From there to Hadejia ... to Kano and from Kano to the whole world. The Prophet said there will be disaster of the wind, poverty, death of sheep and illhealth of women and men. The illhealth of women and men will affect their womanhood and manhood respectively. It would effect the old and the young of women and men East and West, South and North.
>
> —Letter circulated by Maitatsine followers[34]

How was this peculiar configuration of surplus money, commodification, and rapid modernization "experienced," and quite specifically, how was it experienced by the urban residents of Kano? I want to suggest that the question of experience contains two aspects. On one hand, the oil boom was experienced in class terms, and yet the social and cultural character of this class experience in Kano was, to use Marx's language, inherited from the past and was irreducibly local. The central social class we must consider is the self-conscious popular stratum in northern Nigerian society identified locally as commoners or *talakawa.* On the other hand, the roller-coaster ride on Nigeria's fast capitalist track was experienced explicitly in moral and symbolic terms, and the discursive frame of reference is Islam itself, a subject to which I shall turn in the following section.

To begin with the question of class experience. According to a World Bank study in the early 1980s, 52 to 67 percent of Kano's urban population existed at the "absolute poverty level." This amorphous subaltern class embracing small traders, workers, informal sector workers, and the unemployed was diverse but had a socially unified popular self-identity in Hausa society as commoners or *talakawa.* A *talaka* is "a per-

---

[34] Published in *The New Nigerian*, 3 March 1984.

son who holds no official position ... a man in the street ... a poor person."[35] As an indigenous social category, it is of considerable antiquity, emerging from the social division of labor between town and countryside associated with the genesis of political kingdoms (the *sarauta* system) in the fifteenth century and subsequently the emirate system under the Sokoto caliphate (1806–1902), in which a lineage-based office-holding class (*masu sarauta*) exercised political authority over subject populations. *Talakawa* refers, then, to a class relationship of a precapitalist sort but also a political relationship among status honor groups with distinctive cultural identities and lifestyles. Naturally, the *talakawa* have been differentiated in all sorts of complex ways through the unevenness of proletarianization—the industrial working class (*leburori*), for example, constituting an important social segment of the *talakawa* as such.

While there is a generic sort of subaltern identity embodied in the notion of *talaka*, I wish to identify two distinctive social segments that are key to an understanding of Maitatsine's effort to "reshuffle" Muslim identity—namely, to return to a scripturalist form of piety based on the Qur'an. Both are of some antiquity and are fashioned by locally distinctive social and cultural processes. The first concerns dry-season migrants (*'yan cin rani*), who circulate through the urban economy during the long dry season, relieving pressures on domestic grain reserves in the countryside and perhaps generating limited savings, which are typically of great value to dependent sons preparing for marriage. I would include in this category migrants who were, strictly speaking, not participants in seasonal circulatory networks but, as a consequence of the urban construction boom and the collapse of agriculture, were drawn into the Kano labor market in huge numbers. Almost wholly male, single, and young, and typically drawn from the densely settled and land-scarce northern provinces, they became semipermanent city residents, characteristically working in the construction sector as cart pushers, refuse collectors, itinerant laborers, and so on. This floating population expanded dramatically in the 1970s not only because of the construction boom but because of the devastating impact of drought and food shortage in the early 1970s, and because of the dispos-

---

[35] G. A. Bargery, *A Hausa-English Dictionary* (London: Oxford University Press, 1934) 983.

session of peasants associated with land speculation, fraudulent land claims, and inadequate state compensations in the
peri-urban areas and in the vicinity of the huge state irrigation
schemes. In any event, the '*yan cin rani* were shuttled into the
northern cities such as Kano during the oil boom, filling niches
in the secondary labor market, constituting a sort of lumpen-
proletariat.

The second segment of the *talakawa* is rooted in the informal Muslim schooling system (*makarantar allo*), what has
been termed Qur'anic networks by Paul Lubeck.[36] These networks long predate the nineteenth-century *jihad* and refer to a
peripatetic tradition, rooted in the human ecology of the Sahel,
in which students study with lay clerics (*mallams*) during the
dry season. Students (*almajirai*) migrated to centers of Muslim
learning and typically studied the Qur'anic science of exegesis
at the feet of notable scholars, often living in the entry ways
(*zaure*) of influential merchants and notables. Maitatsine was
himself a product of this system. These networks were sustained by a sort of urban moral economy—begging and alms-
giving as part of the normative set of relations between rich
and poor—which served both to extend Islam into the countryside and to provide a measure of social and ideological integration for Hausa society as a whole. The students themselves
often worked in the textile industry, acquiring important commercial and craft skills. In Kano these students are referred to
as *gardawa*, although this is a semantically dense term and
also refers to adult Muslim students, aspirant *mallams* of
sorts, who may not be seasonal migrants as such but longer-
term urban residents. As an ancient center of learning, of vigorous brotherhood activity, and of enormous mercantile
wealth, Kano was quite naturally a major center of *gardawa*
activity.

If the *talakawa* as a class category (and the '*yan cin rani*
and *gardi* as segments of it) represent a key set of structural
preconditions through which many Kano residents experienced
the oil boom, then what were the immediate or proximate
qualities of that experience in urban Kano? I shall focus on

---

36 P. Lubeck, "Islamic Protest under Semi-industrial Capitalism," *Africa*
55, 4 (1985); "Islamic Protest and Oil-based Capitalism, in *State, Oil and Agriculture*, ed. M. Watts (Berkeley: Institute of International Studies, 1987) 268–
90.

three sets of social relations: state mediation in the form of corruption and violent but undisciplined security forces, urban social processes, and the return to civilian party politics in 1979. I have already referred to the growing presence of the local and federal states in social and economic life. To the extent that the state was rendered much more visible in society by virtue of its expanded activities, including road and office construction and contracting of various sorts, its visibility became synonymous with a total lack of moral responsibility and state accountability. In popular discourse, the state and government meant massive corruption on a Hobbesian scale. Graft through local contracts, import speculation, foreign exchange dealings, drug smuggling, hoarding of food, and so on abounded among all levels of local and federal officialdom. It was commonplace to hear the governor referred to as "a thief" or that "*Nigeriya ta lalachi*" ("Nigeria has been ruined"). State ownership even implicated the Muslim brotherhoods who owned shares in companies. The government was also centrally involved in the annual migration of 100,000 pilgrims who participated in the *hadj*, a sacred event that was widely associated with corruption and conspicuous consumption. In the return to civilian rule, state corruption reached unprecedented levels; as the *talakawa* put it, "siyasa ta bata duniya"—"politics has spoiled the world." When the home of the governor was searched in Kano in 1983 U.S.$5.1 million was found stacked up in cardboard boxes; primitive accumulation of another sort. At around the same time, 10 percent of the Nigerian GDP was "discovered" in an unnamed private bank account in Switzerland.

To put the matter bluntly, state mediation of the oil boom meant corruption, chaos, and bureaucratic indiscipline. The *talakawa* were systematically excluded from access to the state, which they experienced as morally bankrupt, illegitimate, and incompetent. The police, who had been placed under federal jurisdiction, and the internal security forces were widely held to be particularly corrupt, disorganized, and violent; they embodied the moral and political degeneracy of state legitimacy. In the context of rising urban crime, it was the police who proved to be the trigger for all sorts of community violence; they were uniformly feared and loathed by Kano's urban poor. Indeed, it was the antiriot police who perpetrated the slaughter of at least fourteen peasants at Bakalori irrigation project, in a conflict over land compensation, six months prior to the Maitatsine insurrection. In the popular imagination the police were feared and were explicitly referred to as *daggal*— literally, "the devil."

At another level, modernization was experienced throughout the urban community. The central issue here is not simply the anarchic and chaotic growth of Kano City—a terrifying prospect in itself—but the changing material basis of *talakawa* life and what it implied for the brute realities of urban living. First, urban land became a source of speculation for Kano merchants and civil merchants, reflected in the fact that the price of urban plots in the working-class Tudun Wada neighborhood increased twenty times between 1970 and 1978. Land records invariably disappeared (usually through mysterious fires), and compensation for land appropriated by the state was arbitrary and a source of recurrent conflict. Second, the escalation of food prices, typically in the context of price rigging, hoarding, and licensing scandals, far outstripped the growth of urban wages. The inflationary spiral in wage goods went hand in hand with the internationalization of consumption by Kano's elites—car ownership, for instance, grew by 700 percent in six years—and with the erosion of many of the traditional occupations within the secondary labor market taken by *gardawa* and *'yan cin rani.*

Finally, the state-funded Universal Primary Education (UPE) program represented both an ideological attack by proponents of "Western education" on its Qur'anic counterpart and an assault on the *mallams* and the *almajirai* system, which sustained the informal Muslim schooling system. In Kano State, enrollment increased by 491 percent between 1973 and 1977, and in Hadejia emirate the number of primary schools leapt from 36 in 1970 to 392 in 1980. In the 1970s the *mallams* and lay clerics were vigorous critics of UPE, a discontentedness suggestive of a much broader crisis in the *gardawa* system itself.

There is one final circumstance that is central to an understanding of the space—one might say, the discursive space—in which Matatsine could flourish, and that speaks to the return to civilian rule in Nigeria in 1979 following a long period of military governance. In spite of the fact that the National Party of Nigeria (NPN)—the party of the conservative northern oligarchy—were victorious at the federal level and dominated several state legislatures, a populist/socialist party—the People's Redemption Party (PRP)—swept to power in Kano State elections. The local government reforms of the 1970s had virtually eliminated the once-powerful Native Authority officials, who were replaced by university-educated administrators, but the triumph of PRP on a strong antiaristo-cratic (i.e., anti-*sarauta*) platform marked a qualitatively new political environment for the *talakawa*. Much could be said about the PRP—not least its political split between "radical" and "conservative" factions—but in essence the assertion of a populist, procommoner state government in Kano provided a political space in which the radical discourse of popular Islam could operate and indeed be encouraged, not least insofar as it took as its starting point a critique of the Sufi brotherhoods most closely associated with the traditional emirate authorities and the feudal elements of the old northern ruling classes.

The Moral Economy of Islam

At the heart of the revivalist worldview is the belief that the Muslim world is in a state of decline.

— John Esposito[37]

[W]hat the 'ulama [divines] are doing is to attempt a defini-tion of orthodoxy—a (re)ordering of knowledge that governs the "correct" form of Islamic practices.... This like all practical criticism seeks to construct a relation of discursive domi-nance .... [But] "Orthodoxy" is not easy to secure in condi-tions of radical change.

—Talal Asad[38]

Let me then turn to the question of modernity in relation to Islam. In Nigeria, as elsewhere in the Muslim world, Islam is not a monolith but contains important institutional, ideologi-cal, and social tensions within its circumference. There have been struggles between and against the Sufi brotherhoods in Nigeria since the 1950s, and the effort by Ahmadu Bello to cre-

---

[37] *The Islamic Threat* (New York: Oxford University Press, 1992) 19.

[38] *Genealogies of Religion* 210–11.

ate the Jama'atu Nasril Islam (the Organization for the Victory of Islam) in 1962 can be understood as an attempt to unite a *divided* Muslim community as a way of securing northern political hegemony in the newly independent Nigerian federation. But over the past thirty years the fissiparous nature of the Muslim community has deepened. A primary axis of difference and debate links the Darika brotherhoods—Quadriyya and Tijaniyya—to which many Nigerian Muslims are aligned, and newer so-called fundamentalist groups such as the powerful Jama'atu Izalat Al-Bidah Wa Iqamat Al Sunnah or Izala (roughly translated as the Removal of False Innovations and the Establishment of Orthodox Tradition), headed by Abubakar Gumi with strong connections to King Faisal of Saudi Arabia, and the Muslim Students Society, itself split between pro-Iranian and pro-Saudi factions.[39] These local divisions and debates are not unrelated to the extraordinary ferment throughout the Muslim world during the last two decades and must be seen as exemplary of a much longer reformist debate within the ranks of Islam. Indeed, Islam possesses a long tradition of revival (*tajdid*) and reform (*islah*), rooted *within* its own traditions as much as responding to Westernization in its various forms. In other words, the clerics, scholars, and religious leaders—representing in the Nigerian case differing Sufi and anti-Sufi constituencies—attempt to redefine Muslim orthodoxy in the context of radical social, economic, and political change by engaging in a long-standing Muslim tradition of public criticism. As Muslims, in other words, "their differences are fought out on the ground of [orthodoxy]"[40] in an attempt to establish a discursive dominance.

Like other great traditions, Islam is also paradigmatic for its followers, and its origins provide the normative basis of Muslim governance and personal conduct. At the heart of this paradigm, insofar as it shapes attitudes toward state, society, wealth, and poverty, is the concept of justice. As Burke and Lubeck note:

> popular Islamic ideas of justice ... inhibit the flaunting of wealth and the taking of interest, and encourage charity. The

[39] J. Ibrahim, "Religion and Political Turbulence in Nigeria," *Journal of Modern African Studies* 29, 1 (1991): 115–36.

[40] Asad, *Genealogies of Religion* 210.

scripturalist tradition ... thus constrains the choices open to Muslim actors ... and also provides repertories of popular action and cultural vocabularies for their expression.[41]

Of course, these abstractions derived from texts and scripturalist discourses are filtered through local experiences and through quite contrary models of the Islamic polity. In the Sunni tradition (of which Nigeria is part), Burke distinguishes between the Rashidun model, which roots justice and moral virtue in the early Muslim community and the strict application of the Shari'ah, and the imperial model of the later Arab caliphate, which has been typically invoked by incumbent Islamic governments to justify *raison d'état* policies.[42] Despite the distinctions and historical differences in political practice within the Sunni tradition, there is a normative thread that runs through the great tradition, a search for justice in an unjust world that is analogous to the West European notion of a moral economy.[43] Like the European counterpart, the Islamic moral economy was a configuration of symbols and traditions to be interpreted, struggled over, and fought for but also represented a series of cultural and moral norms that imposed particular expectations upon the rich, the clergy, and the ruling class more generally, as well as the commoners.

In light of my emphasis on flexibility, diversity, and moral economy, how might one characterize the Muslim landscape in northern Nigeria on the eve of the oil boom, when Maitatsine was already active within Kano? I want to draw attention to two basic orientations within Kano Islam. The first concerns the shifting influence of the Sufi brotherhoods, most especially the Qadriyya, which is associated with the holy war (*jihad*) of Usman dan Fodio in the early nineteenth century and more generally with the traditional northern Nigerian Hausa-Fulani aristocracy, and the Tijaniyya, which had grown and flourished

[41] E. Burke and P. Lubeck, "Explaining Social Movements in Two Oil-exporting States," *Comparative Studies in Society and History* 29, 4 (1987): 643–65.

[42] E. Burke, "Understanding Arab Protest Movements," *Arab Studies Quarterly* 8, 4 (1986): 333–45.

[43] M. Watts, "The Devil's Excrement," in *Money, Power and Space*, ed. R. Martin and N. Thrist (Oxford: Blackwell, 1994) 406–45; Lubeck, "Islamic Protest under Semi-industrial Capitalism."

in the fertile soil of colonial politics and merchant capitalism. Unlike the Qadriyya, which was part of a class alliance between the local Muslim ruling class (*sarauta*) and the colonial state, Tijaniyya contained specific radical, anticolonial beliefs that appealed to a traditional merchant class operating in the interstices of the colonial economy.[44] Since the 1960s, however, the hegemony of both brotherhoods has been contested by a number of anti-Sufi reformist sects in northern Nigeria—notably the Izala, founded in 1978 by Mallam Idris in Jos in central Nigeria—whose aim is to abolish innovation and to practice Islam in strict accordance with the Qur'an and the *sunna*. Anti-Sufi sentiment in Nigeria can be traced to the 1930s but proliferated during and after World War II with the growth of a class of new elites who articulated the virtues of the modern social transformations in contradistinction to the vices of tradition.[45] Sa'ad Zungur (1915–58), for example, was an early critic of Sufi belief insofar as it rested, in his view, on the introjection of superstition (for example, polygamy, saint veneration, wife seclusion) into pristine Islam as practiced by the Prophet and the caliphs. Since 1960, the anti-Sufi movement has accelerated largely through the leadership of Sheikh Abubakar Gumi, who has employed the Nigerian Broadcasting Corporation and the Kaduna-based Hausa-language newspaper *Gaskiya ta fi Kwabo* to great effect in promoting his message that Sufism is not part of Islam because it emerged long after Islam had been completed. Referred to as the new jihadists, Gumi and the Izala share identical views, but, while critical of the West's decadence, they are neither antimodern nor antimaterialist in any simple sense., Hence they are widely supported by northern Nigerian intelligentsia and by aggressive new modernists and businessmen. In some senses, Izala ideology "is to the Islamic brotherhoods what Protestantism is to Catholicism."[46] But it is also a form of protest against traditional noncapitalist values and against the perceived corruption of religious values and practices in the context of what

[44] J. Paden, *Religion and Political Culture in Kano* (Berkeley: University of California Press, 1973).

[45] M. Umar, "Changing Islamic Identity in Nigeria from the 1960's to 1980's," in *Muslim Identity and Social Change* 154–78.

[46] E. Gregoire, "Islam and Identity of Merchants in Maradi (Niger)," in *Muslim Identity and Social Change* 114.

Umar calls a "shift from communal to an individual mode of religiosity ... in tune with the rugged individualism of capitalist social relations."[47] Whether Izala is simply a cathartic response to the tensions and frustrations of Nigerian capitalism[48] is less relevant for my concerns than the fact that its *tafsir* broadcasts and polemical pleas for the separation of mosques contributed to a growing sense of cleavage within Nigerian Islam and to the wider legitimacy of anti-Sufi sentiment.

The second dimension speaks to the shifting relations among the lay clerics (*ulema*), the teachers (*mallams*), and their institutional networks. Many *mallams* are of course spokespersons for the brotherhoods and, to the extent that they are affiliated with state patronage, can be seen as proestablishment (*malamin soro*). There is nonetheless a relatively independent laity associated in particular with the local Qur'anic schools, of which there are in fact three different forms. First, the primary schools (*makarantar allo*), for which the Qur'an is the main (and sometimes the only) text, typically learned by rote at a seminary. Many of Maitatsine's followers were products of this system, and the *allo* teachers are typically independent, customarily sustained through alms. Second, the higher school (*makarantar ilimi*), which ranges widely over theological and legal matters and interpretation of the religious texts such as the *hadith* and the Qur'an. Most of the *ilimi* teachers are members of the brotherhood orders and are paid for their instructional activities. And third, the so-called Islamiyya schools are primary and secondary, set up in the 1930s (and expanded in

---

[47] Umar, "Changing Islamic Identity" 178.

[48] The critique focuses especially on certain innovations: the folding of arms while praying, not facing Mecca while praying, collections of fees by *mallams*, and the wearing of amulets. The latter is especially interesting because it speaks to the popular belief across many segments of society in non-Muslim spirits and powers. It is precisely this source of power (often associated in northern Nigeria with non-Muslim Hausa [Maguzawa] and the urban underworld) that Maitatsine drew upon; indeed, Maitatsine was recognized as a sort of sorcerer. Several of Maitatsine's lieutenants carried talismens (one quoted in the *Aniagolu Report* spoke of: "if I were cut into pieces and die I shall come back to life").

the 1950s) with a syllabus comparable to Western forms of education but focusing on Arabic and Islamic studies.[49]

I want to emphasize the growing tensions between these Muslim networks, and how these frictions reside within a larger debate over the differing significance attributed to the Qur'an, the *hadith*, the *sunna* and to distinctive religious practices such as prayer, dress, and ritual. The *gardawa* were seen as ignorant and traditional by both the *ilimi* and the Islamiyya scholars, the latter, however, enjoying the prestige and patronage of the state and characteristically being appointed as *alkalis* (local judges). The 'Yan Izala and the *gardawa*, conversely, occupied the same terrain in their anti-brotherhood beliefs.[50] The *ilimi* and the *gardawa* were both marginalized by the fact that the proliferation of Islamiyya schools (in conjunction with the growth of state-funded universal primary education during the oil years) systematically eroded their traditional networks.[51] As Murray Last observes:

> No longer now are there the eventual posts as respected village scholars now that the primary schools have their own religious instructors. No longer is there the ready hospitality (particularly in towns) and the same respect (or casual work) for the migrant students. Worst of all, perhaps, the class of austerely pious, very learned yet public scholars, who once were the models for a particular way of life, has all but disappeared.[52]

---

[49] Graduates of the Islamiyya schools are accredited (i.e., recognized by the state—indeed are state funded in part), typically employed as judges and scribes in the northern emirates, and normally can gain entry into Nigerian universities. Many of the 'Yan Izalas are in fact products of the Islamiyya system, and Sheikh Gumi is perhaps its most distinguished and influential graduate. The Muslim Students Association, many members of which are connected to the Islamiyya schools, also has a scripturalist reading of Islam.

[50] Associated with the brotherhoods, *darikat* practice involved daily prayer and meditation, strict discipline, and obedience to saints.

[51] I have not mentioned here the important tradition of millenarian and Mahdist revolt in Nigeria. The year 1979 also marks the onset of the new century in the Muslim calendar, which was widely held to promise the coming of the Mahdi.

[52] Cited in Barkindo, "Growing Islamism in Kano" 96.

The injection of oil revenues through the state further destabilized this complex force field and had the effect of deepening resentments and divisions within the Muslim community, not least by marginalizing a laity and its followers many of whom were drawn into the irregular and chaotic labor market of urban Kano in the 1970s.

To recapitulate my argument, Nigeria's oil-based fast capitalism was mapped onto, and partially experienced through, a complex, heterogeneous, and, one should add, transnational Muslim community in Nigeria.[53] Debates over Islam and modernity long predated the oil boom, but the social, political, and economic transformations rendered by oil contributed to a serious and deep reformist debate within an ideologically diverse Muslim population. The growing popularity and following of Izala, the Muslim Students Society, and other fundamentalist groups in relation to the powerful brotherhoods suggests an important struggle over orthodox Islam was already in train in Nigeria by the early 1970s, and that cultural and religious capital relevant to these debates was drawn from a transnational Muslim diaspora. Participation in the pilgrimage to Mecca, the geographic circulation of religious clites through transnational networks such as the brotherhoods, and the consumption of new ideas through radio and circulated tape cassettes were all relevant to this vibrant, and not infrequently acrimonious, public discourse within Islam. Maitatsine was, in this regard, legitimately part of a wide-ranging public debate—occasionally violent and divisive—within the northern Nigerian Muslim community. The language of Muslim reformism resonated with large sections of northern Nigerian society, and Maitatsine enjoyed success, as Bawuro Barkindo properly put it, "partly because many ... people who did not join him agreed with the content of his preaching."[54] Marwa was not, in other words, simply an "isolated fanatic." But powerful economic and political forces marginalized the popular laity and their followers (the *gardawa*) whom Maitatsine spoke to and in some sense represented in Kano City, and this permitted Maitatsine to resurrect a debate dating

---

[53] This is to make the point that Nigerian clerics, students, and Muslims more generally traveled to (via the *hadj*) and were familiar with debates within Islam across North Africa and the Middle East.

[54] Barkindo, "Growing Islam in Kano" 98.

back at least to the colonial conquest—but which has in a sense never ceased—designed to condemn the European and to return to a world in which Islam could be practiced without hindrance. It was the marginalization of the *almajirai/gardawa* system and the exploitation of the Maitatsine movement by larger political forces that ultimately propelled Marwa to establish and violently defend an *independent* religious community within the old city walls of Kano capable of realizing this long-standing vision.

Constructing Community and Identity

> Every religion is in reality a multiplicity of distinct and contradictory religions.
>
> —Antonio Gramsci[55]

> [Identity] is not something which already exists, transcending time, place, history and culture…. Far from being eternally fixed in some essentialized past, [identities] are subject to the continual interplay of history, culture and power.
>
> —Stuart Hall[56]

The appeal of Marwa, and the refashioning of local identity that he represented, must be located in a series of complex articulations: between Islam and capitalism, between precapitalist and capitalist institutions, and between class and culture. It would be much too facile to see the millenarian qualities of the movement as a lumpen insurrection plain and simple. The 'yantatsine were uniformly poor; 80 percent had incomes well below the minimum wage. But the "fanatical" qualities of the social explosions that occurred between 1980 and 1985 can only be fully comprehended in terms of the material and status deprivation of 'yantatsine recruits scrambling to survive in an increasingly chaotic and Hobbesian urban environment and

---

[55] Antonio Gramsci, *Selections from the Prison Notebooks* (New York: International Publishers, 1971) 420.

[56] Stuart Hall, "Cultural Identity and Cinematic Representation," *Framework*, 1989, 70.

the unprecedented ill-gotten wealth and corruption of the dominant classes in urban Kano.

Marwa was, first of all, a long-time resident of Kano and was witness to the extraordinary transformation in the political and cultural economy of urban Kano during the oil years. As a charismatic preacher with a compelling, if idiosyncratic, reading of the Qur'an, Marwa recruited followers from the influx of migrants and students into the city and from the marginal underclass of Kano. His disciples recruited at the lorry parks and railway stations in Kano, where they typically sustained themselves by selling tea and bread.[57] His followers (migrants, itinerant workers, *gardawa*) were products of the same Qur'anic system as Marwa himself; most of his Kano followers were educated in the *makarantar allo* system. Furthermore, Marwa's use of syncretist and pre-Islamic powers resonated strongly with migrants from the countryside, where vestiges of ancient Hausa metaphysical belief remained quite influential. Slowly, Marwa was able to build up an enclave in 'Yan Awaki fashioned around a disciplined, and self-consciously austere, egalitarian community of Muslim brothers (*'yan'uwa*) who supported themselves largely through alms, though land and urban gardens were appropriated to support the devotees.[58] Marwa's unorthodox and literalist interpretation of the Qur'an focused specifically on the icons of modernity: bicycles, watches, cars, money, and so on. But it would be mistaken to view Maitatsine as antimodern or simply harking back to some earlier uncontaminated tradition of Islam. The movement employed modern arms when necessary and Marwa emphasized the ill-gotten quality of goods, not their inherent illegitimacy. Likewise his desire to seize key institutions in Kano City—the radio, the state electricity company—is hardly antimodernist. Kano merchants, bureaucrats, and elites were implicated in his critique, but it was the state that was the embodiment of moral bankruptcy and the police its quintessential representatives. Any affiliation to the state naturally contaminated Islamic practice.

---

[57] Federal Government, *Report of the Tribunal.*

[58] According to H. Saad, "Urban Blight and Religious Uprising in Northern Nigeria," *Habitat International* 12, 2 (1988): 118, a survey conducted among the arrested *'yantatsine* revealed that 95 percent believed themselves to be Muslim.

The *'yantatsine* did not necessarily stand in opposition to the popular classes, or indeed the merchants and shopkeepers among whom they lived. In the 1980 conflicts, for example, *'yantatsine* who had occupied a cinema on the Kofar Mata Road told local residents that their fight was strictly with the police, while young immigrant workers living in Fagge "appeared to be just as fearful of the police and of the vigilantes as they were of 'yantatsine."[59] Marwa himself scrupulously returned property to its rightful owners if appropriated by his followers.

Commodification and money are clearly central to the question of identity and community. David Harvey notes in *The Condition of Postmodernity*, "the progressive monetization of relations in social life transforms the qualities of time and space,"[60] and the same argument may be made, I think, during periods of rapid change within peripheral capitalisms. There is a long line of thinking, of course, on the erosive, glacial qualities of money and on money as a form of domination,[61] but it is striking how the social relations of money cut to the core of Maitatsine and his ideological appeal. The *gardawa mallams* were conspicuously nonsalaried and *'yantatsine* carried little or no money on their persons. Further, there was a strong sentiment among *gardawa* that wealth, especially in the 1970s, was ill-gotten (*haram*); in the popular imagination, behind every wealth there is a crime. Indeed, this builds upon an important cultural distinction embedded in Hausa society between fruitful and barren capital. Money capital (literally, "mother of money," *uwa*) may be fertile (*uwa mai amfani*) or ominous (*jarin tsiya*), a distinction rooted in cultural notions of work and proper conduct. Certain money is bitter and illegitimate (for example, interest for Muslims), and this is powerfully expressed in popular reactions to the petro-naira in Nigeria.

Commodities and money, in fact, loomed large in Marwa's preaching. His provocative reading of the Qur'an as the *only* valid guide to human conduct rested on the revelation of hid-

---

[59] A. Christelow, "Three Islamic Voices in Contemporary Nigeria," in *Islam and the Political Economy of Meaning*, ed. W. Roff (London: Croon Helm, 1987) 377.

[60] Harvey, *Condition of Postmodernity* 228.

[61] G. Simmel, *The Philosophy of Money* (London: Routledge, 1978); M. Watts, "The Devil's Excement."

den meanings within the sacred text and on his rooting of verse in local conditions. Marwa's vehement denunciation of cigarettes, motor vehicles, buttons, apparels, and so on was revealed within the text through his careful textual analysis. Marwa deconstructed Qur'anic texts in part by playing on the meanings and phonetic associations of certain Hausa and Arabic words. Furthermore, he played creatively with the relations between signs and their referents. In his public preaching he pointed to the physical similarity between the Arabic character for Allah and a simple graphical depiction of a bicycle. This homology not only validated his accusation that all persons who rode bicycles were by definition pagan but also confirmed his far-reaching attack on the corruption and degeneration of Islam at the highest levels. This sense of moral crisis in a curious way lent both credibility and legitimacy to Maitatsine's ideas because there is within Islamic eschatology a strong belief in "Signs of the Hour," the idea that at the end of every century (which in the Muslim calendar fell in 1979) a renewer may appear to restore order, to regain the world that has been lost.

Place, Space, Identity

[A]ll identity formation is engaged in this habitually bracing activity in which the issue is not so much staying the same, but maintaining sameness through alterity.

—Michael Taussig[62]

Islam is taking on new meanings as Muslims assert the centrality of Islam in public and private life .... Understanding Islamic fundamentalism as an expression of modernity rather than tradition yields insights into its powerful appeal and draws attention to the social and economic processes associated with its spread.

—Victoria Bernal[63]

---

[62] *Mimesis and Alterity* 129.

[63] "Gender, Culture and Capitalism," *Comparative Studies in Society and History* 36, 1 (1994): 38.

The ferocious, Muslim-inspired movements that surfaced between 1980 and 1985 in several cities of northern Nigeria represent a dramatic political expression of the changing geography—or perhaps more properly, the changing cultural geography—of Nigerian capitalism. It is this "fast capitalism," grounded in a deep Muslim tradition, that provided the material and symbolic raw material from which new identities and new communities were forged. To put the matter starkly, the oil boom fashioned a period of "space-time compression," to employ David Harvey's language. In Kano, however, the creative destruction wrought by oil-dependent capitalist industrialization was constituted by a specific articulation of two world-systemic processes: Islam and capitalism. Each world system was both global and local in its constitution; as a global abstraction each force field was experienced, transmitted, and, as it turns out, contested in demonstrably local ways. I have tried to show how each of these force fields mapped onto each other through the unstable and complex dialectics of place and identity.

The Maitatsine insurrection represented a powerful, if counterhegemonic, reading and critique of the Nigerian oil boom and of the Nigerian ruling classes. To this extent one should not be diverted by the syncretist character of Marwa himself, by his purported use of magic, by possible Mahdist overtones, and by accusations of cannibalism. Marwa's self-identity, including his prophethood, is perhaps less relevant than his inconsistently antimaterialist, class-based reading of the moral superiority of the Qur'an, which led him to attack decadence, profligacy, and corruption. His antimaterialism was nonetheless ambiguous and contradictory: on the one hand, he rejected modernity in his invocation of a simple disciplined life, and yet he also invoked a political vision in which the control of modern institutions was central. Critical of corruption, the police, and private property, he fashioned a community of largely young men—unskilled migrants, Qur'anic scholars, and rural destitutes—who were products of the shifting relations between town and countryside during the 1970s. As a result, the community built in 'Yan Awaki was a peculiar and parochial affair, with little said about political horizons beyond the ward in which he and his followers resided. But this was also not a simple return to some mythical past; rather, it is about contesting Islamic traditions and creating new ones by a direct engagement with capitalist modernity read through new scripturalist understandings of Islam.

Oil and Islam no more determine revolutionary, or indeed insurrectional, outcomes than does a mixture of copper and Christianity. But Maitatsine's form of Muslim populism possesses a great capacity to resist co-optation, providing in his case a culturally convincing critique of "oil prosperity," a powerful ideology in weak Islamic states experiencing the radical dislocation of the petroleum boom. The Maitatsine followers constituted a certain disenfranchised segment of the northern popular classes who experienced, handled, and resisted a particular form of capitalism through a particular reading of Islamic tradition. It is a truism that Islam is a text-based religion, but we need to grasp the relationships between texts and the meanings they are purported to provide, what Lambek calls "local hermeneutics":

> The specific problems raised by the translation of objective meaning of written language into the personal act of speaking ... [is an act of] appropriation.... The nature of texts and the knowledge to be drawn from them in any given historical context are shaped by a sociology or political economy of knowledge: how textual knowledge is reproduced ... what social factors mediate access to texts, who is able to read and in what manner, who has the authority to represent ... and how challenges to such authority are manifested.[64]

Islam is a text-based religion that is made socially relevant through citation, reading, enunciation, and interpretation, and in this sense Islam is not prescriptive in simple ways providing unambiguous guidance for its adherents.[65] Indeed, as Fischer and Abedi have brilliantly shown in their book *Debating Muslims*, there is a dialogic and hermeneutical tradition within Islam rooted in the enigmatic, oral, performative, and esoteric qualities of the Qur'an. The same religious symbols can be infused with radically different meanings. Tradition itself is constantly negotiated, contested, and reinvented in the context of

---

[64] M. Lambek, "Certain Knowledge, Contestable Authority," *American Ethnologist* 17, 1 (1990): 23–24.

[65] M. Fischer and A. Abedi, *Debating Muslims* (Madison: University of Wisconsin Press, 1990).

efforts by rulers and clerics (*ulema*) to enforce other meanings in a world turned upside down by oil money. There is a multiplicity of Muslim voices, and it was the mapping of local Islam onto local capitalism that threw these religious multiplicities into bold relief, generating intense struggles over the meaning of Islam and the Muslim community.[66]

In conclusion, I wish to return to the remarks by Harvey and Schorske on territorial identity and the shuffling of the self in emergent modernism with which I began this essay. The Maitatsine movement contained both progressive and exclusionary politics in a vision that fused religion and class. Its limited perspective and reach—Maitatsine never talked about managing the economy, regulating foreign policy, or processes of globalization—had much to do with the limited horizons of Maitatsine and his followers, who were steeped in the traditions of informal Muslim schooling. At the same time, their projection into the maelstrom of fast capitalism compelled Maitatsine to engage his scripturalist concerns with the much larger world of contemporary capitalism. To this extent, as Schorske suggests, there was revising of beliefs and a search for an identity that took the form of a specific, and contradictory, reshuffling of the self. The dramatic way in which oil threw together the old and the new—a sort of combined and uneven development—makes this reshuffling, and the place-based identities so produced, a curious and in some respects fantastic sort of enterprise. And it was this fantasy that Walter Benjamin, in his great study of Baudelaire, spoke of in relation to what he called the tradition of the oppressed:

> To the form of the means of production, which to begin with is still dominated by the old (Marx), there correspond images in the collective consciousness in which the new and the old are intermingled. These images are ideals, and in them the collective seeks not only to transfigure, but also to transcend, the immaturity of the social product and the deficiencies of the social order of production. In these ideals there also emerges a vigorous aspiration to break with what is outdated—which means, however, with the most recent past.

---

[66] For similar arguments within Muslim discourse in relation to capitalism see A. Ong, "State versus Islam," *American Ethnologist* 17, 2 (1990): 258–76, and Lambek, "Certain Knowledge."

These tendencies turn the fantasy, which gains its initial stimulus from the new, back upon a primal past. In the dream in which every epoch sees in images the epoch which is to succeed it, the latter appears coupled with elements of prehistory—that is to say of a classless society. The experiences of this society, which have their store-place in the collective unconscious, interact with the new to give birth to the Utopias which leave their traces in a thousand configurations.[67]

The fantastic intermingling of the old and new encompasses the Maitatsine community and its limited, contradictory, and ultimately inadequate utopian vision. Indeed, it provides a powerful metaphor for the complex intersections of place, space, and identity, for the global sense of place required to grasp Maitatsine's reformist project.

---

[67] Walter Benjamin, *Charles Baudelaire* (London: Verso, 1973) 159. For a further discussion of Benjamin's work in this regard see S. Buck-Morss, *The Dialectics of Seeing* (Cambridge, MA: MIT Press, 1989).

KATHMANDU AS TRANSLOCALITY:
Multiple Places in a Nepali Space

Mark Liechty

Introduction

Among the throngs of mango vendors, cows, tourists, taxi drivers, beggars, and would-be tour guides that congregate every day in Kathmandu's Durbar Square, one denizen stands above and apart. In the garb of a Shaivite *sadhu*—an ascetic Hindu world-renouncer—he can often be seen striking picturesque poses on the corners of temple platforms or sitting meditatively before the awesome devotional images that clutter the ancient pagoda temples and palaces that make the square Kathmandu's main tourist attraction. Carrying a staff in the shape of a three-headed cobra, his beard a knotted mat, and sporting a ragged leopard skin wrapped around his mass of ropelike hair, *sadhuji* waits for shutters to click before producing a large cardboard notice from beneath the flowing folds of his saffron robes. In a half dozen European and East Asian languages tourists are informed of the price per exposure and, while money changes hands, *sadhuji* proposes other photo opportunities for which tourists may wish to engage his services. Ostensibly a "local," an "authentic" holy man, and a sacred manifestation of a "local place," *sadhuji* turns out to be literally a consumable object and a figment of the tourist's imagination. But, then, whose authority determines the authentic? Whose imaginary sense of place may lay claim to the meaning of this public space?

This is an essay about the placing of spaces, about how localities are rendered meaningful, and more particularly about how certain spaces become overpopulated with places. If "place is space to which meaning has been ascribed,"[1] I am con-

Thanks to Laura Hostetler, Pratyoush Onta, Deborah Tooker, Mary Des Chene, Prabhu Mohapatra, Will Derks, and Peter Pels, as well as Patricia Yaeger, who read and made helpful comments on drafts of this paper. Remaining errors and omissions are my responsibility. Research for this paper was conducted during sixteen months between 1988 and 1991 with the help of the

cerned here with how one space becomes the site for a host of places, each claiming the same ground for its own configuration of meanings, or with how layers of signification (multiple places) come to envelope the same referent (a particular space). Localities are typically thought of as social constructions; social relations generate the shared experiences and histories that transform space into place. But in an increasingly "deterritorialized" world, where imaginations are increasingly mass-mediated and "liberated" from the confines of the locale, the meanings and experiences that construct places are often no longer limited to the shared social relations of particular local histories. Arguably, the pseudo-*sadhu* of Kathmandu's Durbar Square is a part of the tourist's memory of Kathmandu before ever arriving in Nepal since *sadhuji* is an important feature of the place, or the configuration of meaning, they have come to see. He is part of a geographic imaginary generated in the minds of foreign tourists at least as much as he inhabits any "local place" that emerges from "authentic" social relations. Here I consider how Durbar Square and a few other spots in Kathmandu have become spaces that are simultaneously multiple places, and particularly how in a deterritorialized world the production of places, or meanings ascribed to locales, is increasingly "freed" from the historical and political conditions of the locations that these meanings claim.

Cities are by definition zones of difference, both in relation to their hinterlands and internally—comprised as they are of neighborhoods, districts, communities. Kathmandu was, and to a considerable extent still is, comprised of a heterogenous cluster of relatively homogenous zones. Indeed, so orderly was

---

Departments of Anthropology and South Asia Regional Studies of the University of Pennsylvania and a Fulbright-Hays Doctoral Dissertation Research Abroad grant. Special thanks go to Som Raj Ghimire, Krishna and Ganu Pradhan, Ang Tshering Sherpa, and Surendra Bajracharya. Finally, my sincere thanks to the International Institute for Asian Studies (IIAS) in Leiden, The Netherlands, for providing me the time and support for writing this paper.

[1] Erica Carter, James Donald, and Judith Squires, "Introduction," in *Space and Place: Theories of Identity and Location*, ed. E. Carter, J. Donald, and J. Squires (London: Lawrence and Wishart, 1993) xii. This is not to say that space is meaningless. The meaning of space lies in its known-but-unknown character.

this social geography that the premodern city has been likened to a *mandala*, or sacred image, in which harmony emerges from the meaningful (and politically sanctioned) configuration of social difference.[2] Arrayed out in concentric circles from the king's residence (Durbar Square) lived citizens of progressively lower ritual and political rank. Even now, when income, not ritual status, usually determines where one lives, members of particular occupational castes still cluster in their "traditional" neighborhoods: oil pressers here, dry goods merchants there, and untouchable animal skinners and butchers in areas once just outside the now-vanished city walls. Even up until 1951, when a popular revolution ended two centuries of autocratic, isolationist rule, strict prohibitions on internal migration made Kathmandu a city of relatively stable (if not "natural") homogeneous communities, inhabiting collectively constructed local places.

From this relatively isolated mountain backwater, Kathmandu has in the 1990s become one of South Asia's busiest transportation hubs, hosting well over a quarter of a million tourists a year. The city's shops and boutiques are jammed with imported consumer goods, making Kathmandu "the Hong Kong of South Asia." For both long-term residents and the tens of thousands of Nepalis who have moved to the city in the past decades, features of Kathmandu's earlier social geography must still be navigated, but communities and their places tend increasingly to reflect the growing precedence of a market economy and the logic of class over a ritual economy and the logic of caste.

Perhaps the single most important factor in the transformation of the city's semantic topography—its map of meaning—has been tourism. According to a retired Nepali civil servant, in the late 1950s, when American diplomats suggested that Nepal promote Kathmandu as a tourist destination, Nepali officials responded by asking, "Why would tourists want to come?" When the Americans replied that foreigners will pay to see temples, festivals, and mountains, the officials "looked at each other trying not to laugh, thinking these Americans are mad!" Mad or otherwise, tourists came, transforming the city's

---

[2] Mary S. Slusser, *Nepal Mandala: A Cultural Study of the Kathmandu Valley* (Princeton: Princeton University Press, 1982).

economy, colonizing certain districts and public places, renaming streets and temples, and radically reconfiguring the semantic geography—the urban *mandala*—of Kathmandu.

I am particularly interested in a few specific localities in this new urban landscape. "Durbar Square" is one, but just as important are the new tourist areas of Jhochen (commonly known by Nepalis and tourists as "Freak Street") and Thamel. These are sites where an astonishing array of places—"texts" of imported, domestic, and unknown provenance—cohabit a particular spatial "context." A semantic "thermograph" of the city would show these as denotative hot spots, zones of complex images or imaginary hyperactivity. As sites that carry a heavy imaginary burden, spaces such as these might be instances of what Marshall Berman calls "modern environments" and what Renato Rosaldo calls "border zones." According to Rosaldo, the "border" is a "zone between stable places," the "site of the implosion of the Third World into the first." On the other hand, the locations described in this essay are perhaps zones in which the First World implodes into the third.[3] Following Arjun Appadurai, I will call these areas "translocalities," or areas characterized by "complex conditions for the production and reproduction of locality in which … work, business, and leisure weave together various circulating populations with various kinds of 'locals.'"[4] As transitory, commercialized, even liminal zones, these are spaces in which the controlled management of meaning is next to impossible.

In this essay I stress that areas such as Freak Street and Thamel are not simply "tourist ghettoes," if by these words we mean spaces only of, by, and for tourists. Rather, as translocalities, these are spaces in which a variety of Nepalis and a variety of foreigners interact, playing roles (wittingly or otherwise) in a space where multiple imaginations of "others" meet.

---

[3] Marshall Berman, *All That Is Solid Melts into Air: The Experience of Modernity* (London: Verso, 1983) 15; Renato Rosaldo, "Ideology, Place, and People without Culture," *Cultural Anthropology* 3, 1 (1988): 85. See also Renato Rosaldo, *Culture and Truth: The Remaking of Social Analysis* (Boston: Beacon Press, 1989).

[4] Arjun Appadurai, "The Production of Locality," in *Modernity at Large: Cultural Dimensions of Globalization* (Minneapolis: University of Minnesota Press, forthcoming).

These are simultaneously places that foreigners imagine from a distance and sites from which Nepalis imagine distant places. Just as films, travel books, and newspapers have helped to produce the memories of Kathmandu that tourists bring with them to Nepal,[5] Nepalis also have mediated memories of other places and seek to live other lives by inhabiting these liminal spaces. In these semantically unstable zones people are relatively free to enact the scripts and roles playing in their own imaginations—even if a political economy of places (mirrored in the pathways of global tourism) guarantees that most Nepalis will only experience "flights" of the imagination. Thus these translocalities are often highly dramatic, performative spaces in which both tourists and Nepalis experiment with identities and practices that would be inappropriate in other locations where the meaning of place is more rigidly controlled.[6]

My aim here is to provide some sense of the imaginative action that transpires in Kathmandu's translocalities. The first part considers a few aspects of the story of Kathmandu's emergence as a tourist destination particularly the links among media representations, tourism, and the meaning of place. I describe how, as representations have changed, so also have tourists and ultimately the "local places" they imagine. From tourist dramas, part two turns to dramas enacted by Nepalis in

---

[5] "[I]dentity, memory and nostalgia—are inextricably interlinked with patterns and flows of communication. The 'memory banks' of our times are in some part built out of the materials supplied by the film and television industries." David Morley and Kevin Robins, "No Place like *Heimat*: Images of Home(land) in European Culture," in *Space and Place* 8.

[6] Part of what I am suggesting is that translocalities are places where the project of disciplinary modernity is difficult to carry out. As highly commercialized spaces with extremely transient populations (upon which both state and commercial interests depend), translocations are those where the circulation of meaning is difficult to regulate or "police." I use the term "liminal" to suggest the fluidity of meaning in these in-between zones, even though to imply "antistructural" intent to the cultural practice that goes on there is perhaps wishful thinking. As I argue below, the "scripts" that people experiment with in these spaces are often either of commercial origin or are quickly appropriated by commercial interests. Yet because they are enacted in liminal zones, these zones attract marginal characters and others eager to explore the margins of acceptability and are thus "dangerous" both to local middle-class sensibilities and to the state.

these same spaces. Tourist zones have become sites where marginalized people such as drug addicts find safe haven and escape in dreams of foreign places. But they are also spaces where middle-class youth experiment with fantasies of tough-ness and action. I conclude with some thoughts on how in Kathmandu's translocalities both visitors and Nepalis share in a middle-class project of mass-mediated dramatization that, while ostensibly uniting groups in a deterritorialized space, ultimately reproduces the structures of global inequality in *re*territorialized spatial imaginaries.

Doing Kathmandu: Dramatic Tourism in Nepal

By the time Bob Seger stuttered out the name of the Nepali capital in his hit song of the mid-1970s, many thou-sands of his North American and European age mates had al-ready gotten out of there and gone to Kathmandu. The story of "hippie tourism" in Nepal (or elsewhere) has yet to be written, even though in the mid to late 1960s these young people were the pioneers (the avant-garde) of a new era of global mass tourism. The seedy tourist area near Kathmandu's Durbar Square—christened "Freak Street"—was by the late 1960s the mecca of Hippiedom, a spot prized beyond competing centers like Marakesh, Kabul, or Goa because of its remoteness and reputation for pristine exoticism. Kathmandu was often *the* destination, with other places just stops along the way.

As the new tourists climbed out of ramshackle airplanes on the cow pasture that served as Kathmandu's first airport or fell out of buses and minivans after driving overland from Europe (half dead from intestinal parasites and Afghan hash-ish), they were met by local residents quick to capitalize on the visitors' needs and desires. With savvy entrepreneurs offering everything from apple pie to yak cheese pizza, Kathmandu quickly became known as the "Alice's Restaurant" of the East, a place where "you can get anything you want." With good cli-mate, good food, exotic surroundings, and plenty of cheap hashish, Kathmandu was a place where Westerners settled in for months and even years.

Though Kathmandu residents remember the 1970s as the hippie decade, people in the tourism business insist that even at their peak, hippies never accounted for more than a quarter of the city's tourists. Yet ironically, by the early 1970s hippies themselves had become tourist attractions, drawing the world's attention as much or more than the city itself. In American and European pop songs, magazine spreads, and films, Kathmandu acquired a reputation for being as "far out" as it was far away. For a generation of newly mobile middle-class Western young people, Kathmandu was the ultimate "alternative" destination.

Media fascination with hippies brought Kathmandu publicity that led to escalating numbers of tourist arrivals. In 1973 a French adventure film entitled *Way to Kathmandu* immortalized the overland trip to Nepal,[7] and in the years that followed a disproportionate number of young French tourists showed up in the city. At about the same time, a young Nepali student who had studied in the U.S. thought of compiling a guidebook for budget travelers. For a year and a half he hung out in Kathmandu's budget-class restaurants and lodges collecting information and interviewing visitors. "I remember meeting many French people who had seen *Way to Kathmandu*," he recalled.

> I remember talking to them and I remember many who said they had been attracted by that film. And even now when I go to France, they say they had never heard about Kathmandu until they saw this movie!

Prakash A. Raj's guidebook went through two editions in as many years before it was snatched up by Lonely Planet—the world's leading publisher of budget-class guidebooks[8] —who turned it into a glossy bestseller for yet another generation of youthful tourists.

---

[7] Following in the tracks of the hippie caravans, organized overland bus service from Europe to Kathmandu had been established by the early 1970s, depositing thousands of exhausted tourists onto Kathmandu streets.

[8] Jon Krakauer, "Making the Planet a Little Less Lonely," *Smithsonian* 25, 7 (1994): 132–44.

Even before Lonely Planet published Prakash A. Raj's Kathmandu guidebook, the company's owners, Tony and Maureen Wheeler, had already been smitten by Kathmandu. The city was a highlight of their own maiden voyage, an overland tour from London to Sydney in 1972, which resulted in their original guidebook. Recalls Maureen Wheeler of their first visit to Kathmandu, "I remember how peaceful and magical it looked. The whole valley was twinkling with the glow of a million butter lamps. It seemed like Shangri-la."[9] In his introduction to Kathmandu in one of the earliest Lonely Planet publications, Tony Wheeler encouraged tourists to see the city as not just a charming Shangri-la but a place where local history could be conveniently (re)placed by their own fantasies. Wheeler wrote, "Nepalese history is really non-history. While things were happening elsewhere they weren't in Nepal, which accounts for the way things are today."[10] It would seem that destinations with "non-history" make for happier touristic hunting grounds. Even today "the Wheelers remain enthralled with Kathmandu," and "Tony ruminates about the glorious, ineffable complexity of Kathmandu, and the hopelessness of illuminating the city's wonders in even the finest guidebook."[11] Hopeless or not, in the early 1970s "the city's wonders" allowed the Wheelers to cash in on "the tremendous pent-up demand for a good guidebook to the so-called Hippie Trail."[12] It is difficult to know to what extent guidebooks like these respond to, or create, demand for the kind of place the Wheelers imagined: Kathmandu as nonhistorical, ineffable, Shangri-la. In any case, peddling imagined places is big business, as Lonely Planet's 22 million dollars in annual sales suggests.[13]

But even in the early 1970s the popular image of Kathmandu as a place of oriental mysticism, free love, and hash brownies had some powerful competition. From 1968 the Nixon administration pressured Nepal to make "drugs" illegal. Fearing the prospect of withdrawal symptoms from its own growing dependency on foreign development aid and suddenly realizing

---

[9] Quoted in Krakauer, "Making the Planet" 144.

[10] Tony Wheeler, *West Asia on a Shoestring* (Victoria: Lonely Planet, 1973) 190.

[11] Krakauer, "Making the Planet" 144.

[12] Krakauer, "Making the Planet" 136.

[13] Krakauer, "Making the Planet" 134.

its already established reputation as a hippie kingdom, the Nepali government decided to clean up its act in time for King Birendra's coronation in 1975. In the mid-1950s Nepalis had been surprised by the global media attention garnered by King Mahendra's coronation, an event immortalized in high-profile publications like *National Geographic*[14] and in at least one steamy popular romantic novel.[15] Yet by the 1970s the government saw in the upcoming celebrations a chance to project a "stately" image—in addition to a now-studied exoticism—to the assembled press hordes. Birendra's coronation earned another wave of media coverage, helping to cement Kathmandu's exotic reputation but without the embarrassing hippie riffraff.

The city's more "respectable" reputation helped produce a different breed of tourist, a different brand of exoticism, and even a new tourist district in Kathmandu. The city itself remained a tourist attraction, but Nepal was becoming more and more known as a land of mountaineering and natural beauty. In television travelogues, coffee-table books, spellbinding accounts of Himalayan expeditions, and even Tintin comic books,[16] Nepal became the land of adventure and the destination of "adventure tourists." Unlike the mountains of North America, the Nepal Himalaya is both populated and crisscrossed with superbly engineered trails that have been the lifelines of transhimalayan trade for millennia. Even if they were

---

[14] E. Thomas Gilliard, "Coronation in Kathmandu," *National Geographic* 114 (July 1957): 138–52. Since 1920 *National Geographic* has published nine illustrated articles on Nepal, most of which focus on Kathmandu or at least feature the city prominently, placing the nation and its capital among the magazine's most privileged sites and helping to locate these places in the imaginations of American middle-class readers. Cf. Catherine Lutz and Jane Collins, *Reading National Geographic* (Chicago: University of Chicago Press, 1993).

[15] Han Suyin, *The Mountain Is Young* (London: Jonathan Cape, 1958).

[16] After visiting Durbar Square, one French tourist exclaimed, "I feel just like Tintin in Tibet!" referring to the popular comic book adventures of Tintin. In fact, the episode *Tintin in Tibet* is set partly in Kathmandu, where the city's ancient buildings serve as backdrops for Tintin's adventure. For Europeans especially, *Tintin in Tibet* is often an important part of their imagined Nepal, and embroidered "Tintin in Tibet" T-shirts are among the most popular souvenir items in Kathmandu tourist shops.

not interested in technical climbing, just about anyone could enjoy "trekking" from village to village in Nepal, an enterprise that did not require carrying anything more than a sleeping bag and a change of clothes. After Prince Charles trekked through west-central Nepal, "So many British housewives came to us asking for 'Charlie's Trek'," recalled one tour operator. Similarly, Americans flocked to Lukla following media coverage of Robert Redford's trek to the Everest base camp.

Adventure tourists came to Nepal with a different romantic complex in mind, one that wanted nothing to do with the psychedelic seediness of their hippie predecessors. Again, Nepali business people were quick to capitalize on the new tourists' desire to distance themselves from the freaks of Freak Street. In 1973 a young Nepali naturalist—employed by the Nepali government but unable to support himself on his tiny salary—decided to transform his family home into a "guest house," a concept he had become familiar with while a student in Australia. Although then in a somewhat out-of-the-way neighborhood on the northern edge of the city, Karna Shakya's "Kathmandu Guest House" in Thamel attracted Peace Corps Volunteers and soon gained a reputation for being a clean, quiet alternative to the dark and dirty flophouses of Freak Street. The Kathmandu Guest House was looking for the new tourists (the owner had a strict no-hippie policy),[17] and it turned out to be exactly what the new adventure tourists were looking for.

Within a few years property values in Thamel skyrocketed, as lodges, restaurants, and curio shops sprouted in every direction. Offering clean sheets, private baths, and hot water, Thamel appealed to yuppies as Freak Street had appealed to hippies. If in the 1970s Kathmandu was a "bargain" because one could live for months on almost nothing, by the 1980s

---

[17] Recalls the owner,

> I gave strict instructions to my staff. There was a definition of hippies in my hotel. The one who doesn't come with shoes. The one who shows his buttocks—you know, sometimes we see the jeans with the holes—the man who has no respect for his own body cannot be respected by other people. And the man who never washes, and has weird kind of things [makes gestures around his head indicating long, filthy, matted hair]. So that kind of three characters, we never put them up from the beginning.

Kathmandu had acquired a reputation for "bargains," and Thamel became the budget shopper's paradise: hand-made carpets, paper goods, masks, jewelry, statuary, thankas, clothing, and ethnic exotica of all kinds. Whereas hippies often spent months in Kathmandu and left with little more than the clothes on their backs, adventure tourists spent a few weeks and left with bulging bags of bargains.

In spite of serious overpopulation, air pollution, garbage problems, and periodic political instability, in the 1990s Kathmandu, and in particular Thamel, continues to host ever-growing numbers and varieties of Western and East Asian middle-class tourists. No longer the primary destination for most visitors, Kathmandu is still the starting point for a wide range of romantic adventures and the location of many romantic places. Constantly scanning tourists' imagined scripts, Thamel business people are quick to create suitable stages and props through which different tourists can live out a variety of romantic dramas. The "outdoorsy" types (run-of-the-mill trekkers and the more radical "eco-tourists"), dressed in khaki, goretex, hiking boots, and glacier glasses, find their adventure on the mountain trails but share their romance in the special mountaineers' bars and health food restaurants (brown rice and tofu) of Thamel. For those who did not come dressed for the part, dozens of secondhand shops in Thamel sell world-class equipment (jettisoned by big-budget climbing expeditions) at low prices.

Others come looking for spiritual romance. When the "Dharma Bums," dressed in loose cotton clothes and sandals, are not studying Tibetan Buddhism, Tantrism, Yoga, or "Ayurvedic Massage," they tend to congregate in a few Thamel garden cafes. One afternoon in 1991, while waiting for a friend in one of these cafes, I sat down at a table near a young man who was sipping tea and earnestly "journaling" in a thick, tattered notebook. Soon a similarly attired young woman sat down across from him, also equipped with a well-worn notebook. After a few minutes of silent writing, a conversation began. The two seekers (an American and an Australian) soon found they shared a metaphysical wavelength and spent more than half an hour affirming each other's impressions of Kathmandu's mystical aura and the spiritual beauty of the Nepali people. They departed, shoulder to shoulder, to collect information on English-language meditation courses at a popular

Buddhist monastery that has its own convenient information office in Thamel.

On a plane into Nepal a young American in tie-dye and ponytail boasted of his recent exploits on a cycling tour of mainland China. Responding to his questions about lodging in Kathmandu, my wife suggested a cheap, clean hotel in Thamel. "But I heard about a place called Freak Street," he replied, with a hint of nostalgia in his voice. Looking for a retro or sixties throwback experience, tourists like this man usually head for Freak Street first, even if they end up in a Thamel hotel with hot showers before long. Regardless of where they stay, those looking to (re)inhabit a "far-out" psychedelic Kathmandu have no trouble procuring the officially banned substances (from the city's ubiquitous curbside hashish vendors) that aid in efforts to produce such a place.

Still others come looking to capture and live the "local" or "ethnic" experience. Most settle for a few items of "ethnic" clothing—a wool felt "Tibetan" jacket, a "Bhutanese" cap, a "Nepali" skirt—and a few visits to Thamel restaurants specializing in Tibetan and Nepali cuisine. Of those who go more "native," women tend to favor the tight-fitting, midriff-baring blouses worn under *saris* by Nepali women. I also encountered a number of Japanese men sporting *lungi*, singlet, and head scarf—the unmistakable (and by Nepalis much-derided) garb of the north Indian fruit peddlers who occupy the bottom of the local labor market. "Going native" is not so easy when it is unclear just which "natives" belong in any particular "native place."

And finally some tourists come to Nepal expecting nothing in particular, having arrived more or less by accident. In the summer of 1991, at the peak of the monsoon season, I visited a friend in a hill village in central Nepal. On the way I spent an evening in a damp trekker's lodge along one of the main tourist trails leading north out of Pokhara. I was relieved to find a lodge open in the off season and surprised to find two other foreign guests already present. Dressed in biking shorts and muscle shirts, Al and Gus were middle-aged professionals from San Francisco on a one-month vacation. Thirty-six hours earlier they had been lying on a beach in Phuket (a resort in southern Thailand), where, having read a tourist flier, on a whim they decided to visit Nepal.

They jumped on a plane, landed in Kathmandu, and were instantly traumatized. Unlike many tourists for whom even before arrival Nepal is prepackaged in layers of imagination, Al and Gus had little or no imaginary armor and saw nothing more than what is at least part of the reality of Kathmandu: squalor, poverty, mud, chaos, and pollution. They could not believe what they were seeing. "How can people live like that?" "Why don't they do something?" they asked. They knew they had to get out of Kathmandu and within hours had arranged with an agency to "go trekking" north of Pokhara. Another short plane ride, a wet six-hour climb, and there we were, eating rice and vegetables by candlelight in a Gurung village high on a mountain ridge in central Nepal. Al and Gus did not complain about the food, the rain, the climb, or the leeches but were genuinely distressed—even moved—by what they were experiencing. It seemed never to have occurred to them that in Nepal they might encounter something unusual or different. They struggled to make sense of what they saw but without great success. Nepal, and especially Kathmandu, had not been the experience they had in mind, and they planned a hasty re-treat back to Phuket, their Thai beach resort.

Two things struck me about this encounter. The first is that we live in an age in which, in a matter of days, on a whim, two North Americans can find themselves in a remote Nepali hill village in a befuddled daze. But more to the point of this essay, I was also struck by the way in which tourists arriving with no preparation or forethought are unshielded from the facts of Nepali poverty and underdevelopment. Al and Gus had not carried out the preliminary imaginative labor necessary to transform Kathmandu into the nonhistorical and classless *place of their dreams*. All of us work to construct places—both "our own" and "others"; we work to imagine and naturalize difference; and we work to maintain and inhabit these fictions of place. But for tourists, those who must transport their sensibilities and dreams through space, the labor of producing places is a task of particularly heroic proportions. Without this prefiguring labor, Kathmandu was an abomination.

Why had Al and Gus not been shocked by their experiences in Thailand? Part of the answer may lie in a peculiar feature of tourist talk. On a holiday or world tour people "go to" places like Hawaii, Majorca, Cyprus, or Thailand, but they "do"

Nepal.[18] "Going to" someplace is a more or less passive enterprise, but "doing" Nepal means work. Compared with Phuket,
"doing" Kathmandu is "roughing it." In Phuket a tourist can
enjoy an exotic scene without having his/her sensibilities ac-
costed. But Kathmandu—with its garbage, hustlers, intestinal
parasites, dope dealers, black marketeers, and labyrinthine
bureaucracy—is a different story. Before they arrive, tourists
know it will be "tough," and simply surviving their allotted two
or three weeks gives them a sense of accomplishment. Tourists
proudly don T-shirts that proclaim, "I did the Annapurna Circuit," even though over ten thousand others trek the same
route every year.

Every year hundreds of thousands of Euro-American and
East Asian middle-class young people "do Nepal" as part of,
and often the climax to, a kind of bourgeois "vision quest."[19]
"Doing Nepal" is the centerpiece of their own personal "hero's
journey" of self-empowerment and transformation, which will
be recounted for decades in travelers' tales and snapshots. In
other stops along the international youth travel circuit young
people learn that it takes physical and mental "toughness" to
"do Nepal." Thus by the time they wade into the throng of hotel
touts, taxi drivers, and baggage boys at the Kathmandu airport
exit, most tourists have steeled themselves to the demands of
Kathmandu and have carefully rehearsed the dramatis persona
that they wish to enact. In the drama of their vision quest they
themselves play the leading role in the pursuit of a "vision" of
romance and adventure they have already imposed on the
imaginary place of Kathmandu. In order to "find" this vision
they must be tough and able to discipline themselves and their
surroundings into conformity. Most tourists find the place they
are looking for, even if that place comes and goes with them.

Strangely absent from the Thamel tourist scene are any of
the 100,000 plus Indians—mostly wealthy and middle-aged—
who visit Nepal in a good year. In fact, even in a small city the

---

[18] Thanks to Nick Nickson for pointing out the significance of this usage.

[19] For example, in 1992 out of 334,353 tourist arrivals 227,779 were
from countries outside of South Asia. Out of the total arrivals 70 percent were
below age 45 (Central Bureau of Statistics, *Statistical Pocketbook 1994*
[Kathmandu: CBS, 1994] 121), but if statistics were available on the Euro-
American and East Asian tourists alone, it is almost certain that up to 90 percent would be between ages 15 and 35.

size of Kathmandu, the two groups of tourists rarely cross paths or interfere in each other's "quests." Throughout the year on Friday afternoons charter flights from Delhi and Bombay arrive in Kathmandu and by 6:00 the city's Super Market shopping mall and New Road retail district are crowded with Indian shoppers, who strip the walls of imported (mostly East Asian and European) clothing, housewares, and consumer electronics.[20] After dinner at their multistar hotels, the visitors gamble through the night in a Kathmandu casino and in the morning stagger onto buses bound for Pashupatinath, one of the subcontinent's most important Hindu pilgrimage centers, located on the outskirts of Kathmandu. Sunday morning they do last-minute shopping before boarding planes in the mid-afternoon.

For many Indians Kathmandu is a hill resort with a difference: no import restrictions, a major airport, legalized gambling, and a pilgrimage site to boot. Ironically, for these South Asian visitors Kathmandu is like an off-shore island of glitzy cosmopolitan consumer excess where visitors can live out fantasy roles as big spenders and high rollers, even while for many Western and East Asian tourists the city has precisely the opposite ethos, of oriental spirituality, exoticism, and ascetic simplicity. These contrasting images are a particularly vivid illustration of how the movement of people also involves the movement of places—that is, the movement of meanings with which people distinguish separate places within the same space. In the material I have presented we see how modern mass tourism intermeshes with modern mass media in the creation of these spatial imaginaries and how "texts" of many imagined places may occupy a shared spatial "context."

To conclude this section let me underline the fact that the dramaturgical language in this essay is not meant to be taken only metaphorically. When I suggest that various visitors to Kathmandu act out scripts that have been rehearsed and preimagined, I mean it quite literally. Yet whereas some suggest that modern "daily life" is a project of continuous drama-

---

[20] One businessman who runs a hotel just off of New Road spoke fondly of an Indian family he sees three or four times a year, or every time they need to restock their supply of disposable diapers.

turgical "presentation of self,"[21] my aims here are both more limited and more specific. I want to suggest that certain zones (such as Kathmandu's translocalities) are conducive to dramaturgical "play" or "presentation" that renders those spaces meaningful places in the mind of the actor. Furthermore, I want to suggest that the link between mass media and the imagination of distant places, which has been a recurring theme so far in this essay, is not coincidental. Obviously, people have imagined distant places forever—places are only meaningful in contrast to other places—but it is modern technology of the imagination and modern means of representation that have forever altered the nature of our geographic "imaginative resources." Neither *Tintin in Tibet* nor romantic travel novels, nor even television travelogues, are *necessarily* or *essentially* different from earlier representations of different places.

What *is* different is the scale or abundance of these representations in a host of representational modes—oral, aural, written, and visual—through commercial mass media, as well as the huge numbers of people able to travel to "other places," and the way these movements of images and people resonate with and reinforce divisions of political and economic power. Enormous numbers of first-world tourists now flit around the globe, taking with them imagined places that would previously only have been imagined *from* a distance. In importing their imagined places into foreign spaces, they (re)enact as personal drama (and indeed embody) a conceptual disciplinary labor that mirrors the violence of inequality upon which global power differentials are based. To the extent that modern mass tourism mirrors earlier patterns of colonial surveillance and exploitation,[22] it also guarantees who may engage their fantasies of "other places" on location and who must fantasize from a distance.

---

[21] Erving Goffman, *The Presentation of Self in Everyday Life* (New York: Anchor Doubleday, 1959).

[22] Dean MacCannel, *The Tourist: A New Theory of the Leisure Class* (New York: Schocken, 1976).

Locating the Periphery: Nepali Views from Thamel

Thamel is one of those places where both sides of this touristic coin coexist. Having discussed some of the dramatic places, the geographic imaginaries that tourists bring with them to areas like Thamel, I turn now to some of the dramatic Nepali lives (both heroic and tragic) enacted in the foreign-but-local space—the translocality—of Thamel. Although Thamel is often so crowded with young tourists that Nepalis sometimes refer to it as "*kuire* country"—using a derogatory term for fair-skinned foreigners—it is not a place that attracts large numbers of *local* young people. Even if they could afford the tourist goods and services available in Thamel, most young people in Kathmandu would have little interest in what is for sale.

But more than price, a reputation for toughness, drugs, and danger keeps many Nepali young people out of Thamel. Those Nepalis one sees in Thamel are mostly young men from the rural districts around Kathmandu who work long hours for low wages as cooks, waiters, and dish washers in the dozens of Thamel cafes and restaurants. Sharing cramped rented rooms in other parts of town, they send whatever money they can to their families in the hills. But those young men one sees "hanging out" on the streets and in certain cafes and bars are often representatives of two categories: tourist hustlers (who are often drug users) and "*punks*"[23]—middle-class young men who cultivate a tough but suave and fashionable persona.[24] For many Kathmandu young people, to frequent Thamel is to claim a vaguely sinister tough-guy reputation associated with drug use and/or violence. Most of the city's

---

[23] Words appearing between asterisks in quoted material designate English usage in colloquial Nepali.

[24] In the translocation of Thamel, as a zone for the extraction of resources from tourists, state and commercial interests must either put up with the "symbiots" and even "parasites" that "infest" this economic/cultural "niche" or risk destroying—through disciplinary actions—the extremely fragile cultural medium on which tourism thrives. As I suggested in the first part of this essay, tourism flourishes so long as the delicate ahistorical, apolitical places that tourists imagine are not threatened by the unpleasantries of social unrest.

middle- and upper-middle-class young people congregate in other parts of town; to be in Thamel one should be tough and ready to prove it. "Why ask for trouble?" wondered one young man who said he might visit Thamel once or twice a year. Many of the young people I met simply avoided Thamel.

Down and "Out Here" in Kathmandu: Drugs and Dreams from the Bottom. Although a generation ago drugs were an important part of Kathmandu's tourist allure, by the early 1990s drug use among tourists was not that common. One Thamel dealer in his thirties remembered "better times" but noted that now maybe only two or three out of a hundred tourists showed any interest in his whispered offers of "hash, real cheap." Ironically, Kathmandu's drug market is now mostly propelled by local demand, and the substances of choice are often "harder" drugs like heroin and various commercially produced (and unregulated) pharmaceuticals.

Thamel's reputation for drugs is only indirectly related to tourism; tourists help finance local users. While white heroin from Thailand and Burma is too expensive for Kathmandu users, the brown or unrefined heroin from India and Afghanistan makes up most of the local market. In 1991 a gram of "*brown sugar*" cost 400 Nepali rupees (compared to Rs. 1,200/gram for white).[25] At this rate, an "average" habit of one-half gram per day required a monthly cash outlay of at least 6,000 rupees, close to double the monthly salary of most civil servants. With the prospects for getting *any* job, let alone a high-paying one, abysmally low for even privileged young people, it is not surprising that most addicts eventually ended up pursuing tourists on the streets of Thamel. Taking profits on hashish or pot, changing hard currency on the black market, or acting as a tour guide, a skilled street hustler can make enough for a daily fix in a matter of hours. In the chaotic flow of Thamel tourists it is fairly easy to buy and sell drugs. With so many lodges and so few permanent residents, Thamel is a convenient liminal zone where addicts, prostitutes, and other demimondaines can find refuge, away from the prying eyes of the city's residential areas. For addicts Thamel offers both an extractive

---

[25] In the early 1990s 400 Nepali rupees was equal to roughly 10 U.S. dollars. In 1991 Nepal's average annual per capita income was only 180 U.S. dollars (Central Bureau of Statistics, *Statistical Pocketbook* 260).

resource (tourists) and a (relatively) safe haven. For these people the constantly transient chaos of Thamel makes it a place of freedom, a place to be invisible but also a place where one can exchange the stigma of the outcast for fantasies of other, more valued lives.

Ramesh was one such person.[26] Although I had encountered him several times in previous years, when I met Ramesh on a Thamel street one chilly spring morning in 1991, his gaunt and tired appearance seemed to confirm reports that he had relapsed into a heroin habit. As we walked together through Thamel in the months that followed, Ramesh threw light on a dimension of the reality around us that was completely new to me. In Ramesh's company places I had imagined and inhabited for years would suddenly evaporate, as glimpses of other (and others') places came briefly into view. For example, in the same Thamel garden cafe where I had encountered the two young mystical seekers described above, Ramesh pointed out drug transactions, police surveillance, school boys drinking codeine cough syrup, and a junkie tottering out of the bathroom, his face flush from retching, unable to keep down any food. Here was a kind of violence—usually quiet and self-destructive—that, once seen, shattered the tranquil imagined place that I and other foreigners imposed on that space, though our imaginations rendered this violence invisible and inaudible.

Ramesh introduced me to friends and fellow street hustlers. For these young men, supporting addictions meant maintaining the precarious balance between presenting a "clean," nonthreatening image to potential tourist clients and successfully procuring a daily fix. Losing one's composure meant losing customers, which meant missing a fix and further damaging one's ability to make money. One victim of this truly vicious cycle was Tamding, a Tibetan refugee and former monk with a severe heroin addiction. When I met him, Tamding was in his late twenties and sleeping on the streets: thin, filthy, and with a full-gram-a-day heroin habit, he was close to

---

[26] Some of the ethnographic material on Ramesh appears also in an earlier article on youth culture in Kathmandu: Mark Liechty, "Modernization, Media, and Markets: Youth Identities and the Experience of Modernity in Kathmandu, Nepal," in *Youth Cultures*, ed. V. Amit-Talai and H. Wulff (London: Routledge, 1995).

death. Reduced to begging and unable to support his habit, he used what money he had on incredible "pharma-cocktails"—seemingly deadly combinations of powerful sedatives, synthetic opiates, and psychiatric drugs that would temporarily induce sleep and mask the effects of heroin withdrawal. In tears Tamding described how a few months earlier his younger brother had died after eating refuse out of a Thamel restaurant dumpster, and it was clear that he himself would not survive the next intestinal parasite he encountered.

Ramesh was in better shape, though his personal background would not have suggested his current condition. Ramesh's parents had moved to Kathmandu from an eastern hill district when he was in his early teens. He had attended a respected English-medium high school in the valley and learned to read and speak English. By the time I met him in 1991, he had been in and out of drug rehabilitation seven times and had little more than the clothes on his back and a few rupees in his pocket. He lived by his wits day to day, hustling tourists, selling drugs, taking profits on petty commodity transactions, and running a variety of scams like sewing foreign labels into locally produced garments.

From a middle-class family, the product of an English-medium school, and a heavy consumer of imported Hindi and English mass media from videos to detective novels, Ramesh had much in common with his peers. As with many others, consuming foreign media had made Ramesh painfully aware of the limitations of his life as a Nepali, a life that he constantly compared to those lived in distant power centers. Ramesh constantly evaluated his Nepaliness through his media awareness of life in the West and Far East, even though he himself had never traveled farther than north India. In my presence, he repeatedly brought up images of "America," compared to which he found his own life one of extreme deprivation.

> Out here young people like me, we want a *fast* life, not this slow life.
>
> *What do you mean a "fast" life?*
>
> I mean like in the States where you can stay out all night until you drop. Here there's nothing, no [late-night] bars, and we can't even go anywhere to play video games.

When I asked how he knew about bars and video games, he explained that he had learned all about these things from movies and novels.

Indeed, Ramesh was a special connoisseur of films, books, magazine articles—anything he could find—especially those having to do with New York City. He knew all the city's boroughs and landmarks, but he was especially intrigued by "the Bronx," a place he brought up again and again in our conversations. From dozens of tough-guy movies and gangster novels, Ramesh had constructed a detailed image of a New York street culture full of drugs and gangs. He frequently compared Kathmandu's street life with that of New York, as when he explained how Kathmandu "gangs" take "tabs" (specific prescription drug tablets) before going to a fight, "just like in the Bronx." Ramesh could quote lines from Mafioso novels, and he frequently spoke of how one's face should never show feeling, a lesson he learned from *The Godfather.* Ramesh's ultimate goal was to move to "the States" and live in New York City. He often spoke in vague terms of a cousin living in Seattle who might help him get there.

Ironically, it sometimes seemed as though Ramesh already lived in New York. "The Bronx," in particular, seemed to be a kind of shadow universe where his mind roamed while his body navigated the streets of Thamel. "The Bronx"—with its street smarts and antiheroic codes of valor—was often the standard of reality against which he measured his own existence. At times it seemed that Ramesh was only imagining his life in Kathmandu against the reality of "the Bronx," not vice versa. For Ramesh "the Bronx" seemed to offer a way of understanding his own life, a life that he hated yet could link with a way of existence at the modern metropole. Ramesh's vision of "the Bronx" allowed him to identify his own existence as at least some version of "modernity," even if it lacked the all-night bars, video games, and a host of other modern accouterments that he had never seen in more than two dimensions.

The mediated images in Ramesh's imagination have important implications for his experience of place. Like many other young adults I met in Kathmandu, when speaking in English Ramesh constantly referred to the place he had spent most of his life as "out here." "Out here in Kathmandu" prefaced so many of his comments that in the course of time the words barely registered in my mind. This persistent self-pe-ripheralization is almost unimaginable outside the context of global media and a host of other marginalizing transnational cultural forces, including tourism and commodity imports. Mass media (as well as tourists and foreign goods) act like a lens that situates the local in an implicitly devalued and dimin-ished "out here" place, while at the same time seeming to pro-vide a window onto modern places that are distant in both time and space. But if the video screen is like a window, it is one with bars that keep viewers like Ramesh outside, "out here," looking in.

But media and tourism only work in conjunction with the Nepali state and its ideology of progress (*bikas*) and moderni-zation. By assuming the role of recipient and dependent in the global development aid economy, the Nepali state also lan-guishes in this "out here," self-peripheralizing mentality, in which modernity is essentially a foreign commodity. Hence in schools and in the government-run media young people are frequently reminded of Nepal's status as a "Least Developed Country." By almost all the standards that their education teaches them to value, whether through formal education or consumption of commercial mass media, Nepali conditions are deemed inferior in an evolutionary sense. The rhetoric of backwardness, development, foreign aid, and education col-lapses time and space, such that Nepali youth learn to situate themselves on the margins of a meaningful universe as con-sumers of an externally generated material modernity.[27] The entire discourse of modernization, progress, and development fuses with the image worlds of media to give young people an acute sense of marginality. For people like Ramesh, Thamel becomes a liminal wasteland between two worlds: the lived ex-perience of "out here" and the mediated dreams of modernity.

In a recent article, David Morley and Kevin Robins write that identity is "a question of memory, and memory of 'home' in particular."[28] Yet unlike the nostalgic longing for an ideal-ized "home" that Morley and Robins discuss, "home" for people like Ramesh is increasingly constructed at the confluence of

---

[27] Cf. Johannes Fabian, *Time and the Other* (New York: Columbia Uni-versity Press, 1983).

[28] Morley and Robins, "No Place like *Heimat*" 10.

various state and commercial discourses as devalued, stigmatized, and outdated. Morley and Robins talk about the power of
the state and media to construct an ideal "home" in the past,
yet in Kathmandu the state and media seem to construct home
as a place stigmatized in the present precisely because it represents (ostensibly) someone else's past. Removed from the apparent production zones of modernity, and unable to follow the
power lines back through time and space to the tourist homelands, people like Ramesh are stuck in the archaic "home
place" they imagine: "out here in Kathmandu."

Thamel Tough Guys: Fighting Boredom. While Ramesh often seemed to be moving through Thamel even while occupying
a foreign place, other young Kathmandu men came to Thamel
to live out fantasies that were much more localized. If part of
Thamel's reputation for "toughness" and danger is tied to its
drug culture, the area is also infamous for its gang activity and
violence. Ramesh often starred in his own internal dramas, but
other young men are tied into a variety of loosely organized,
hierarchical factions or "*gangs*," which occasionally enact
group dramas of toughness that may become violent. Though
by no means the only spot in town that sees gang activity,
Thamel is known for having more, and more serious, violence.

For Europeans and North Americans "gangs" and "idle
youths" hanging out on street corners ("corner boys") are
usually associated with lower- or working-class backgrounds,
but in Nepal the poor do not have the luxury of becoming what
are known in Nepali as "*punks*." Ironically, in Kathmandu
the "tough-guy," "street-fighter" persona is the privilege of a
kind of "leisure class." They are members of a middle class
that, while not wealthy by first-world standards, would rather
have its educated young people unemployed than engaged in
anything but white-collar labor. In an enormously glutted
middle-class labor market, young people are more or less idle
for years between high-school graduation and the beginning of
any meaningful employment.[29]

Leading lives of essentially forced inactivity and boredom,
young people, especially young men, often experiment with
fantasies of "action," with scripts loosely based on the media

---

[29] Liechty, "Modernization, Media, and Markets."

images that fill much of their day-to-day lives.[30] Of the many "action" fantasies available, some are more active and potentially violent than others. Thamel is a popular hangout for a certain kind of middle-class action seeker willing to "*fight* khelnu"—literally "to play at fighting."[31] A Kathmandu journalist in his early thirties described a fight he had recently witnessed in Thamel:

> I saw those people, and they weren't the types who have nothing, you know. They were like me, just a little younger, that's all. I didn't see anyone who didn't look like [their family owned] a house in Kathmandu. It's all these people who at least have a house and their parents are working—basically middle-class types.

Said another young man, only half-sarcastically, "The poor kids have gangs in America; then they make movies about them, and it's the rich kids who watch them here!" In Kathmandu the areas that have the worst reputations for juvenile violence—where taxi drivers hesitate to go at night—are usually the wealthy neighborhoods in the suburbs, not the poverty-stricken areas in the old city.

In many respects the young men who hang out in Thamel are similar to the Japanese bosozoku described by Ikuya Sato.[32] Bosozoku are young middle-class men who live for the

---

30 For a detailed discussion of middle-class youth and media consumption in Kathmandu, see Mark Liechty, "Fashioning Modernity in Kathmandu: Mass Media, Consumer Culture, and the Middle Class in Nepal" (Ph.D. dissertation, University of Pennsylvania, 1994), especially chaps. 1–5.

31 Unlike kusti khelnu (to wrestle), mudki hannu (to punch), or jhagada garnu (to quarrel, or tussle), "*fight* khelnu" is a term/concept that entered local language and practice through films. "*Fight* khelnu" refers both to the surrealistic choreographed fight sequences in films and also to the dramatic role acting between individuals and "*gangs*," which occasionally escalates into serious physical violence, especially when weapons are involved. When I asked one tough-looking 18–year-old Newar from a neighborhood near Thamel whether he was ever involved in gang violence, he replied, "kheleko chaina," or "No, I don't play that game."

32 Ikuya Sato, Kamikaze Biker: Parody and Anomy in Affluent Japan (Chicago: University of Chicago Press, 1991).

thrill of dressing up in tough-looking clothes and driving their modified cars and motorcycles at suicidal speeds (known as "*boso* driving") down the city streets of Japan. In certain times and places becoming an antisocial and dangerous *bosozoku*, like becoming a "*punk*" in Kathmandu, offers young people an expressive experience in what would otherwise be "extraordinarily boring and purposeless" lives.[33] Yet whereas *bosozoku* culture revolves around modified vehicles and the potential dangers of hot-rodding, Kathmandu "*punks*" are much more likely to fixate on what one might call "modified bodies"—disciplined through regimens of martial arts and body-building—and the potential dangers of fighting. *Bosozoku* idolize characters from films like *Mad Max* and fantasize about the "fierce-looking Kawasaki 1000 vehicles they use in the movie,"[34] while Kathmandu tough guys are more likely to be avid Kung-fu film consumers, focusing on the moves and bodies (of both "heroes" and "villains") depicted in those movies.

The "toughness" projected by these young men in Thamel has an important history in Nepal. From "Gurkha" soldiers to "Sherpa" mountaineers, many Nepalis literally make a living off of the now-global image of the fearless, robust, and tireless Himalayan hill man. Indeed, "Gurkha" and even "Sherpa" are now essentially professional titles, as often as they designate "authentic" ethnic or regional identities. Although the image and rhetoric of the brave "Gurkha" soldier is more than simply a colonial fantasy, the fact that British colonizers identified several populations in west-central and eastern Nepal as among the subcontinent's innately warlike "martial tribes" is an important factor in both the historical construction and continued salience of an essentialized image of the brave, courageous, *bahadur* Nepali male. The British and Indian armies still recruit Nepali "Gurkha" fighters, and many parts of rural Nepal are dependent on this form of labor migration.[35]

It is perhaps no coincidence that among those young men in Thamel with the "toughest" reputations, many are from the very "martial tribes" that have traded in toughness for centu-

---

[33] Sato, *Kamikaze Biker* 4.

[34] Sato, *Kamikaze Biker* 77.

[35] Mary Des Chene, "'Relics of Empire': A Cultural History of the Gurkhas, 1815–1987," (Ph.D. dissertation, Stanford University, 1991).

ries (Gurung, Rai, etc.). Precisely where and how an indigenous notion of "toughness" articulates with colonial constructs and new media-generated images such as the Kung-fu hero is difficult to say. But perhaps most important is how a deterritorialized global media genre like the Kung-fu film becomes embedded in a highly idiosyncratic local history that is itself already inflected by centuries of transnational cultural process.

In informal interviews conducted in a Thamel restaurant two young men talked about (among other things) their tastes in films. The first—a twenty-year-old Gurung with long hair, fashionable clothes, and a muscular build—explained which kind of "*English*" films he liked most:

> I like certain kinds, like *Rambo*, *commando* films, and the *Kung-fu*, *Karate* films, you know, Bruce Lee, Jackie Chan, and all that stuff.

> *Why these kinds?*

> Now, while I'm a youth, I like to be brave and active. This is what I like to do.

> *How did you get into watching *English* films?*

> My friends all watch only English films, and at first I didn't really like them, but after a while, I got into the habit, and I could understand what was going on. At first I didn't like them. But now I like them a lot.

His friend, a few years younger but equally well-dressed and extremely fit, also claimed English films as his favorites.

> *For example, what kind?*

> Let's see.... Well, there's *Kung-fu*. I like Bruce Lee so much. If I feel *bored*, like if there is some really *boring* time,[36] I like to go watch a Bruce Lee film.

---

[36] When used in spoken Nepali, various forms of the English word bore can have meanings slightly different from common usage in the West. In addition to tedium or monotony, in Nepali feeling "*bored*" can imply sadness,

> If I do, *automatically* I begin to feel very energetic, very strong and eager. All these feelings start to rise up! I've probably seen six different Bruce Lee movies already. There was *Enter the Dragon*, *Way of the Dragon*, and others too.

For both of these young men film preference had to do with imagining themselves as particular kinds of youth, ones who are tough, active, brave, and eager. When the boredom of everyday life became overpowering, films like these "*automatically*" gave them feelings of energy and strength. But most importantly, these films offer youth an image or outline of an active, exciting, and meaningful way of being: they offer dramatic alternatives to otherwise "*boring*" lives. Borrowing a few terms from Sato, one could argue that films like these help certain young people in Kathmandu construct "play worlds" in which to imagine themselves as "picaresque heroes, that is, strange combinations of picaro (rogue) and hero."[37]

Part of this "picaresque" persona involves adopting a studied presentation. In addition to fashioned bodies and fashionable clothing, young "*punks*" in Thamel cultivated a kind of expressionless countenance (like Ramesh), slow, fluid body movements, and a variety of striking postures and actions. A tricky way of lighting a cigarette, smoking in a sensual and suave manner, a sophisticated demeanor, effortless performance of intricate dance movements: many of these young men more than cut across my anthropological efforts to make Thamel an "other place," raising in me uncomfortable feelings of cultural inferiority and provinciality. In certain Thamel bars, at certain times, I had the unpleasant feeling of tables turning as people around me enacted a modernity that was all too close to home. If, as a Western anthropologist, I imagined Kathmandu as a place called "the field," at these times and places it became especially difficult to maintain the ethnographic fiction distinguishing "field" from "home." In these places—where Nepalis often surpassed "first-world" visitors in cosmopolitan sophistication—the "work" of "fieldwork" became an effort to stifle feelings of intimidation and the urge to leave.

---

depression, and frustration. In fact, the two sets of feelings are not antithetical and seem to be common features of life for many middle-class youth.

[37] Sato, *Kamikaze Biker* 5, 30.

In addition to the often-mediated fantasies of toughness, bravery, and violence, perhaps the ultimate fantasies pursued in Thamel are sexual, and in particular, fantasies of sexual relations between Nepali men and foreign women.[38] An essential part of any claim to distinction in the "play world" of the Thamel tough guys is the ability to attract foreign women (or at least a reputation for doing so). With its bars, music cafes, and hotels, Thamel is the prime location in Kathmandu for engaging in these transnational sexual fantasies. Even if many tales of sexual prowess are exaggerated, there is no doubt that out of the roughly one hundred thousand Euro-American women who visit Nepal each year, a few bring with them romantic fantasies of a kind that compliment those of some young men in Thamel.[39] Compared with male fellow-travelers, young female tourists from Europe and North America seemed more interested in having a "local experience" that included friendships with Nepalis. Because the Nepali people they encounter are likely to be in Thamel, there are fairly frequent opportunities for young "*punks*" to meet foreign women. What for these women may seem like a pleasant local friendship may, for the young men involved, be very sexually charged. Even if there is no sexual contact, these relationships may be the stuff of erotic fantasies and boasting among friends.

One young man I met came close to epitomizing the Thamel sophisticate. When I met Pradip, the friend of a friend, he was only in his late twenties and already owned a restaurant/bar and small lodge in a prime Thamel location. Having owned land in Thamel, Pradip's family was able to cash in on the tourist boom of the 1970s and '80s. Pradip had received a first-rate English education, had grown up around foreigners,

---

[38] As I discuss in detail elsewhere, these sexual fantasies of "other women" are at least in part tied into the heavy consumption of Euro-American and East Asian pornography in Kathmandu. See Liechty, "Fashioning Modernity" chap. 14.

[39] Because Nepali women have far fewer opportunities to interact with foreign men, there seems to be very little sexual contact across this divide. Unlike places like Bangkok, and increasingly Hanoi, Kathmandu is not a destination for Euro-American or East Asian male sex tourism, even though it has an active prostitution scene. According to my sources (social workers, medical personnel, journalists, hotel managers) the only foreigners that employ Kathmandu prostitutes are Indians (truckers, businessmen, tourists).

could converse in several European languages, and was a re-fined and engaging conversationalist by any standards. His reputation for sexual conquest was probably based more on speculation than evidence, but on several occasions he spoke of his relationships with foreign women. Pradip identified one woman in particular as his "girlfriend"—an American from California, whom he had met several years earlier. She came to Nepal at least once a year, and they were in regular phone contact. Clearly, they had a sincere relationship, but, Pradip confessed, deep down he knew it could not work. He described how one evening on her most recent visit she had been out smoking hash with friends and did not return to the lodge until the early morning. When Pradip angrily demanded an explanation, she exclaimed, "You don't own me! I can do what I like." Furthermore, his girlfriend assumed that he would eventually move to the United States. "Why should I go to America?" he asked.

> There I couldn't get a very good job but would just have to work all day for little money. Here I have plenty of money, and I don't have to work! Here I have my bar and my lodge. They are both in profit.... Why would I want anything differ-ent?

In the mean time Pradip introduced me to a young woman from the consular affairs office of the French Embassy whom he had been "dating for the past six months." It was clear that ultimately Pradip was not interested in marrying a Western woman, even though he greatly enjoyed such company. Push-ing thirty, Pradip was thinking of "settling down" and had real-ized that while Western women—witty and unreserved—were good to have in a Thamel restaurant (and possibly in a hotel room), a Nepali woman—obedient and demure—was good to have at home. For Pradip different kinds of imagined women belonged in different imagined places.

As for many others, for Pradip Thamel is a distinctive place in the overall urban geography of Kathmandu. Thamel is a place with its own distinctive ethos, a place in which to pur-sue a dramatic public lifestyle built around entertainment, lei-sure, and commercialized/mediated images of sophistication, glamour, and sexuality. Thamel is a quasi-foreign place, a place in which to experiment with, and for those "lucky" enough, to indulge in images and fantasies of foreignness. Thamel is a place conceptually distinct from "home," even if "home" might occupy the same physical space. For Ramesh— the heroin addict who came to Thamel to hustle tourists and dream of life on the streets of New York—dreams of foreign places made "home" a place to flee. But for those at the top, who successfully enacted the ethos of the Thamel transnational "play world," "home" was a place to retreat to away from Thamel, a place to escape from the dramaturgical mode or at least lapse into a more familiar "local" drama.

"Stars of Action": The Politics of Dramatization

During the late 1980s and early 1990s Star Beer (produced in Nepal) staked its claim in the increasingly competitive Nepali national alcohol market with an interesting jingle that ran frequently on Radio Nepal. Even though almost all of Radio Nepal's programming is in Nepali, the Star Beer jingle was in English:

> It takes a star of action,
>   to satisfy a man like you,
> Smooth reaction,
>   to satisfy a man like you,
> Men like you who want to see,
> Men like you who want to be,
> Stars of action with Star Beer.

It struck me as no coincidence that advertisers would wish to capitalize on the desire to "see" and "be" "stars of action." The ad seemed to capture, in caricature, the "smooth reaction" of the middle-class, suave, Kathmandu tough-guy persona and then play on the related longing for "action." "Men like you" not only "want to see" the media stars of imaginary action but also "want to be" those "stars of action."

But in this essay I have tried to show that in Kathmandu it is not only certain "locals"—people like Ramesh and Pradip— whose lives have "become inflected, even afflicted, by cosmopolitan scripts"[40] but tourists as well. Indeed, it is a shared project of mass-mediated dramatization that seems to tie both tourists and "locals" together in spaces like Thamel. In this modern translocality youthful members of a now-global middle class flow through and past one another's mediated quests for "adventure" and "action." In this regard Susan Sontag's observation that "boredom is just the reverse of fascination" is intriguing. Of boredom and fascination, Sontag continues, "both depend on being outside rather than inside a situation, and one leads to the other."[41] United in their experience of middle-class boredom (in the modern zone of "youth" between child and adulthood),[42] young people long for the fascination of romantic "action adventures," whether at home or abroad. In translocalities like Thamel it is precisely the fantasies/ images of "action" and "adventure" that construct places in complex layers over the same space. In these localities an array of mediated memories, rather than shared social relations, inscribes a host of meaningful places onto a shared space.

Another peculiar feature of Kathmandu as translocality is the strange symmetry between the middle-class dreams of toughness shared by tourists and Nepalis. There is a kind of dramatic violence on both sides of the equation. On the one hand, there is the perceptual violence that most tourists conduct in order to cleanse the Nepali spaces they occupy of the historical and class contradictions that would prevent them from imposing their own preimagined place onto this space. There is violence embedded in the toughness of "doing Nepal," in the work necessary to imagine, maintain, and inhabit the "other place" of one's dreams. On the other hand, there is "local" violence: the seductive self-destruction that is dependence, whether on drugs or foreign aid; and the seemingly non-referential violence of middle-class youth fighting boredom.

---

[40] Appadurai, "Global Ethnoscapes" 208.

[41] Susan Sontag, *On Photography* (New York: Delta/Dell, 1977) 42.

[42] Elsewhere I have suggested (building on an argument by Joseph Kett, *Rites of Passage: Adolescence in America* [New York: Basic Books, 1977]) that "youth" (the "teen," the "adolescent," etc.) as a category between child and adult is largely a modern phenomenon emerging both from middle-class demands for distinction (prolonged education) and market demand for a new consumer category. See Liechty, "Modernization, Media, and Markets."

Whether foreign or Nepali, all of these middle-class youth share in a fantasy of toughness and the dramatization of "other roles" in "other places," even if for young people in Kathmandu the dramatic journey's destination must be closer at hand. Yet though they share a dramatic mode and even a space in Kathmandu, the distance between their imagined places only reproduces the distance they have traveled (and the privilege, or lack, that it represents), guaranteeing that the two groups, though elbow to elbow, fail to find each other. Thus the shared drama is ultimately a tragedy to the extent that members of a globally connected middle class lead lives as media-inspired "actors" rather than creative agents and pursue scripted representations of difference rather than the possibilities of a just and equitable global common ground.

Scholars typically cite contemporary trends in the global circulation of mass media, tourists, money, and commodities as prime instances of cultural deterritorialization—the severing of culture from locale and the rise of global interdependency. Yet far from eliminating difference around the world, cultural deterritorialization has witnessed the widespread, often violent, (re)emergence of cultural difference. In a recent critical essay, Akhil Gupta and James Ferguson suggest that we look beyond deterritorialization to explore "the production of difference within common, shared, and connected spaces," and that we must look for "a shared historical process that differentiates the world as it connects it."[43] In translocalities such as those in Kathmandu we catch glimpses of these shared historical processes that reterritorialize the world even while ostensibly transcending its boundaries. In these localities space is reterritorialized as tourists and locals imagine places and long for meaning. But in this process of reterritorialization the imagined is not imaginary. To the extent that transnational economic and cultural hierarchies continue to generate a longing for "other" meaning—whether nostalgia for the "exotic" periphery or the periphery's desire for the "modern"—imaginations will continue not simply to reflect but to reinforce global structures of inequality. Even in translocal spaces such as Thamel, where both tourists and locals share a middle-class

---

[43] Akhil Gupta and James Ferguson, "Beyond 'Culture': Space, Identity, and the Politics of Difference," *Cultural Anthropology* 7, 1 (1992): 16.

project of mass-mediated dramatization, the very boundaries apparently "deterritorialized" by transnational media industries are reinscribed in contrasting imagined places that reproduce the contours of global power.

IDENTITY IN THE GLOBAL CITY:
Economic and Cultural Encasements

Saskia Sassen

Profound transformations in the organization and spaces of the economy have produced what we might think of as an unmooring, a disembedding of identities. Today's major cities are strategic sites for the exploration of this process and the partial refiguring of identities that ensues. This is especially so in the type of city I refer to as global, that is, cities that have become the location for key global processes ranging from international finance to immigration. Here I want to explore one particular angle of this process and to do so from the perspective of the economy.

The organizational and spatial transformation of economic activity in the global city has strengthened the power of the economic center; the city is a site for the overvalorization of the leading corporate sectors, which now operate globally. On the other hand, that transformation has reduced the economic status of an increasing range of workers and firms; the global city becomes the site for their devalorization, as in the much-noted increased poverty of the urban working class. These changes capture in a somewhat tentative and ambiguous way what is potentially the beginning of a fundamental shift in highly developed economies. How to describe these changes, how to represent them is thus no easy matter if one is to go beyond a mere description of patterns and produce a new account of what constitutes an advanced economy. Current representations in the mainstream press and in much conventional economic analysis of the organizational and spatial changes evident in the most advanced economies have come to a) restrict the terrain of "the economy" to an increasingly narrow spectrum of economic actors, notably corporate firms and highly educated workers, and b) expel a variety of economic actors, recasting them in terms of cultural representations (for example, immigrant community, ethnic group, underclass) that marginalize them as economic actors.

Restricting the notion of the economic in an advanced system to the corporate sector is a partial account of real-life economics. It is so in terms of the actual workings of the corporate sector of the economy. And it is so in the sense that it sidesteps the whole question of what Sennett refers to as the culture of the form, that is to say, the fact that any institutional form has a culture.[1] Thus the duality economy-culture is fundamentally flawed to start with. Confining economic activities and organizations that do not fit the image of the advanced information economy to the realm of "culture" clearly also creates a partial account. I think of these conceptual operations as encasements of identity. What I want to develop here is a specific usage of the concept of identity—we might say, a political economist's usage.

Insofar as the organizational and spatial transformations in the economy are confined to certain types of places—notably major cities, which account for only a fraction of people in the developed world—this encasement of identities may well be, in turn, a confined event. Yet it may also signal the beginning of a more general transition.

In the following sections I explore these issues in an effort to reframe the terrain within which we understand economic activity. Central to such an effort is the need to examine critically the specific transformations typically grouped under the notion of the global information economy, an economy seen as resting on the most advanced forms of technical and scientific inputs. For purposes of clarity I will use the term *corporate economy* or *corporate sector* to refer to the narrower definition of what is usually recognized as the advanced economy or the economic center; and I will use the more general term *urban economy* to designate that broader terrain within which economic activity operates.

Exclusion: Actual and Represented

In the last twenty years we have seen the expulsion and continuing exclusion from the "center" of significant components of the economy, notably much of manufacturing and many industrial services. One manifestation of this exclusion is the sharp increase in earnings inequality between corporate-sector professional and managerial workers, on the one hand,

---

[1] R. Sennett, *The Conscience of the Eye: The Design and Social Life of Cities* (New York: Norton, 1992).

and manual service and production workers, on the other. We see a similar increasing inequality in the profit-making capacities of firms in different sectors, notably financial firms compared with factories. Such inequalities in earnings and profit-making capacities have long existed; it is the sharpening of these inequalities evident over the last decade that signals a departure from older trends. There is today a generalized impression that manual workers and factories are basically obsolete in an advanced information economy. The fact is that many of those workers and firms are actually servicing the economic center. These trends are particularly evident in the economy of large cities.

Exclusion from the center makes economic survival precarious for excluded firms and workers. It also makes them appear either invisible or backward, unnecessary, anachronistic. These devalorized components/subjects need to be recovered in our accounts of the advanced economy, thereby transforming our understanding of the "center." This eviction and devaluing coincide with a sharp demographic transformation: the growing presence of women, immigrants, and people of color generally in the urban economy. One important question is whether this demographic transformation has facilitated eviction and devalorization. If so, we can speak of the demographic embeddedness of processes of exclusion from the economic center.

What I have sought to do in much of my politico-economic work on cities is to valorize components of the economy that have been devalorized because evicted from the center or never installed in the center. I have sought to show that they are articulated with sectors considered central but in ways that present them as marginal, backward, unnecessary. Thus it is the form of this articulation rather than some sort of intrinsic value that produces their marginality. By revealing the facts of this articulation and the multiplicity of forms it assumes, I hope to begin the process of valorizing these sectors, firms, and workers that constitute the devalorized part of the urban economy.

What are the conceptual operations that make such partial accounts possible?

Current mainstream representations of the economy have several key elements through which the system is constructed and explained. I will focus on three of them. Probably fundamental is the notion of continuous flow, also referred to as the trickle-down: the idea that there are no structural barriers to the circulation of economic growth or no discontinuities to be negotiated in this circulation and installation of economic growth. Thus growth emanates from the leading sectors and flows down to the rest of the economy through a series of mechanisms and intermediaries. Politically, this establishes the superiority of the leading sectors; these are the ones that should receive support from the larger polity and the government when necessary. Sectors that lack technological development and have a preponderance of low-wage workers and small, low-profit firms are considered as backward and not really belonging to an advanced economy. Hence the location of each component, whether at the top or the bottom, reflects its value. In some sense one could say that the leading sector occupies the privileged location of the positioned viewer in theories of visuality. This account of the economy creates a "white-knight" theory of economic growth: one sector is privileged as the one that will rescue the economy. Again, there are resonances with accounts in other disciplines. In the U.S. this white-knight version of economic growth was apparent in the hope and fanfare surrounding high tech industries in the 1970s and finance in the 1980s as the sectors that would pull the economy ahead, making us strong, beautiful, and happy.

At times the center has incorporated a majority of workers and firms under its regulatory umbrella and therewith empowered workers and their families—for example, in the 1950s and 1960s, through well-paying unionized jobs and subsidized housing for the suburban middle class. When this protected center shrinks and begins to expel a growing number of workers and firms, another situation obtains. And this distinction clearly is important within the conventional account and policy debate.[2] We must immediately note that much of that expanded, protected center in the economy—epitomized by the two decades after World War II—privileged men over women, whites over blacks; and that the expanded exclusion and devalorization of the last decade are embedded in a sharp demo-

---

[2] The shrinking of the protected center has engendered considerable debate and caused much impoverishment. It is an important subject unto itself, and there is a whole policy discussion that could eventually become of interest in the more theoretically oriented examination I am seeking to develop here.

graphic transformation in the urban workforce: women, immigrants, African-Americans now constitute a numerical majority of this workforce in our large cities.

A second important aspect in current representations of the advanced economy is economic internationalization. The account of the economy that takes off from the internationalization of transactions and firms is in many ways an empirical description. It privileges certain elements, such as global telecommunications capacity, and keeps silent about others. It also privileges the reconstitution of capital as an internationalized presence and emphasizes the vanguard character of this reconstitution. At the same time it remains absolutely silent about another crucial element of this internationalization, one that some, like myself, see as the counterpart of the internationalization of capital: this is the internationalization of labor. We are still using the language of immigration to describe this process. Elsewhere I argue that this language constructs immigration as a devalued process insofar as it describes the entry of people from generally poorer, disadvantaged countries in search of the better lives that the receiving country can offer; it contains an implicit valorization of the receiving country and a devalorization of the sending country.[3] It is furthermore a language derived from an earlier historical period and proceeds as if the world economic system were the same today as it was one hundred years ago.

A third aspect, a variant on the preceding one, is the conception of the global information economy as placeless. Key concepts in this account—globalization, information economy, and telematics—all suggest that place no longer matters. And they suggest that the type of place represented by major cities may have become obsolete from the perspective of the economy, particularly for the leading industries, which have the best access to, and are the most advanced users of, telecommunications and computer networks. This account privileges the capacity for global transmission over the concentrations of built infrastructure that make transmission possible; information outputs over the work of producing those outputs, from specialists to secretaries; and the new transnational corporate

---

[3] See S. Sassen, *The Mobility of Labor and Capital: A Study in International Investment and Labor Flow* (New York: Cambridge University Press, 1988).

culture over the various cultural environments, including reterritorialized immigrant cultures, within which many of the "other" jobs of the global information economy take place.

The overall effect is to lose the place-boundedness of significant components of the global information economy. This loss entails the eviction from the account of globalization of a whole array of activities and types of workers that, I argue, are as much a part of it as is international finance. And by evicting these activities and workers, this narrative excludes the variety of cultural contexts within which they exist, a cultural diversity that is as much a presence in processes of globalization as is the new international corporate culture.

A fourth aspect of the economic system and its representation has to do with the tendency towards concentration—of power, of control, of appropriation of profits. This tendency, produced and reproduced through different historical periods under different specific forms and contents, clearly feeds the valorizing of the center of the economy. That is, it constitutes a center and then valorizes it. Elsewhere I explain how this formation and reproduction of a center in the economy takes place through a variety of mechanisms and intermediaries.[4] A general question we need to address is whether an economic system with strong tendencies toward concentration in ownership and control can have a space economy that lacks points of physical agglomeration. That is, does power lack spatial correlates?[5]

This dominant narrative about the economy can be usefully explored in large cities, such as New York and Los Angeles or any of the major Western European cities, for at least two reasons. First, cities are the site for concrete operations of the economy. Much of what goes by the name of economic globalization materializes in major cities. Cities are strategic places that concentrate command functions, global markets, and, I would add, production sites for the new advanced information industries. Further, an examination of the day-to-day work in the leading industrial complex, finance and specialized serv-

[4] S. Sassen, *The Global City: New York, London, Tokyo* (Princeton University Press, 1991), and *Cities in a World Economy* (Thousand Oaks, CA: Pine Forge/Sage, 1994).

[5] See Sassen, *Global City*, parts 1 and 2; Sassen, *Cities in a World Economy*, chaps. 1 and 4.

ices, makes it clear that a large share of the jobs involved in finance, for example, are low-paid clerical and manual jobs, many held by women and immigrants. Such workers and jobs do not fit the representation of what finance, the premier industry of this period, is about—complex financial instruments and expertise.

Secondly, the city concentrates diversity.[6] Its spaces are inscribed with the dominant corporate culture but also with many other cultures and identities. The slippage is evident: the dominant culture can encompass only part of the city. And while corporate power inscribes these cultures and identities with "otherness," thereby devaluing them, they are present everywhere. This presence is especially strong in our major cities, which also have the largest concentrations of corporate power. This interesting correspondence between great concentrations of both corporate power and an amalgamated "other" invites us to see that globalization is not only constituted in terms of capital (international finance, telecommunications, information flows) but also in terms of people and cultures.

The Global City

Changes in the geography, composition, and institutional framework of economic globalization over the last two decades have led to sharp concentrations of economic functions in major cities.[7] Some of this concentration reflects the reinvigora-

---

[6] An important point made by A. D. King, *Urbanism, Colonialism, and the World Economy: Culture and Spatial Foundations of the World Urban System,* The International Library of Sociology (London and New York: Routledge, 1990), is that during European colonization different cultures and races met in the colonial cities. The cities of Europe and North America have only recently become places where such diversity is concentrated.

[7] The term *globalization* requires some clarification. R. Robertson, "Social Theory, Cultural Relativity and the Problem of Globality," in *Culture, Globalization and the World-System,* ed. A. D. King, Current Debates in Art History 3 (Department of Art & Art History, State University of New York at Binghamton, 1991) 69–90, posits that concepts of globalism are not economically fixed; I agree with this. A very common way of defining globalization is to see it as having come to mean the world is "systematic or one place." But authors as

tion of old functions; but much of it consists of new functions. Major cities have emerged as strategic places in the world economy. In the past cities were centers for imperial administration and international trade.[8] Today they are transnational spaces for business and finance, where firms and governments from many different countries can transact with one another, increasingly bypassing the firms of the "host" country.

I note two other economic operations, not sufficiently recognized in the literature on economic globalization. One is that global cities are a new kind of production site. They contain the combination of industries, suppliers, and markets—including labor markets—necessary for the production of highly specialized services: from financial innovations to international accounting models, international legal expertise, management and the coordination functions for just about any transborder flow. Emphasizing production foregrounds a broad range of presences that are usually lost in discussions of

---

diverse as S. Hall on culture ("The Local and the Global: Globalization and Ethnicity" in *Culture, Globalization* 19–40) and me on the economy do not work with this version of the global. Detailed research on globalization makes it clear that it is a highly diversified and contested process, with many geographies and events, narratives and self-reflexive mechanisms. See A. Giddens, *The Consequences of Modernity* (Oxford: Polity Press, 1991) on the self-reflexivity of modernism. It seems to me that it is not simply a question of choosing between two extremes: either a singular, nonreflexive narrative of globalization or a series of concepts that only exist in terms of the discourses that contain them and that can never be the expression of a real process of globalization. Once one begins to work with the clay of that multiplicity of geographies, events, and contradictions that constitute globalization, one can indeed see the gravitation of discourses (see the discourse of the global information economy, which I have sought to critique in much of my work) but also the concrete specificities of lived experience. The question for me is how globalization is constituted, not just as a narrative but in terms of concrete, specific, often place-bound, operations. Thus the narrative about globalization that is centered on the information economy and telematics is, in my analysis, a very partial and distorted representation because it leaves out a variety of elements that are part of globalization; secondly, what it leaves out tends to be overwhelmingly that which lacks power (see Sassen, *Global City*).

[8] King, *Urbanism, Colonialism*, notes that a major instrument of European colonization was the colonial city. It played a different role from that of the imperial capital cities.

globalization and the information economy. These presences range from the material conditions underlying global telecommunications to the various types of workers and firms not usually associated with globalization and the information economy: secretaries, manual workers, the truckers who deliver state-of-the-art software (and that old-fashioned xerox paper). It is particularly important, it seems to me, to effect these analytic operations in the case of the leading sectors of the information economy because the mainstream account of this economy is so radically distorting in its privileging of information flows over the material and concrete conditions through which it operates, in its privileging of the advanced professional workforce, in its exclusion of nonprofessional workers and firms. In accounts of other sectors such as manufacturing or transportation, by contrast, these "other" types of workers, firms, and places are less likely to be excluded; indeed, they are often put at the center of the account and used to devalorize much of manufacturing. The exception is high tech, and here again we see a privileging of the research and professional staff and a veiling of the production workforce, which is mostly low-wage, female, and immigrant. Technology and the different classes of workers that embody, enact, or use its components—whether technicians, professionals, clericals, manual workers—are not a preexisting condition in the organization of the economy but are constituted by that economic organization.

The third aspect that matters in the discussion is that global cities are also internationalized spaces in terms of people. The emphasis on production discussed above foregrounds place-bound aspects of globalization.[9] And a recovery of place in a discussion of globalization reveals that not only firms from many different countries meet there to do business. It is also the terrain where peoples from various third world countries are most likely to meet and a multiplicity of cultures come together. The city is not only the material infrastructure, the jobs and firms: it is also the many different cultural environments in which these workers exist. One can no longer think of centers for international business and finance simply in terms of the corporate towers and corporate culture at its center.

---

[9] Cf. Robertson's notion of the world as a single place, or the global human condition, in "Social Theory, Cultural Relativity."

Thus I would say that globalization is also a process that produces differentiation, but the alignment of differences varies greatly from that associated with such differentiating notions as national character, national culture, national society. For example, the corporate world today has a global geography, but it isn't everywhere in the world: in fact, it has highly defined and structured spaces; secondly, it is increasingly sharply differentiated from noncorporate segments in the economies of the particular locations (a city such as New York) or countries where it operates. There is homogenization along certain lines that cross national boundaries and sharp differentiation inside these boundaries. This is also apparent in the geography of certain built forms—from the bungalow to the corporate complex or the landscapes of American theme parks, which are global yet highly localized in certain places. Globalized forms and processes tend to have a distinct geography.[10]

Increasingly, the dominant narrative of the economy posits the formation of an international professional class of workers and of environments that are highly internationalized due to the presence of foreign firms and personnel, the formation of global markets in the arts, and the international circulation of high culture. What has not been recognized is the possibility that we are seeing an internationalized labor market for low-wage manual and service workers. This process continues to be couched in terms of immigration, a narrative rooted in an earlier historical period.

I think that certain representations of globality have not been recognized as such or are contested. Among these is the question of immigration, as well as the multiplicity of cultural environments it contributes in large cities, often subsumed under the notion of ethnicity. What we still narrate in the language of immigration and ethnicity, I would argue, is actually a series of processes having to do with the globalization of economic activity, of cultural activity, of identity formation. Elsewhere I argue that the current post-1945 period has distinct conditions for the formation and continuation of international

---

[10] On the bungalow see A. D. King, *The Bungalow: The Production of a Global Culture* (London and New York: Routledge and Kegan Paul, 1984). On the corporate complex see S. Sassen, *Cities in a World Economy.* On the landscapes of American theme parks see S. Zukin, *Landscapes of Power* (Berkeley: University of California Press, 1991).

flows of immigrants and refugees. I show that the specific forms of internationalization of capital we see over this period have contributed to mobilize people into migration streams and build bridges between countries of origin and the U.S. The first took place through the implantation of Western development strategies, from the replacement of small-holder agriculture with export-oriented commercial agriculture to the Westernization of educational systems. At the same time the administrative, commercial, and development networks of the former European empires and the newer forms these networks assumed under the Pax Americana (international direct foreign investment, export processing zones, wars for democracy) have not only created bridges for the flow of capital, information, and high-level personnel from the center to the periphery but, I argue, also for the flow of migrants.[11]

In the conventional narration immigration and ethnicity are constituted as otherness. Understanding them as a set of processes whereby global elements are localized, international labor markets are constituted, and cultures from all over the world are de- and re-territorialized puts them right at the center, along with the internationalization of capital, as a fundamental aspect of globalization.[12] This way of narrating the migration events of the postwar era captures the ongoing impact of colonialism and postcolonial forms of empire on major processes of globalization today, and specifically those binding emigration and immigration countries. The major immigration countries are not innocent bystanders; the specific genesis and contents of their responsibility will vary from case to case and period to period.

Today's global cities are in part the spaces of postcolonialism and indeed contain conditions for the formation of a post-

---

[11] See Sassen, *Mobility of Labor and Capital.* On this last point, see also Hall's account in "The Local and the Global" of the postwar influx of people from the Commonwealth into Britain and his description of how England and Englishness were so present in his native Jamaica as to make people feel that London was the capital where they were all headed sooner or later.

[12] That is why in a book mostly on immigration, I refused to use the concept immigration in the title and sought to link the internationalization of capital and labor.

colonialist discourse.[13] An interesting question concerns the nature of internationalization today in ex-colonial cities. King's important analysis of the distinctive historical and unequal conditions in which the notion of the "international" was constructed shows that during the time of empire some major old colonial centers were far more internationalized than the metropolitan centers.[14] Internationalization as used today is assumed to be rooted in the experience of the center. This brings up a parallel contemporary blind spot, well captured in Hall's observation that contemporary postcolonial and postimperialist critiques have emerged in the former centers of empires and are silent about a range of conditions evident today in ex-colonial cities or countries. Similarly, the idea that the international migrations now directed largely to the center from former colonial territories, and neocolonial territories in the case of the U.S. and Japan,[15] might be the correlate of the internationalization of capital that began with colonialism is simply not part of the mainstream interpretation of that past and the present.

Methodologically speaking, this conception of the global city contains one way of addressing the question of the unit of analysis. The national society is a problematic category. But so is the "world economy."[16] Highly internationalized cities such as New York or London offer the possibility of examining globalization processes in great detail, within a bounded set-

---

[13] See Hall, "The Local and the Global," and King, *Urbanism, Colonialism.*

[14] King,*Urbanism, Colonialism.*

[15] See Sassen, *Global City.*

[16] I tend to agree with Robertson's comment in "Social Theory, Cultural Relativity" that the proliferation of the ideas of nation, nationalism, and national culture, especially in the twentieth century, is connected to globalization processes. Various forms of nationalism and subnationalism are speaking with increasingly loud voices today precisely because the nation-state and national society are eroding from within *and* without. This erosion assumes distinct modalities and degrees of intensity in different countries. It is by no means a uniform and universal process. The new nationalisms range from reemergence of older nationalisms in extreme forms, as evident in the former territories of Yugoslavia, to the renewed intensity of statements about the American people, the American character, and English as the official language in the last two decades in the U.S.

ting, and with all their multiple, often contradictory aspects. Such an examination would begin to address some of the questions raised by King about the need for a differentiated notion of not only culture but also the international and the global.[17]

We need to recognize the specific historical conditions for different conceptions of the international. There is a tendency to see the internationalization of the economy as a process operating at the center, embedded in the power of the multinational corporations today and colonial enterprises in the past.[18] Yet the economies of many peripheral countries are thoroughly internationalized due to high levels of foreign investment in all economic sectors and heavy dependence on world markets for "hard" currency. What center countries have is strategic concentrations of firms and markets that operate globally, the capability for global control and coordination, and power. This is a very different form of the international from that found in peripheral countries.

Globalization is a contradictory space; it is characterized by contestation, internal differentiation, continuous border crossings.[19] The global city is emblematic of this condition.

---

[17] King, *Urbanism, Colonialism.*

[18] Similarly, in the social sciences such categories as economic power, leading industries, or economic globalization are most commonly studied from the top down. I agree with Janet Abu-Lughod (ed., *Contested Turf* [Oxford: Blackwell, 1994]) that we also need to proceed from the bottom up. The central assumption in much of my work has been that we learn something about power through its absence and by moving through or negotiating the borders and terrains that connect powerlessness to power. Power is not a silence at the bottom; its absence is present and has consequences. The terms and language of the debate force particular positions and preempt others.

[19] There are many examples. Global mass culture homogenizes and can absorb an immense variety of local cultural elements. But this process is never complete. Manufacturing of electronic components shows that employment in lead sectors no longer inevitably constitutes membership in a labor aristocracy. Thus third world women working in Export Processing Zones are not empowered: capitalism can work through difference. In the case of "illegal" immigrants, national boundaries have the effect of creating and criminalizing difference. These kinds of differentiations are central to the formation of a world economic system. See I. Wallerstein, "Culture as the Ideological Battleground of the Modern World-System," in *Global Culture: Nationalism, Globali-*

Contested Spaces in the City

Space in the city is increasingly inscribed by the dominant corporate culture. Sennett observes that "the space of authority in Western culture has evolved as a space of precision." And Giddens notes the centrality of "expertise" in today's society, with the corresponding transfer of authority and trust to expert systems.[20]

Corporate culture is one representation of precision and expertise. Its space has become one of the main spaces of authority in today's cities. The dense concentrations of tall buildings in major downtowns or in the new edge cities are the site for corporate culture—though, as I will argue later, they are also the site for other forms of inhabitation, which have been rendered invisible. The vertical grid of the corporate tower is imbued with the same neutrality and rationality attributed to the horizontal grid of American cities.

Much has been said about the Protestant ethic as the culture through which the economic operations of capitalism are constituted in daily life. Sennett opens up a whole new perspective both on the Protestant ethic and on the American city by suggesting that what is experienced as a form of rational urban organization, the grid, is actually far more charged. It is the representation in urban design of "how a protestant language of self and space becomes a modern form of power."[21] Clearly, the neutralization of place brought about by the modern grid contains an aspiration to a modern space of precision. The same aspiration is evident in the self-inscription of corporate culture as neutral, as ordered by technology, economic efficiency, rationality. This contrasts with what is thought of as the culture of small businesses or, even more so, ethnic enterprises. Each of these is a partial representation, in one case of the city, in the other of the economy.

The dominant narrative presents the economy as ordered by principles of technical and scientific efficiency and in that

---

zation and Modernity, ed. Mike Featherstone (London, Newbury Park, and Delhi: Sage, 1990).

[20] Sennett, *Conscience of the Eye* 36; Giddens, *Consequences of Modernity* 88–91.

[21] Sennett, *Conscience of the Eye* 50.

sense as neutral. The emergence and consolidation of corporate power appears, then, as an inevitable form that economic growth takes under these ordering principles. The impressive engineering and architecture evident in the tall corporate towers that dominate our downtowns are a physical embodiment of these principles. And the corporate culture that inhabits these towers and inscribes them is the organizational and behavioral correlate to these ordering principles.

Authority is thereby "divorced from community.... The visual forms of legibility in urban designs or space no longer suggest much about subjective life."[22] Subjective life is installed in a multiplicity of subjectivities, and this undermines the representation of the advanced modern economy as a space of neutrality, the neutrality that comes from technology and efficiency: the ordering principles of a modern economy.

Both the neutralization of place through the grid in its aspiration to a modern space of precision and the self-inscription of corporate culture as neutral, as ordered by technology and efficiency, are partial representations of the city and the economy. This inscription needs to be produced and reproduced, and it can never be complete because of all the other presences in the city that are inscribed in urban space. The representation of the city contained in the dominant economic narrative can exclude large portions of the lived city and reconstitute them as some amalgamated "other."

The lived city contains multiple spatialities and identities, many indeed articulated with and very much a part of the economy but represented as superfluous, anachronistic, or marginal. Through immigration numerous once highly localized cultures now have become presences in many large cities whose elites think of themselves as cosmopolitan—that is, as transcending any locality.[23] An immense array of cultures

---

[22] Sennett, *Conscience of the Eye* 37.

[23] Hall, "The Local and the Global," makes an important observation when he uses the term *ethnicity* to describe that which is grounded, rooted and notes two aspects: 1) the inevitability of this if a group is to recover its own hidden history to enter into representation; 2) that ethnicity, while necessary, is also about exclusion of all others. Politics should not be reduced to the politics of ethnicity, which risks becoming yet another form of fundamentalism. The discussion of culture as increasingly deterritorialized offers additional narratives to encompass certain aspects of the immigrant experience.

from around the world, each rooted in a particular country or village, now are reterritorialized in a few single places, such as New York, Los Angeles, Paris, London, and, most recently, Tokyo.[24]

The space of the amalgamated other created by corporate culture is constituted as a devalued, downgraded space in the dominant economic narrative: social and physical decay, a burden. In today's New York or Los Angeles, this is the space of the immigrant community, of the black ghetto, and increasingly of the old manufacturing district. In its most extreme version it is the space of the underclass, welfare mothers, and drug addicts. Corporate culture collapses differences, some minute, some sharp, among the different sociocultural contexts into one amorphous otherness—an otherness that has no place in the economy, the other who holds the low-wage jobs that are, supposedly, only marginally attached to the economy. It therewith reproduces the devaluing of those jobs and of those who hold the jobs. By omitting these articulations and focusing only on centrally placed sectors of the economy, the dominant economic narrative can present the economy as containing a higher order unity.

The corporate economy evicts these other economies and workers from economic representation, and the corporate culture represents them as the other. It evicts other ways of being in the city and in the economy. What is not installed in a corporate center is devalued, will tend to be devalued. And what occupies the corporate building in noncorporate ways is made invisible. The fact that most of the people working in the corporate city during the day are low-paid secretaries, mostly women, many immigrant or African-American women, is not included in the representation of the corporate economy or corporate culture. And the fact that at night a whole other

---

[24] Tokyo now has several, mostly working-class concentrations of legal and illegal immigrants coming from China, Bangladesh, Pakistan, the Philippines. This is quite remarkable in view of Japan's legal and cultural exclusion of immigrants. Poverty alone cannot explain this immigration, since these countries have long had poverty. I posit that the internationalization of the Japanese economy, including specific forms of investment in those countries and Japan's growing cultural influence there, have created bridges between them and Japan and have reduced the subjective distance from Japan. See Sassen, *Global City* chap. 9.

work force, the cleaners, installs itself in these spaces, including the offices of the chief executives, and inscribes the space
with a whole different culture (manual labor, often music,
lunch breaks at midnight) is an invisible event. As I have argued elsewhere, an infrastructure of low-wage, nonprofessional
jobs and activities constitutes a crucial part of the so-called
corporate economy: printers, truckers, repair workers, nighttime clerical workers.

In this sense, corporate architecture assumes a whole new
meaning beyond the question of the economy of offices and
real estate development. The built forms of the corporate economy are seen as representing its "neutrality"—the fact that it is
driven by technological development and efficiency, which are
considered neutral. Corporate architectural spatiality is one
specific form assumed by the circulation of power in the economy, and specifically in the corporate economy. Wigley notes
that the house is not innocent of the violence inside it.[25] And
we now have an excellent literature showing how the design of
different types of buildings—homes, factories, "public" lob-
bies—is shaped by cultural values and social norms. This
"rational" organization of office space illustrates Foucault's mi-
crotechnologies of power.[26]

But the changes in the details of inhabitation—institutional practices, the types and contents of buildings—indicate
there is no univocal relation between these and built form. I
agree with Rakatansky's observation that the play of ideologies
in architectural form is complex. And I would add that this
conception is essential if we are to allow for politics and agency
in the built environment. Yes, in some sense buildings are frozen in time. But they can be reinscribed. The only way we can
think of these towers now is as corporate giants if they are located downtown and as failed public housing projects if they
are in poor ghettos.

Another dimension along which to explore some of these
issues is the body "as the site of inscription for specific modes

---

[25] M. Wigley, "Untitled: The Housing of Gender," in *Sexuality and Space*,
ed. B. Colomina, Princeton Papers on Architecture (Princeton: Princeton Architectural Press, 1992) 327–90.

[26] M. Rakatansky, "Spatial Narratives," in *Strategies in Architectural
Thinking*, ed. J. Whiteman, J. Kipnis, and R. Burdett (Chicago: Institute for
Architecture and Urbanism; Cambridge: MIT Press, 1992) 198–221.

of subjectivity."[27] The body in large cities is citified, urbanized as a distinctively metropolitan body, unlike the body in a small town or rural area. The particular geographical, architectural, municipal arrangements constituting a city are one particular ingredient in the social constitution of the body; Grosz adds that they are by no means the most important one. She argues that the structure and particularity of the family and neighborhoods are more influential, though the structure of the city is also contained therein.[28] I would add that the structure, spatiality, and concrete localization of economic activities are also influential. In these many ways the city is an active force that "leaves its traces on the subject's corporeality."

But the body is citified in diverse ways: it is inscribed by the many sociocultural environments present in the city, and it, in turn, inscribes these. There are two forms in which this process weaves itself into the space of the economy. One is that these diverse ways in which the body is inscribed in the city's many sociocultural contexts works as a mechanism for segmenting, and in the end for devaluing, immigrant or African-American workers. This happens in very concrete ways. For example, research by the anthropologist Philippe Bourgeois details the case of an eighteen-year-old Puerto Rican from East Harlem who gets a job as a clerical attendant in an office in downtown Manhattan. For this young man, walking over to the xerox machine, past all the secretaries, is humiliating. The way he walks, the way he is dressed, the way he moves present him to the secretaries and managers as someone from the ghetto, someone who "doesn't know the proper ways." This particular young man eventually fled the downtown world and entered

---

[27] E. Grosz, "Bodies-Cities," in *Sexuality and Space* 241–53.

[28] She suggests a model of the relation between bodies and cities that sees them not as distinct megalithic total entities but as assemblies or collections of parts, capable of crossing the thresholds between substances to create new linkages. She does not stress the unity and integration of body and city or posit their ecological balance. Rather, what she posits is a fundamentally disunified series of systems and interconnections, disparate flows, events, entities, spaces, brought together or drawn apart in more or less temporary alignments.

the ghetto economy, where at least his gait, speech, and dress were the norm.[29]

This diversity also weaves itself into the economy by reentering the space of the dominant economic sector as merchandise and marketing. Interestingly, contemporary forms of globalization are different from earlier ones: the new global culture is absorptive, a continuously changing terrain that incorporates the new cultural elements whenever it can. In the earlier period, the culture of the empire, epitomized by Englishness, was exclusionary, seeking always to reproduce its difference.[30] At the same time, today's global culture cannot absorb everything; it is always a terrain for contestation, and its edges are certainly always in flux. The process of absorption can never be complete.

One question is whether the argument developed above regarding the neutralization of space brought about by the grid, and the system of values it entails or seeks to produce in space, also occurs with cultural globalization. As with the grid, culture never fully succeeds in this neutralization; yet absorption does alter the absorbed. An interesting issue emerging out of my work on the urban economy is whether at some point all the "others" (at its most extreme, the informal economy) carry enough weight to transform the center. In the case of culture, the absorption of multiple cultural elements, along with the cultural politics so evident in large cities, has transformed global culture. Thus unlike English imperial culture, which was highly exclusionary, today's global culture is inclusionary. Yet it is still centered in the technologies and images of the West. Thus absorbed, the other cultures are neutralized. And yet they are also present. Today's cultural politics creates vast spaces, especially in large cities, for numerous other cultural presences—some eventually absorbed by the machinery of "global culture," some not.

We can perhaps see this most clearly in urban space, where many other work cultures, cultural environments, and culturally inscribed bodies increasingly inhabit a built terrain that has its origins visibly in another culture, the culture lying

---

[29] P. Bourgeois, *In Search of Respect: Selling Crack in El Barrio*, Structural Analysis in the Social Sciences Series (New York: Cambridge University Press, forthcoming).

[30] Hall, "The Local and the Global."

behind the grid.[31] Here again, I ask, at what point does the "curve effect," as social scientists would put it, take hold and bring the center down?

Conclusion

In the preceding sections I have tried to show that the dominant economic sectors represent themselves through narratives and spaces that are partial representations of the urban economy. These representations pivot on notions of precision, neutrality, technical proficiency—all considered attributes of an advanced economy. In that sense we can speak of an economic encasement of the identity of these dominant sectors. Left out are the various attributes of power and the often irrational (counterproductive) pursuit of profits at all costs. Also left out is the possibility that precision, neutrality, and technical proficiency are embedded in a distinct culture and that its recognition would conceivably redefine those supposedly neutral attributes.

Secondly, I sought to show that devalorized economic sectors are servicing the corporate center of the economy and hence are necessary to that center even though represented as marginal. In large cities particularly, the identity of these sectors has been encased in cultural forms associated with marginality or inscribed as such by the larger society. This devalorization and cultural encasement of the identity of growing sectors of the urban economy has been embedded in a massive demographic transition toward women, African-Americans, and immigrants in the urban workforce.

---

[31] Similarly, the informal economy, when acknowledged, which is rare, is conceived of as a distortion, an import from the third world. Elsewhere I have documented the diverse ways in which goods and services produced in the informal economy circulate in the mainstream economy and can be shown to meet the needs of a broad variety of firms and households in the mainstream economy. Thus I posit that informalization is one way of organizing a range of activities that, on the one hand, produce goods and services in demand in the overall economy and, on the other hand, have been devalorized and hence are under immense competitive pressures.

Further, I have sought to argue that globalization—one of the key processes reshaping the advanced urban economy—needs to be thought of as a series of processes that materialize in places and are constituted by people as much as capital. Our large cities, and increasingly the large cities in Western Europe, are the terrain where a multiplicity of globalization processes assume concrete, localized forms, some seen as global and others not. These localized forms are, in good part, what globalization is about.

Large cities have emerged as strategic territories for these developments. On the one hand, they are crucial cogs in the new global economic system: they function as command points, global marketplaces for capital, and production sites for the information economy. On the other hand, they contain the varied economic activities and types of workers and cultural environments that are never represented as part of the global economy but are, in fact, as much a part of globalization as is international finance and corporate culture. These joint presences have made cities a contested terrain.

PART TWO: THE CRISIS IN THE NATION-STATE

FIGURES OF THE SUBJECT IN TIMES OF CRISIS

Achille Mbembe and Janet Roitman

Moi, quand quelque chose me dépasse, je ris seulement.
—Douala, August 1993

The following remarks are about subjectivities of "the crisis" and their corollary, the crisis of the subject. The first term refers to the crisis as a constitutive site of particular forms of subjectivity. The second term invokes the crisis of the very act of signifying this moment. These two instances, constitution and signification, are decisive elements in the generalized production of violence in the world today. They are also instances of its specificity.

The moment being considered, then, is not without date, place, or name. In fact, the object of our commentary is a precise phenomenon: contemporaneousness. Its real time can only be called the "immediate present." And it is the spirit (*esprit*), visibility, and profanity of this immediate present that is at the heart of our inquiry. This "immediate time" and "present duration" are defined by the acute economic depression, the chain of upheavals and tribulations, instabilities, fluctuations, and ruptures of all sorts (wars, genocide, large-scale movements of populations, sudden devaluations of currencies, natural catastrophes, brutal collapses of prices, breaches in provisioning, diverse forms of exaction, coercion, and constraint) that make up the fundamental experiences of African societies over the last several years.[1] The specific con-

The following study results from time spent in Cameroon: from March 1992 to December 1993 (J. Roitman) and June to August 1993 (A. Mbembe). J. Roitman acknowledges the generous support provided by the SSRC-MacArthur Program on Peace and Security during this period. A. Mbembe acknowledges the support of the History Department, University of Pennsylvania. We benefited from the assistance, commentary, and criticism of J. M. Ela, T. Mouctar Bah, V. Ombe Ndzana, S. Zoa, H. Bouba, A. Inoua, A. Ayissi, and A. Ashforth. C. Breckenridge offered insightful remarks and encouragement.

[1] For some examples of these events, S. Commins, M. Lofchie, and R. Payne, *Africa's Agrarian Crisis: The Roots of Famine* (Boulder: Westview Press,

juncture referred to here, this age that merges with immediate time, this contemporaneousness is what Africans and others have called "the crisis." That is to say—and this is what we hope to demonstrate—the entanglement of a plurality of real and not wholly distinct transformations; the combining and packaging of experiences lived by people at all levels of society; and the physical and mental violence that issues from the disjunction between the everyday practice of life (facticity) and the corpus of significations or meanings (ideality) available to explain and interpret what happens, to act efficaciously and, in so doing, attempt to overcome the specter of nothingness (*le néant*, in the double sense of nothingness and meaningless).

This inquiry responds to several questions, some theoretical, others less so, but all concern the general problematic of the constitution of specific regimes of subjectivity in the context and as a result of the specific conjuncture described below. By regime of subjectivity, we mean: a shared set of imaginary configurations of "everyday life"[2] —imaginaries that have a material basis; systems of intelligibility to which people refer in order to construct a more or less clear idea of cause and effect, to determine the domain of what is possible and feasible, as well as the logics of efficacious action. More generally, a regime of subjectivity is an ensemble of ways of living, representing, and experiencing contemporaneousness while, at the same time, inscribing this experience in the mentality, understanding, and language of a historical time.

According to this formulation, we are not interested primarily in the problematics of resistance, emancipation, or autonomy.[3] We distance ourselves from these questions in order better to apprehend, in today's context, the series of op-

---

1986); R. Sandbrook, *The Politics of Africa's Economic Stagnation* (Cambridge: Cambridge University Press, 1985); T. Callaghy and J. Ravenhill, eds., *Hemmed In: Responses to Africa's Economic Decline* (New York: Columbia University Press, 1993); C. Geffray, *La Cause des armes au Mozambique: Anthropologie d'une guerre civile* (Paris: Karthala, 1990); T. Allen, "Understanding Alice: Uganda's Holy Spirit Movement in Context," *Africa* 61 (1991): 370–99.

[2] M. de Certeau, *The Practice of Everyday Life* (Berkeley: University of California Press, 1984); F. Braudel, *The Structures of Everyday Life. The Limits of the Possible* (New York: Harper and Row, 1979).

[3] C. Castoriadis, *Philosophy, Politics, Autonomy* (Oxford: Oxford University Press, 1991).

erations in and through which people weave their existence in incoherence, uncertainty, instability, and discontinuity; then, in experiencing the reversal of the material conditions of their societies, they recapture the possibility for self-constitution, thus instituting other "worlds of truth." By setting our sights on the domains of the unforeseen and the unexpected, the productive moments during which the incomplete nature of things coincides with the reversibility of that which has been acquired, and by attending to the stupor associated with terror, where individuals and societies are taken aback, defigured and without stable referents, we hope to apprehend an apparent paradox: in Africa today, becoming a "subject" involves a splitting of identities, which fuels a certain pragmatics of subjection, both of which make up a simultaneous moment. Subjectivity does not evade but rather issues from positions of subjugation.

This approach, contrary to typical discourses on politics and the economy in Africa, does not reduce the crisis to an event whose meaning is exhausted once it has been analyzed and deciphered statistically, becoming then simply an object of proposed reform, as in the framework of structural adjustment programs.[4] Against statistical representations, this is an attempt to treat the crisis as, above all, lived experience. Secondly, this attempt suggests that it is in everyday life that the crisis as a limitless experience and a field dramatizing particular forms of subjectivity is authored, receives its translations, is institutionalized, loses its exceptional character, and in the end, as a "normal," ordinary, and banal phenomenon, becomes an imperative to consciousness. Such "normalization," which is also the tautology involved in explaining the crisis by the crisis, results from a combination of repertoires. The very notion of the crisis widely serves as a structuring idiom. In this sense, it constitutes almost in and of itself a singular mode of apprehending (and hence narrating, or living) immediate agonies. The crisis also operates as a figure of rationality and an existential device. In other words, by relegating the crisis to the realm of the inexplicable, people likewise simultaneously circumscribe a field of both constraints and possible, reasonable,

---

[4] Cf. The World Bank, *Sub-Saharan Africa. From Crisis to Sustainable Growth: A Long-Term Perspective Study* (The World Bank: Washington, DC, 1989).

and legitimate action. Through acting on the basis of these rationalities, in the midst of these entangled fields of action, they themselves end up participating in the very process of the production of the crisis: a self-referring chain.

Yet we do not wish to underestimate the weight of external factors and the role of global forces in the origins and course of what has been called the crisis. The nature of these constraints has largely been explored and documented and their historical underpinnings brought to light,[5] even if their present mutations still essentially defy analysis.[6] The question for research is no longer simply measuring the impact of the crisis on society or measuring the disparities between prescribed reforms and their realization, as in the case of classical analyses. Unlike readings of the crisis that are limited to socioeconomic indicators commonly used to describe, understand, and explain the current situation in Africa, the approach outlined here obliges the scholar to "return to the field."[7] Return to the field does not signify, however, a mechanical turn to "local knowledge"; people themselves claim that they no longer understand what is happening to them, much less that they have mastered the ins and outs of the processes in which they are implicated. The problem is, indeed, that the determining forces of the societies we study are not located where inquiries founded on a static epistemology have until now sought to find

---

[5] Read, for example, F. Cooper, "Africa and the World Economy," *African Studies Review* 24, 2–3 (1981). See also J. Lonsdale, "States and Social Processes in Africa," *African Studies Review* 24, 2–3 (1981).

[6] See, however, Z. Laïdi, *L'Ordre mondial relâché* (Paris: Seuil, 1992); "Points de vue sur le système monde," *Cahier du GEMDEV* 20 (1993); A. Appadurai, "Disjuncture and Difference in the Global Cultural Economy," *Public Culture* 2, 2 (1990): 1–24.

[7] By "return to the field" we are not necessarily referring to anthropologists' debates on the construction of the object of study and their trenchant critique of the supposed objective character of that object. In our opinion, the point that the researcher is implicated in the demarcation and construction of the object of study goes without saying. Cf. G. Marcus and M. J. Fischer, *Anthropology as Cultural Critique: An Experimental Moment in the Human Sciences* (Chicago: University of Chicago Press, 1986); J. Clifford and G. Marcus, *Writing Culture: The Poetics and Politics of Ethnography* (Berkeley: University of California Press, 1986).

them.[8] Thus, contrary to an approach based on linear perceptions of cause and effect, one must, in a self-reflective move, apprehend what the analyst defines in terms of the destructuring "effects" of the crisis as in fact *already there* or in the process of being unevenly constituted. Thus one approaches the crisis not as a system but as a prosaic: the routinization of a *register of improvisations* lived as such by people and, in this sense, belonging at most to the domain of the obvious or self-evident and at least to the banal or that which no longer evokes surprise.

This, then, is what we shall examine through examples taken, for the most part, from urban life in Cameroon. In the first part of this discussion, we will outline a geography of the crisis by detailing, from examples lived and known by a large number of people, the way in which the crisis is inscribed in the everyday urban landscape—in its material structures such as roads, residences, and buildings and in social interactions and relations of power, profit, and subsistence. This description serves two purposes. First, it gives a concrete indication of the living space of the subject, the forms of inscription of the crisis in public space, the body, and material life—in brief, its physicality[9] . It also serves as an introduction to the very field of representations of the time and imaginary of the crisis, paying heed to its supposed abrupt and sudden character. In the remaining part of the text, we underscore the relationship that exists between these representations and the destabilization of certain historical referents for action and understanding. And since in the present context this relationship also opens the way for a remarkable proliferation of criteria for judgment, we will examine how this proliferation affects logics of efficacious action and renders recourse to paradoxical logics

---

[8] This epistemological problem also concerns claims to knowledge based on founding oppositions, which impose order on, and preclude the legitimate status of, unrelatedness and unsystematicity, reversibility and surprise, inconclusiveness and the plurality of social time and space, which in turn leads to often problematic distinctions between levels of reality, everyday practices and extraordinary experiences.

[9] We are not describing havoc in Cameroon. We are trying to underline the materiality of the crisis in order then to look at its representational effects.

more likely.[10] Finally, we shall indicate how all of this leads to a crisis of the subject and thus of meaning and produces conditions favorable to forms of violence that are specific to the present juncture.

The Crisis in Space and Matter

Of all African countries, Cameroon was considered and considered itself, until the mid-1980s, to be a land endowed with economic assets such as petroleum, lumber, cocoa, coffee, cotton. Its annual rates of growth were among the highest on the continent. The implementation of a series of five-year development plans led to numerous investments, expanded the mass of wealth, and accelerated the process of social stratification. A powerful urban middle class emerged. On the whole, however, this class depended on its incorporation in the state apparatus, and especially the army and civil service, for its reproduction. A private sector was developing, and its dynamism varied according to regions and sectors of activity.[11] Furthermore, this relative prosperity had been made part and parcel of official and popular representations of national identity and Cameroonian singularity.

These representations were based on the idea that Cameroon was on a continuous and irreversible path of progress in a context in which the creation of wealth and material welfare seemed without limits. In concrete terms this progress translated for urban and rural families into possibilities for investing in children's education, attaining health care, buying real estate or a car, building a house, or even engaging in entrepreneurial activities—in brief, for raising their standards of liv-

---

[10] We are not asserting that this proliferation is without precedent. At this point in the discussion, what is important is to show the relationship that exists between the crisis in meaning and references, on the one hand, and the problem of criteria for efficacious action.

[11] On certain aspects of these processes, consult the cases in P. Geschiere and P. Konings, *Itinéraires d'accumulation au Cameroun/Paths of Accumulation in Cameroon* (Paris: Karthala, 1993).

ing.[12] This set of potential and real possibilities included both specific possessions that had been acquired and that which was so assured that one imagined the present and the future and thus elaborated ideas about society and community on the basis of these possibilities. Moreover, a tacit pact, guaranteed by the single party and founded on the principle of the reciprocal assimilation of elites into the centers of power, allowed for the unequal redistribution of material and symbolic rents between different social strata and regions. This in turn assured a certain legitimacy for the ruling regime.[13] And it is this entire material and symbolic architecture that has crumbled under the weight of the crisis.

Its most physical and visible mark, that which captures the eye and is instantaneously frozen as a vision, what one might call its iconicity, is the image of abandonment and general decomposition, which contrasts so starkly with the picture of affluence and prosperity that prevailed only a few years ago. The apparently abrupt nature of this rupture is most obvious in Yaoundé, where, as Cameroon's capital, the markers of modernity are supposed to be exhibited. Since the colonial period, roads have been one of the most distinctive signs of modernity. Today, Yaoundé's roads are in near total disrepair and dilapidation. Central avenues are as bad as streets in peripheral neighborhoods. Many roads that were paved a few years ago are now paths of beaten earth. They are broken up by sections that juxtapose efforts of resurfacing with potholes, crevices, and precarious ditches. Most traffic circles are nothing more than a heap of old tires or empty, rusted barrels.

The traffic lights no longer function. Some are still intact but no longer light up. Due to the absence of maintenance, vandalism, or, most often, traffic accidents, others have either toppled over, exposing their massive cement base, or lean dangerously over the *ad hoc* sidewalk or over the road itself. Although they are all still there, sometimes in the very spot where they were erected, they are now masses of useless "traces," outliers of bygone days.

---

[12] J.-P. Warnier, *L'Esprit d'entreprise au Cameroun* (Paris: Karthala, 1993).

[13] This process has been best described and interpreted by J.-F. Bayart, *L'État au Cameroun* (Paris: Fondation nationale des sciences politiques, 1977).

Such conditions incite a very particular economy of traffic circulation.[14] At first glance, its seems to lack rules or order. The chaos is undeniable even if it is sometimes misleading. In fact, drivers combine manners proper to the bush and those of the town, those of the military with the civilian. These produce deviations from recognized norms, ignore specific rights of way, and, of course, lead to accidents. The road is a disputed space, where private cars, taxis, public transportation, truck drivers, military jeeps, police cars, mopeds, bicycles, rickshaws, pedestrians, cattle, sheep, goats, and fowl intermingle and confront one another. Sudden stops and random parking, collisions that block traffic and cause congestion, the exchange of insults and physical abuse are par for the course. Furthermore, now that the automobile has become increasingly rare, the figure of the pedestrian is again firmly rooted in the urban landscape. With every passing vehicle the partly dirt, partly paved roadway becomes a "whirlwind of red dust which suffocates the pedestrian and sticks to their clothing, even becoming a stickier, thick muck with the least bit of intemperate if not infrequent rainfall."[15] The absence of traffic lights and thus of explicit rules of right-of-way, combined with the teeming atmosphere, render the road a particularly productive disciplinary device; experience on and familiarity with the road give rise to an array of dispositions and arts of negotiation that are constitutive of subjectivities of conflict.[16]

The other attribute and metaphor of progress and modernity was, until recently, the automobile itself. Today, the passenger is never sure about arriving at the desired destination. This is partly due to the innumerable breakdowns resulting from the vehicle's age and problems such as sagging shock

---

[14] For a purely geographic point of view on this subject, see the study by E. Tazo, "La Circulation routière à Yaoundé," Mémoire de maîtrise de géographie, Yaoundé, Université de Yaoundé, 1980.

[15] "un tourbillon de poussière rouge dont le piéton suffoque et qui colle aux vêtements, quitte à se transformer en une boue épaisse, plus collante encore, à la moindre pluie, intempérie plus que fréquente." Mongo Beti, *La France contre l'Afrique: Retour au Cameroun* (Paris: La Découverte, 1993) 61, our translation.

[16] For a technocratic reading of these practices, cf. X. Godard and P. Teurnier, *Les Transports urbains en Afrique à l'heure de l'ajustement* (Paris: Karthala-INRETS, 1992).

absorbers, missing windshields and doors, car bodies riddled with holes, faulty soldering and makeshift repairs leading to defective joints as well as dead starters that require a car to be pushed to get it going. Factors as prosaic as lack of servicing, the artisanal installation of spare parts,[17] and the impossibility (without a salary) of paying for gas must also be taken into account. In fact, most cars run on the reserve tank. Parsimony prompts drivers to turn off the engine and coast down hills in order to save gas. The wreckage of automobiles, bus cemeteries, passengers who strain behind a wheezing car: all of this has been from day to day so etched onto the urban landscape that it no longer creates a spectacle. It ceases to surprise. And so the physicality of the crisis reduces people to a precarious condition that affects the very way in which they define themselves.

The automobile, however, continues to "be useful for something." It is still an object of appropriation as a sign, belonging to a logic that is partly inspired by class affiliations.[18] This is evident from the attraction for, and fascination with, the most luxurious and expensive models. But, at the same time, and because it is most often broken down and immobilized, the car no longer takes part with the same intensity in the logic of ostentation, at least for the middle classes. Its presence can be more of a monument than anything else: a broken-down machine; a vestige of a shattered career; a once prosperous commerce now bankrupt; and a social status from which the owner was seemingly ejected. At most, then, it has become a figurative object.

Like roads and cars, the crisis has reconfigured another sign of modernity and economic progress, electric lighting. There are very few neighborhoods where all houses, buildings, and streets have electricity. With dusk, the city dimly spreads over its vast expanse of hills and valleys, gaping in places with black holes and shadows, brightened elsewhere with small pockets of light, sometimes emanating from kerosene lamps.

---

[17] The point is not that they are done wrongly but rather that they are done under certain circumstances and according to a particular level of infrastructure.

[18] In the sense in which J. Baudrillard speaks of a "sign function" (fonction-signe), a function that refers to a "class logic." See *Pour une critique de l'économie politique du signe* (Paris: Gallimard, 1972).

These pockets are magnets for various passersby who participate in the city's nocturnal life. On the edges of the *ad hoc* sidewalks, the commerce of the night proceeds. An entire urban food economy controlled by women selling foodstuffs like beans and fish provides subsistence to those on the margins and, increasingly, entire families struck by the irregularity of revenue and rarity of money. Public lighting, and the lack of it, also has other meanings. Associated with violence, the lack of public lighting and entry into a state of darkness also throw into question the specificity of Cameroonian national identity, which rested in part upon the idea that violence belonged to countries like Rwanda, Somalia, Chad, Zaïre, or Liberia but not in Cameroon. The failure of public lighting and the plunge into darkness are now perceived as intimating that such violence is now on the order of the possible (*de l'ordre du possible*).[19]

The widespread dilapidation creates a ubiquitous landscape of decay. This is a landscape unfolding and arranging itself like a fold in a fabric on the edge of the world; in the midst of an almost surrealist decor, transformations are enveloped in quasi-magical effects. The city is laced in a string of litter and refuse that is rarely collected.[20] Mounds of rubbish

---

[19] J. Roitman, "Notes," Maroua, 1993. At a meeting of public officials and merchants, one official commented, "SONEL [Société nationale d'électricité] va couper. C'est la honte; le chef lieu de Province est dans l'obscurité.... Les touristes, les espions vont venir voir ... et la SONEL agit toujours avec sa soeur, la SNEC [Société nationale des eaux du Cameroun]. Elle va couper l'eau. C'est la vie de l'humanité, c'est la vie du bétail, c'est la mort, c'est un drame." Later, he commented on the rise of vandalism, noting that "Si la SONEL coupe, il y aura l'obscurité, les vols, les meurtres ... vivre en peur. C'est vous qui allez vivre dans l'insécurité." A merchant responded that, "ils peuvent même entrer chez nous arracher ce qu'ils veulent. Alors vous avez vu au Zaïre. Alors je vous demande de payer [les impôts] si vous ne voulez pas de problèmes comme au Zaïre où il y a la famine qui a commencé à déranger, et puis les fonctionnaires qui ont commencé à faire du bruit." Maroua, Cameroon, 15 April 1993.

[20] See the studies by A. S. Zoa, "Les Ordures à Yaoundé: Jalons pour une garbéologie africaine," Mémoire de maîtrise de sociologie, Yaoundé, Université de Yaoundé, 1993; and T. Tang, "L'Evacuation des eaux usées à Yaoundé," Mémoire de maîtrise de géographie, Yaoundé, Université de Yaoundé, 1990.

have become the capital's landmarks, replacing street names and main crossroads. When they spill over in all directions and infect the air with their stench, the garbage is set on fire. Its smoke rises from entire parts of the city and can be seen from miles away. It is testimony to this work of Sisyphus; this devouring and omnivorous force cannot be ensnared and becomes practically autonomous. Vegetation overruns not only the capital city but also most of the secondary towns, which were once prosperous due to their integration in economic and transportation circuits. The following passage describes one of these towns:

> Today, what once was the river quay is now overrun with tufts of wild grass; the arrival of lumber by floating, a spectacle that always brought reveling schoolchildren, of which I was one, belongs to the past. A mysterious scourge chased away the white exploiters of the forest. The trading posts and general stores that swarmed with rustic and avid clients have disappeared, as have their light-skinned managers, always disdainful and never attentive. Mbalmayo is only a phantom of what it once was, a sort of dusty and flea-ridden Far West.[21]

The same is true for certain gigantic industrial projects dating from the era of abundance, notably the Cellucam paper pulp factory at Edea, which is located in the very heart of the equatorial forest on a plateau overhanging the cutoff of the Sanaga River. The part of the forest granted to the company contained more than twenty-five species that are highly valued on the world market (*bubinga, doussié, sipo, sapelli, mahogany, iroko,* and *azobé*). Aside from the actual industrial infrastructure, the site includes a residential complex. The executive housing estate contains about fifty whitewashed villas sur-

---

[21] "Aujourd'hui, ce qui fut le quai aux grumes est envahi par les buissons d'herbes folles; l'arrivage du bois par flottage, spectacle dont venaient se repaître les écoliers de la ville, dont j'étais, appartient au passé. Un fléau mystérieux a chassé les exploitants forestiers blancs. Les comptoirs et les bazars grouillant de chalands rustiques et avides ont disparu ainsi que leurs gérants à peau claire, toujours dédaigneux, jamais empressés. Mbalmayo n'est plus que le fantôme de ce qu'il fut, sorte de Far-West poussiéreux et pouilleux." Beti, *La France contre l'Afrique* 56–57, our translation.

rounded by fir trees, and the workers' housing development consists of about one hundred buildings. The encampment, which was reserved for expatriate and bachelor workers who helped build the factory, includes an impressive edifice over fifty meters tall. It towers majestically in the middle of a collection of other colossal structures covering over sixty hectares and cordoned off by a practically insurmountable hedge.

Over this site, now taken over by rampant grass, reigns the silence of a cemetery. It looks like a ghost town, completely deserted by its inhabitants. Luxurious vegetation has invaded up to the asphalt paths that once gave the encampment the look of a modern city. The buildings, with their dilapidated walls and rusted antitheft window coverings, have lost their openings and, for the most part, their electricity meters as well. All metal apparatus is heavily damaged; immense machines are now almost completely jammed and inoperable. The most gripping image of this "cannibalism" and spectacular destruction of wealth is the factory's parking lot. D. Nouwou describes the debacle:

> Imagine several hundred rotted vehicles (trucks, buses, personal cars, lumber haulers, tractors of all kinds) barely visible, buried in a tawny vegetation that has established its right to the city. When walking amongst them, one discovers that the vehicles were geometrically arranged, certainly being in perfect condition at the time. Today they are 100 percent deteriorated. Only the bodies held up by the wheel rims attest to the car models. They say there are hundreds of vehicles thus abandoned in the different zones of the forest where companies operated; scores of others being sold off or stolen.[22]

And the stock of over one thousand blocks of wood stored by the company before its closure was devoured, over a one-month period, by a gigantic brush fire, thus transforming the area into an immense Gehenna.

This state of decay and destitution can also be gleaned from the numerous construction sites that have been abandoned long before completion of their projects. The phenome-

---

[22] See the narrative of D. Nouwou, "Voyage au coeur d'un monstre économique mort," *La Nouvelle Expression* 56 (June–July 1992): 11.

non is so extensive and so significant that it is worth introducing a few distinctions. First, some of these are public construction sites that were initiated by the government. These are mostly administrative office buildings; their construction began when the state had more or less stable sources of revenue. Today these work sites, which are in the city center, look as though the construction workers left one day for lunch and never returned. Tools are strewn about, often fixed in positions as if they were still in use.

Other buildings seem, from the outside, like modern skyscrapers. When night falls they are even lit up. Sometimes a security service prevents thieves from making off with the precious objects found within. But these buildings are not at all operational. For instance, an edifice located on the Boulevard John Paul II was to be the headquarters of the Cameroonian Development Bank. Its cost was estimated at 5 billion francs CFA (or $20 million).[23] In 1991, while this luxury building was being raised, the bank was dissolved by presidential decree. The bank had financed unprofitable projects, and various dignitaries of the regime owed large sums to the bank.

Other similar buildings project massive cement columns into the sky. Ironwork, doors, shards of broken windows, even shredded curtains clutter these buildings; the rest of their contents, such as doors, tiles, locks, sanitary material, have been pillaged, sometimes right in front of passersby and public authorities. Some of these places, now used by squatters, have been transformed into hideouts for all sorts of marginalized people. The Interministerial Building at the Central Post Office crossroads is one example. Work on this building was interrupted in the middle of the 1980s, even though it was nearly finished. Its cost was estimated at more than 20 billion francs CFA ($80 million). It was being financed with public funds, and the work was being executed by a group of French and Cameroonian companies. Today, small-scale informal trade flourishes in front of this incomplete twenty-story undertaking. Street vendors have colonized this space and sell pedestrians an array of merchandise, from shoes, audiocassettes, books and diverse documents, pharmaceutical products and beauty aids to trinkets and cheap kitsch. And besides serving as a refuge for

---

[23] All figures are based on exchange rates prior to the devaluation of the franc CFA in 1994.

the marginalized, the interior of the building is now a public urinal and depository for excrement.[24]

Like the official buildings discussed above, homes and palaces of disinherited notables and historical figures of Cameroonian society are also in various states of dilapidation. A particularly prominent example is the old presidential palace on the slopes of Mont Febe. The palace had been built by Ahmadou Ahidjo, who was head of state from 1958 to 1982 and died in exile in 1989 after having been condemned to death, then pardoned by the successor he himself had selected.

Abandoned projects include not only factories, offices, and residences but also places of worship. Two examples are the Catholic cathedral of Mvolye and the mosque at Tsinga. The cathedral seems hardly begun; its collection of icons, pillars, and columns might almost be excavated from a Greco-Roman archaeological site. The mosque, which seems hardly finished, features a decapitated minaret. Both administrative and religious buildings, with their massive amounts of cement buried in the ground or rising into the sky, attest not only to a form of architecture entirely dedicated to grandiloquence and baroque majesty adored by postcolonial power in Cameroon but also to its corollary, an extravagant and unproductive economy of public and private expenditures. Central to this unproductive economy was a system of public contracting (*marché public*).

According to its generally accepted definition, a *marché public* is one that is open to public bidding. It issues from a contract concluded between a legally public or private entity and a public establishment or collectivity, or even a parastatal body. By contract, the former makes a commitment to the latter to perform, either for their benefit or under their surveillance, work defined by a common agreement, or to furnish goods and services. In principle, and at the level of regulation, an offer to tender was an obligatory procedure for all Cameroonian public contracts that exceeded costs totaling 50 million francs CFA ($200,000). For lesser amounts, a letter from the minister or head of the establishment sufficed, at least until recently. The open call to tender generally involved a public call for competitive bidding, unless it was addressed to a limited number of candidates chosen for apparent economic or

---

[24] Refer to the observations made by D. Atangana, "Des milliards enterrés," *Galaxie* 48 (June 1993): 6.

technical reasons. In this case, it was termed "limited" or "restrained."

A central structure, the *Direction Générale des Grands Travaux du Cameroun* (DGTC) was charged with initiating invitations to tender on behalf of the administration and local collectivities, as well as public and parapublic firms. It was also responsible for giving advice on how to rank the submitting parties during the period of examination. This was done upon completion of the work of a technical subcommission, composed of representatives of the DGTC and those of the ministry or organization involved. This subcommission established a first ranking on the basis of ostensibly technical criteria. The portfolios were then submitted to the National Commission of Markets for scrutiny before passing for signature to the representative of the presidency. After this procedure for making a public contract was concluded, the DGTC was responsible for monitoring the project, providing technical assistance, and signing accounts and bills presented by the firm for reimbursement.

This bureaucratic framework for negotiating and monitoring contracts gave rise to an entire social commerce with forms of political exchange and modes of appropriating public goods that were widely known. The architectural text of unfinished edifices stands as a reminder of this political subtext. This commerce involved a diverse set of Cameroonian and foreign actors, including businessmen, high-ranking officials, firms, French negotiators, and brokers. Together, and often in competition and conflict, they plotted a structure of interests and set in motion a regime of ownership and modalities for gaining private revenues. The specificity of this regime was that it relied neither on imposing obligatory labor on subjects nor on directly using the labor force itself. This network of predatory interests, brokers, and local agents rendered the state less a public good than a social relation of domination founded essentially on coercive exchange, plunder, and consumption. In other words, this manner of appropriating wealth created its social meaning through the very act of destroying and dissipating wealth.

This system allowed public contracts to be concluded with firms that had not presented any submission. Other contracts were offered without a call to tender; that is, without a call to competition and hence in violation of regulatory statutes that defined them as restrictive and prescribed that their signing be authorized by the president of the republic. Overinvoicing was also a common practice for overhead and assignment costs, especially when they involved expenses accruing to so-called expatriate personnel.[25] To these practices must be added those involving large expenditures for a fleet of cars, with the Land Cruiser, Renault 19, Peugeot 405 and 605 the preferred models. In short, this was the nature of an array of officially acknowledged practices that were not, however, sanctioned and were ultimately directed at circumventing regulations. In many ministries, one tactic involved dividing all contracts worth over 50 million francs ($20,000) into packages with costs below this amount, thus bringing them under the jurisdiction of the letter of order. Other methods of circumventing regulation were invented under the guise of "privatization." Fictitious firms and warehouses were created to recycle gains and avoid customs. Resulting income and properties were converted into ornamental and prestige goods and objects. These goods could be displayed. In any case, they were circulated on the market of symbols and used by those in power to dumbfound, stupefy, and politically subjugate their dependents, or simply to mark the glamour of their social position, especially through ceremonies and other forms of grandiose expenditure.[26]

To be sure, according to economic calculations of loss and profit, this capacity for waste and the spectacular destruction of wealth is, as Bataille would have it, of a purely excremental order.[27] Yet the experience examined here also indicates that such an interpretation is insufficient. In fact, the very meaning

---

[25] Until recently, the six French directors of the DGTC cost, unto themselves, a grand total of 22.5 million francs CFA ($90,000) per month. Cf. J. D. Sibafo, "Bâtiments et travaux publics: DGTC, l'édifice s'effondre inexorablement," *La Nouvelle Expression* 81 (July 1993): 8.

[26] Yamdeu, "Grande bamboula pour Tchouta Moussa," *Soleil d'Afrique* 24 (July 1993): 6–8. The author describes ceremonies organized to "salute in grand pomp" the nomination of Tchouta Moussa to the head of the Office National des Ports du Cameroun. To celebrate this nomination "with éclat," Tchouta Moussa was able to mobilize members of the government, thirty-six traditional chiefs, and businessmen. In a more general sense, see A. Mbembe, "Provisional Notes on the Postcolony," *Africa* 62, 1 (1992): 3–37.

[27] G. Bataille, *La Part maudite: Précédé de la notion de dépense* (Paris: Éditions de Minuit, 1967) 29.

of loss must be elucidated in order to respond to the question of the logics of efficacious action posed at the beginning of this discussion. And, as we have seen, the loss in question implies enormous material and physical investments. Likewise, an important part of the life of private and public institutions, as well as the various networks that gravitate around them, is organized according to these very acts of dissipation. Furthermore, the country's integration in the world economy is based on these logics, which combine consumption and national debt. That this immense work of material, physical, and symbolic investment leads to the depository for excrement described above confirms some of Bataille's intuitions. And yet another aspect of this situation is that, through this evaporation of wealth, people also construct relations of cause and effect, thus circumscribing fields of possible action and elaborating forms of behavior that accentuate the crisis.[28]

Public expenditure can also be interpreted as one of the registers of sovereignty. It provides the sites where the state endeavors to combine the monstrative exercise of physical violence and arbitrary symbolic acts. In this way, expenditure is part of an omnivorous political configuration, where public and private forces mingle; where spoils, salaries, exactions, fees, and monopolies are inseparable; and where the state apparatus and framework for extraction are one and the same. Hence, during the "forced recovery" (recouvrement forcé), or collection of taxes (automobile stickers, small merchant licenses, the head tax), the police, militia, and army set up barriers all along the national roads, through cities and villages, giving Cameroon the atmosphere of a country at war.[29] All these forces are charged with "closing establishments and firms, impounding vehicles and locking up thousands of young, unemployed youth who are incapable of attending to their basic needs let alone paying their taxes."[30]

Finally, the crisis seems to have seized people in the very interiors of their homes, becoming a part of their domesticity.

---

[28] But one could also argue that, since this opens contradictory fields of potential action, certain forms might counter this tendency.

[29] E. Ngangue, "Péage routier: Les Limites d'un nouveau racket," Le Messager 326 (September 1993): 5.

[30] A. C. Fomi, "Lettre ouverte au ministre des finances," Dikalo 82 (July 1993): 15.

Between 1984 and 1988, Cameroon witnessed a boom in the building industry. The years of relative affluence (1979–86) following the injection of a portion of oil revenues into the economy led to a frenzy in construction that was not limited to the state. And even though credit remained tight, numerous executives, managers, and officials who once rented their houses decided to invest in property. At the same time, large-scale urban renewal was initiated. This run on property was still underway when the crisis hit; but the crisis abruptly ended it. Every neighborhood in the city is now studded with half-built villas and abandoned houses, sometimes with belongings and furniture left inside or overrun with undergrowth that the rainy season sends to vertiginous heights. Families living in semiconstructed houses and villas have become so commonplace that one is regularly ushered into homes with "Welcome to our construction site!" "Excuse us, we live in a construction site." Obsolete and rundown furnishings and appliances have become a constitutive feature of home decor; often a telephone sits mutely on a pedestal, with service terminated due to unpaid bills.[31]

The sudden nature of this intrusion is well illustrated by popular expressions: "The crisis fell on our heads" (*La crise est tombée sur nos têtes*) and "I've got the crisis" (*J'ai la crise*).[32] This experience, which is at once intimate and dramatic, gives rise to narratives that no longer locate the crisis in an evolutionary history; that is to say, in a causal description of an event that develops over a relatively long period of time. The experience and the imaginary of time that results are of a condensed, compressed, and abrupt duration. Because of this contraction, the transformations taking place are not necessarily correlated to precise factors and historical referents, even if one is aware that these elements do in fact exist. For lack of these referents, the crisis is exiled to the domain of the inexplicable.

---

[31] H. L. Bateg, "Impayés du téléphone: qui va payer la note?" *Dikalo* 83 (July 1993): 7. Also, M. Waffo, "La SIC aux trousses des locataires indélicats," *Challenge Bi-Hebdo* 95 (July 1993): 8.

[32] The latter is intoned in the same way one says, "I have a cold."

Explanation by the Inexplicable

When asked to explain the events described above, and to render "intelligible" the lived experiences these situations incite, people generally respond that they no longer understand at all what is happening. Yet it would be wrong to regard this answer as a simple claim to ignorance. To the extent that this statement tends to become, for those involved, an answer that is valid in and of itself and is hence legitimate, it deserves further consideration. On the one hand, it is important to retrace the path that leads to such a response (how does one arrive there?). On the other hand, if people "understand" their lived experiences as incomprehensible, what forms of (in)action does such an understanding or even such a mental disposition lead to? And at the same time to what extent can this complex of dispositions and conduct itself be said to aggravate the crisis?

Without responding directly to these questions, we can gain insight by recalling the historical context and intellectual moment from which they arise. The historical context is that of a society knocked about and mistreated by a succession of instabilities, shortages, constraints, and blockages. Some of these phenomena are external in origin, others are from within, but all bring about several types of incoherence. As noted above, these discontinuities and contradictions (*incohésions*) are becoming more and more systematic, to the point that what results from mere chance or accident can no longer be distinguished from what results from the "normal" state of affairs. The examples outlined above also demonstrate that the conditions of the very material reproduction of society are being intensely modified. This movement appears to be taking place in a manner that is so unexpected and sudden, at least in people's consciousness, that it induces "surprise," "perplexity," and even a sort of "stupor." Because it is lived as an abrupt experience, this bundle of events provokes entry into other categories of reference, other systems of causality, or, in brief, other regimes of intelligibility. Cameroonian society's long-standing capacity to "imagine" itself in a certain manner, mentally to author and thence institute itself,[33] has been con-

---

[33] C. Castoriadis, *L'Institution imaginaire de la société* (Paris: Seuil, 1972).

tradicted and seems now thrown into question. As indicated above, at the time when annual growth rates were on the order of 6 to 7 percent, Cameroonians perceived themselves as a part of a rich nation, with infinite possibilities before them. This was, to be sure, part of a deliberate effort to imagine a national identity founded on economic attributes. Today's bankruptcy thwarts this mode of imagining, leaving in its wake certain forms of nostalgia. There is the incessant reminder: "Only a few years ago, things were not as they are now."[34] This attests to a sense of loss, both in the material sense of waste and dilapidation as well as in the sense of existential deprivation and disorientation.

From within this dislocation Cameroonians attempt to articulate new forms of rationality based on emergent understandings of efficacious action, which often issue from ambiguous and contradictory situations. For example, consumers of electricity provided by the national company, sometimes with the complicity of its own agents, have their meters jammed so that they can consume as much energy as desired for free. The same practice applies to water consumption. The rationing of water and the segmentation of its sale have also become widespread: the consumer of water, no longer able to pay for the service, is obliged to buy it from itinerant vendors or from private parties who subcontract it out. Furthermore, agents of the urban transport company have established parallel services for the sale of tickets. Similarly, train passengers, instead of buying tickets at the normal price, "make arrangements" (*s'arrangent*) with conductors at much lower prices. In a like manner, during a roadblock inspection, a common occurrence, police and militiamen pocket the fines for citations and "warnings."

Fraudulent identity cards; fake policemen dressed in official uniform; army troops complicit with gangs of thieves and bandits; forged enrollment for exams; illegal withdrawal of money orders; fake bank notes; the circulation and sale of false school reports, medical certificates, and damaged commodities: all of this is not only an expression of frenetic trafficking and "arranging." It also manifests the fact that, here, things no longer exist without their parallel. Every law enacted is sub-

---

[34] "Il y a seulement quelques années, les choses n'étaient pas comme maintenant."

merged by an ensemble of techniques of avoidance, circum-
vention, and envelopment that, in the end, neutralize and invert the legislation.[35] There is hardly a reality here without its
double. Hence acting efficaciously requires that one develop an
extraordinary capacity to be simultaneously inside and outside, for and against, and constantly introduce changes in the
reading and usage of things, playing, in this way, with the
structures and apparatuses, capturing them where possible,
eluding them where necessary, and, in any event, amputating
them and almost always emptying them of their formal and
designated functions in order better to reconcile them with desired goals and expected gains.

Without denying the scattered and inchoate character of
most of these acts, their ultimately unsystematic, chaotic, and
inconclusive nature, it should be noted that they are repeated
so often at all levels of society that they are well known to almost everyone. They are widespread and are, in this sense, no
longer simply isolated incidents or simple tinkerings with the
system in order to survive.[36] Instead, they have become "ways
of doing" that belong to the register of new forms of public
knowledge: the constitution of a prosaic that is not specifically
African but is rather particular to all times of crisis in a general sense. Certainly, for now, the legitimation of such practices is an object of dispute. They are vehemently condemned
by the public authorities (without leading to effective sanctions) as well as by the general public, even while they themselves continue to resort to such practices.

To a large extent, it is the daily negotiation with the absurd in order to subsist and survive that induces people to say
they "no longer understand." The paradoxical situations in
which they find themselves are thus qualified as "incredible,"
"unimaginable," and even "insane."[37] The density of the constraints that grip everyday life is no doubt such that one is

---

[35] Here, we are referring to combinatory effects and, eventually, the production of another "kind" of system, not simply a "parallel" one.

[36] In this sense, it is fallacious to consider them purely and simply in
terms of survival strategies or as acts of resistance as in the case of J. Scott,
Domination and the Arts of Resistance: Hidden Transcripts (New Haven: Yale
University Press, 1990).

[37] Conversations with J. M. Ela, V. Ombe Ndzana, T. Mouctar Bah,
Yaoundé, July 1993.

never sure to get by, as the following narrative of a train ride demonstrates:

> It was the station at Belabo. We wanted two seats on the night train to Ngaoundere. The station teemed with people. Some were standing, others lay on the ground or sat on the edge of the rails, sometimes in the shadows. Itinerant vendors, legal and clandestine transporters, an entire mass of people came and went in indolence and numbness, punctuated by abrupt waves. A long line of travelers waited wearily; their wait would last an eternity. Finally, at 11:00, the ticket window opened. Yet the line remained as immobile as before; while purchasers advanced, other travelers tacked on to the end so that the length of the line seemed always the same. The sale of a ticket took about fifteen minutes, including the designating of destination, the choice of seating, the unrolling of the tickets, unfurling of bank notes and coins, the search for change, calculating the difference, the manual inscription of the price and other information, and the inevitable rubber stamp officializing the document. From entry into the line to arrival at the ticket window, we spent over an hour. Upon leaving the window, it was evident that the train's estimated arrival time had long passed.
>
> Hoping to have a minimum of comfort but not wanting to pay the price of a berth, we had twice requested access to the first-class car. And the cashier twice responded favorably. We consequently paid the required fee. The train arrived at about 1:40 in the morning. We immediately sought out the first-class car. It was nowhere. The second-class car and bunk car were all that were to be found. The train had hardly come to a halt when the crowd, once nonchalant and dozing, suddenly arose. Unleashed, the mass took the second-class car literally by assault. People pushed, swore, hurled abuses, and tossed bags, packages, children, and animals through doorways and windows, in tumultuous confusion.
>
> We located the conductor and, with the requisite deference, noted that the agent of the rail company had sold us tickets for services that were nowhere to be found. We thus had no seats for a night journey of over 400 kilometers. A first-class car for night trains? No such thing existed, he informed us, adding that we could have access to the berth for a sum. We could have discussed it all night, but the fact was

that the agent had consciously sold us fake tickets for services that did not exist. We journeyed standing up, caught
between travelers who, overcome with fatigue, were strewn
along the aisles, knocking the knees of those who constantly
flowed from one end of the car to the other, in a quest for
what, we never knew.[38]

In this specific instance, a formal agreement such as paying a precise sum for a precise service on the basis of information given by the railway company employee resulted in a loss
of money and frustration. But this is not because formal rules
and conventional procedures are not publicized or not respected. One can respect them very well. But this in no way
automatically implies that the prescribed results will be at-
tained. To the contrary, those who follow the rules scrupulously sometimes find themselves in a snarl, facing figures of
the real that scarcely correspond to what is publicly alleged or
prescribed at the point of departure. Whether this involves a
bureaucratic or a purely private transaction, every single step
must be negotiated. Thus when people refer to "insanity," they
are not referring to a lapse of reason but rather to the unbear-
able discrepancy between publicly announced reality and that
other constantly changing, unstable and uncertain, quasiellip-
tical realm that is always pursued and always elusive, often
emerging only after a long and exhausting bargain. It follows
that "the real" of the crisis is "ephemeral" since it is marked by
and punctuated with false starts, hyperbolic and highly eccen-
tric rules, all of which require a particular theory not only of
uncertainty but also of causality and error. Every step or effort
made to follow the written rule may lead not to the targeted
goal but to a situation of apparent contradiction and closure
from which it is difficult to exit either by invoking the very
same rules and authorities responsible for applying them or by
reclaiming theoretical rights supposed to protect those who
respect official law.

Furthermore, even where contracts and engagements are
made, they are almost never definitive; they are always liable
to renegotiation. Thus every contract or negotiation constitutes
in itself a vast field of ambiguity, which, as such, leaves enormous potential for dispute, argument, and discord. This pro-

---

[38] The experience of the authors, Cameroon, July 1993.

foundly provisional and revisable character of things is at the heart of the proliferation of criteria for efficacious action. The ensuing conduct ranges from pure and simple infractions to violations, evasion, avoidance, deviation, figuration, use of circumlocutions, improvisation, tossing the dice, and turning things inside out. Sometimes one and the same operation requires several levels and forms of negotiation with several kinds of authority. This is, in part, due to the absence of institutional and material infrastructure: the telephone is not working; the electricity is temporarily cut; the attendant is out or absent; money or a letter has not arrived; the schedule has changed or is broken; the chain of command is defective; the person responsible did not complete the required task; another document or official stamp is necessary.

Such conditions also relate to the extraordinary fragmentation and redundancy of administrative services: for a single service, A can only give you certain information; B can only give you the application; C can give you advice about general formalities. D can sell you the stamp, but his services are located elsewhere and you must go in person. Only E can verify that the application has been properly filled out before transmitting it to F, who types it and sends it to G, who submits it to H, who is the supervisor. H then authorizes G to apply the rubber stamp. After the document is stamped, it is brought back to the supervisor, H, for signature. One must then return, often several times, before getting it back. Or, when it is not necessary to "come back tomorrow," one must stay and wait.

These examples clearly demonstrate that extreme bureaucratization and specialization (Weber) do not necessarily lead to increased productivity.[39] In the context being considered here, this gives rise to a particular mode of managing "public goods," where users become the agents who undertake tasks and services usually rendered by public power. When trying to obtain an official document in a police station or ministry, one must purchase the application, furnish paper and writing utensils, find stamps, photocopy documents, and gather exact change before presenting oneself to the cashier.

---

[39] In an entirely different context, this point is also suggested by D. Rejali, *Torture and Modernity: Self, Society, and State in Modern Iran* (Boulder: Westview Press, 1994) 42–44, 61.

The same process also applies to other public institutions. In hospitals, it is not unusual that to "be served" the patient must obtain cotton and alcohol, furnish instruments for surgery, and pay the doctors and nurses beyond their salaries. And schoolchildren must often bring chalk, tables, and chairs to class; their parents also contribute in cash or kind to the salary of the teacher. This is what we have labeled "do-it-yourself bureaucracy." What we wish to underscore, however, is not the extraordinary but the routine. In constructing the frameworks of everyday life, these now-common practices destabilize the referents once considered intrinsic to the constitution of order and hierarchy. One consequence of this is the corrosion of long-standing conceptions of causality and responsibility, or the dissolution of authority itself.

The Crisis of the Subject and Historical Violence

The dissolution of authority, and the unhinging of its associated hierarchy and order, first takes the form of a dispersal of the attributes of public power. This, however, does not mean that there are no longer mechanisms and agents of power. Soldiers, policemen, and the militia continue to lead the "fiscal war": they survey documents, extort goods, and confiscate commodities. This kind of violence does not necessarily imply an opposition between a dissipating form of authority and an emergent one. As the following example shows, it proceeds rather from the monopolization and reinterpretation of roles in directions that were, in the past, either unthinkable, reprehensible, and reprimanded or impracticable:

> After the inspection of documents, the police officer asks the taxi driver to put his foot on the brakes. If the brake lights fail, the poor driver falls through the trap. If not, the inspection continues. Everything is subject to it: tires, brakes, shock absorbers, headlights, blinkers, bumpers. Tired of insisting, the cops have recourse to their last card, the missing fire extinguisher and first-aid kit, before asking all of the passengers for their papers. The second de-vice is simply to waste time. The policeman stops a taxi, asks for "the documents," and moves away from the vehicle. He talks with his

colleagues with-out even deigning to glance at the papers.
Hurried and tired of waiting, the passengers get out of the
taxi one by one and hitch rides with other cars.... As soon as
the taxi driver gives "500," the policeman returns his documents, and the pigeon is free to fly away and be plucked
elsewhere.[40]

The decline of public authority and its dereliction of duty
has led to a situation of confusion and chaos that people im-
pute not only to the crisis but also to "democracy": "Now everyone does what they please." The state of the garbage in
Yaoundé offers a good example. Common responses to the
problem are: "It's uncontrollable"; "it's ungovernable"; "we don't
know whom to address"; "we no longer know who is responsible for what"; "we don't know what to do any longer"; "it's beyond us." Generally speaking, the expression, "we no longer
know what to do," implies that one has tried in vain to transform existing conditions until the capacity to produce concrete
effects has been exhausted. "We no longer know whom to address" implies that one can no longer identify pertinent
authorities or, in any case, be heard by them. This also indicates that some sites of power now escape all control; that is,
they are now endowed with immunities.

Such conditions structure forms of violence in daily transactions and relationships, which include the transgression and
forced alienation of rights as well as purely physical abuse.
Practices that are perhaps most likely to entail violent confis-
cation of goods and property are those involving the systematic
sale of public services. Here, for example, is a description of an
everyday scenario:

In certain magistrates' courts, retrieval of official documents,
such as form number 3 from the criminal record, requires
one to respond to superfluous demands for stamps [which,
once] applied, will be immediately recovered and resold by
administrators. [Amongst other requests, there are] so-called
"research expenses." Their costs multiply with the number of
copies requested by the user. And this, without counting the
eventual inflation of the final bill, is much influenced by the

---

[40] E. Ngangue, "Taximen contre policiers: Combat de rue ou guerre de
tranchées?" *Le Messager* 315 (July 1993): 11.

appearance of the client. Attempts at fraud are now assured at all levels.... At the treasuries, the little swindlers continue systematically to apply a "commission" of 5 to 25 percent on bills and salaries to be paid. Furthermore, it is now difficult to mobilize the police for a problem under their jurisdiction if one has not "greased their palms." In all sectors of public service, there is always a slightly illegal way to "get by." Fewer and fewer bosses who have not maintained their small network of "fakes" have conserved their aura.... Women try to sell their colleagues as many tidbits and trinkets as possible in order to make ends meet.[41]

To apprehend clearly how these developments are implicated in the general enactment of power, and moreover, in the structuration of violence thus contributing to the specific content of that power, analyses proceeding from normative concepts such as corruption are to be avoided. Indeed, state services and functions that are thus sold are, above all, a series of formalities. The user is constrained to carry out or fulfill these formalities each time he or she must retrieve a salary, pass an official examination, go before the courts, obtain a visa, or renew a license. In perfect colonial tradition, the height of the formality is the signature, itself authenticated by the rubber stamp.[42] And here public power surely has the monopoly, at least in principle. In a sense, the formalities, the signature being the one that perhaps most efficiently reduces power to the sign, are what users must buy at public prices applicable to all. The purchase allows users access to formal "rights" or, even better, to "authorizations" corresponding to domains covered by the object bought.

For now, we will simply consider what is exercised at the precise moment when agents of so-called public service sell formalities to users on behalf of the state. In this instance, various phenomena are brought together, each contributing to the specific character of the exercise of violence in a time of

[41] J. M. Soboth, "Fonctionnaires: La Fin des patates," *La Nouvelle Expression* 87 (August 1993): 6.

[42] J. Roitman, "Notes," Maroua, 1992–93. In a more general sense, cf. B. Fraenkel, *La Signature: Genèse d'un signe* (Paris: Gallimard, 1992), even though she considers the signature only in the sacred terms of a new conception of identity and recognition of the singularity of the human being.

crisis. First, there is the generalization of favors and privileges: one wants access to officially prescribed rights and authorizations but by circumventing required formalities. This can be accomplished in many ways. Private arrangements can be made with the agent responsible for the public service. Or, in a context where agents of public power are paid episodically and public power itself no longer has the necessary infrastructure to exercise its command, the user is often forced to purchase the materials necessary for an official institution to function. Thus in a private capacity, one directly assures the financing of a public service. Also, in buying the formality, one directly compensates the public servant who is supposedly remunerated by the state. Otherwise, one pays stamps and other formal taxes and sometimes even assumes the very task of the bureaucrat. What we termed *do-it-yourself bureaucracy* is a site where, on the one hand, functions assigned to public power are exercised by private users (a formal substitution) in an official capacity; and, on the other hand, the user is *de facto* no longer served but pays to "self-serve." The formalities that are at the origin of these transactions continue, however, to be the property, so to speak, of public power and are not, strictly speaking, the object of an individual appropriation or a definitive alienation. What is important for our argument is that, at the heart of such a structure of action, the existence of these formalities is neither disputed nor does it determine the nature of day-to-day violence in the public sphere. Governing the specific content of the violence of the crisis is the interpretation of formalities and the determination of where and when they must be fulfilled, for example what papers one must have when one drives a car. This interpretation is sufficiently underdetermined so that substantial margins are open for the intensification of impositions or levies, as well as their generalization. The violence of the crisis emerges as much from the dissolution and dispersion of authority as from within official sites themselves.

But this excess, this proliferation of legitimate interpretations and the attendant violence itself rests on specific material conditions and a singular political economy. To be sure, in the public mind, the state is no one's property, not even the autocrat's. It is an anonymous and vacant domain. By the discretionary path of "nomination" and "the decree," the autocrat can nonetheless cede a portion of this anonymous domain to obliged subjects. Nomination to a position of responsibility or command, that is, to control over a part of the apparatus of authorizations and formalities, is lived as an allocation in kind from which one can, by being astute, organize levies and parallel fiscal mechanisms. The present circumstances, where the autocrat endowed with the power of nomination finds himself no longer able to settle accounts, favor the emergence of a particular type of domination that might be described as "discharge" (*décharge*). Through discharge, operations once solely executed by the state are allotted to henchmen who generalize, in this manner, the extortion of dues and fees. Here, extortion seems to be a substitute for forced labor. It is based on the idea of the enactment of fiscal relationships in kind. But discharge in no way implies the permanent appropriation of state property, anonymous as it is. At most, it only involves a concession; at best, a *beneficium*. It does not, however, guarantee immunity to those who profit in a precarious or provisional manner. These practices should then be interpreted more in terms of dispensation than privatization.[43]

But one of the most flagrant signs of the decline of public power is surely what appears to be "the end of the salary" and its replacement by occasional payments, the amounts of which are steadily declining. This state of affairs, never before known in the history of the country, extends beyond agents of public service. It includes the entire salaried population and is linked to the problems of disaccumulation and illiquidity that now sap the country. The shortage of money affects the urban centers, as well as the rural areas that have lived by the monetary rhythms of specific seasonal cycles of cocoa, coffee, cotton. Two points illuminate the magnitude of the dislocations that followed and the ways in which they have structured the subjectivities of the crisis. The first is that a major part of Cameroonian economic and political life was, until recently, organized around the "end of the month." The regularity of salary payments allowed for the regulation of the lives of not only those who earned them but also those who depended on them for their survival, according to the principles of redistribution, allocations, transfers, and reciprocity studied by Mahieu in the

---

[43] N. van de Walle, in Callaghy, *Hemmed In.*

case of the Ivory Coast.[44] The cycles of debts, contracts, and obligations were stimulated in this way, as was most formal and informal economic activity.

At the present time, the decrease in salary levels and irregularity of payments have introduced ruptures and discontinuities into these cycles, obliging people to negotiate forms of uncertainty and instability unknown heretofore. One of these uncertainties is the date of salary payments. A large part of social life, particularly in cities, has been reorganized around this now-unpredictable moment. Many live on the look-out, plunged in anxious anticipation. They look for signs: a mob in front of the Treasury building or the bank, rumors, and news of dates. People insist that they can no longer plan their lives or even make commitments. And this concerns events and phenomena as ordinary and vital as children starting the new school year, all sorts of ceremonies, health prevention and care, and even death and burial. All contracts become, of course, a risk. New forms of migration have appeared: every month numerous government employees head for the capital from distant provinces in search of their salaries. From time to time, soldiers and policemen, and even regular citizens, take bank managers and treasurers hostage, demanding to be paid on the spot. Because salaries allowed people to procure the necessities and even conveniences of life and assured subsistence for recipients and their dependents, allowing them to clothe themselves as well as prevent illness and hunger, this uncertainty leaves them exposed to the pressures of need and to the specific form of violence constituted by shortages and scarcity.

Because of the contradictory nature of subject positions and conduct (being inside and outside, for and against) described above, the response to this situation has not been uniform. Organized and silent protest alternate with accommodation and acceptance of a *fait accompli*. To understand the violence inherent in this debilitated situation, it is important to remember that, in postcolonial Cameroon, besides being one of the privileged sites for the structuration of inequality and social stratification (because all remunerations are not equal), the relationship among salary, work, and wealth has led to a

---

[44] R. Mahieu, "Principes de l'économie africaine" *Tiers-Monde* 30, 120 (1989): 725–53.

more or less legitimate form of domination, a particular form of civility that itself merits discussion.

For the general public, the equivalence between wealth and work—understood as "toil and time, the working-day that at once patterns and uses up man's life"[45]—was unclear since it is obvious that people become rich without submitting to fatigue and hunger and without being exposed to death. Thus bureaucratic "work" was neither perceived nor lived as a specifically or necessarily productive activity. It was therefore not conceptualized as a commodity or ware that one sold to the state, which purchased it for the price of a salary. Consequently, the quantity and value of work, as such, was not what was remunerated by these payments.

In the precrisis system, the salary was, like the public expenditures examined above, a positivity not reducible to remuneration for productivity or the formation of wealth. It was a resource of the state insofar as it served to purchase obedience and to settle the population in disciplinary mechanisms. The salary, then, legitimated subjection by establishing a particular type of civility: authoritarian civility.[46] In this sense, it constituted a purely ascriptive and juridical allocation, as well as an indispensable cog in the dynamics of the relationship between state and society and the constitution of a particular type of citizenship. This type of citizenship was not, above all, founded on the principle of political equality and representations thereof. It was based on "claims," with the salary as the most significant, from which the state created social debts. The construction of the political relationship was thus enacted in redistribution and not on the basis of representations of equivalence among human beings endowed with their own natural and civil rights and thus able to weigh in on political decisions. By transforming the salary into a claim and a formality, the state granted subsistence to its subjects. But these means did not sanction a conversion of energy into wealth; they resulted in a specific figure of obedience and domination.

---

[45] M. Foucault, *The Order of Things: An Archaeology of the Human Sciences* (New York: Vintage Books, 1973) 225.

[46] A. Mbembe, "Prosaics of Servitude and Authoritarian Civilities," *Public Culture* 5, 1 (1992): 123–48.

This is, moreover, why, in public discourse, these claims are sometimes represented as favors or, at least, privileges.[47]

This is perhaps why the "end of the salary," and its replacement with occasional payments, has not provoked the kind of outright, contentious mobilization one might expect. Civil workers continue to go to their offices even though they are not paid. Certainly, their reasons for doing so are complex. Many still hope that their salaries will arrive, betting that they are simply "late." Fear of losing the little that one has is, no doubt, a persuasive factor since large-scale layoffs have taken place and continue to be announced. From a strictly sociological point of view, it is important to note that the workplace is also a social site, not unlike a cafe or salon. One goes there to make phone calls, visit people, sell things, converse. It is also a place for *rendez-vous*. It marks off, in this sense, the frontier between "life inside," with its domestic and familial pressures, and "life outside."

What has developed is a form of protest by inertia. Few people come to their offices on time. Many are almost never there, preoccupied with the salary chase or out "getting by" to make up for what is lacking at the end of the month. The disorganization of schedules is such that being present at work does not necessarily mean that one actually works nor that one is actually there.[48] Here the absence of a violent popular reaction arises from two factors. For one, there is a profound memory of fear and real trauma associated with the defeat of historical movements of insubordination.[49] Also, since the failure of the civil disobedience movements of 1992 (*Opération Villes Mortes*), all protest is now thought to be ineffective. In this context but on another level, the idea of ineffectiveness results from a certain conceptualization of relations of cause

---

[47] This part of the discussion owes much to a series of conversations with J. M. Ela, Yaoundé, July–August 1993.

[48] Present practice involves signing a roll call at various times during the day to establish theoretical presence while not actually being physically in the office or workplace during the entire day.

[49] Cf. R. Joseph, *Radical Nationalism in Cameroon: Social Origins of the UPC Rebellion* (Oxford: Oxford University Press, 1977); J.-F. Bayart, *L'Etat au Cameroun* (Paris: Presses de la Fondation nationale des sciences politiques, 1977); A. Mbembe, *La Naissance du maquis dans le Sud-Cameroun: Histoires d'indisciplines* (Paris : Karthala, forthcoming).

and effect that is related to the experience of dissipation, or material loss and existential disorientation, discussed above.

It is important to underscore that irregular payment of salaries is not the only visible dimension of this violence. The other aspect, which affects innumerable high school, university, and technical graduates, is the large-scale layoffs implemented in response to recommendations made by international financial institutions such as the World Bank and the International Monetary Fund. This phenomenon is so massive that it has inspired an immense sense of anguish among an entire generation of young, educated persons. Those who still have a job live under the permanent threat of losing it. In response, a vast array of forms of protection have emerged, drawing from popular modes of Christianity and Islam—exorcism, purification and anointing, having offices blessed, wearing sacred objects and medications—as well as from the autochthonous world of the night and the invisible.[50] This atmosphere of insecurity and tension is not limited to public places; the rise in domestic conflict, the rapidity with which people resort to anger, verbal abuse, and physical violence is evident in intimate and daily interactions. Aggravating the situation are new forms of urban violence, inspired either by the quest for subsistence or attempts to eradicate the very sources of perceived danger. Such violence includes the lynching of thieves and presumed bandits by the citizenry, the repression of protesters and assassinations of taxi drivers by the police, armed attacks, and highway robbery.[51] In sum, a situation marked by extraordinary tension (*nervosité*) prevails: the proliferation of all kinds of rumors; the escalation of credulity; the unleashing of an imaginary of marvel (*le merveilleux*) and evil (*malheur*), bad luck and pain. This deployment of violence has plunged a large part of the population into a prolonged state of anxiety and perplexity.

All of this goes, however, hand in hand with an extraordinary capacity to turn violence, the absurd, and even terror it-

---

[50] Cf. P. Geschiere, *La Viande de l'autre: Etat et sorcellerie au Cameroun* (Paris: Karthala, forthcoming); E. de Rosny, *L'Afrique des guérisons* (Paris: Karthala, 1992).

[51] Read "Un Macchabée calciné à Yaoundé," *Challenge Bi-Hebdo* 106 (August 1993): 9; or C. Yaho, "Gangstérisme urbain: la justice populaire comme réponse à l'insécurité," *La Nouvelle Expression* 81 (July 1993): 4.

self into a source of derision.[52] In the context described above, laughter is inseparable from the fear inspired by the immediate present, populated, as we have shown, by "evil spirits," that is, those that are out of control, such as traffic flow, garbage, underbrush, construction sites, authorities, and people on the margins. The proliferation of criteria for judgment induces a state of uncertainty and contradictory or easily reversible forms of behavior, which, in turn, lead to increased levels and new forms of violence. Fear, and the laughter it provokes, are often an effect of the ambiguity of lived experience: one is subject to this violence and yet, often in spite of oneself, one participates in its very production.

To the extent that in a time of crisis relations of domination conceal themselves behind figures of monstrosity, the absurd (*l'absurde*), and suffering, *to laugh* means not only to hypostasize domination but also to mark the disjunction between objectified violence and the fear that one endeavors to admit and avert. But as a magical imaginary and particular figure of superstition, laughter, derision, and mockery themselves harbor enormous possibilities for substitution, imitation, and falsification. They aim to travesty, avenge, scare the evil spirits and appease them or to exercise reprisals on "the signs of the thing"[53] (*exercer des représailles sur les signes de la chose*) that cannot be overcome otherwise. As rites of expiation, laughter and derision give way to an imaginary well-being; they allow for distance between the subject who laughs and the object of mockery. The division thus realized is precisely what permits the laughing subject to regain possession of self and to wear the mask, that is, to become a stranger to this "thing" (*la chose*) that exercises domination—and then to deride torture, murder, and all other forms of wretchedness.

---

52 Cf. the popular caricatures found in the weekly *Le Messager-Popoli: La Version-image de l'actualité.* Also F. Oyono, *Une Vie de boy* (Paris: Julliard, 1957) and *Le Vieux nègre et la médaille* (Paris: Julliard, 1956).

53 M. Heidegger, *Qu'est-ce qu'une chose?* (Paris: Gallimard, 1971).

CONTRASTING NARRATIVES OF PALESTINIAN IDENTITY

Rashid I. Khalidi

I

Any serious consideration of the identity of the Palestinian people raises a number of questions. What are the limits of Palestine? Where does it end and where does Israel begin, and are those limits spatial or temporal or both? More specifically, what delimits the modern history of the Palestinian people from that of the Israelis, who over the past half century have come to dominate the country both peoples claim? Finally, what is it that demarcates Palestinian history from the larger canvas of Middle Eastern and Arab history and from the history of the neighboring Arab states—Lebanon, Syria, Jordan, and Egypt? In other words, what in Palestinian identity is specific and unique, and what must be understood in the context of broader historical narratives, whether those of Zionism and the state of Israel or those of Arabism and the neighboring Arab nation-states or those of Islam and the Muslims?

Notwithstanding its undoubted uniqueness and specificity, Palestinian identity can only, I contend, be fully understood in the context of a sequence of other histories, a sequence of other narratives. Stuart Hall and others have argued that this is true generally, that identity "is partly the relationship between you and the Other."[1] Moreover, it can be shown that this interrelatedness of narratives is characteristic of many peoples in the Middle East and elsewhere, particularly those in the numerous nation-states established since World War I. For all of them, transnational identities (whether religious or nationalist), local patriotism, and affiliations of family and clan

---

[1] In Stuart Hall, "Ethnicity: Identity and Difference," *Radical America* 23, 4 (1989): 16. As Edward Said puts it in the new afterword to *Orientalism* (New York: Vintage, 1994) 331–32: "the development and maintenance of every culture require the existence of another, different and competing *alter ego*. The construction of identity ... involves the construction of opposites and 'others' whose actuality is always subject to the continuous interpretation and reinterpretation of their differences from 'us'."

have competed for loyalty. But one of the central themes of this essay is that the pull of competing loyalties has been considerably stronger for the Palestinians than for others and that the existence of these multiple foci of identity is one of the characteristic features of their history.

Why is this the case? Part of the answer is relatively simple: unlike most of these other peoples, the Palestinians have never achieved any form of national independence in their own homeland. In spite of some success in asserting their national identity inside and outside Palestine, they have consistently failed over the years to create for themselves a space where they are in some measure sovereign.[2] This has denied the Palestinians control over the state mechanisms—education, museums, archaeology, postage stamps and coins, and the media, especially radio and television—which, as myriad recent examples show, is essential for disseminating and imposing uniform "national" criteria of identity. Explaining this failure to achieve statehood and sovereignty, in terms of both the external and internal factors responsible, is a central problem of modern Palestinian historiography.

The Palestinians resemble a few other peoples in the modern era who have reached a high level of national consciousness and have developed a clearly defined sense of national identity but have long failed to achieve national independence. In the Middle East, these include the Kurds and (until their recent achievement of independence) the Armenians. All three peoples had reason to expect the self-determination promised by Woodrow Wilson's Fourteen Points in the wake of the breakup of the multinational Ottoman state during World War I, and all were disappointed. In spite of the sufferings of Kurds and Armenians, however, they are now in some respects freer than the Palestinians and less subject to domination by others. The

---

[2] The Palestinian "state within a state" in Lebanon from the late 1960s until 1982 was a partial exception and ultimately not a particularly happy one for any of those concerned, for it was not in Palestine and existed at the expense of the Lebanese. For more on this episode, see R. Khalidi, *Under Siege: PLO Decision-making during the 1982 War* (New York: Columbia University Press, 1986) chap. 2, and "The Palestinians in Lebanon: The Repercussions of the Israeli Invasion," *Middle East Journal* 38, 2 (Spring 1984): 255–66; and Rex Brynen, *Sanctuary and Survival: The PLO in Lebanon* (Boulder: Westview, 1990).

Armenians finally have an independent republic, albeit one engaged in bitter border conflicts with neighboring Azerbaijan and located in only part of their ancestral homeland. The Kurds, although denied statehood, currently enjoy an ambiguous international protection in northern Iraq, while a decade-long conflict with the authorities in Turkish Kurdistan continues. In spite of these differences, all three Middle Eastern peoples are in some ways comparable, having been denied self-determination by the great powers in the settlements they imposed on the Middle East after World War I[3] and living in disputed homelands that overlap with those of other peoples and have ambiguous and indeterminate boundaries.

An exploration of Palestinian identity thus has the potential to clarify the specific history not only of Palestine and its people in the modern era nor indeed of all those with whom the Palestinians have been so intimately involved. It touches as well on broader questions of national identity and the overlapping frontiers of national narratives, national myths, and national histories that are relevant far beyond the Middle East. It thus uses the history of a people that in some measure has still not successfully defined itself in the eyes of others to illuminate the processes at work in the self-definition of more "successful" peoples, including the neighbors of the Palestinians themselves.

What follows is not a reinterpretation of the history of Palestine or the Palestinian people, grounded in new research in primary sources (although it is partly based on such research). It is not even an attempt to define fully these heavily contested

---

[3] The Kurds and Armenians were candidates for self-determination during the negotiations over the postwar settlements, notably in the unratified 1920 treaty of Sèvres, but were ultimately abandoned to their fate by the European powers. Alone among the inhabitants of the Arab lands that fell under the League of Nations mandate system, the Palestinians were never considered for self-determination by the powers. Unlike the mandates for Syria and Iraq, which were to become "independent states," the mandate for Palestine omitted mention of independence or self-determination for the Palestinians, referring rather to the establishment of a "national home for the Jewish people" in Palestine. As in the Balfour Declaration (which was incorporated into the mandate), the Palestinians were only referred to as "existing non-Jewish communities in Palestine," whose civil and religious (but not political or national) rights were to be protected by the mandatory power.

terms. It is, rather, an exploration of the interplay between the different narratives that make up Palestinian history, meant to illuminate aspects of the identity of a people about which much has been written and said but little is understood. Why such a great deal of attention has produced such a small amount of useful scholarship is worth considering, for the degree of heat that is often generated by the very mention of the terms *Palestine* or *Palestinian* is notable in itself. It is even more striking in contrast to the small amount of light cast on the subject by these copious writings.

The best explanation for this phenomenon of intense polemical heat combined with scant intellectual light is that in Palestine are conjoined many powerful and contradictory views of self and of history. These may be religious—whether Jewish, Christian, or Muslim—or secular—as, for example, the focus of Masonic ritual on the Temple in Jerusalem; or they may be national or supranational, whether Arab or Jewish. Whatever their nature, however, these narratives of self and history that focus on Palestine have an influence far beyond its boundaries, reaching millions who know of this land only through the texts produced by these various currents of thought and belief, or perhaps in consequence of brief pilgrimages. All of them nevertheless feel that they know the country intimately, whatever name they give it and however they visualize its boundaries.

Moreover, those who hold these views often do so with an intense passion combined with a dogmatic certainty about their beliefs but against a background of nearly complete ignorance of Palestine and its history. This unique combination of deeply held beliefs related to Palestine and little real knowledge of it helps to explain the level of conflict the country has witnessed in the past and witnesses today. To take a distant example, an otherwise almost incomprehensible series of events like the Crusades—a series of ultimately futile attempts over more than two centuries by northern Europeans to conquer and colonize part of West Asia—can only be understood in terms of such a combination of passion with ignorance. Thus the fervor of the Crusaders' yearning for Palestine, which was apparent in the willingness of so many to set off on such a daunting endeavor, was matched only by these northern European knights' obliviousness to the complex political, cultural, and religious realities of Palestine and adjacent parts of the Islamic world in the eleventh, twelfth, and thirteenth centuries.

Their ignorance, however, was no bar to their lengthy and intense involvement in the affairs of the region.

To this day, the Crusades have a powerful resonance both in Palestine and far beyond its confines. For Palestinians and Israelis in particular, the Crusades hold special meaning, for one people as representing the ultimate triumph of resistance to alien invasion and colonization and for the other as an episode to be contrasted unfavorably with the more successful Zionist enterprise. Each side thus sees in the Crusades only what it wants to see. This continuing resonance is a testament to the power of self-contained and self-reflective narratives like that of the Crusades. Such accounts are grounded in the history of the country—for it was of course the Christian connection to Jerusalem and the holy land that originally provoked the Crusades—but they have an autonomous dynamic, growing out of forces and passions whose original locus is elsewhere, and a *raison d'être* all their own, defined primarily in terms of medieval European history. Thus the story of the Crusades is often told in isolation from its context, neglecting the social implications of these massive military campaigns inside Europe as well as their powerful and often disastrous impact on the Jewish communities of Europe, the Byzantine Empire, and the Islamic societies affected.[4]

II

It is certainly not a coincidence that virtually all these narratives about Palestine—religious and secular; Jewish, Christian, and Muslim; Palestinian and Israeli—revolve around the

---

[4] Most scholarly literature on the Crusades, like the magisterial work of Sir Steven Runciman, *A History of the Crusades*, 3 vols. (Cambridge: Cambridge University Press, 1951–54), depends on Western sources rather than the voluminous Islamic and Eastern Christian sources. For the Arabic sources see Francesco Gabrieli, *Arab Historians of the Crusades* (London: Routledge, 1969); Amin Maalouf, *The Crusades through Arab Eyes* (New York: Schocken, 1985); and Philip Hitti, *An Arab-Syrian Gentleman and Warrior in the Period of the Crusades* (Princeton: Princeton University Press, 1987). Most of this literature treats the Crusades as an extension of Western European history, albeit taking place in an exotic locale.

city of Jerusalem, which has long been the geographical, spiritual, political, and administrative center of Palestine. Indeed, it is in and over Jerusalem, which has such great significance to so many people in so many different ways, that the contrasting narratives regarding Palestine come most bitterly into conflict. It is in Jerusalem as well that one sees the most extreme instances of the various local parties' attempts to assert physical control over the country and to obtain validation of their conflicting claims.

In Palestine, as elsewhere, such validation is achieved notably by the act of naming. This process is already strikingly evident in the disputed naming of Israel/Palestine: most Israelis and Palestinians today have in mind essentially the same country—from the Mediterranean to the Jordan River and from the deserts in the south to the southern foothills of the Lebanese mountains and Mount Hermon in the north—although they have different names for it. It is most fittingly symbolized, however, by the unremitting struggle over the naming of Jerusalem. The city is called Yerushalaim in Hebrew (a word derived from the Aramaic, meaning, ironically, "city of peace"). The English derivative of this Hebrew name is Jerusalem, while translated into Arabic it is rendered Urshalim. In Arabic, however, since early in the Islamic era Jerusalem has generally been called Bayt al-Maqdis, the House of Sanctity (a term that may itself be drawn from the original Hebrew term for the Temple), or al-Quds al-Sharif, the Noble Holy Place.[5]

But while Jerusalem might be expected to have different names in different languages, what is at issue here is an attempt to impose on one language a name based on usage in another language. Thus in its Arabic-language broadcasts, Israeli radio refers to the city exclusively as Urshalim/al-Quds, and this is the name found on all official Israeli documents in Arabic. Israeli television weather forecasts in Arabic shorten this to Urshalim. Those who have mandated this usage seem to want to force Palestinians to recognize the Hebrew name for the city, although speakers of Arabic have had a perfectly serviceable name of their own for the city for well over a millennium.

---

[5] Early Muslims also called the city Ilya, derived from the Roman name, Aelia Capitolina, which was used before the Islamic period.

Although such measures may seem petty, they are related to the significant process of attempting to signal control by imposing place names. This has, for example, rendered the West Bank as Judea and Samaria in the official terminology used for Israel's Hebrew, English, and Arabic pronouncements and publications.. For the past few decades many such archaic or invented place names have been imposed throughout Palestine over the Arabic ones employed for many centuries and still used by much of the present-day population (many of these Arabic names, ironically, are based on earlier Hebrew, Aramaic, Greek, Latin, or French Crusader names for the same sites).[6] This process of naming is an attempt to privilege one dimension of a complex reality at the expense of others, with the ultimate aim of blotting the others out or decisively subordinating them to Israeli hegemony.

Another aspect of this process is visible in the sphere of archaeology. Attempts to privilege one archaeological stratum over others are predicated on a belief both that one stratum is "superior" or unique and that the past can be manipulated to affect the present by "proving" this superiority. Thus if one specific stratum of a city can be privileged, if one set of names derived from that stratum (or taken from the Bible or another ancient text and applied to that stratum) can be given pride of place over all others below or above it, then a certain contemporary "reality" that claims roots in the past can be imposed on the present and further consecrated.[7]

---

[6] See Meron Benvenisti, *Conflicts and Contradictions* (New York: Villard, 1986) 191–98, who writes that under the Israeli map of the country, there lies another Arab map. As deputy mayor of Jerusalem, Benvenisti played a part in Israeli settlement of Arab areas in the newly expanded municipality of Jerusalem after 1967; earlier, his father was one of the geographers assigned to give Hebrew names (some of them Hebrew versions of the original Arabic names) to localities throughout the country, a process that accelerated after 1948, when over three hundred Arab villages were obliterated after their inhabitants had fled. See the illustrated study of these villages compiled under the direction of Walid Khalidi, *All That Remains* (Washington: Institute for Palestine Studies, 1992).

[7] A striking attempt to do this in Jerusalem is the slide show for visitors to the excavations along the western wall of the Haram al-Sharif, which are controlled by the Israeli ministry of religion, the Israel Antiquities Authority, and the Jerusalem municipality. This extraordinary excavation involves a war-

This phenomenon is illustrated in the Arab village of Silwan, adjacent to and immediately south of the walls of the Old City in Jerusalem. There Israeli settlers, who have occupied several homes in the midst of Silwan, are attempting to impose exclusive use of the name City of David (after the hillside where King David is supposed to have built his city), thereby giving their current claims the patina, prestige, and legitimacy of a connection some 3000 years old. In this they are aided by various maps and road-signs produced by the Israeli government, the Jerusalem municipality, and the Israeli tourist authorities, which use the archaic name City of David wherever possible in place of Silwan, the name used for centuries by the village's Arab inhabitants (ironically, this Arabic name is derived from the biblical Siloam, site of the pool of the same name!).

This conflict through names has in the past had other than Palestinian-Israeli dimensions. For example, books in Arabic published in Jerusalem by Catholic presses in the early nineteenth century referred to the place of publication as Urshalim (the name for the city used by Eastern Christian churches that utilize Arabic in their liturgy) rather than as al-Quds al-Sharif or Bayt al-Maqdis. A work published in Arabic by the Franciscan press as late as 1865 still uses the term Urshalim for the place of publication, even though the work is a petition presented to the local government, which is described in the text of the petition itself as that of "al-Quds al-Sharif."[8] Similarly, a book on the history of the Orthodox Church in Je-

---

ren of subterranean tunnels driven through a substructure of arches constructed by Umayyad and Mameluke master builders as foundations for several superb monuments of Islamic architecture, yet the powerful slide show blots out everything but one segment of the city's history, linking the present to a "privileged" period 2000 years ago. See Nadia al-Hajj's ongoing Duke University dissertation on Israeli archaeology, notably chap. 3, "The Power of Knowledge: Discovery Scholarship and the Making of a Past for Contemporary Jerusalem."

[8] The cover of the pamphlet reads: "Tarjamat al-kurras al-mad'u muhamat 'an huquq Terra Sancta fil-maghara al-mad'uawa magharat al-halib al-ka'ina bil-qurb min Baytlahm. Mu'alafa wa muqaddama ila hukumat al-Quds al-Sharif min al-ab Rimigio Busayli, katib Terra Sancta, haziran sanat 1865. Tubi'a bi-Urshalim fi Dayr al-Ruhban al-Fransiscan." The pamphlet, which defends the rights of the Franciscan Terra Sancta order to a cave located in Bethlehem, is addressed to the Ottoman authorities.

rusalem, published in 1925 in Jerusalem, uses the term Ur-shalim in the title and the term al-Quds al-Sharif to describe the place of publication.[9]

This vestigial reluctance to use the common Arabic name, with its Islamic overtones, even in works using that name somewhere on their title page, represents the last flickering of a rivalry for control of the city between Islam and Christian-ity—a rivalry that began in the seventh century with its con-quest by Muslim armies from Byzantium, was greatly intensi-fied during the Crusades, and abated only in the early twenti-eth century.[10] More recently, the devotion of some fundamen-talist Christians to Israel, and their visceral hostility to Islam and the Arabs, shows that a few embers of this ancient rivalry have not been entirely extinguished.[11]

The conflict over names in Jerusalem goes beyond the name of the city itself. Jerusalem's most prominent geographi-cal feature, as well as its most important site historically and religiously, is the vast manmade plateau in the southeast cor-ner of the Old City within its Ottoman walls. This spacious rectangular platform (about 480 by 300 m) is located around a huge stone, which is all that remains of the peak of Mount Moriah, where Jews, Christians, and many Muslims believe Abraham to have been commanded by God to sacrifice his son.[12] From this stone, Muslims believe, the Prophet Muham-

---

[9] The book is *Khulasat tarikh kanisat urshalim al-urthoduksiyya*, by Shehadi and Nicola Khuri, published by Matba'at Bayt al-Maqdis.

[10] The leader in *The Times* on 11 December 1917, the day General Al-lenby entered Jerusalem, begins by stating that "The deliverance of Jerusalem . . . must remain for all time a most memorable event in the history of Chris-tendom," describes the war itself as "a crusade for human liberties," states that "the yoke of the Turk is broken for ever," and discusses at length the history of the Crusades, indicating that a consciousness of this religious ri-valry still remained alive. See *Orientations* (London: Weidenfeld & Nicholson, 1945), the autobiography of Ronald Storrs, British military governor of the city from 1917 until 1920, for further evidence of this consciousness.

[11] For analyses of this phenomenon, see Hassan Haddad and Donald Wagner, eds., *All in the Name of the Bible: Selected Essays on Israel and American Christian Fundamentalism* (Brattleboro: Amana, 1986).

[12] Most later Islamic traditions—the text of the Qur'an is not explicit—place the sacrifice at Mecca, although the commentators state that Abraham was "in the fertile land of Syria and Palestine" at this time, in the words of the

mad made a night journey to paradise described in the Qur'an
(17:1). The entire site, known in Arabic as al-Haram al-Sharif—
the Noble Sanctuary—encompasses a number of strikingly
beautiful Islamic structures, notably the al-Aqsa Mosque and
the Dome of the Rock, which have dominated and adorned this
space for the past thirteen centuries. The mosque was first
constructed some time between 636 and 670, and the dome
was erected in 692 by the Umayyad caliph 'Abd al-Malik.[13]

The same site is known to Israelis and others as the Temple Mount. Six centuries before the advent of Islam, it was
dominated by the great Temple built by Herod.[14] This structure, destroyed by Titus in 70 AD, was built in turn on what
was believed to be the site of earlier structures, going back to
the Temple described in the Bible as having been constructed
by Solomon. Much of the outer enclosure wall of the Herodian
Temple compound survives in its lower courses of finely finished cyclopean masonry, which constitute the foundations for
the eastern, southern, and western walls of the Haram al-
Sharif enclosure, built in its present form on the identical site
by the Umayyads in the seventh century.

Needless to say, Arabs and Israelis recognize only their
own respective names for this site, demonstrating that in
much of what it does, each side chooses to be oblivious to the

---

commentary on this passage appended to the official Saudi translation of the
Qur'an (Medina, 1405/1985). Otherwise, the only divergence among the beliefs of the three different faiths is that the Muslim commentators unani-
mously consider Isma'il, Abraham's eldest son, to have been the intended victim rather than Isaac. Although the relevant verses of the Qur'an (37:100–12)
are ambiguous in not mentioning Isma'il by name, the subsequent reference
to Isaac and the clear implication that the intended victim was Abraham's
eldest son bear out the traditional interpretation of these verses as concerning
Isma'il.

[13] See R. Khalidi, "The Future of Arab Jerusalem," *British Journal of
Middle East Studies* 19, 2 (Fall 1993): 133–43, for more details on problems
related to areas around the Haram al-Sharif.

[14] Herod, who was imposed on Judea as a ruler by the Romans after the
extinction of the Hasmonean dynasty, was "a Jew by religion" but not by origin, whose father was Jewish but whose mother's family came from Idumea, in
what is today Jordan. The words are those of the Israeli archaeologist Meir
Ben Dov, *In the Shadow of the Temple: The Discovery of Ancient Jerusalem*
(Jerusalem: Keter, 1985) 62.

existence of the other.[15] In a sense, each party to this conflict, and every other claimant, operates in a different dimension from the other, looking back to a different era of the past and living in a different present, albeit in the very same place. These two peoples, however, live cheek by jowl perforce, and their awareness of this enforced coexistence is occasionally illustrated in striking and bloody fashion, ranging from the so-called Wailing Wall riots of 1929 (although ostensibly about the rights of the respective communities to this site, most of the violence took place elsewhere) to the October 1990 clashes in which Israeli security forces shot and killed eighteen Palestinians and wounded over three hundred others inside the Haram al-Sharif.[16]

The conflict over this site, and over its name, extends down to levels of even greater detail. Thus the southernmost section of the western wall of the Haram al-Sharif includes in its lower courses part of the outer enclosure of the Temple compound built by Herod. Known as the Wailing Wall or the Western Wall, ha-Kotel ha-Ma'ravi in Hebrew, this site has been the scene of public Jewish worship since the sixteenth or seventeenth century, before which time such worship took place on the Mount of Olives overlooking the eastern walls of

---

[15] This is true even in a relatively enlightened work such as that of Ben Dov, *In the Shadow*. In it he devotes 380 pages to a study of excavations around the southern end of the Haram al-Sharif, including his own discoveries of a series of massive and hitherto unknown Umayyad buildings of great significance, without once mentioning the term *Haram al-Sharif*, the name used by Muslims for thirteen centuries for what he calls the Temple Mount.

[16] The pretext later invoked for the shootings was that the Palestinians inside the Haram were throwing stones at Jewish worshippers at the Wailing Wall plaza below, an allegation that careful journalistic investigation later revealed was false. It is impossible to see the plaza from the Haram, given the high arcade that surrounds the latter, and the Palestinians were in fact throwing stones at Israeli security forces shooting at them from the Haram's western wall and adjacent roofs. It has since been established that most worshippers were gone before stones thrown at the soldiers went over the arcade and into the plaza. See Michael Emery, "New Videotapes Reveal Israeli Cover-up," *The Village Voice*, 13 November 1990, 25–29, and the reportage by Mike Wallace on *60 Minutes*, 2 December 1990. For a detailed account based on testimonies of eyewitnesses, see Raja Shehadeh, *The Sealed Room* (London: Quartet, 1992) 24–29.

the Haram.[17] Precisely the same section of this western wall is considered by Muslims to be the site where the Prophet Muhammad tethered his winged steed al-Buraq on the night journey to paradise described in the Qur'an (17:1) "from the Masjid al-Haram [in Mecca] to the Masjid al-Aqsa [in Jerusalem]." As such, the spot has long been venerated by Muslims.[18]

The very same wall is thus among the holiest of sites to two faiths and is naturally considered by each to be its exclusive property. Immediately inside the wall of the Haram, near the Bab al-Maghariba gate, is a small mosque called Jami' al-Buraq, commemorating the spot where al-Buraq was supposedly tethered.[19] The entire area to the west of the wall, until

---

[17] 14. For details, see R. Khalidi, "The Future." Moshe Gil writes in *A History of Palestine, 640–1099* (Cambridge: Cambridge University Press, 1992) 646–50 of a Jewish synagogue during the early Muslim period and locates it in the vicinity of the western wall, but his pinpointing of its location seems singularly vague. On the other hand, he states (646) that in Jewish sources of the same period, "we find that the Western Wall is mentioned almost not at all," while with regard to Bab al-Rahme (sometimes known as Bawabat al-Rahme, or Gates of Mercy) on the eastern side of the Haram, he notes (643) that "the Jews of this period ... used to visit the gate and pray alongside it, and write about it, mentioning its name (in the singular or the plural) in letters."

[18] Moshe Gil, in *A History*, a revised version of his Hebrew-language work, *Eretz Israel during the First Muslim Period* (a more apt title than the English one, given the book's focus on the history of the Jewish community in Palestine) 90 ff., states that the Muslims' veneration for Jerusalem began decades after they took the city but fails to account for manifold indications of its sanctity to the earliest Muslims. These include the attention supposedly paid to Jerusalem and to the Haram by the caliph 'Umar, which Gil himself describes; the building of a large mosque on the site of the present al-Aqsa mosque, traditionally ascribed to 'Umar but historically datable at least as far back as 670, when a large wooden structure was described in an account by a Christian pilgrim, Bishop Arculf; the sanctity attached to Jerusalem by the Prophet Muhammad in making it the first direction of prayer before Mecca was finally chosen; and the reference to al-Masjid al-Aqsa ("the farthest mosque") in the Qur'an. Gil argues that traditions relating this verse to Jerusalem are late ones, begging the question of how early Muslims understood this verse, if not as referring to Jerusalem.

[19] Ben Dov claims (*In the Shadow* 286) that Muslim devotion to this site dates back only to the nineteenth century and was a response to the growth of Jewish interest in the adjacent Wailing Wall. He refers to the fifteenth-century

1967 a residential quarter called Haret al-Maghariba, or the Moroccan quarter, was established as a Muslim *waqf*, or inalienable pious endowment, in 1193 by al-Malik al-Afdal, the son of the Ayyubid Sultan Salah al-Din (Saladin), who retook the city from the Crusaders. A few days after Israel's occupation of East Jerusalem in 1967, the entire Haret al-Maghariba, including the four Muslim religious sites it encompassed, was demolished and its approximately 1000 residents evicted, in order to create the large open plaza that now exists west of the wall.[20] In addition to its frequent use for Jewish religious observances, this plaza has since 1967 become the site of Israeli national and patriotic mass gatherings, such as torch-light ceremonies celebrating graduation from training for recruits to elite army units and political demonstrations by right-wing parties.

This disputed site thus displays elements of the various conflicting narratives—going back to those relating to the patriarch Abraham, venerated by followers of all three monotheistic faiths—that lie behind the complex identity of the Palestinians, and of many others. This conflict is illustrated by the archaeological excavations carried out for many years after 1967 immediately to the south of the Haram al-Sharif, on a site immediately abutting the al-Aqsa Mosque and the Western Wall/al-Buraq plaza. According to Meir Ben Dov, the Israeli field director of the dig, this site "contains the remains of twenty-five strata from twelve distinct periods."[21] Each stra-

---

work of Mujir al-Din to show that Muslims earlier connected al-Buraq to Bab al-Rahme on the eastern side of the Haram. Mujir al-Din (d. 1521) does suggest this in *al-Uns al-jalil bi-tarikh al-Quds wal-Khalil* (Amman: Maktabat al-Muhtasib, 1973) 2, 28. But a source from two centuries earlier, *Ba'ith al-nufus ila ziyarat al-Quds al-mahrus* (manuscript located in the Khalidi Library in Jerusalem) 26, by Ibrahim b. Ishaq al-Ansari, known as Ibn Furkah (d. 1328), states that al-Buraq was tethered outside Bab al-Nabi, an old name for a gate that Gil (*A History* 645) locates at the southwest corner of the Haram and that Mujir al-Din (2, 31) identifies with Bab al-Maghariba, at the southern end of the western wall of the Haram, the very site venerated by Muslims today! All that is clear from this dispute about the tethering place of an apocryphal winged horse is that otherwise-sober scholars risk getting carried away where religious claims in Jerusalem are concerned.

[20] See Khalidi, "The Future," for more details on the destruction of Haret al-Maghariba.

[21] Ben Dov, *In the Shadow* 378.

tum is part of the identity of the Palestinian people as they have come to understand it over the past century—encompassing the biblical, Roman, Byzantine, Umayyad, Fatimid, Crusader, Ayyubid, Mameluke, and Ottoman periods.[22] At the same time, several strata have special importance to others who revere Jerusalem (the Byzantine and Crusader strata for Western Christians, for example, or the stratum containing the southern steps of the Herodian Temple—where Jesus encountered the money changers—for Christians and Jews alike), and they are not treated equally by any means.[23]

Most importantly, central though Jerusalem is to the Palestinians and to their self-image, it is also central to the self-image of their Israeli adversaries. Yet the Israelis control Jerusalem and are able to expropriate, excavate, label, and describe antiquities there as they please. They can thus put the stamp of authority on narratives that give extraordinary weight to selected strata, generally in pursuit of a clear nationalist political agenda. Their success can be seen from the tides of foreign

---

[22] Two contrasting but complementary perspectives on the role of history and archaeology in the construction of Palestinian identity can be found in Meir Litvak, "A Palestinian Past: National Construction and Reconstruction," *History and Memory: Studies in the Representation of the Past* 6, 2 (Fall/Winter 1994): 24–56; and Albert Glock, "Cultural Bias in the Archaeology of Palestine," *Journal of Palestine Studies* 24, 2 (Winter 1995): 48–59.

[23] For details on how Christian and Muslim antiquities unearthed at this and other sites in the Old City of Jerusalem are treated, and the "privileging" of some, see Abu al-Hajj, chap. 3. Another perspective on the significance of Jerusalem can be found in Jerome Murphy-O'Connor's *The Holy Land: An Archaeological Guide from Earliest Times to 1700*, 2nd ed. (Oxford: Oxford University Press, 1986), a work of erudition whose otherwise restrained tone occasionally betrays the author's preference for biblical antiquities over those of succeeding eras. Fr. Murphy-O'Connor sometimes goes beyond the mere expression of preferences, as with his occasional derogatory comments on structures associated with the Eastern churches, such as parts of the Holy Sepulcher (49, where he describes the monument over Jesus' tomb as a "hideous kiosk") or his description of Nablus: "the town has nothing to offer visitors, and the uncertain temper of the populace counsels speedy transit" (309). Besides needlessly slighting the inhabitants of Nablus, this judgment ignores the late Mameluke-era Qasr Touqan, an extensive palace-fortress in the heart of the old *qasaba*, which was dynamited and partially destroyed by the Israeli military in reprisal for the killing of a soldier in 1989.

tourists that choke the narrow alleys of the Old City, most of them in groups led by Israeli tour guides propagating one version of the city's history. It is interesting to speculate what a Palestinian version would look like, and even more interesting to contemplate the possibility of a multidimensional narrative that would reproduce all of Jerusalem's ambiguity and the overlapping traditions it represents instead of reducing the complexity of the city's history to a single narrow dimension.

III

One of the central arguments of this essay is that several overlapping senses of identity have been operating in the way the Palestinians have come to define themselves as a people, senses that are not contradictory for the Palestinians themselves but can be misunderstood or misinterpreted by others. As Palestinian identity has evolved over time, its elements have varied, with some eventually disappearing and others emerging to take their place. What follows is a discussion of this process and of the ways in which both collective traumas and major obstacles have played a role in shaping and expressing a separate Palestinian identity, even while problems internal to Palestinian society have helped prevent—thus far at least—the realization of the Palestinian "national project."

It is characteristic of both time and place that the intellectuals, writers, and politicians who were instrumental in the evolution of Palestinian identity at the end of the last century and early in this century—figures such as Sa'id al-Husayni, Ruhi al-Khalidi, Najib Nassar, 'Isa al-'Isa, Muhammad Hassan al-Budayri, 'Arif al-'Arif, Khalil al-Sakakini, and Musa al-'Alami—identified with the Ottoman Empire, their religion, Arabism, their homeland Palestine, their city or region, and their family, without feeling any contradiction or sense of conflicting loyalties.[24] By the late 1920s and the 1930s, the way

---

[24] Sa'id al-Husayni and Ruhi al-Khalidi were members of the Ottoman Parliaments elected in 1908 and put forward Palestinian and Arab concerns there, while remaining loyal to the Ottoman state; Najib Nassar and 'Isa al-'Isa were the most prominent newspaper editors of the period, whose papers, *al-Karmil* and *Filastin*, were instrumental in shaping early Palestinian national

in which such individuals related to these foci of identity had changed greatly. The Ottoman Empire had disappeared; the importance of religion in public life had declined; Arab nationalism had suffered defeats at the hands of the French (whose troops drove an Arab nationalist government out of Damascus in 1920); and Britain had received a mandate for Palestine within fixed frontiers, wherein national rights had been promised for the Jewish minority but not mentioned for the Arab majority. All these changes strengthened the preexisting identification with Palestine of such people, their contemporaries, and the generation that followed them into politics, education, and journalism, although they still continued to identify with religion, Arabism, and their localities and families.

In this there was nothing particularly unusual for its time and place, except that unlike Egyptians, Iraqis, Syrians, or Lebanese, all of whom developed a loyalty to nation-state nationalism over approximately the same period,[25] the Palestinians not only had to fashion and impose their identity and political existence in opposition to a European colonial power. They also had to match themselves against the growing and powerful Zionist movement, which was motivated by a strong, highly developed, and focused sense of national identification and which challenged the national rights of the Palestinians in

---

consciousness and in stirring opposition to Zionism; Muhammad Hassan al-Budayri and 'Arif al-'Arif were the editors of a paper called *Suriyya al-Janubiyya*, a pan-Arab journal of the post–World War I era and the main nationalist organ before its suppression by the British in 1920; Musa al-'Alami was a prominent lawyer and educator whose autobiography, *Palestine Is My Country: The Story of Musa al-Alami* (London: Murray, 1969), shows how he looked at these different sources of identity.

[25] On the way this process developed in these countries, see, *inter alia*, Israel Gershoni and James Jankowski, *Egypt, Islam and the Arabs: The Search for Egyptian Nationhood, 1900–1930* (New York: Oxford University Press, 1986), and *Redefining the Egyptian Nation, 1930–1945* (Cambridge: Cambridge University Press, 1995); Hanna Batatu, *The Old Social Classes and the Revolutionary Movements of Iraq* (Princeton: Princeton University Press, 1978); Philip Khoury, *Syria and the French Mandate: The Politics of Arab Nationalism, 1920–1945* (Princeton: Princeton University Press, 1987); and Kamal Salibi, *A House of Many Mansions: The History of Lebanon Reconsidered* (Berkeley: University of California Press, 1988).

their own homeland. While this challenge helped to shape the specific form Palestinian national identification took, it is a mistake to suggest that Palestinian nationalism was mainly a response to Zionism.[26] This should be obvious from the fact that an increasing identification with the new states created by the post–World War I partitions, one based on preexisting loyalties as in the Palestinian case, was a universal process in the Middle East during this period. Moreover, Lebanese, Syrians, Egyptians, Iraqis, and Jordanians all managed to develop their respective nation-state nationalisms during the same period without the dubious benefit of a Zionist challenge.[27]

The existence of overlapping senses of identity—including transnational, religious, local, family, and nation-state loyalties—found in the peoples of all these Arab states, is in fact common in polities where new national narratives have developed out of many separate strands. In some cases champions of different elements of national identity have come into conflict, which has resulted in the absence of even a minimal consensus on national identity, as was long the case in Lebanon.[28] Most often, however, such a consensus has eventually emerged. Although the phenomenon of overlapping senses of identity characterizes all the neighbors of the Palestinians, including the Israelis, there is one vital difference: these neighboring peoples have lived for most of the past half century under the rule of increasingly strong independent states, which gave substance to their national narratives and propagated

---

[26] For an example of this view see M. Curtis, J. Neyer, C. Waxman, and A. Pollack, eds., *The Palestinians: People, History, Politics* (New Brunswick: Transaction, 1975) 4: "Palestinian Arab nationalism, stimulated by and reacting to the Jewish national liberation movement of Zionism, is even more recent.... Its chief impetus has come from opposition to Jewish settlement and to the State of Israel."

[27] For more on some of the stimuli to Palestinian nationalism other than Zionism, see Muhammad Muslih, *The Origins of Palestinian Nationalism* (New York: Columbia University Press, 1990).

[28] The best analysis of conflicting Lebanese national narratives is by Kamal Salibi, in his *A House of Many Mansions* (Berkeley: University of California Press, 1988). This is one of the most radical critiques extant of the national myths of any Arab country and of some shared Arab national myths. See also Ahmad Beydoun's perceptive *al-Sira' 'al tarik Lubnan* (Beirut: Lebanese University Press, 1989).

them domestically and internationally in an authoritative fashion. In contrast, the lack of a strong state—indeed of any state of their own—has clearly had a great impact on the Palestinian sense of national identity.

The major currents that swept the Middle East during this century, such as the Western powers' definition of state boundaries, as well as Arabism, Islamic trends, Zionism, and the growth of nation-state nationalisms in the Arab states, all affected the process of Palestinian self-definition, but so did several more parochial factors. These included a strong religious attachment to Palestine among Muslims and Christians;[29] the impact over time of living within long-standing administrative boundaries;[30] and enduring regional and local loyalties, involving attachment of the urban population to their cities and towns and of the peasantry to their villages and lands. While studies of Palestinian nationalism have concentrated on its development in recent decades, in fact most elements of Palestinian identity—particularly the parochial ones—were well developed before the climactic date of 1948, although they continued to overlap and evolve both before and after that date.

In 1948 half of the country's 1.4 million Arabs were uprooted from their homes, and the traditional Palestinian political leadership was scattered and discredited, not to be replaced

---

[29] In *Palestine in Transformation, 1856–1882* (Washington, DC: Institute for Palestine Studies, 1993), Alexander Schölch shows how the idea of the holy land, which had developed over centuries among Christians and Muslims, helped to shape the modern concept of Palestine as a unit in the minds of its Arab inhabitants.

[30] The Ottomans in 1874 elevated the Jerusalem *sanjaq*, or district (including the area from the Jordan to the sea and from a line above Jaffa and Jerusalem to south of Beersheba and encompassing Jerusalem, Jaffa, Gaza, Beersheba, Hebron, and Bethlehem), to the status of an independent administrative unit reporting directly to the capital. Earlier, Palestine was usually included as the separate *sanjaq*s of Jerusalem, Nablus, and Acre in the Sidon *vilayet*, or province, or in the *vilayet* of Syria. Under the Ottomans, Palestine was always administratively separate from the area east of the Jordan, which was governed from Damascus. The administrative boundaries of Ottoman Palestine were finally fixed in the 1880s, when the *sanjaq*s of Nablus and Acre were attached to the new *vilayet* of Beirut, an arrangement that remained stable until 1918.

for over a decade and a half. Were a basic core sense of national identity not already in place among key segments of the Palestinian people, the catastrophic shock of these events) might have been expected to shatter the Palestinians as a people, eventually leading to their full absorption into the neighboring Arab countries. This indeed was what many of their opponents hoped would happen.[31] After 1948 the Palestinians were to some degree integrated into the Arab host countries, whether socially, economically, or politically, as might be expected given the overlapping identities of the Palestinians. But instead of scattering them and causing their absorption into these countries, the trauma of 1948 reinforced preexisting elements of identity, which amounted to a Palestinian self-definition. The shared events of 1948 thus brought the Palestinians closer together in terms of their collective consciousness, even as they were physically dispersed all over the Middle East and beyond. The experience of 1948, and its impact on different segments of the Palestinian people, is still a common topic of discussion among Palestinians of diverse backgrounds and generations, and ultimately a source of shared beliefs and values.

The overt obstacles to the expression of a separate Palestinian identity in national terms are thus worth considering, alongside the ideologies that competed for the loyalty of the Palestinian people or exerted influence on them, from Ottomanism and Arabism to Islam to the nation-state nationalism of the neighboring Arab nation-states. Whether as elements of the Palestinians' overlapping sense of identity or as obstacles to the expression of this identity, all of these "others" contributed, albeit in markedly different ways, to the Palestinians' self-definition.

The main obstacles to the expression of a separate Palestinian identity included the external powers that have dominated the region during this century, Britain and the United States, both of which perceived Palestinian nationalism as a threat to their interests. As we have seen, the Balfour Declaration and the League of Nations Mandate for Palestine (which

---

[31] This was the premise of the Johnston Plan, which American policy makers in the 1950s hoped would lead to the assimilation of the refugees into the surrounding countries. In this context, John Foster Dulles expressed the belief that within a generation the refugees would forget Palestine.

governed British policy in Palestine for three decades) explicitly excluded Palestinian national rights and did not even mention the Palestinians *per se*, whether as Palestinians, Arabs, or Syrians. They were referred to rather in negative terms, as "the non-Jewish communities in Palestine." This negation was an important prerequisite both for the denial of self-determination to the Palestinians and for the British decision to favor Zionism: for if the Palestinians had no determined identity,[32] they were unworthy of self-determination or at least less worthy than the Jews, who clearly had a determined identity, now being posed in national rather than religious terms. At the same time as they denied Palestinian identity, both documents enshrined the establishment of a Jewish "national home" as Britain's primary responsibility in governing Palestine. Except for a brief period following the issuance of the 1939 White Paper, Britain remained essentially faithful to this dual approach until 1947–48, when it successfully colluded with Jordan (and indirectly with Israel) to prevent the emergence of the Palestinian state provided for in the 1947 United Nations General Assembly's partition plan, embodied in resolution 181.[33]

As for the United States, although in 1947 it supported the partition of Palestine and the creation of a Palestinian state alongside Israel, it did nothing to help that state come into being against the machinations of Jordan, Britain, and Israel but instead materially helped the nascent state of Israel. Since 1948, the United States has followed essentially the same

---

[32] On this many Zionist leaders and British officials were agreed in 1918, when Chaim Weizmann wrote that "The present state of affairs would necessarily tend towards the creation of an Arab Palestine, if there were an Arab people in Palestine," and William Ormsby-Gore (assistant secretary of the war cabinet and later colonial secretary) stated that "west of the Jordan the people were not Arabs, but only Arabic-speaking." Cited in Doreen Warriner, comp., *Palestine Papers, 1917–1922* (London: John Murray, 1972) 32–33.

[33] The details are recorded in Avi Shlaim, *Collusion across the Jordan* (New York: Columbia University Press, 1990), and Mary Wilson, *King Abdullah, Britain and the Making of Jordan* (Cambridge: Cambridge University Press, 1988). Although the British in 1939 modified the unconditional support they had shown for Zionism for over two decades, this change was limited by the presence as prime minister from 1939 to 1945 of Winston Churchill, perhaps the most ardent Zionist in British public life, and by the fact that British hostility to Palestinian aspirations and leadership remained unabated.

course as Britain, supporting Israel but never conceding the validity of Palestinian national rights or the self-determination and statehood that would entail and indeed often making efforts to prevent their implementation. This policy was consistent although different administrations edged ambiguously toward accepting certain Palestinian political rights, while invariably excluding the right of national self-determination. Thus in the 1978 Camp David agreement, which includes the phrase "the legitimate rights of the Palestinian people," it is clear from the context that these are less than full rights of self-determination and independence. Little has changed since then, even in the PLO-Israel Declaration of Principles signed on the White House lawn in September 1993, which fails to provide for Palestinian statehood.

The obstacles to the achievement of Palestinian national rights also included the Zionist movement, which since its implantation in Palestine at the end of the last century has strongly opposed any expression of independent Palestinian nationalism, Palestinian claims to the country, and the exercise of Palestinian national identity. With few exceptions (Ahad Ha-Am and Judah Magnes stand out among them), early Zionist leaders, and Israeli politicians since the founding of the state, have tended to see their conflict with Palestinian nationalism as a zero-sum game.[34] Beyond winning most of the early rounds of this game on the ground in Palestine, they were able to carry their battle back to the international "metropolises" of the era, whether London and Paris before World War II or Washington and New York since then, and to succeed in gaining support for their own national aspirations, while at the same time delegitimizing the national aspirations of their Palestinian opponents.

From very early in the history of the Zionist movement, Palestinian intellectuals and political figures perceived that Zi-

---

[34] Although much past writing on this subject has been devoted to blurring this harsh reality, more recent research has borne it out: e.g., Anita Shapira, *Land and Power: The Zionist Recourse to Force, 1881–1948* (New York: Oxford University Press, 1992); Nur Masalha, *Expulsion of the Palestinians: The Concept of "Transfer" in Zionist Political Thought, 1882–1948* (Washington, DC: Institute for Palestine Studies, 1992); see also Zachary Lockman, *Comrades and Enemies: Arab and Jewish Workers in Palestine, 1906–1948* (Berkeley: University of California Press, 1996).

onism had objectives that could only be achieved at the expense of Palestinian aspirations, whether framed in Ottoman, Muslim, or Christian, Arab, Syrian, or narrowly Palestinian terms (and they too generally came to hold a zero-sum view of the conflict).[35] One of the earliest recorded Palestinian reactions to Zionism was a letter written to Theodor Herzl in 1899 by Yusuf Dia Pasha al-Khalidi, former mayor of Jerusalem and deputy for the city in the 1877–78 Ottoman Parliament. He warned Herzl that the Palestinians would resist the aspirations of political Zionism, which they understood could only be achieved at their expense, and concluded, "let Palestine be left in peace."[36]

It may be asked why, given this early awareness, the Palestinians were not more effective in their resistance to the Zionist movement. For the effective and successful expression of Palestinian identity—meaning the achievement of a greater measure of independent national existence, up to and including sovereignty—was not obstructed solely by external obstacles, powerful though these were. Internal factors, resulting from the social structure of Palestine in the nineteenth and twentieth centuries, also contributed to maintaining the Palestinians in a state of dependence until the present.

The general outlines of this social structure, fragmented along regional, class, religious, and family lines, were not peculiar to Palestinian society; indeed they were common to many others in the Arab world in this period. Other Arab countries, however, generally succeeded in transcending these divisions, at least in times of national crisis. At similar times, the lack of cohesion of Palestinian society repeatedly hindered effective, unified responses to the challenges posed by the formidable foes of Palestinian nationalism.

It is illuminating to study the differences between the Palestinians and the Arab peoples who over the past century developed national frontiers and state structures and secured

---

[35] Neville Mandel's *Arab Reactions to Zionism 1882–1914* (Berkeley: University of California Press, 1986) is the best work on this early period. See also R. Khalidi, "The Role of the Press in the Early Arab Reaction to Zionism," *Peuples Méditerranéans/Mediterranean Peoples* 20 (July–Sept. 1982): 105–24.

[36] Mandel, *Arab Reactions* 47–48, discusses this letter, sent via the chief rabbi of France, Zadok Khan. See Herzl's reply in Walid Khalidi, ed., *From Haven to Conquest* (Beirut: Institute for Palestine Studies, 1970) 91–93.

independence from the same Western powers that denied these things to the Palestinians. Both Egypt and Tunisia showed a high degree of cohesiveness in spite of deep societal divisions and managed to negotiate the difficult transition from foreign occupation to independence with limited instability, dissension, or domestic repression. In Syria and Iraq, the passage was stormier, with national consensus harder to build and less mutual tolerance and pluralism in political life than in Egypt or Tunisia. The result was that, before and after independence, internal sectarian, social, and political tensions repeatedly exploded in bloody domestic strife, leaving both Syria and Iraq with repressive, authoritarian states as the price of this transition.[37]

In the Palestinian case, what had to be achieved was more difficult than in other Arab countries, for the opposition of both Britain and the Zionist movement had to be taken into account. But from 1918 until 1948, the Palestinians also demonstrated less ability to transcend local, family, and political rivalries and to unify their efforts against their common enemies than did Egyptians, Tunisians, Syrians, Iraqis, and even the religiously divided Lebanese. In all these cases, the respective national movements managed to display greater cohesiveness and solidarity at critical moments in the struggle with the colonial power than did the Palestinians—Egypt in 1919 and 1936; Tunisia in the mid-1950s; Syria in 1925–26 and 1936; Iraq in 1941 and 1946–48; and Lebanon in 1943. At times, the outcome was not an unequivocal victory, but in all cases the ultimate result was independence.

Certainly, the lack of access after 1918 to state structures (or to any meaningful level of government: the top posts in the

---

[37] Iraq was far more afflicted by these problems than Syria, partly because the three Ottoman provinces, Basra, Baghdad, and Mosul, out of which the British created Iraq had little in common, with their population deeply divided on sectarian and ethnic grounds—between Sunni and Shi'a, Arab and Kurd, urban and rural, settled and tribal populations. See Batatu, *Old Social Classes.* Syria suffered from some of these problems but was a more homogenous society than Iraq, with a larger urban and settled population, a clear Sunni majority, less diversity among regions, and only two Ottoman provinces, Damascus and Aleppo, to be subsumed under the structure of a single state.

mandate administration were reserved for the British)[38] hindered the Palestinians by comparison with their Arab neighbors. Most other Arab countries either had a preexisting state with a degree of independence, as in Egypt or Tunisia, which had autonomous hereditary regimes under the Ottomans before European occupation in the 1880s and retained them afterwards; or the European powers were bound by the terms of League of Nations mandates to create such state structures and eventually to hand over power to them. We have already seen that this was not the case with regard to the Palestine mandate. Moreover, in Palestine the Zionists built their own exclusive, well-funded parastate structures with the blessing of the mandatory authority and in keeping with the terms of the mandate, even while benefiting inordinately from the administrative structures of the Government of Palestine created by the British.

But in addition to these special disadvantages affecting the Palestinians, it might also be argued that Palestine, and especially the hilly central Nablus-Jerusalem-Hebron axis whence came most of the political leaders, was simply less developed economically, and therefore had evolved less socially and politically, than had the urban areas of Egypt, Syria, Iraq, and Lebanon during this period.[39] Moreover, even in neighboring Lebanon and Syria, which were most similar to Palestine, political leadership tended to come not from the towns of the relatively isolated hill areas but rather from the middle and upper classes of the larger and more socially, economically, and politically developed cities of the coast and the interior plains: Beirut, Aleppo, and Damascus. In 1942, these cities

---

[38] For the best account of how the mandate excluded Palestinians from positions of responsibility, see Bernard Wasserstein, *The British in Palestine: The Mandatory Government and the Arab-Jewish Conflict, 1917–1929*, 2nd ed. (Oxford: Blackwell, 1991).

[39] The British tactic of reinforcing traditional social structures in rural areas as a prop for their rule is examined by Ylana Miller, *Government and Society in Rural Palestine 1920–1948* (Austin: University of Texas Press, 1985). This policy was continued by Jordan in the West Bank from 1948 until 1967 and by Israel in Arab areas incorporated into Israel after 1948 and in the occupied West Bank after 1967. For an analysis that stresses the dichotomy between the coastal plain and the hill areas, see Baruch Kimmerling and Joel S. Migdal, *Palestinians: The Making of a People* (New York: Free Press, 1993).

had populations of 233,000, 257,000, and 261,000, respectively, while the three largest cities in Palestine with Arab populations—Jerusalem, Haifa, and Jaffa—had populations of 143,000, 116,000, and 89,000, with only about 180,000 of the three cities' total population of 348,000 being Arabs.[40]

In Palestine, by way of contrast, while Jaffa and Haifa were the commercial and economic foci of the country, as well as centers of intellectual and cultural life and of press activity (and had the largest Arab populations of any cities in the country—larger even than Jerusalem), Jerusalem, Nablus, and other cities and towns of the hills tended to dominate political life. The implication is that Palestinian politics tended to be most influenced by these hill areas, where religious, clan, family, and parochial perspectives were more prevalent, rather than by the coastal cities, where working-class associations, radical urban religious groups, commercial and business concerns, and intellectual and social organizations were most active.[41]

Certainly, political party organization, sustained mass political mobilization, a vigorous independent political press, and many other features of "modern" politics, which had burgeoned rapidly at this time in other Arab countries, were relatively underdeveloped in Palestine when the crucial test of the 1936–39 revolt arose.[42] Palestinians showed great solidarity in the opening phases of this revolt, which was started and sustained by the grassroots rather than the traditional political leadership. It is also true that the strong religious, family, and local loyalties that characterized this society were initially a great asset during the revolt. Nevertheless, in the end the lack

---

[40] Population estimates are from Alfred Bonne, ed., *Statistical Handbook of Middle Eastern Countries*, 2nd ed. (Jerusalem: Economic Research Institute of the Jewish Agency for Palestine, 1945) 3, 99.

[41] For more on the coastal cities, see the forthcoming books of May Seikaly on Haifa (London: I. B. Tauris) and Zachary Lockman on Arab and Jewish working-class organizations, cited in n. 34, as well as Kimmerling and Migdal, *Palestinians*.

[42] Although the press was extremely active and a number of political parties existed in Palestine in the 1930s, most of these parties were essentially vehicles for narrow family or individual interests, as were some of the newspapers. Hizb al-Istiqlal, founded by 'Auni 'Abd al-Hadi, was probably the most developed example of a modern political party in Palestine.

of organization and the urban-rural, class, and family divisions that bedeviled Palestinian society reemerged, splintering the internal front even as the British mounted a fierce campaign of repression in late 1938. The result was a crushing military and political reverse for the Palestinians. This reverse was perhaps inevitable, since it is difficult to imagine the British Empire accepting defeat at the hands of the Palestinians, however sophisticated their leadership and organization, at this crucial juncture just before World War II and in an area that the British considered to be of vital strategic importance to them. It was nevertheless devastating.

This decisive defeat in 1936–39 fatally weakened the Palestinians on the eve of their desperate final post–World War II struggle with the Zionist movement to retain control of some part of what they passionately believed was their country. In consequence, by the time expeditionary forces of four Arab armies entered Palestine on 15 May 1948, the Palestinians had already been militarily overwhelmed by the forces of the Haganah, the Palmach, and the Irgun in a series of sweeping routs, which ended in the loss of Jaffa, Haifa, Acre, Tiberias, and many other cities, towns, villages, and strategic communications routes. The result was a political and military vacuum, which the nascent Israeli state rapidly filled, together with the armies of several Arab states, which proceeded to lose much of the rest of Palestine to the victorious Israelis.

It was not until the mid-1960s that the rebirth of Palestinian nationalism would put the Palestinians back on the political map of the Middle East. By this time, a new middle-class leadership had emerged at the head of effectively organized political structures like Fatah and the Movement of Arab Nationalists, eclipsing the traditional leaders who had failed during the mandate period.[43] The legacy that the traditional leaders left to their successors included the heavy burden of repeated political defeats culminating in the disaster of 1948 and the frustration of Palestinian aspirations for independence and sovereignty. Yet these setbacks, far from weakening it, seem to have reinforced the sense of Palestinian national identity that

---

[43] It remains to be determined to what degree this new leadership has managed to overcome the persistence of personal, family, regional, and sectarian rivalries through the development of effective modern institutions and structures that transcend these parochial divisions.

had emerged over the preceding decades out of the disparate strands of religious and local attachments to Palestine, commitment to Arabism, and resistance to what Palestinians perceived was the creeping encroachment of the Zionist movement on their homeland. The Palestinians held fast to this strong sense of identity after 1948—both those who became refugees and those who remained in their homes inside Palestine. Even while it continued to evolve and change, it remained the foundation upon which the Palestinian nationalist groups that emerged after 1948 were to build.

IV

Given this background, how has the way Palestinians define their identity changed over time? It is difficult to date precisely when a distinct sense of Palestinian identity first emerged. There is little doubt that it emerged unevenly, in different ways among different groups and in different areas, and that it always coexisted with other forms of identification, such as religion or family. And important roots of this identity go back before the development of modern national consciousness. But there is considerable evidence that much of the population of Palestine became, in Benedict Anderson's phrase, an "imagined community" in the early decades of this century.[44] This section recapitulates some of the stages in this process, concluding with a warning of the pitfalls that threaten the study of this topic.

The incipient sense of community-as-nation can be seen in an article by Najib 'Azoury, a former Ottoman official in Palestine, in the newspaper *Thamarat al-Funun* on 23 September 1908. 'Azoury suggested that the newly restored Ottoman Parliament expand the existing *sanjaq* of Jerusalem, stressing that an expansion of this district's frontiers northwards to include the northern parts of Palestine then part of the *vilayet* of Beirut was necessary because "the progress of the land of Pal-

---

[44] In *Imagined Communities: Reflections on the Rise and Spread of Nationalism*, 2nd ed. (London: Verso, 1991) 6, Anderson defines a nation as "an imagined political community ... imagined as both inherently limited and sovereign."

estine depends on this."[45] The idea of a clearly defined "land of Palestine," with frontiers approximating those given to the country under the mandate, must have been clearly present in 'Azoury's mind, and also in the minds of his readers, for him to make such a proposal. His proposal specifies a primary unit of territory to which the residents of Palestine belonged and owed their loyalty and through which they should be represented in the Ottoman Parliament. In 'Azoury's case, we know from his book *Le Reveil de la nation arabe*[46] that he had a clear sense of Palestine as a country—it contains an entire chapter on the history, geography, population, and administration of Palestine—and of the potential impact on it of the rise of the Zionist movement. There are many other indications that such an "idea of Palestine" existed at this time, among them the founding in Jaffa in 1911 of the influential newspaper *Filastin* (meaning Palestine), which in the decades to follow was instrumental in spreading this idea.

Before the twentieth century, as we have seen, Ottoman Palestine had been subject to a variety of administrative arrangements. The existing sense of Palestine as a country, however, was little affected by Ottoman administrative changes, in part because this sense was based on the long-standing and firmly held religious idea that Palestine within generally recognized borders was a holy land common to all three monotheistic faiths. The importance of this idea for shaping the nascent nationalist consciousness of Palestinians in the late nineteenth century has been well traced by the late Alexander Schölch in his masterful study, *Palestine in Transformation: 1856–1882*.[47] As he points out, this sense of Palestine as a country went back to the *fada'il al-Quds* literature, which described Jerusa-

---

[45] The article was published after the Ottoman Constitutional Revolution of July 1908, which liberated the press from the censorship of the old regime, making possible the freer expression of nationalist ideas.

[46] *Reveil de la nation arabe* (Paris: n.p., 1905) predicted an inevitable collision between Zionism and Arabism. On 'Azoury, Lebanese by origin, see Mandel, *Arab Reactions* 49–52.

[47] Cited in n. 29. References to "the land of Palestine" are widespread in the Arabic-language press in Palestine and elsewhere before 1914. A typical example is an article in the Beirut newspaper *al-Ittihad al-'Uthmani*, no. 559, 19 July 1910, 2, which warns against "Zionist colonization, in other words foreign seizure of the land of Palestine" in a lengthy article on Zionism.

lem and holy sites and places of note throughout Palestine, including Hebron, Jericho, Bethlehem, Nablus, al-Ramla, Safad, Ascalon, Acre, Gaza, and Nazareth, for pilgrims and visitors to Palestine and for the devout and inquisitive elsewhere.[48] These place names suggest that a clear idea of the rough boundaries of Palestine, as a sort of sacred—if not yet a national—space, already existed in the minds of authors and readers of this Islamic devotional literature.

This sense of Palestine as a special and sacred space recurs in the historical record. In 1701, the French consul in Sidon paid a visit to Jerusalem, an innovation never before permitted by the Ottoman authorities. This produced a strong reaction from the local Muslim population, whose representatives met in the Haram al-Sharif. There, more than eighty Muslim leaders representing the city's main families, together with several local military officials and large numbers of the populace "including poor and rich," deliberated and signed a petition demanding that the Ottoman sultan, Mustafa II, revoke permission for such a visit.[49]

The terms this document uses are telling.[50] The petitioners remind the sultan that Jerusalem, called Bayt al-Maqdis, is

---

[48] These sites are mentioned repeatedly, e.g., in Mujir al-Din's al-Uns al-jalil and in earlier works. They refer also to sites throughout Syria that are seen as having a certain sanctity, although a special place is reserved for Palestine, and Jerusalem in particular. There are eleven sayings, or ahadith, attributed to the Prophet Muhammad that have this same focus recorded in the standard compilations: Husni Adham Jarrar, al-Hajj Amin al-Husayni (Amman: Dar al-Dia', 1987) 6–8.

[49] For background on the situation in Palestine, see Amnon Cohen, Palestine in the Eighteenth Century (Jerusalem: Hebrew University, 1985). For more general background on this incident see Fatma Müge Göçek, East Encounters West: France and the Ottoman Empire in the Eighteenth Century (New York: Oxford University Press, 1987).

[50] This undated document in Arabic was located in the Khalidi Library in Jerusalem, together with more than 300 legal documents that originate in the local court, the mahkama shar'iyya, from the seventeenth through the early twentieth centuries. During this time, members of the Khalidi family often held the senior local post in this court, as deputy to the qadi, who was appointed from Istanbul and generally served for one year. For details, see Madeleine Zilfi, The Politics of Piety: The Ottoman Ulema in the Post-Classical Age (Minneapolis: Biblioteca Islamica, 1988), and R. C. Repp, The Mufti of Istanbul:

the first of the two *qiblas*, or directions of prayer, and the third of the Islamic holy places.[51] Those present salute the sultan using his various titles, prominently including that of protector of Jerusalem (*hami Bayt al-Maqdis*). They state that the consul carried with him an imperial document issued in Istanbul, which gave him permission to remain in Jerusalem, something that had never been allowed to a foreign diplomat under Islamic rule since the conquest of the city by 'Umar Ibn al-Khattab in the seventh century or its reconquest by Salah al-Din in the twelfth.

Those present at the meeting argued to the *qadi* and the governor that the consul's visit to Jerusalem violated the conditions imposed by 'Umar Ibn al-Khattab and later caliphs and that his behavior was a great evil, "especially since our city is the focus of attention of the infidels," suggesting considerable concern that the events of the Crusades could be repeated. The petition warned that "we fear that we will be occupied as a result of this, as happened repeatedly in past times," another clear reference to the Crusades. The *qadi* and the governor agreed with those present and requested the consul to leave, which he did. In conclusion, the petitioners asked that foreign consuls continue to be posted in Sidon, as had always been the case in the past, and requested that the sultan prevent the French consul from remaining "in this holy land" (*al-diyar al-qudsiyya*).[52]

This petition recapitulates the idea of Palestine as a special and sacred land with Jerusalem as its focus. Such a notion is found throughout the *fada'il al-Quds* literature and

---

A Study in the Development of the Ottoman Learned Hierarchy (London: Ithaca Press, 1986).

[51] "Awwal [*sic*] al-qiblatayn wa thalith al-haramain al-sharifain."

[52] The wording could also mean "this region of Jerusalem," but the other reading is more likely, and there is an implication of sanctity in both cases. That this petition was not exceptional in its stress on the sanctity of Jerusalem is indicated by another more routine one in Ottoman Turkish, dating from later in the eighteenth century. In this petition a large number of Jerusalem notables complain about the misbehavior of local military personnel in Jerusalem. The petition begins by stressing that Jerusalem is the "third of the holy places, its nobility protected until the day of Resurrection." The document, signed by the *qadi* of Jerusalem, Ma'nzade Muhammad, is also located in the Khalidi Library in Jerusalem.

shows that the sense of Palestine as an entity, whose importance Schölch stresses for the late nineteenth century, was in fact clearly present at least two centuries earlier. A careful reading of the petition shows that this idea of Palestine's special importance is, at least in part, rooted in the heightened Islamic concern for Jerusalem and Palestine that followed the traumatic episode of the Crusades and persisted long afterwards. Thus the assertion that Palestinian nationalism developed in response to the challenge of Zionism embodies a kernel of a much older truth: this modern nationalism was rooted in long-standing attitudes of concern for Palestine as a sacred entity in response to perceived external threats. The incursions of the European powers and the Zionist movement in the late nineteenth century were only the most recent examples of this threat.

These themes are recapitulated during one of the earliest cases of organized opposition to Zionist land purchase in Palestine: the al-Fula incident of 1910–1911. Many newspaper articles written in opposition to this sale stressed the special place of Palestine, for it was one of the biggest purchases up to that point and one of the earliest to lead to the eviction of large numbers of Palestinian peasants. In two anonymous articles in the Damascus paper *al-Muqtabas*, later reprinted in newspapers in Haifa, Beirut, and elsewhere, much is made of the presence on this land of the "fortress" of al-Fula, supposedly built by Saladin and shown in an illustration accompanying one article.[53]

This ruin, located at the center of the present-day Israeli settlement of Merhavia, was what remained of the Crusader castle of La Fève. Although not built by Saladin, it was captured by his forces in 1187 and is not far from Mount Tabor, a site dominated in the twelfth century by a still-extant Crusader fortress. The important thing was not whether the ruin had originally been built by Saladin: it was that these newspapers' readers believed that part of the heritage of Saladin, savior of Palestine from the Crusaders, was being sold off (by implica-

---

[53] See Khalidi, "The Role of the Press" 105–24. The two articles were in nos. 551 and 552, dated 19 and 20 December 1910. Two later articles deal with the sale, the first of a series by the wealthy Sursuq family of Beirut of property in the fertile and strategic Jezreel Valley.

tion, to the "new Crusaders") without the Ottoman government lifting a finger.

The government's alleged dereliction of its duty to restrict Zionist colonization was the focus of speeches made in Parliament on 16 May 1911 by Ruhi al-Khalidi and Hafiz Sa'id, deputies for Jerusalem. They were joined in their critique by Shukri al-'Asali, the newly elected deputy of Damascus and former governor of the Nazareth district, who had fought the al-Fula land sale in his previous post (and was probably the author of the anonymous articles about it) and who specifically mentioned the fortress in his intervention. But while this use of the Saladin/Crusader theme evoked the danger of Zionism in the Palestinian press,[54] it evoked only derision in the Ottoman Parliament, where other speakers demanded that the three deputies stop wasting the chamber's time with nonexistent problems such as that of Zionism.

In Palestine, by contrast, such ideas were seriously received, for al-Khalidi was reelected the following year in an election rigged by the government to rid itself of opposition in the Arab provinces, even though government loyalists described the debate on Zionism that he initiated as an antigovernmental ploy.[55] He retained his seat at a time when other critics of the government lost theirs, at least in part because in his speeches on Zionism before Parliament, which were widely reprinted in the local press, al-Khalidi appealed to ideas that resonated with his Palestinian constituents.[56] These longstanding ideas about Palestine as a holy land under threat from without, to which these men and others appealed, offered a focus of identity that was central to the local Palestinian patriotism that was the forerunner of the modern Palestinian nationalist movement.

---

[54] Articles on the subject were widely reprinted in such papers as *Filastin* in Jaffa and *al-Karmil* in Haifa, as well as *al-Nafir* in Jerusalem. *Filastin*, 27 May 1911, for example, carries extensive citations from the texts of the Parliamentary speeches, having earlier carried summaries.

[55] For more on this election, see R. Khalidi, "The 1912 Election Campaign in the Cities of *Bilad al-Sham*," *International Journal of Middle East Studies* 16, 4 (November 1984): 461–74.

[56] Zionism concerned al-Khalidi so much that he made an extensive study of the subject, about which he had just completed a book when he died in 1913.

This local patriotism could not yet be described as nation-state nationalism for the simple reason that the prerequisites for modern nationalism did not yet exist—notably, the means for mobilizing large numbers of people and rapidly winning them over to a single set of ideas, especially the idea that they partook of the same fate and were a single community. Yet the ideas represented in the 1701 petition were not restricted to the elite, as attested by the mass nature of the meeting at which it was adopted. This continuing attachment to Palestine in the face of an external threat constituted the basis upon which modern Palestinian nationalism was built when its pre-requisites—the press, historical novels, modern communications, the spread of education, and mass politics—appeared in the early decades of the twentieth century.

Following the 1908 Ottoman revolution, all these factors began to function together. As before, Jerusalem was the focus of Palestinian concern and the center of their responses to all external challenges. As in 1701, many Palestinians feared the territorial ambitions of external powers, albeit with more reason than their eighteenth-century predecessors. They expressed this fear in the 1911 Parliamentary speeches: al-Khalidi warned that "the aim of the Zionists ... is the creation of an Israeli kingdom [mamlaka isra'iliyya] whose capital will be Jerusalem," while al-'Asali declared that the Zionists intended "to create a strong state, for after taking possession of the land they will expel the inhabitants either by force or through the use of wealth."[57]

In spite of these early warnings, the Palestinians were less successful in confronting the external and internal challenges they faced in the twentieth century than their ancestors had been in 1701. Although recent Palestinian leaders have had access to newspapers and rapid means of communication and organization, as well as wielding new ideological tools giving them more power than their predecessors to mobilize people, these instruments of modern politics were not yet fully developed, nor had society changed rapidly enough to respond to them fully. Moreover, the Palestinians now faced foes with considerably greater abilities to organize and mobilize than they possessed.

---

[57] These speeches are quoted in *Filastin*, cited in n. 54.

Conclusion

To obtain a nuanced understanding of Palestinian history, we need to comprehend how the Palestinians reached this point and why, in consequence, the Zionist movement triumphed at their expense. This project demands that we give proper weight to all the different narratives that intertwine to make up Palestinian identity. Our objective should be scholarship that respects the specificity of the Palestinian experience without sacrificing the sophistication derived from an appreciation of how all these disparate narratives interact. This may help prevent the study of Palestinian history from sinking to the level of shameless chauvinistic self-glorification prevalent in much nationalist-influenced Middle Eastern historiography, whereby the writing of Arab, Turkish, Iranian, and Israeli history has yielded to ideological distortion and a blindness to the different strands that comprise the current reality of each modern nation-state in the region.

In the Arab world what has often been lacking—partly as a result of the influence of early Arab nationalist historiography—is an accurate appreciation of the importance of the Ottoman and Islamic heritage in the genesis of existing Arab nation-states. This deficiency is frequently combined with an overemphasis on even the most tenuous Arab connections and a tendency to "Arabize" much Islamic and pre-Islamic history. Turkish historiography has similarly slighted the Ottoman roots of the modern republic, as well as the Islamic and non-Turkish contributions to the Ottoman heritage, while rewriting earlier history in light of modern Turkish nationalist canons. Much Iranian historiography has minimized the influence of either non-Iranian or non-Islamic elements in Iranian history, while overstressing that of either Iranian or Islamic factors (the Islamic revolution of 1979 is the demarcation line between these contradictory trends). Israeli historiography and archaeology have often looked obsessively for evidence of the Jewish presence in Palestine, the majority of whose population for millennia were non-Jews, while neglecting elements of the larger pattern, except as background to Jewish history.[58]

---

[58] For a discussion of all of these problems, see R. Khalidi, "Arab Nationalism: Historical Problems in the Literature," *The American Historical Re-*

The possible pitfalls for the study of Palestinian identity include similar obsessions with elements of a larger pattern, in the Palestinian case usually Arab or Islamic ones. Another, unique pitfall is the tendency to focus on the external reasons for the failure of the Palestinian people to achieve self-determination to the exclusion of internal ones. The alignment between Britain and Zionism for thirty years of this century, and between the United States and Israel since then, engendered a daunting set of external challenges. But this cannot absolve students of Palestinian history from asking whether the Palestinians could not have improved their chances at certain critical junctures, and if they could have, what structural or other reasons prevented them from doing so.

Focusing on Palestinian social dynamics, I have suggested answers to these questions, and while there are other possible avenues of investigation, this would seem to be a fruitful one. It is hard for historians who are part of a society still suffering from the direct effects of such a series of historic failures to look self-critically at that society's flaws, and the consequences of not doing so are obvious. Much of the historical writing on this subject has been done by Israelis and others who harbor little apparent sympathy for their subject. But the defects of history written without empathy should be equally obvious. It is necessary for those with such empathy, as well as the unique access to and understanding of sources that often go with it, to address such questions rigorously. Without rigor, the writing of Palestinian history risks being tainted by the same chauvinism and disguised emotionalism that have already affected the writing of much other modern Middle Eastern history. These factors are partly responsible for leaving the Middle East field behind others, mired in naked partisanship, engaged in provincial debates of little interest to others, and

---

view 95, 5 (December 1991): 1363–64. Gil's *A History* illustrates the last ones mentioned perfectly: of its 840 pages, the last 350 are devoted almost exclusively to the history of the tiny Palestinian Jewish community, as are generous sections of the earlier parts of the book.

cut off from trends that affect the wider historical community. Although the study of Palestinian identity is far from a *tabula rasa*, perhaps it is not too late to avoid these pitfalls.

CRISIS OF CULTURE, CRISIS OF STATE:
André Malraux Ministers to French Culture, 1959–1969

Herman Lebovics

In recent years French intellectual life has been agitated to an unprecedented degree by a sense of cultural crisis. This is not the usual cultural hysteria of Left Bank intellectuals, which they, their friends, and obliging enemies spread in the press and the media to hype a new book or performance. Both the intensity and the self-absorption of the new mood are evident in Ariane Mnouchkine's denunciation of Eurodisney as a "cultural Chernobyl." Mnouchkine heads Le Théâtre du Soleil, which refreshes classical pieces in daring avant-garde performances. Drowning in U.S. sitcoms, ordered about by European Community bureaucrats, and apparently unable to assimilate a Muslim population of over two million as it has assimilated other immigrants in the past, France and her civilization are at risk of losing their historic identity, or so many literary intellectuals aver.

Moreover, today's alarms are being read back into the history of our half-century. In his wonderfully named *How New York Stole the Idea of Modern Art*—from Paris, to be sure—Serge Guilbaut argues that, soon after World War II, the U.S. State Department, the Office for International Information and Cultural Affairs (until 1953, precursor of the USIA), and Henry Luce at *Life* magazine conspired to promote American abstract expressionist artists as harbingers of the new and as part of an American hegemonic project after the victorious war to consolidate what Luce named "The American Century."[1] So not the German occupation nor postwar disorder but rather the unholy trinity of NATO, the Marshall Plan, and the artists who frequented the Cedar Bar in Greenwich Village united to de-

---

[1] Serge Guilbaut, *How New York Stole the Idea of Modern Art: Abstract Expressionism, Freedom, and the Cold War* (Chicago: University of Chicago Press, 1983). See also his edited volume, *Reconstructing Modernism: Art in New York, Paris, and Montreal, 1945–1964* (Cambridge, MA: MIT Press, 1990), especially Guibaut's "Introduction" (ix–xvii), his essay "Postwar Painting Games: The Rough and the Slick" (30–84), and the piece by John-Franklin Koenig, "Abstraction Chaude in Paris in the 1950s" (1–16).

throne the admittedly waning creative leadership of the School of Paris and thereby threaten France's historic role as cultural leader of the West, and by extension its standing as a world power. For all the bitter conflicts between them, in the postwar years the Gaullists shared with French Communists that vision of the danger to France.

Of all the high cultural worries American conservatives write about, contamination from foreign cultures is not one of them. By their lights, it is the vulgar innovations of domestic culture that are to be feared. Indeed, the secular-academic wing of American conservatism prizes borrowings from foreign and ancient high cultures as America's most beneficial imports. And I am persuaded that foreign cultural influences—more than Frederick Jackson Turner's frontier—have profoundly marked American civilization. Until the end of World War II, at least, we ran a deficit in international cultural accounts: we borrowed more from other cultures than we produced and exported of our own.

Historically, the rewards to those who embrace such syncretism have been splendid. The French anthropologist Marc Augé reminds us that great moments of cultural creativity come at times of great cultural exchange and mixing—even the mixing engendered by wars or social conflict. Following Lévy-Strauss, Augé names Italy during the Renaissance as one locus of such intense cultural exchange and hence creativity. I would add Europe in the thirty years between 1914 and 1945 and the United States in the decades after 1945.[2] So what today, and indeed for nearly half a century now, fuels the anxieties and cataclysmic utterances of French intellectuals and cultural policy officials? Hasn't France's role as the second homeland of humankind enriched French culture? Why in the last half-century has there been fear for the life of the culture, and how has this threatened cultural identity been defended?

---

[2] Marc Augé, concluding remarks of the plenary session, "Actes des colloques de la Direction du Patrimoine: Patrimoine et société contemporaine," held in Paris 7–11 October 1987 (Paris, 1988) 55–57. It is clear that the arts do not march or retreat together. The years between 1914 and 1945 were generally glorious for literature and theater in Europe, and even for art and architecture in Germany. But compared to what had come before, French art—especially the School of Paris—produced little that was innovative or notable.

I want here to propose that perhaps the most important innovation in French culture since World War II was not existentialism, the new novel, or the New Wave in films, nor even the various philosophical movements that have had so great an impact on contemporary American letters, but rather the creation of an organization to protect and spread French culture at home and abroad. France's first Ministry of Cultural Affairs was initiated by Charles de Gaulle in the early days of the Fifth Republic. From 1959 to 1969 its organizer and first minister was the novelist, art writer, war hero, and mystical left-Gaullist, André Malraux.

Peter Bürger's idea of the "institution of art," the socio-aesthetic norms that validate cultural life and inform concrete art institutions and practices, will guide what follows. Without coercion or travail these norms work to include or exclude certain practices, movements, ideas, and critical positions in the arts. What, for example, would have been the fate of a painter who did history paintings in France in the 1920s and 1930s? A more complex analysis is needed to understand the institution of art in the era of de Gaulle and Malraux, which stressed not so much artistic style but rather the place of art in society and the relation of the arts to one another in a new discourse of culture. André Malraux tried to save the hegemonic institution of art in 1960s France. I will say more about this at the end.

I think that at least three historical moments came together to make the crucial cultural project that, upon taking office, Malraux embraced: 1) The culture of the Classical Age and its derivations were the "glue" of modern France. In the unstable political situation from 1945 to 1959, this *imaginaire* of classical, humanist France served as an important component of national unity and class harmony; 2) in a social transformation vast enough for some specialists to speak of a Second Revolution in the thirty years after the war, France experienced an economic development that detached its citizens from their old lives and cast them adrift in potentially anomic modernity. The familiar historic culture eased the transition *and* furthered modernization. Finally, 3) passing after the war from the status of a weak major power to something rather less, and stripped of its colonies, France deployed its culture—especially its language and arts—to give it a comparative advantage in the new international competition.

Let us first consider the unique role of culture in the making of modern France. We do not have to endorse the old-book fetishism of J. D. Hirsch, Allan Bloom, or the French supporters of the ideas of Leo Strauss such as Tzvetan Todorov and Marc Fumaroli[3] to see the centrality of culture in the creation, expansion, and preservation of France. France was not made out of an alliance of peoples with self-conscious identities who worked out a political union, as was the Dutch Republic, Switzerland, the United States, or, since 1989, Germany. Rather, a small royal power created a state in the course of the Middle Ages and, for the sake of its domination and glory, set out to create a people. Because this state's power was at all times as centralized as the means of communication and coercion permitted, struggles about what was France and who spoke for the French people tended to be claims for hegemonic domination rather than proposals for inclusion. Thus during the Revolution, and indeed building on the heritage of monarchical Absolutism, the Jacobins set out to make a land of many regions and diverse populations a unitary republic. Just as the *ancien régime* saw as part of its responsibilities— however sporadically or faintheartedly carried out before 1789—the regulation of religious belief and practice, rules of language, aesthetic standards of theater, art, and architecture, and what might be published, so the Jacobins attempted to create a different, but equally total, definition of France to negate the weakened old order and contradict that of the counterrevolution to come.

During the Revolution sovereignty, the embodiment of France, was transferred from the king to the male members of the nation and in the Restoration back again to the king, in a combat that continued in subsequent centuries. Using Disraeli's image for what was wrong with Britain, Pierre Nora has characterized this struggle over French identity as that of the

---

[3] See his recycling of the "moderate humanism" of Montesquieu as the antidote for contemporary intolerance in a book that represents something of a leap backwards for a man known earlier for his contributions to structuralist and semiotic writing. Tzvetan Todorov, *On Human Diversity: Nationalism, Racism, and Exoticism in French Thought* (Cambridge, MA: Harvard University Press, 1993), trans. by Catherine Porter of *Nous et les autres: La Réflexion française sur la diversité humaine* (Paris: Seuil, 1989). Marc Fumaroli, *L'Etat culturel: Essai sur une religion moderne* (Paris: Editions de Fallois, 1991).

two nations of France. Politically, France reconciled its two selves, its dual personality, according to Nora, when from 1959 onward de Gaulle united the authoritarian monarchical tradition with that of the republican nation. His new presidential republic was accepted and left intact by the socialists when they came to power in 1981.[4]

Culturally, national unity took the form of assimilating the population to a common culture, which from the late nineteenth century was classical in content and republican in its prescriptions.[5] French republicanism interpreted the logic of the nation-state as requiring that political boundaries approximate cultural ones or, even more exactly, that to share in the life of the nation one had to be a part of the national culture. This imperative of unity, then, required the French state to concern itself deeply with the culture of its citizens in the areas of language and aesthetics, the policy inherited from the *ancien régime*. But also for the last hundred years, in view of the strong pulls of regionalism, the many immigrants, the ever-evoked menace of clericalism, and, most important, the need to conduct government under the constraints of universal male, then female, suffrage, the national society had to be brought along to think of itself as one.[6]

Accordingly, to violate this cultural unity with American words and food, Islamic beliefs and exclusiveness, and European Community agricultural standards and policies was to threaten the cohesion—perhaps the existence—of the French nation. In France, at least, postmodern multiplicity threatens the inherited vision of national life. There are, and have always been, foreign cultural borrowings to be sure; but to love first

---

[4] Pierre Nora, "Nation," in *Dictionnaire critique de la Révolution française, 1780–1880*, ed. François Furet and Mona Ozouf (Paris: Flammarion, 1988).

[5] Gérard Noiriel, *Le Creuset français: Histoire de l'immigration, XIXe-XXe siècles* (Paris: Seuil, 1988) 50–67. Eugen Weber, *Peasants into Frenchmen: The Modernization of Rural France (1870–1914)* (Stanford: Stanford University Press, 1976).

[6] De Gaulle decided to liquidate France's political control of Algeria in 1959–60 when he realized that the price of keeping Algeria French had to be to give Arabs and Berbers full citizenship. He did not want natives of the colonies voting and influencing the fate of his France. Jean Lacouture, *De Gaulle: The Ruler, 1945–1970*, trans. Alan Sheridan (New York: Norton, 1992) 243–50, 487.

Jerry Lewis, then Woody Allen, and recently Sylvester Stallone enough to admit them as Chevaliers de l'ordre des Arts et des Lettres, for example, was not such a threat, since these were (each in his way) Americans to laugh at.

So in 1959 in the crisis over whether Algeria would remain France, Charles de Gaulle, called back from writing his memoirs in his farmhouse outside of Paris to become president of the new Fifth Republic, combined the various offices charged with oversight of French cultural production into a new Ministry of Cultural Affairs. As he explained to the new premier Michel Debré, he put the ex-red and now fervent mystical Gaullist André Malraux at its head to give the new administration a "high profile."[7]

We know Malraux primarily as an author of political-existential novels about the Spanish Civil War and the communist movement in China. Many of his works drew from his own experiences. He had organized a group of French flyers to aid the Spanish Republican government during the Civil War and had taken part in bombing missions against Francist targets. And although he played no role in the revolutionary movement in China, he had edited an anticolonial newspaper in Indochina (actually, Vietnam) until the French governor general shut it down.

But the main political experience that shaped his future thinking about the relation of culture to politics was the French Popular Front of the mid-1930s. From his deep involvement with the left in those days, he learned two ideas that he retained into his Gaullist years: first, the state had to assume a large and continuous responsibility for the life of the nation's culture; and second, culture needed to be spread down the social ladder, a process understood in the 1930s as democratization of the high culture. Just as in the 1880s Jules Ferry had created a school system to make education available to all, so in the 1960s Malraux wanted culture to be equally universal.

---

[7] Michel Debré, *Gouverner, Mémoires*, vol. 3 (Paris: A. Michel, 1987) 246. Geneviève Poujol, "The Creation of a Ministry of Culture in France," *French Cultural Studies* 2 (1991): 251–60. Ministère de la Culture et de la Communication, "Journées d'étude sur la création du ministère de la culture, 30 novembre-1er décembre 1989," photocopied talks by former coworkers of Malraux and researchers (Paris, 1989).

In 1959 Malraux had never run anything larger than his small band of volunteer flyers in Spain and the tank brigade made up of Alsatian volunteers he formed during the last months of the French Liberation. And neither of these did he lead sitting at a desk. But as the novelist, art critic, idealist, and patriot whom de Gaulle saw as the best contemporary personification of French aesthetic values, he was the perfect choice to orchestrate state management of culture. By the late 1930s Malraux had become disenchanted with Moscow and French Communism. In the war years he responded deeply to de Gaulle's call for French renewal. A soldier-existentialist, he saw art as the only enduring value in the face of death. A searcher, he saw the arts as the twentieth-century way to fill the void left by the death of God. Within this vision art museums could become, for him and he believed for his fellow citizens, the new cathedrals. Still imbued with the spirit of the old Popular Front and now adding a Gaullist authoritarian overlay, he believed that the people had to be given access by the provident state not just to the old mandarin *civilisation française* but to *the* culture: this new inclusive, total involvement of all the French in a common spiritual destiny, in a certain idea of France.

Initially, Malraux staffed his new ministry with some individuals willing to transfer from National Education. But the biggest part of the new team came—with fascinating implications of a domestic *mission civilisatrice* guided by top-down rule—from the colonial service. With France rapidly losing its colonial empire, many colonial civil servants were suddenly available to employ their skills at home. Administratively, Malraux directed the Beaux Arts (museums and national art school), the national theaters, opera, and ballet, the Paris Conservatory of Music, the state cinema administration and cinematography school, and—his special interest—the regional Houses of Culture. With the possible exception of the cinema branch, which he inherited from the Ministry of Commerce and which was initially concerned with more technical than creative matters, Malraux set out to guide the heritage of France's high, Paris-defined culture. This was a large responsibility for a man who never finished high school and who had gained entry into the world of arts and letters by working as a *chineur*, a person who scavenges the quays and small bookshops for rare books and prints to resell to fine book dealers.

But since France had managed all these centuries without such a ministry, why create one now? With the exception of the cinema office and the regional Houses of Culture he created, the other fine arts activities had been unified under one administration since before the Revolution. Moreover, wasn't the Opera packed every night? Didn't the Comédie Française fill its hall for every performance of Molière or Racine? The long lines of visitors from all over the world waiting to enter the Louvre bespoke the treasures inside. But the reassuring continuation of these old habits of cultural consumption masked the deep cultural problems France faced.

The rest of this essay probes the three major existential challenges that confronted France in the years leading up to the cultural rebellion of May 1968 and Malraux's attempts to respond to them. The challenges were, first, that of keeping a True France alive in culture; second, and paradoxically, modernizing France; and third, making it once again a great power in the world. These tasks were interconnected.

Malraux had witnessed the fall of France to the technically sophisticated military prowess of the Germans in 1940 and, after the war, the decline of France as a major power. Now he confronted the prospect of the cultural fall of France in the face of science, technology, the famous American Way of Life, but above all internal disunity. Largely an autodidact, he realized that the *civilisation* of the Classical Age and its emanations was limited to a tiny stratum of the population; in 1959 it could not unite a divided people, let alone represent the true France abroad. The current generation of young people was finding the old humanist and authoritarian France not to its liking. An overburdened educational system oriented toward the humanities was creating individuals ill-fitted for life in modern industrial culture. Much of the thematic content and intensity of French intellectual life in the second half of this century may be traced to the social angst of the best students who studied philosophy or literature—France's scholastic princes—as they discovered their verbal skills increasingly devalorized in prestige and devalued in market worth in a new scientific and technologically sophisticated society. Education—not Malraux's portfolio—needed reform, to be sure. But taking a word that French intellectuals had contemptuously associated with German holistic thinking, Malraux and his co-workers concluded that only *the culture* of France could bring together generations, regions, and classes. Confronted with an ill fit between population and culture, Malraux wagered that he could reconstruct the people to fit the culture. It is altogether appropriate that France at this period formed a thinker like Michel Foucault, the analyst of the controlling discourses of the Classical Age.

By the end of the 1950s, once the physical and economic reconstruction of France was well underway and people had begun to experience postwar prosperity, France's political elite started to realize that the inherited culture was in institutional disarray. Badly staged, badly played and sung, performances at the Opera were musical jokes; and those at the Comédie Française attracted primarily tourists and schoolchildren marched there by their teachers. Art created in France after 1900 could be seen either in American museums—the French state had not purchased France's great modern artists—or in a few samples crowded together in the Jeu de Paume, the tiny narrow hall off the Place de la Concorde that had been built as a court for an early variant of indoor tennis. Workers and peasants who dared cross the threshold of museums described feeling awed before the great cultural treasures, as in a church—not a positive comparison in an increasingly irreligious country.[8] Great monuments of French architecture were collapsing from neglect, and historic districts, quarters, and even whole towns and villages[9] were beginning to be targeted for urban renewal by French real estate developers. Most potent symbolically, Coca-Cola had just built its first bottling plant on French soil.[10]

Second, the rapid and sustained economic development of France from 1945 to about 1974, especially in the regions—

---

[8] Pierre Bourdieu, Alain Darbel; with Dominique Schnapper, *The Love of Art: European Art Museums and Their Public*, trans. Caroline Beattie and Nick Merriman (Stanford: Stanford University Press, 1990).

[9] Examples include the Marais in Paris, Aix-en-Provence, Amien, Avignon, Chartres, Sarlat, Troyes, Rousillon (Laurence Wylie's Village in the Vaucluse).

[10] On the symbolism of Coca-Cola in French public life see Richard Kuisel, "Coca-Cola and the Cold War: The French Face Americanization," *French Historical Studies* 17 (1991): 96–116, and his *Seducing the French: The Dilemma of Americanization* (Berkeley and Los Angeles: University of California Press, 1993).

aerospace around Toulouse, high-tech around Grenoble and in the South, urbanization everywhere with the modernization of agriculture and the plummet of the farming population—generated higher incomes and amenities for all classes but also a national crisis of identity. French advertising tried to master the contradictions with the famous television and print ads in which la Mère Denis, a ruddy, hearty peasant woman, the sort one still saw doing their wash in the public basins in small towns after the war, extols the virtues of the new electric washing machines. But what goes as cultural change in advertising does not always capture the deeper anomies of great social transformations.

Nor could national television and advertising replace the solidarity of culture in a nation like France, where, unlike the United States, the school system was still decisive in socializing participants in the *civilisation française*. On the contrary, the extent to which the old learned print culture infiltrated television programming, corrupting the purity of the new medium, is remarkable. There were, for example, primetime discussions of scholarly books,[11] the national *dictée* (a spelling bee *cum* grammar quiz), and casts-of-thousands Hollywood pharaoh movies followed by long, learned, and passionate discussions about the archaeology of the New Kingdom period by Egyptologists.

In a word, to create a modern industrial society in this historically capital-centered nation, the talented and educated—the new middle class, called *cadre*—would have to live either in Paris or *as if* in Paris. De Gaulle and Malraux began the process, today largely completed, of "decentralization," in effect multiplying the culture and sophistication of Paris in all the urban centers of France. Just two years ago, in the continuation of this policy, the National School of Administration was moved from Paris to Strasbourg. The highest strata of the state's elite civil service will now be trained in the provinces to rule France. May we reasonably see this move as a blow to what the French term *Parisienisme*? Sometimes, as here, decentering strengthens the forces of tradition rather than defeating them.

---

[11] Such scholarly discussions propelled Emmanuel Le Roy Ladurie, among other academics, to media stardom.

Internationally, too, there was work for culture to perform. In brief, if the elites of the ex-colonies continued to write in French, they might more readily sign commercial contracts written in that language; and if cultured elites everywhere continued to be open to the charms of French civilization— including the export to the United States of French cooking as both taught and complicated by Julia Child and associates and the traveling exhibitions representing France's trusteeship of European culture (for example, the *Mona Lisa* to New York and Washington, the *Venus de Milo* to Japan)—then France could certainly expect to bank a good deal of what Pierre Bourdieu calls "symbolic capital."[12]

The main task of Malraux's new ministry, then, was to address these three areas: maintaining national unity, cushioning and furthering economic development, and enhancing France's standing among the nations. His actions in these spheres bear on the qualities of the institution of art during the 1960s. Malraux was convinced that "the civilization of machines and of science, the most powerful civilization the world has ever known, has been able to create not a temple nor a tomb. Nor, stranger still, its own *imaginaire*." There was only the culture of the past to guide the French, for the cultural production of the machine age, such as it was, he disdainfully dismissed: "for the first time dreams are made in factories."[13] Hollywood films, radio, records, television—all products of the factories of dreams. With this grand judgment, meant to repudiate the effects of "Americanization," Malraux in effect also dismissed France's rich aesthetic encounters with the machine

---

[12] Pierre Bourdieu, *Les Régles de l'art: Genèse et structure du champ littéraire* (Paris: Editions du Seuil, 1992) esp. 393–430; *The Field of Cultural Production* (New York: Columbia University Press, 1993) 29–141; and, with Loic Wacquant, *An Invitation to Reflexive Sociology* (Chicago: University of Chicago Press, 1992). A chapter in my forthcoming book on the origins of France's first Ministry of Culture deals with how and when the French got the idea that France was the trustee of Western civilization.

[13] "La civilisation des machines et de la science, la plus puissante civilisation que le monde ait connue, n'a été capable de créer ni un temple ni un tombeau. Ni ce que est plus étrange, son propre imaginaire"; "pour la première fois les rêves ont leurs usines." The address given by André Malraux at the inauguration of the House of Culture at Grenoble, 6 February 1968, as originally carried by *Le Monde*; rpt. *Le Monde*, 6 August 1986.

age in the 1920s and 1930s through Fernand Leger, the makers of the ballet *Parade*, and the Surrealists. In any case, when he concretely addressed the growing irrelevance and/or challenges to France's most treasured inherited values, that is, the general crisis of classical French culture in the postwar years (of which existentialism was both a symptom and an attempted cure), Malraux could offer only weak and belated responses, as the explosion of May 1968 showed.

He tried to make the institutions in place run better: asking Jean Vilar to reform the state theaters of Paris and the Opera, for example—largely without success, except for the appointment of Madeleine Renaud and Jean-Louis Barrault to head a new Théâtre de France. His strategy for democratization—cheap reproductions of great masters, night hours at state museums, legally protecting historic buildings and sectors, advancing domestic archaeological work for the sake of the *patrimoine* (the cultural heritage) and of tourism—was, in retrospect, like trying to upgrade the accommodations of steerage passengers as the ship sinks. For the real problem of France was not so much the old French republican and leftist charge that access to cultural capital in France was undemocratic but the growing general depreciation in the value of accumulated old culture. Or more precisely, de Gaulle's drive to modernize France to make it a stable and powerful state was undermining the classical cultural tradition Malraux was trying to save and diffuse.

To be sure, a similar decanonization was occurring in other parts of Europe and America. Daniel Bell has termed the social dilemmas of maintaining inherited cultural values and submitting to the logic of modernization "the cultural contradictions of capitalism."[14] But the special place of culture in the construction of the French nation made, and makes, the crisis both more profound and more dangerous there.

Not content just to conserve the best of old France, Malraux dedicated the Ministry of Cultural Affairs to the work of modernizing the nation as well. His efforts primarily took the form of encouraging national culture in the hinterlands of Paris: a kind of *dirigiste*, or top-down, regionalism.

---

[14] Daniel Bell, *The Cultural Contradictions of Capitalism* (New York: Basic Books, 1976).

He could build on the experience of the war years. The exigencies of the German occupation of first part, then all of France made decentralization an unalterable fact of French public life. This fact, however, both encouraged old-fashioned conservative regionalists to entertain great hopes for transcending the territorial organization created by the Revolution and at the same time gave Vichy modernizing technocrats the opportunity to develop new ideas for regional planning. After the war, Gaullism could mine both the backward-looking and modernizing traditions in French economic, political, and above all cultural policies.

Malraux tried to reform music and art training in provincial centers. Where it existed, he tried to encourage local initiatives, such as Jean Vilar's Avignon Festival. But the centerpiece in his regional strategy was to create little Paris cultural hubs all over the country. The armature of a truly national French culture began to take form as, one after another, Malraux built Houses of Culture (modeled after the PCF-created one during the Popular Front) in different parts of France to provide local people the theater, arts, music, and classic cinema that in the past had only been accessible to Parisians. With his Houses of Culture he hoped finally to abolish the phrase he detested above all others—*the provinces*. At the heart of these institutions—some dozen were built before May 1968 united their directors and staffs against Gaullism—were theaters, often with resident companies. In significant ways under Malraux and in the realm of high culture, France changed from Paris and the French desert to a multicentered interconnected nation, still steered, of course, from Paris.

Finally, Malraux tried to package French civilization for foreign consumption. By the twentieth century France had a secure reputation as the great exporter of finely wrought, elegant consumer goods, wines, fashion, impressionist art, and tourism (which counts as an export in international balance of payments accounting). The use of culture as a weapon of diplomacy, war, and commerce is not new, and France, since at least Francis I in the Renaissance, has been a brilliant strategist of the game. But the military and political deadlock of the Cold War years of the 1960s made cultural policy more important than ever before: what one well-connected commentator at the time called the "fourth dimension" of foreign policy, equal to diplomatic, military, and economic strategies.[15] With most of the European belligerents still nursing fragile economies, with the proliferation of atomic weapons and power-bloc diplomacy giving nations little free play or room for error, ideology was an arena of possible and important contestation. The political rise of the so-called "third world" made contests over the hearts and minds of people central in the postwar years. And cultural display, sparring, and influence were the weapons of choice.

France had a cultural service in its diplomatic arsenal, but André Malraux was France's not-very-secret new weapon. On the model of de Gaulle presenting himself as the voice of the essential French nation, Malraux presented himself as the embodiment of France's civilizing mission. He traveled all over the world: to charm Jacqueline Kennedy with compliments on her French and on the holdings of the National Gallery in Washington, to talk over past parallel struggles against injustice with Nehru, to be celebrated in the People's Republic of China for his *Condition humaine* (translated in English as *Man's Fate*), and to remind nationalist leaders in colonial France what heritage they risked losing if they broke completely with France. When in January 1963 he inaugurated the Washington exhibition of the Louvre's *Mona Lisa*, jokingly referring to the Gaullist project of making France an independent nuclear power, President John Kennedy paid tribute to the power of the Louvre's most visited painting by calling it France's "own independent artistic strike force."[16] As Malraux told the members of the Assemblée nationale after the triumphal Japanese tour of the Louvre's *Venus de Milo*, "Four million Japanese saw the French flag hung behind this statue. In Japan as in Brazil when people come to applaud France, they come to applaud the generosity [*générosité*] of spirit expressed by the French genius."[17] Malraux here seems to have conferred French citi-

---

[15] Philip H. Coombs, *The Fourth Dimension of Foreign Policy: Educational and Cultural Affairs* (New York: Harper & Row for the Council on Foreign Relations, 1964).

[16] From Malraux's report to President de Gaulle and the Council of State, 16 January 1963. Alain Peyrefitte, *C'était de Gaulle*, vol. 1: "*La France redevient la France*" (Paris: Fayard, 1994) 358.

[17] "Il y a ... eu quatre millions de Japonais pour aller voir le drapeau français placé derrière cette statue. Au Japon comme au Brésil, lorsque les

zenship retroactively on the Greek statue, while at the same time holding to the special French mission of representing Western civilization abroad.

As provisional conclusions, or more accurately a progress report on a project in process, I will propose a number of insights that might guide further reflections on the themes I have raised. First, we see in the France of the thirty years of post–World War II economic and social development the completion—that is, both the perfection and the finale—of its inherited *grande Civilisation*. In more than one way, de Gaulle had put Malraux in charge of museums.

Second, the notion that New York stole the idea of modern art from Paris obscures a much more interesting story of French *and* American cultural crisis, but one not confined to a few years after World War II. The blow-up of May 1968 marks the judgment that Paris was unsuccessful in keeping its old culture alive. An aesthetic vanguard needs an establishment both to attack but also to orient itself. We may observe, as the intellectual prelude to the 1968 Refusal, that in the late 1950s and 1960s an avant-garde with no great aesthetic bastions to overthrow (certainly none in art) was searching for other means of orientation while indulging in the unprecedented possibilities for aesthetic anarchy like truants at an untended candy counter.[18]

---

gens viennent applaudir la France, ils viennent applaudir la générosité de l'esprit exprimé par le génie français." Assemblée nationale, 7 November 1964. See further Charles-Louis Foulon, "L'Etat et le gouvernement des Affaires culturelles de 1959 à 1974," *Culture et Société: Cahiers Français*, no. 260 (March–April 1993): 18–31.

[18] Since at least the Revolution, the French state, although powerful in the cultural realm, has rarely favored aesthetic innovation. Patricia Mainardi suggests that, just because art-creating was heavily controlled before the Revolution, stylistic innovation represented few risks to the regime so it was welcomed and encouraged. When in the nineteenth century aesthetic rebellion threatened to converge with political upheaval, the state—especially the Republics—showed little interest in encouraging arts troublemakers. The important role of writers and theater people in May 1968 suggests that the leaders of the Fifth Republic were right to be nervous about the political undependability of even state-sponsored artists. Conversation with Mainardi, 6 December 1993. On the normalcy of changes in styles in the Old Regime and pastiche and no style in the nineteenth century, at least in French furniture, see

The upheaval of 1968 made it evident that a cultural return to order was impossible. It ended the Malraux ministry
and the de Gaulle government. The movements of the 1970s
and 1980s whose names begin with *post* signified the attempt
by the French cultural elite to celebrate the end of the hegemony of both classicism *and* the modernist avant-garde. Despite
their insurgent rhetorics, however, the discourses of poststruc-
turalism, postmodernity, and postcolonialism were conceptual
moves to bring *some* coherence to a world without cultural
authority.

For its part, the French state since the 1970s has poured
millions into reviving the old cultural ideals/idols. Under the
new president, Georges Pompidou, France in the 1970s finally
established an important museum of modern art and music,
the Centre Beaubourg. Paris could now participate once again
in the world of modernism, even if it could no longer lead it or
keep it alive. In a space Le Corbusier had wanted to build a
new hotel, Valéry Giscard d'Estaing had the nineteenth-
century Gare d'Orsay transformed into a museum of nineteenth-century culture. And after 1981 the *grands travaux* of
the Socialist president François Mitterand manifested the same
cultural conservatism: the expansion and renovation of the
entrance to the Louvre, the creation of a new socialist arch of
triumph at the edge of the city, and, most amazing in this new
computer age, construction of a massive new national library
with corner towers designed like four open books sunning
themselves.

Third, the place of French culture in creating France's
world standing, the importance of reproducing cultural Paris
all over France for the labor and investment mobility required
for French economic development, the very role of culture in
making France, have been little appreciated by scholars innocent of exactly how the state, social institutions, and economic
determinants interact with the language of texts and images
embedded in discourses both to make and to change cultures.
I have here briefly sketched a number of dominant values in
the French state's idea of French culture, the norms that both
validated French cultural practices and made alternative aesthetics, institutions, and practices impossible, or at best mar-

Leora Auslander's new *Taste and Power: Furnishing Modern France* (Berkeley:
University of California Press, 1996).

ginal. I have also suggested some concrete, material connections between this structure of values and institutions and practices in postwar France.

I wish to propose that the hegemonic "institution of art" in the Malraux years was the idea of French aesthetic culture as a unity. This idea of French culture understood as a *totality* repressed the diversity of real art forms with different creative trajectories and audiences; it gave the different art forms and styles their meanings and licensed the actual social-cultural organizations and practices of arts production, reproduction, and consumption. The idea of French culture in Malraux's sense was integrally connected to national life in France rather than being merely a way of generalizing about what writers, artists, and theater people were doing. So for de Gaulle and Malraux there was high culture and no culture. Nonculture included kitsch, of course, and the products of the machine age—for example, television, which was only good for news, political messages by the General, and mere entertainment. Neither de Gaulle nor Malraux took the media seriously as cultural expression, with the possible exception of film. Malraux had himself made a film about the Spanish Civil War and as minister helped fund the making and distribution of French films. The Gaullist regime systematically censored or tilted the news transmitted by the state-owned broadcast media.

The Malraux-era institution of art privileged the word over the visual or the musical.[19] Looking in this way at the institution of art in 1960s France, it seems to me, makes sense of the policies and emphases of France's first cultural ministry, as I have sketched them. And this approach might help us get beyond current word play yet not fall into a reductionist institutionalism. Certainly, both André Malraux and his critics believed that language, life, art, politics, and the annual budget of the Ministry of Cultural Affairs were deeply connected.

---

[19] Peter Bürger, "Literary Institution and Modernization," in his *Decline of Modernism*, trans. Nicholas Walker (Cambridge: Polity, 1992) 3–18; in *Institutions of Art*, published with Christa Bürger, trans. Loren Kruger (Lincoln, NE: University of Nebraska Press, 1992) his sections, 4–5, 16, 23, 71. See further the same line of argument in Roland Barthes—which Bürger draws upon—in Barthes's essay "Histoire ou littérature?" *Sur Racine* (Paris: Seuil, 1963) 149–52.

An episode from the student-initiated uprising of May 1968 may serve as a useful metonymy of Malraux's cultural project and an appropriate conclusion to this essay. In the headiest moments of the Great Refusal of '68, the intellectuals and those who joined them wished the movement of May to inaugurate a cultural revolution that would dethrone tradition and bring imagination to power. Accordingly, the students at the Beaux Arts did the posters for the rebellion. In a dramatic gesture from the stage of the nation's most prestigious theater, Jean-Louis Barrault declared that henceforth Jean-Louis Barrault was dead; by this piece of early performance art, he joined the student mob occupying his building. The directors of Malraux's Houses of Culture met to vote support of the students and to denounce the Gaullist government.

At a meeting of his senior staff in the middle of the troubles, Malraux and his department heads discussed what could be done, what had to be done. The students had started to escalate their actions beyond just ripping up trees and paving stones to build barricades in the Latin Quarter; they were moving out of their academic ghetto on the Left Bank and had begun attacking what a ministry staff member called "symbols:" The day before, they had set fire to the Bourse. Malraux began speaking.

> "Take a symbol more spectacular than the archives or the Gobelin tapestry works," he said, "take the Louvre. What if they attack the Louvre as the symbol of the culture...." And all of a sudden, observed with astonishment, Pierre Moinot, the head of the cinema administrator, who reports this account in his memoirs, [Malraux] *saw* the Louvre besieged, the rioters pouring in at the Sunday entrance, invading Classical Antiquity, surging toward the great stairway. "We'll let them get that far," he said, "none of the statues down there are fragile, we have lots of copies; we can let them get that far. But at the grand stairway, before the [statute of the Winged Victory of] Samothrace, I'd be there on the stairway. All of you would be behind me. We'd be there, arms outstretched...."

Malraux employed an image that signifies both a desperate defense of the classical cultural heritage and the final agony of Jesus.

Moinot's sad assessment: "Confronting the mob of idol smashers, in front of the Samothrace, protecting this cold and yet divine piece of stone, A.M. evoked a vision of his own death."[20]

---

[20] Pierre Moinot, *Tous comptes faits* (Paris: Quai Voltaire, 1993) 137–38.

PART THREE: THE URBAN HETEROCLITE

QUEER SITES IN MODERNISM:
Harlem/The Left Bank/Greenwich Village

Joseph A. Boone

I

> Thus I lie, and find no peace
> Night or day no slight release
> from the intermittent beat
> made by cruel padded feet
> Walking through my body's street.
> —Countee Cullen, "Heritage"[1]

In contrast to the institutionalization of high modernism that the very names Joyce and Woolf have come to signify over the course of the twentieth century, this essay investigates a much less institutionalized, indeed deviating and deviant mod-

For important help in conceiving and writing this essay, I owe many thanks to Susan Stanford Friedman, who first encouraged me to develop these ideas by inviting me to be part of a series of panels she organized at the 1994 MLA Convention on "The New Modernist Studies"; Dale Wall, who shared with me his extensive knowledge and bibliography of urban design and spatial theory (and without whose influence, indeed, this reading would never have occurred to me); and David Roman, who, at the eleventh hour, provided me with some of my best sentences. I am also grateful to the responsive audiences that this paper met at the MLA and at the Graduate Center at CUNY.

[1] Cullen, *On These I Stand: An Anthology of the Best Poems of Countee Cullen* (1947; rpt. New York: Harper and Row, 1927) 16. "Heritage" is dedicated to Harold Jackman, Cullen's longtime lover, in a volume of verse dedicated, interestingly enough, to Cullen's wife, the daughter of W. E. B. Du Bois. These specific lines are quoted by the gay protagonist of Blair Niles's *Strange Brother*, cited in n. 6 below, to describe his relation to the city life and particularly to Harlem, where he has made peace with his homosexuality. For mentions of Cullen's lifelong relationship with Jackson, see Eric Garber, "A Spectacle in Color: The Lesbian and Gay Subculture of Jazz Age Harlem," in *Hidden in History: Reclaiming the Gay and Lesbian Past*, ed. Martin Duberman, Martha Vicinus, and George Chauncey, Jr. (New York: Meridian, 1989) 327; and David Levering Lewis, *When Harlem Was in Vogue* (New York: Knopf, 1984) 76.

ernist practice, one emanating from the gay and protogay urban spaces of the Left Bank, Greenwich Village, and Harlem in the 1920s and 1930s. I will argue that this alternative modernist enterprise created linguistically complex, highly experimental fictions as well as popular texts of mass culture that are not only worth examining in their own right but whose circulations of sexual and textual desire fascinatingly foreshadow the rise of what is now being called "queer" in current gay studies, arts, and politics. The potentially disruptive power of these visions of modernity cannot be separated from the quintessentially urban experience—an experience unique to the twentieth century—that provides the geographical and textual "sites" within which their depictions of queer identity and community unfold.

Before linking these urban spaces and literary modernism further, however, I need to justify the applicability of the adjective *queer*—until recently a term of violently homophobic disapprobation—to this historically specific context. I will do this, first, by turning to appropriations and redefinitions of the term in today's gay cultural scene and, second, by intimating its relevance to the revisionary modernist project of this essay. Indeed, in what has been an amazingly short span of time, the proliferation of the word *queer* in lesbian and gay politics, arts, and culture, in the academy, and on the street indicates a term whose radical usefulness is quickly superseding its various and sometimes contradictory meanings. "The appeal of 'queer theory'," Michael Warner explains, "has outstripped anyone's sense of what exactly it means."[2] Part of this appeal has to do with the heady perception that queerness is not simply a passing trend but the marker of an epoch-making, historically specific shift in modes of conceiving sexuality, portending the breakdown of the hetero/homo binary within whose confines most of us have grown up. Hence, for Jeff Escoffier and Allan Berube, the term *queerness* (as opposed to *gayness*) includes *all* "people who have been made to feel perverse, queer, odd, outcast, different, and deviant"; it "affirm[s] sameness by defining a common identity on the fringes."[3] By shifting the debate on sexuality from a straight/gay opposition

---

[2] Warner, "From Queer to Eternity: An Army of Theorists Cannot Fail," *Village Voice Literary Supplement*, June 1992, 18.

[3] Escoffier and Berube, "Queer/Nation," *OUT/LOOK: National Lesbian and Gay Quarterly* 11 (Winter 1991): 14–16.

(in which one's sexuality is defined solely by the gender of one's sexual partners) to that of normative/non-normative behaviors (which recognizes the polymorphous fluidity of *all* sexuality), queer thinking thus strategically attempts to free homosexual desire from its dependence on and secondariness to heterosexuality as the privileged term within the dominant sexual regime. Instead, governed by a logic and a politics that is at once radically antiassimilationist (I refuse to be like you) and radically antiseparatist (we are not a single minority defined by one agenda), this embrace of "a common identity on the fringes" positions same-sex desire as part of a more general celebration of difference.[4] As a means of reconceptualizing sexual categories, spaces, and boundaries, then, the queering of identity and academic theory alike also seems a uniquely contemporary phenomenon whose time is *now*: it is not for nothing that a phrase like "the pomo homo" has become a byword of the 1990s, the product of a postmodern aesthetics of performance and pastiche that, in the words of Ann Powers, "has turned the closet inside out, making the projection of a queer attitude enough to claim space in homosexual culture."[5]

Without denying the relevance of the social and psychological transformations signaled by the term *queer* for the lives we are creating now and the futures toward which we are moving, this essay suggests that in another liminal epoch—the 1920s and 1930s—something very like what Powers calls "the projection of a queer attitude" was at work in the making of urban gay and protogay spaces in the early twentieth-century modern city, as well as in the representation of these urban spaces in a series of fictional texts. I especially have in mind, as already indicated, the bohemian enclaves of Greenwich Village and Harlem in New York City and of the Left Bank in Paris, all of whose often complexly intertwined and interchangeable literary communities became the locus in this period of certain modes of alternative modernist writing that

---

[4] In addition to Warner's analysis, my definitions here are especially indebted to Lisa Duggan, "Making It Perfectly Queer," *Socialist Review* 22 (1992): 11–31, and Alisha Solomon, "In Whose Face? A Gay Generation is Not an Age Group," *Village Voice*, July 1991, 18–19.

[5] Powers, "Queer in the Streets, Straight in the Sheets: Notes on Passing," *Village Voice*, June 1993, rpt. in *Utne Reader*, November-December 1993, 75.

presage the principal tenets of contemporary queer theory. In the larger project of which this essay is part, I suggest that this conjunction of sexual subculture, the city, modernist practice, and queer theory provides an intriguing blueprint for rereading the often subversive energies of a series of marginalized "modernist" American texts, several of which receive passing mention in the pages that follow: Bruce Nugent's "Smoke, Lilies, and Jade" (1926), Blair Niles's *Strange Brother* (1931), Charles Henri Ford and Parker Tyler's co-authored *The Young and the* Evil (1933), and Djuna Barnes's *Nightwood* (1937).

A few caveats are in order before I proceed further. First, in speaking of a "queer" modernism of the 1920s and 1930s, I do not mean to suggest that the meanings we now associate with the term *queer* were available, or even latent, in its usage then. To the contrary, rather than signaling a fluidity in excess of the homo/hetero binary, the term *queer* emerged in the interwar period among homosexuals to signal an inalterable, indeed innate, orientation toward persons of the same sex. Those of "us who are born 'queer'," as Mark Thornton, the gay protagonist of Niles's *Strange Brother*, explains, exist "at the opposite pole from the entirely normal man," and, unlike those "borderline cases" that the psychoanalyst can supposedly influence, can never be "push[ed] … over into the safe region of normality—into the happy pasture of the herd": for Mark and his "tribe," queerness is a birthright, not a choice.[6] Second, I am not interested in making a cause-and-effect argument that purports to have uncovered the "origins" of contemporary queer theory in an earlier period—in this case, the modernist era—thereby vitiating the potentially revolutionary impact of the present moment by revealing queerness to have been around all along. Rather, my interest is in the ways in which many of the most challenging implications of contemporary queer identifications, attitudes, and theorizing retrospectively shed light on various questions about same-sex desire and its representations that were current in the early decades of this century and that were intimately linked to the rise of the twentieth-century metropolis. In other words, while the project of this essay may indeed be historiographical, intent on rendering intelligible certain aspects of the past, it does not aim to

---

[6] Niles, *Strange Brother* (1931; rpt. London: GMP Publishers, 1991) 155. All further page references to this novel appear in parentheses in my text.

provide a teleology that traces an unbroken history of influence from "then" to "now."

Crucial to the "siting" of queer desire in these textual manifestations of modernist practice are a specifically modern experience and conception of urban space as uncontrollably vast, internationally diverse, and spectacularly unknowable. Georg Simmel, for one, has argued that the explosion in the size and complexity of the modern metropolis at the beginning of this century fundamentally reshaped the *mental* life of the city dweller, whose psyche responded to the myriad stimuli of the modern city with increased feelings of both anonymity or alienation and unprecedented freedoms.[7] This dual response is confirmed by Raymond Williams's observations in an essay suggestively titled "Metropolitan Perceptions and the Emergence of Modernism," which links the new psychology created by this increase in anonymity/autonomy to the development of modernism itself: if the sense of isolation, of being lost in the crowd, created for many individuals those extreme states of distorting, subjective, alienated consciousness that have since become hallmarks of modernist art, so too the "liberating diversity and mobility of the [modern] city," in Williams's words, awakened in many individuals a sense of openness, of new horizons, and of "exceptional liberties of expression" that also served as a crucial spur to modernist experimentations. Williams also notes that "within the new kind of open, complex, and mobile society" being created in the great international metropolitan centers after the turn of the century "small groups in any form of divergence or dissent could find some kind of foothold, in ways that would not have been possible if the artists and thinkers composing them had been scattered in more traditional, closed societies."[8]

Hence, along with the anonymity and autonomy that Simmel cites as intrinsic to the experience of modern city life, the possibility of establishing such "footholds" served as a

---

[7] Simmel, "The Metropolis and Mental Life," in *Classic Essays in the Culture of Cities*, ed. Richard Sennett (New Jersey: Appleton-Century-Crofts, 1969) 47–60, rpt. from *The Sociology of Georg Simmel*, ed. Kurt Wolff (New York: The Free Press, 1950).

[8] Williams, "Metropolitan Perceptions and the Emergence of Modernism," *The Politics of Modernism* (London and New York: Verso, 1989) 37–48. Quotations are from 43, 44, and 45, respectively.

powerful impetus, on both psychological and practical levels, for attracting increasing (and increasingly visible) numbers of homosexually disposed men and women to the metropolis at the beginning of the century. *Strange Brother* provides a paradigmatic example of this migration: taking to heart the advice of an older gay mentor to leave Iowa for "a place big enough for a man to be different safely," Mark moves to New York City, where the relative tolerance of Harlem's community provides him the space to be most open about his gayness (74). Likewise, the narrative action proper of *The Young and Evil* begins with the disembarking of a homosexual youth named Julian, flushed with "lush expectancy," from a ship that has carried him from the repressive South to the docks of New York City; here he is met by the mascara-eyed Karel, a hitherto unseen pen pal whose body, undulating "like a tall curved building," seems a personification of knowing urbanity itself.[9] The possibility that *any* person moving through the diverse urban landscape might experience hitherto unimagined possibilities of sexual desire and satisfaction, as well as the likelihood that the homosexually aware individual's daily physical movements exponentially increased his or her chances of intersecting with others sharing those desires, gradually helped to map out enclaves within the larger urban grid where, as George Chauncey's recent work has brilliantly documented, increasingly visible gay subcultures took root and flourished into active, indeed self-sustaining, *communities* from the turn of the century forward.[10] "Paris has always seemed to me the only city where you can live and express yourself as you please," Natalie Barney wrote of the city that since the 1890s had gained a reputation as the site of modern-day Mytilene (of which Barney's Sapphic coterie on the Left Bank was a central fixture). Likewise, throughout the first decades of the twentieth century, as Chauncey notes, the reputation of New York City's Village definitively shifted from that of artistic haven to enclave for sexual suspects—a "Mecca," one scholar mourns in an article called "The Degenerates of Greenwich Village," for "ex-

---

[9] Ford and Tyler, *The Young and the Evil* (New York: Sea Horse Book/Gay Presses of New York, 1988) 15. All further page references to this novel appear in parentheses in my text.

[10] Chauncey, *Gay New York: Gender, Urban Culture, and the Making of the Gay Male World 1898–1940* (New York: Basic Books, 1994) 1–29.

hibitionists and perverts of all kinds." Uptown, meanwhile, the popular press was beginning to take note of the "erotics, perverts, inverts, and other types of abnormalities cavorting with wild and Wilde abandon" in the public spaces of Harlem.[11] In measuring the rise of homosexuality in this century, it becomes clear that the geography of gay identity increasingly occupies an urban space.

In the communities and texts that I am considering, however, it is crucial to note that none of these emerging "gay" urban sites is *exclusively* "homosexual" (that is, characterized by same-sex relationships alone). Rather, they exist in a fluid and contingent relation to other disenfranchised populations: the bohemian artist community, political extremists, sexual profligates, the entertainment demimonde, the criminal underground. Similarly, these queer urban sites, as I will be calling them, are characterized by a polymorphous, labile sexuality whose expressions may run in any of several directions.[12] Such characteristics, of course, point toward some of the more salient features of current queer theory, three aspects of which are particularly relevant to the revisionist modernist project of this essay.

First, these texts presage a contemporary understanding of queer subjectivity as the assumption of a defiantly *nonnormative identity* that defines itself primarily in terms of its defiant opposition to the status quo rather than exclusively by the (same-sex) gender of one's sexual object choices. Hence, in addition to lesbians and gay men of various races, classes, and ethnicities, the urban spaces represented in these texts em-

---

[11] Barney's views are quoted in Shari Benstock, *Women of the Left Bank: Paris, 1900–1940* (Austin, TX: University of Texas Press, 1986), who also comments on Paris's growing reputation as a new Lesbos (271 and 289, respectively); the reference to the article "The Degenerates of Greenwich Village," appearing in a 1936 issue of *Current Psychology and Psychoanalysis*, is quoted in Chauncey, as is the reference to "Wilde" Harlem, which appeared in a restaurant review in the *Baltimore Afro-American* (234 and 249, respectively).

[12] Here I have liberally adapted and collapsed the wording of Steven Watson in his excellent introduction to the 1988 Gay Presses of New York/ Sea Horse edition of *The Young and the Evil*, where he writes of the "universe of shifting relationships and labile sexuality" that comprise the backdrop of this novel, which "doesn't present a strictly homosexual world, but one of polymorphous sexuality" (ix).

brace drag queens, straight-identified male hustlers, fag hags, impoverished artists, bisexuals, anarchists and communists, and middle-class straight women exploring their own oppression. Second, and closely related to this diversity, this alternate modernist tradition shares with current queer theory a sense of queerness as a *communal affiliation*, one shared by those sexual dissidents and otherwise marginalized members of society who find in the proclamation and celebration of their common difference the basis on which to begin to build alternative, sustaining worlds. Indeed, the creation of affiliations and identifications that cross and recross hitherto segregated sexual/social categories of oppression becomes a pivotal defining feature of these marginal communities. At the same time— and this is a crucial distinction—the self-proclaimed outcasts who populate these texts also typically find a common rallying point, *whatever* their sexual orientations, under the sign of the "Homosexual," the modern identity category based on same-sex desire. In their embrace of homosexuality as a governing trope, these fictions embody a stance that looks toward Eve Kosofsky Sedgwick's definition of queerness in *Tendencies*, where she argues that any politically viable use of the term *queer* today must acknowledge the centrality of same-sex expression to its present definition. "Given the historical and contemporary force of the prohibitions against every same-sex sexual expression," Sedgwick writes, "for anyone to disavow those meanings of queer, or to displace them from the term's definitional center, would be to dematerialize any possibility of queerness [as something other than the inverse of heterosexuality] itself."[13]

Third, these "fringe" modernist texts share with current theory a sense of queerness *as an effect of representation and hence of style*, whether played out in fantasy, on the body, or in writing. Modernist writing, of course, is nothing if not a self-conscious performance of style, of textual inscriptions that— like the coded gay body—simultaneously flaunt and conceal "meaning" in a masquerade of allusion and self-referentiality.[14] On the textual plane, the appeal of modernist style, lan-

---

[13] Sedgwick, *Tendencies* (Durham, NC: Duke University Press, 1993) 8.

[14] Intriguing in this regard is the conflation of textual and bodily "styles" underlying Parker Tyler's reminiscence of his and Charles Henri Ford's attempt in *The Young and the Evil* to create their own "brand" of avant-garde

guage play, and experimental formats to gay writers who seek both to convey and disguise taboo subject matter is obvious. For example, in the story "Smoke, Lilies, and Jade," Nugent's adaptation of a kind of Joycean stream-of-consciousness technique allows him to record the immediacy of the mental processes by which his protagonist, Alex, slowly works toward an acknowledgment of his homoerotic desires; at the same time the frequent ellipses that connect Alex's short, random thoughts signal the concealments and repressions that accompany the process of his coming out. The manipulation of modernist style for queer ends is also evident in the complex interplay of gay argot and linguistic experimentation in Ford and Tyler's novel, where the text's verbal difficulty—a typical trait of modernist prose—is directly related to the reader's knowledge or ignorance of the camp slang it employs to describe the homosexual subculture it gleefully depicts.[15] If language lends itself to queer readings in such texts, so too do their larger narrative formats, which have often developed modes of narrative desire that defy normative heterosexualizing or oedipalized definitions of textual movement: through patterns of textual intersections, linkages, breakdowns, couplings, and recouplings, these fictions map out a deliberately perverse textual flow or circuitry within which and through whose spaces something akin to "queer" desire is produced and recirculated, reconfiguring the concept of narrative space itself. If a major project of the modernist aesthetic was to reconceive the spatial-temporal coordinates of written and visual art, the queering of narrative movement in the modernist text provides a

---

literature in the late 1920s. Well known throughout the Village for his theatrical self-presentation and sartorial flamboyance, Tyler writes, "We were trying to create our brand [of modernism]. What we didn't realize too consciously was that *we were* (I hope this isn't too much of a boast!) *modern poetry.*" Quoted in Watson, *The Young and the Evil* xx. The italics are Tyler's.

[15] Paul Monette's comments on his early writing style can be taken as representative of the continuing appeal to the gay artist of using modernist-sanctioned stylistic obfuscation in order to escape the judgments of homophobic culture: "Until I came out ... clear was the last thing I wanted my writing to be," he reveals. "The only outlet for the torments of my affliction was poetry, where I could conceal the subject—or thought I could—in the caves of metaphor and monologue." See Monette, *Becoming a Man: Half a Life Story* (1992; rpt. New York: Harper Collins, 1993) 121.

particularly salient instance in which the more general revolution in ways of conceiving space and time in the heyday of modernism is enhanced by a specific if largely unacknowledged subcultural politics of sexuality. At the very least the experimental forms of these texts unsettle the primacy of heterosexuality as the novel's governing trope; at their most they espouse a protoqueer narrative politics by positing their objects of desire as equal to, and part of, the "queerness" that constitutes *all* desire.

II

Such modernist mappings of queer desire in fictional narrative circle us back to the geographical mappings of queer sites in the topography of the early twentieth-century city. In the following pages, I hope to show how an application of theories of social space, particularly those of the city and urban geographies, may expand our understanding of not only the historical formation of such enclaves (such as Chauncey's work on "Gay New York" has already admirably begun to do) but also *the conceptual and imaginative projections* that such spaces may engender. I would like to posit five general directions that such a theorizing of urban gay space might take, with an eye to how these directions enhance our understanding of those "queer sites in modernism" designated by the title of this essay. But, first, I want to suggest that in order to realize the radical potential of such conceptions of queer space, queer theorists may need to reconsider some of the Foucauldian paradigms that have come to be taken for granted in thinking about social space, particularly as regards the relation of (social) space to the (sexual) body. For Foucault, of course, space most often functions, in David Harvey's paraphrase, as a metaphor "for a site or container of power which usually constrains,"[16] and the spatial organization of the post-Enlightenment city is no exception: within its newly organized, disciplinary spaces of social control, the body is subjected to a

---

[16] See Harvey's very helpful positioning of Foucault in relation to theories of time, space, and modernity in *The Condition of Postmodernity: An Inquiry into the Origins of Cultural Change* (Oxford: Basil Blackwell, 1989) 213.

regime of faceless, technocratic surveillance and figurative when not literal incarceration. Foucault does acknowledge the possibility, however circumscribed, that the body may fashion discrete spaces of resistance, temporary heterotopias, from an otherwise totalizing disciplinary world.[17] "Resistance," however, may not provide us with a sufficient theoretical handle for imagining, much less articulating, alternate systems of experiencing, living in, manipulating, and (re)creating social space—systems of being-in-the-world that, it strikes me, the conjunction of the desiring queer body and urban space in all its liberating anonymity, mobility, and diversity holds out as a radically differently configured possibility. Keeping this caveat about Foucault in view, the following paragraphs sketch out five general approaches that might prove useful in attempting more rigorously to theorize and not simply historicize gay urban space, particularly as it comes into being in the 1920s and 1930s and as it enters into modern(ist) textual representation.

Approach #1. First of all, one might consider how the imposition of the ubiquitous city model of the *urban grid and/or axial radius* contributes to the formation of *specific pockets* where cultural difference is not only encouraged but, in its very containment, becomes advantageous to those located both outside and inside its parameters. As Rosalind Krauss notes in her famous monograph on modern art, the grid pattern is *the* quintessential emblem of modernity—"like that other symptom of modernity, the large city." For in spatial terms, the grid—whether imposed over the space of the canvas or the topography of the city—creates an "anti-natural, anti-mimetic, anti-real" flatness that not only replaces "the dimensions of the real ... with the lateral spread of a single surface" but also upholds the absolute autonomy of the artifact, the construct, itself. "The grid is a way of abrogating the claims of natural objects to have an order particular to themselves," Krauss writes of mod-

---

[17] See Foucault, *The History of Sexuality: Volume 1: An Introduction* (1976; rpt. New York: Vintage, 1980) 157 and passim; *Discipline and Punish: The Birth of the Prison* (1975; rpt. New York: Vintage, 1979) 201–3 and passim; and *The Order of Things: An Archaeology of the Human Sciences* (1966; rpt. New York: Vintage, 1973).

ernist aesthetics.[18] This description of the modernist repudia-
tion of the terms of "natural" "order" is particularly evocative
when juxtaposed to the simultaneous creation, within the
modern urban landscape, of communities of homosexually
identified men and women whose collective psychic imperative
is the similarly "modernist" one of dissociating sexual desire
and object choice from the tyranny of the "natural" as reified
within the "order" of heterosexuality.

These aesthetic/spatial considerations have important
correlatives in the social history of city planning as well. As a
facet of urban design, the grid is most often seen as an American innovation, that is, as an utopic attempt to reconceive the
hierarchized space of the European city by using right angles
to create "equal" or "democratic" relations among its sectors
and hence its citizens; the nearly uniform grid of Franklin's
"city of brotherly love," Philadelphia, stands as a quintessential
example of this democratic ideal. As such, the urban grid contrasts to the most common, historically evolved feature of urban organization in Europe: the baroque radial axis, which,
from medieval Italian hill towns to Haussman's restructuring
of Paris in the mid-nineteenth century to Mussolini's Rome,
monumentalizes the city center as the source from which
power flows.[19] The radius serves the practical function, as
well, of controlling the flow and distribution of both citizens
and troops. Indeed, in contrast to the "democracy" of the grid,
the radiating axis is often equated with an authoritarian impulse to police human social relations through a hierarchical
division of space (although, one hastens to add, the monotony
of the grid can prove as tyrannical as the subordinations created by the axial radius). In reality, most cities—even the newly
styled American ones—consist of some overlay of the two pat-

---

[18] Krauss, "Grids, You Say," *Grids: Format and Image in 20th Century
Art* (New York: The Pace Gallery, 1978) no pagination; quotations are from the
first two pages of the essay.

[19] On the European city model of the baroque axial network as "a strategy for the economical application of central power," and as a "way of using
the city as an expression of central power and a strategy for maintaining visual magnificence and control within available means," see Kevin Lynch, *A Theory of Good City Form* (Cambridge, MA: MIT Press, 1981) 280–84; quotations
are from 281 and 283, respectively. My observations in this paragraph are
greatly shaped by discussions with Dale M. Wall.

terns, of which Washington, D.C., provides the most stunning example, as anyone driving in the city for the first time soon learns: an axial grid of streets, radiating from the White House, is laid over a square grid, planting a firm "center" of Power in the midst of this political experiment in establishing democratic relations between parts and the whole.[20]

Indeed, such overlays often create the interstices or pockets within the urban grid where "forgotten" or "invisible" subcultures first take root and flourish. For in terms of the two quintessential cities of modernity that become such evocative sites of queer social and textual innovation—Paris and New York—it is worth thinking about the degree to which the actual physical layout or mapping of street patterns within particular sectors, along with their positioning within the interstices of the larger grid, has worked to make these sites more amenable to protogay and gay lifestyles.[21] Note, for instance, the historical positioning of Greenwich Village as an old-world, virtually-

---

[20] See Lynch, *Theory of Good City Form* 283.

[21] On the most basic level, such pockets or sectors require the proximity of both commercial and residential entities appropriate to unmarried individuals living on their own (this would entail the study of the rise of gay-friendly institutions such as the boarding house and the cafeteria). Relevant here is Chauncey's work on the rise of an urban bachelor subculture in New York City: "Tellingly," Chauncey writes, "gay men tended to gather in the same neighborhoods where many of the city's other unmarried men and women clustered, since they offered the housing and commercial services suitable to the needs of a nonfamily population. Gay male residential and commercial enclaves developed in the Bowery, Greenwich Village, Times Square, and Harlem in large part because they were the city's major centers of furnished-room housing for single men.... Rooming houses and cafeterias served as meeting grounds for gay men, facilitating the constant interaction that made possible the development of a distinctive subculture" (136). On a more theoretical level, such pockets or interstices are reminiscent of Aldo Rossi's hypothesis of the city "as an entity constituted of many parts which are complete in themselves ... one which truly permits *freedom of choice*"; part of this "freedom of choice," tellingly, also lies in the fact that the so-called "city of parts" is also always in process, constituting what Rossi calls the "analogous city" whose "elements are preexisting ... but whose true meaning is unforeseen at the beginning and unfolds only at the end of the process. Thus the meaning of the process is identified with the meaning of the city." See Rossi, *The Architecture of the City* (Cambridge, MA: MIT Press, 1982) 96, 18.

unreconstructed "village" within New York City, whose tangle of small streets, influenced by the curve of the Hudson, defeats the larger grid pattern and creates an insular neighborhood in which it is much easier a) to lose oneself (in all senses of the word); b) to maintain a sense of privacy and therefore safety from outside interlopers; and c) to execute the "cruise," creating an intersection or crossing of glances and looks as often as one recrosses and recirculates among the same streets. Likewise, the Latin Quarter of the Left Bank, literally the "Latin" or medieval quartier of Paris, functions both physically and symbolically to create a similar kind of hidden "pocket" within Paris. As Aldo Rossi notes, a "quartier" implies a residential area that has evolved from *within* a sector of the city rather than one that has been superimposed *upon* it.[22] By and large escaping the fascistic nineteenth-century city planning of Haussman, whose scheme of grand boulevards imposed over old Paris was ostensibly designed to open up city perspectives but actually created routes by which the militia could more easily defeat any popular unrest, the Latin Quarter's labyrinth of ancient, narrow *rues*, *allées*, and *cul de sacs*, peppered with cafes, bars, and seedy hotels, has maintained an atmospheric insularity, mystery, and autonomy conducive to artistic and "alternative" lifestyles.[23] Even Harlem's more recent development and positioning in the grid of New York, while lacking the

---

[22] Rossi, *Architecture of the City* 65n.

[23] As Norma Evenson notes in *Paris: A Century of Change, 1878–1978* (New Haven: Yale University Press, 1979) 65–71, Haussman's plans in fact included a boulevard that would have bisected the Saint Germain and Latin Quarters parallel to the Seine and leveled much of their "ancient fabric" (it was blocked for complicated reasons that Evenson reports). Later attempts were made to revive the Haussman plan, in part because of the association of the physical layout of the Quarter with past political insurrection and present-day sexual sins: "It is impossible to traverse the narrow streets which go from the Quai de Conti to the old abbey of Saint Germain des Pres, without seeing again the horrible days of the revolution of which they were the theater, where the walls themselves have retained the cries of the victims of September.... Where the disorders were [once] unchained, prostitution and disease has [now] elected its domicile. History and a concern for human dignity ... order us, imperiously, to abolish, together with this past, the present-day misery." Andre Menabrea, "Les Enseignements du vieux Pont Neuf," *Urbanisme* 8–9 (November-December 1932): 226, reported in Evenson, *Paris* 70.

small "old-world-village" feel of Greenwich Village or the Left Bank, maintains a physical insularity and symbolic resonance given its location on the "other" side of the "wilderness" of Central Park; its locus functions, quite literally, as the repressed Other of establishment Manhattan. The hierarchizing implications of this spatial distinction are evocatively captured by the title of Carl Van Vechten's novel about Harlem, *Nigger Heaven* (1926)—for "nigger heaven" refers to the balcony to which theater-going blacks were relegated, a position of spatial subordination from which, however, in terms meant to suggest Harlem's uptown relation to midtown and lower Manhattan, those "on top" look down upon and potentially threaten their unaware oppressors.[24]

Approach #2. In addition to the physical spaces carved out by such pockets, one might consider the effect of *the ceaseless mobility* of metropolitan modernity on the evolution of dissident sexual identities and communities. Of obvious importance in this regard is the evolution of those various modern technologies of transportation—such as the underground metro—that not only enhanced the relative ease with which one could move through districts of the urbanscape, making an appearance and then disappearing at will, but that also created a complex layering and simultaneity of movement that radically reordered the early twentieth-century city dweller's spatial experience of urban life. (Think, for instance, of the strata of movements created by the simultaneous existence of the underground, the pedestrian sidewalk, automotive street transportation [cars, buses, taxis], and the overhead "elevated" train.)

Of equal relevance to any discussion of urban mobility and sexual identity is the creative role played by individual pedestrian movements in demarcating and thereby constructing social space. The most prominent theorist of the importance of the individual city pedestrian is Michel de Certeau, who argues in *The Practice of Everyday Life* that the very activity of walking through the cityscape defines a "space of enunciation," resulting in a proliferation of individual "pedestrian rhetoric[s]" that together resist many of the oppressive, totalizing attributes of social space proposed by Foucault. For what appears to be a swarming mass in motion is also, for de Certeau, "an innumerable collection of singularities," individual human agents

---

[24] Lewis, *When Harlem Was in Vogue* 186, explains the title reference.

whose multiple yet intersecting paths throughout the city inscribe "an allusive and fragmentary story whose [very] gaps" make space for nonhegemonic vernaculars and popular street cultures that can in turn give rise to viable social practices.[25] The way in which the multiplication of these pedestrian rhetorics liberates (rather than localizes) social space and social practice, de Certeau asserts, creates the city anew daily.[26] Such an explosion of movement, moreover, renders all urban mobility, to use gay parlance, a form of cruising—indeed, cruising may be said to become the "pedestrian rhetoric" *par excellence* within the modern era, taking the place formerly occupied by the *flâneur* in the nineteenth century.

The interpenetrability of street cruising, urban subjectivity, and nonhegemonic practices lies at the heart of Nugent's "Smoke, Lilies, and Jade." In effect, the mental world of the protagonist—the primary locus of the narrative—functions as one vast thoroughfare, for the associative flow of language that Nugent uses to simulate Alex's thought-impressions is paralleled by the protagonist's physical movements as he wanders the streets of Harlem and the Village by night ("to wander in the night was wonderful ... curiously prying into the dark").[27] Venturing out into Harlem's nightworld to join his African-American artist friends and their white patrons (he proudly claims first-name familiarity with Langston, Zora, and Carl, among others) provides Alex with the perfect mental subterfuge to disguise his "blue thoughts" as he cruises "the narrow blue" of the city streets (104–5) in search, as he tells himself, of poetry—which he ultimately finds at 4 A.M. in the form of a man

---

[25] De Certeau, *The Practice of Everyday Life*, trans. Steven F. Rendall (Berkeley, CA: University of California Press, 1984) 97–98, 102; see de Certeau's refutation of Foucault's totalizing spaces on xiv-xv, 45–49, 96, and passim.

[26] Harvey, *Condition of Postmodernity* 213. Harvey's summary of de Certeau's argument concludes, "[s]paces can be more easily 'liberated' than Foucault imagines, precisely because social practices spatialize rather than becoming localized within some repressive grid of social control" (214).

[27] Nugent, "Smoke, Lilies, and Jade" (1926; rpt. in *Voices from the Harlem Renaissance*, ed. Nathan Irvin Huggins [New York: Oxford University Press, 1995] 102). This story was first published under the name Richard Bruce in 1926 in the inaugural and only issue of the renegade Harlem Renaissance arts magazine *Fire!! A Quarterly Devoted to Younger Negro Artists*.

whom he picks up (or allows himself to be picked up by) and whom he renames, aptly enough, "Beauty." As Alex "aimlessly" wanders the night, his steps leading him toward a sexual goal he cannot consciously admit until he has crossed its threshold, the reader is put in the analogous position of cruising Alex's recorded thoughts, suspecting but never certain of the narrative's sexual destination. Moreover, the abundant ellipses that punctuate the narrative flow—overtly serving as bridges between Alex's thought-sensations but also creating blank spaces in the text that keep their secrets—become a stylistic equivalent of what de Certeau calls the "gaps" within the "allusory and fragmentary story" created by the city's individual urban subjects in their manifold movements. Escaping the totalizing discourse of disciplinary technologies, such gaps provide the clandestine sites within which nonhegemonic social practices—for example, Alex's eventual acceptance of his sexual love for another man—come into being and succeed in occupying social space.

Approach #3. We also might usefully theorize these gay urban enclaves as a series of traversable sites, across which its "native" inhabitants move in a continual flow of desirous possibility that constantly redefines the community's shifting parameters of tolerance and relative safety and though which other segments of society are also always moving, taking with them impressions that thus travel elsewhere. Hence, as a node of transit and point of intersection, the gay enclave participates in the dissemination of "gay knowledge"—that is, knowledge of things gay—to unfamiliar terrains outside its immediate borders and encourages the very cross-identifications that constitute the queerness of its community. "Gayness" thus permeates outside the boundaries of its specific "sites," in the form of information from which no city dweller is absolutely immune.[28]

---

[28] The spread of such knowledge beyond its ostensible "confines" is graphically illustrated in Strange Brother, which opens with the meeting of Mark, a gay artist, and June, a disaffected straight woman, within the liminal and liberating space provided by the "otherness" of Harlem's sexually and racially mixed nightworld. Yet, once the narrative moves beyond the Harlem setting that has provided the opening frame of the text, the "gay knowledge" that it has awakened in June tends to spread everywhere: when Mark leaves Harlem to visit June's mid-Manhattan apartment, the implication of possible

Approach #4. Conversely, it is also fruitful to conceptualize these urban gay "sites" as *mobile, shifting entities.* Greenwich Village, the Left Bank, and Harlem, that is, are imaginary as well as actual sites, whose meanings can float and attach to other locations: thus we find manifestations of "Harlem" in the midst of a midtown jazz and supper club, venerable institutions of Greenwich Village bar life rebuilt twenty blocks to the north, and the expatriate queer world of Paris turning up, in *Nightwood*, in Vienna and Berlin. The latter shift, whereby Berlin metonymically "becomes" an imaginary Paris and vice-versa, also underlines the fluid and interchangeable internationalism of these urban sites, as metropolises whose cosmopolitanism exceeds the patriotic, often parochial boundaries of nationhood. In a profound sense, such "world-class" cities, along with the queer denizens they shelter, share a system of values, an aura of sophistication, a general appreciation of culture, and, due to patterns of immigration and the heritage of imperialism, an awareness of "a wide variety of subordinate cultures," in Raymond Williams's phrase,[29] that makes them more like one another, despite geographical and language dif-

---

homosexuality seems to attach to all the supposedly straight men in June's and Mark's lives, in a vivid demonstration of the processes of connotation that both reinforce homophobia and expose the constructedness, the fragility, of the lines purported to separate the invert from the normal person. One consequence is that all these "straight" men have to start defining themselves either against Mark's homosexuality or June's questions about homosexuality. Homosexuality, which for Niles serves as the rallying trope for all the modes of social oppression her novel explores, cannot be quarantined to one part of the city: it travels everywhere. The classic analysis of the role of connotation in producing gay "meaning" is D. A. Miller, "Anal Rope," in *Inside/Out: Lesbian Theories, Gay Theories*, ed. Diana Fuss (New York: Routledge, 1991) 119–41.

[29] See Williams, "Metropolitan Perceptions" 44–45, on the definition of the metropolis "beyond both city and nation in their older senses" and on the impact of the internationalism of the "imperial capital" on modernist "innovations": "The most important general element of the innovations in form is the fact of immigration to the metropolis, and it cannot too often be emphasized how many of the major innovators were, in this precise sense, immigrants," newly "[l]iberated or breaking from their national and provincial cultures, placed in quite new relations to ... other native languages or native visual traditions, encountering ... a novel and dynamic common environment from which many of the older forms were obviously distinct" (45).

ferences, than like the national populations whose spatial boundaries contain them.

In this regard, it is also interesting to note that the urban spaces under investigation in this essay—Harlem, Paris, Greenwich Village—are often rendered as linguistically analogous to one another in the literature by and about them. During the 1920s and 1930s "downtown" gay New York (or the "fanciful aggregation of Greenwich Village uranians," as Wallace Thurman caustically put it in his novel *The Infants of the Spring*)[30] increasingly came "uptown" to Harlem, particularly to participate in its scandalous rent parties and famed drag balls.[31] And Harlem in this period is often represented as the "Paris of New York."[32] Conversely, jazz age Paris is seen as a version of Harlem, especially given the African-American colony of Montmartre, the sensational presence of Josephine Baker on the Paris stage, and the numbers of expatriate Harlem Renaissance writers—including Hughes, McKay, and Larsen—who took up temporary residence in what was generally perceived as Paris's more racially and sexually tolerant environment.

Approach #5. In addition, we might apply theories relating to *the spatial transformation of the everyday or commonplace* to these queer urban sites, to show how the appropriation of public social space—the park, the cafe, the store window, the subway, the bathhouse—often radically reorganizes what is considered public and private space, and in ways that become especially constitutive of modern gay male identity (normative heterosexual male life, by contrast, has increasingly been defined by the separation of the public and domestic realms from the mid-nineteenth century on).[33] The letters of Parker Tyler

---

[30] Thurman, *Infants of the Spring* (1932; Boston: Northeastern University Press, 1992) 184.

[31] For examples of this migration uptown, see chaps. 11, 13, and 18 of *Strange Brother*, *The Young and Evil*, and *Infants of the Spring*, respectively.

[32] Chauncey, *Gay New York* 246. Lewis, *When Harlem Was in Vogue* 99, also notes that the Negrotarians of the Lost Generation were "drawn to Harlem on the way to Paris": here Harlem quite literally represents a space of transit between the bohemian Village and the expatriate artist's colony established in Paris.

[33] Summarizing his in-depth analysis of the various "public" spaces—restaurants and cafeterias, parks, the street, public bathrooms, etc.—that become sites of gay life in New York City, Chauncey, *Gay New York* 180, writes

describing Village life, for instance, underline the way in which he and his gay friends act out "private dramas" in the public eye that, even when staged as campy public spectacles, nonetheless occlude the (in)sight of those not in the know. Similarly, Chauncey reports how the plate glass windows of the Life Cafeteria, a well-known gay hangout in the Village, provided a sort of stage where gays could perform a "show" for the voyeuristic tourists who have come to the Village to watch the faggot parade; at the same time the cafe's gay clientele are actively appropriating this public venue as a "private" space in which to carry on their domestic gay lives.[34] Walter Benjamin, writing about the way that the Arcades project recreated Paris's public spaces, comments that the creation of these glass-enclosed shopping thoroughfares transformed its city streets into a vast interior.[35] Conversely, we may hypothesize that, in much gay life, *interiorized space becomes one vast street*, a thoroughfare accommodating social, intimate, and anonymous interchanges impossible in the realm of the bourgeois home or its rarefied interior space. Numerous examples abound: the tradition of the Harlem rent party and the buffet flat; the artistic and literary salon (including Gertrude Stein's and Alice B. Toklas's Saturday evening gatherings in the atelier of their home on rue de Fleuris and Natalie Barney's lesbian revelries held in the wooded garden, replete with Temple à l'Amitié, at 20 rue Jacob); the democratizing brotherhood of the YMCA (in which the hallway onto which all the rooms open becomes the public thoroughfare); the public bathhouse.[36]

---

that "gay men devised a variety of tactics that allowed them to move freely about the city, to appropriate for themselves spaces that were not marked as gay, and to construct a gay city in the midst of, yet invisible to, the dominant city." One of the best sources on the rise of new standards of masculine heterosexual normativity in the nineteenth century is Ed Cohen, *Talk on the Wilde Side* (New York: Routledge, 1993).

[34] Chauncey, *Gay New York*, cites Tyler's correspondence on 168–69 and reports on the spectacle afforded by the Life Cafeteria on 166–68.

[35] Benjamin, "Paris, Capital of the Nineteenth Century," *Reflections* (New York: Harcourt Brace Jovanovich, 1978) 146–47.

[36] On the tradition of the rent party and buffet flat in Harlem, and their highly charged sexual—and often gay—atmosphere, see Garber, "A Spectacle in Color" 318–31, esp. 331–23. On Natalie Barney's desire to form a Sapphic circle dedicated to love of beauty and sensuality, and on the particular attrac-

Theorizing urban sexual "subcultures" through these various filters may also help us rethink certain tropes that have become commonplaces in lesbian-gay criticism, including Sedgwick's theory of the closet.[37] For instance, if we think of gay urban enclaves *as physical sites* of intersection through which people of all dispositions travel and *as conceptual sites* with the power to migrate elsewhere, the idea that there is a distinct "inside" or "outside" to "gay life" (an idea that has served to police the hetero/homo divide) begins to lose its descriptive force. Likewise, who is to say that Greenwich Village is a margin, a "closet," or even a "*sub*culture" when the very conditions of its making and dissemination, like those of postmodern queer world-making, call into question the normalizing and hierarchizing assumptions upon which a term like "*sub*culture" is founded?

III

Elsewhere I draw more extensively on the specific textual examples offered by Nugent, Ford and Tyler, Barnes, and Niles to show how the desires that circulate and proliferate on the streets, in the clubs and speakeasies, and in the private residences that comprise these "queer sites" within the urban grid of the 1920s and 1930s became models for the spatial and temporal experimentations characterizing these defiantly perverse fictional narratives—narratives that, in undertaking to represent the nonhegemonic sexual identities that such queer

---

tion of Paris as a modern-day isle of Lesbos, see Benstock, *Women of the Left Bank* 268–307 and passim; and George Wickes, *The Amazon of Letters: The Life and Loves of Natalie Barney* (London: Allen, 1977). On the gay activity prevalent in the YMCA and the public bath, see Chauncey, *Gay New York* 155–57 and 207–25 (chap. 8: "The Social World of the Baths").

[37] In this vein, see also Wayne Koestenbaum's intelligent comments in "Vagabond Blues," his review of *Gay New York* in the *Los Angeles Times Book Review*, 7 August 1994, 2, 13, as well as Chauncey's critique of the closet as the "spatial metaphor people typically used to characterize gay life before the advent of gay liberation," despite the fact that the metaphor was never used by gay people before the 1960s (Chauncey, *Gay New York* 6; see also 375, n. 9, for his comments on Sedgwick's *Epistemology of the Closet*).

spaces at once fostered and made possible, constitute an overlooked modernist practice.[38] But in order to suggest some of the more general ways in which the various ideas about the modern city, and particularly about urban gay space, sketched out in the above axioms might broaden current interpretations of literary modernism, I want to close this essay with an overview of several ways in which these queerly experimental fictions succeeded in translating urban gay experience into quite specific literary equivalents.

The firs, is a move that might be seen as a thematic and formal correlative of Chauncey's evidence that the gay enclave in the urban grid in the first three decades of this century constituted a more self-sufficient and autonomous entity than hitherto suspected; that is, these revisionary modernist texts tend to transform the "footholds" of dissent that they depict into totalizing, self-contained, and self-regulating textual worlds. For, generally speaking, these texts do not merely offer the reader voyeuristic glimpses of the queer community from some safe or superior vantage point. Rather, they make this world the entire, encompassing focus of their representational efforts. In texts like Ford and Tyler's and Barnes's, we *only* see a (very) queer world, from which the world of the status quo is entirely banished, and in texts like Nugent's and Niles's, the privileging of the point of view of their gay protagonists subsumes all other nongay perspectives, facilitating a crossing of multiple categories of identity that results in a queer world-vision if not in an entirely queer world. Consequently, readers must wholly immerse themselves, for the spatial entirety of the text, in its self-contained and self-referential realm of significations, imaginatively entering a space of "otherness" from which the only exit is the closing of the book itself.[39]

---

[38] I examine these texts at greater length in the fourth chapter of a book in progress tentatively titled *Modernity's Fictions of Sexuality*. This essay is taken from the introduction to that chapter.

[39] Such a reading sheds a different light on the commonplace of the modernist writer fighting the meaninglessness, chaos, and randomness of the fragmented post–World War I world by the creative act of willing into being self-contained, self-referential fictional orders; from a queer perspective, the self-referentiality and self-containment of the fictional world creates an otherwise invisible gay reality.

Second, to the degree that these alternative, totalizing visions of urban queerness strategically counterbalance the more usual novelistic representation of quotidian, heteronormative reality, it is not surprising that they repeatedly turn to the world of the night—and, more specifically, to the social activities, summed up by the term "nightlife," made available to the public in unprecedented dimensions by the evolution of the modern metropolis—as a primary locus of their narratives. The one constant in all these texts, indeed, is the number of seemingly insomniac characters who ceaselessly wander the city by night, finding under its cover a realm of less inhibited, polymorphous, fluid desire. This realm of desire often borders on the extravagantly carnivalesque, as the elaborate set pieces and backdrops to the narrative action often illustrate: exotic stage shows, drag balls, circus acts, all-night speakeasies, private parties, sidewalk cafes, illuminated street festivals. Traditionally, of course, the world of carnival served as a ritualized space for the inversion of social order, allowing a temporary suspension of its rules and values.[40] In making the shadow world of night a nearly totalizing realm of feverous activity, these texts also invert the outsider's (and by proxy certain readers') conceptions of what is natural or not: thus in *Strange Brother* June feels, upon her liminal entrance into the homosexual subculture to which Mark's revelations have given her access, as if turned "mentally upside-down" (158), for "what still seemed to her as inverted as skyscrapers pointed earthward, Mark regarded as perfectly natural" (194). As the figure of the skyscraper intimates, this inverted order is intrinsically connected to the modes of life made possible by the form of the modern city itself. And to the degree that the literal space of the text becomes (a container of) an entire world, it represents a world of multiplying difference in which "inversion," as it were, is the norm, that which Mark regards as "perfectly natural."

Third, one may locate various textual manifestations of the two psychological characteristics, anonymity and autonomy, that Simmel associates with modern urban experience. The sense of anonymity that the proximity of and daily encounter

---

[40] See, for example, Terry Castle, *Masquerade and Civilization: The Carnivalesque in Eighteenth-Century English Culture and Fiction* (Stanford, CA: Stanford University Press, 1986).

with sheer numbers of unknown beings forces upon the individual city dweller is often reflected in the anonymity or elusiveness that marks the characterization of the protagonists in these texts. Rendered primarily through their exteriors, their poses of worldiness or sophistication or disaffection, such characters deny the reader easy access to their "inner depths" and demand to be read in terms of the surfaces they have constructed as signifiers of their difference. This resistance to interiorization provides one reason why the characters of such texts as *Nightwood* and *The Young and the Evil* appear so utterly amoral or morally blank: they refuse the logic of a core identity within which prevailing moral values can or should be located. Closely related to this elusiveness is the autonomy these characters exhibit as independent agents, most pronounced in the ease with which they shed not only dominant values but dominant conceptions of fidelity, relationship, or even friendship. Their random physical movements, mirroring their tendency to drift in and out of each other's lives, bespeak a willed freedom from commitments—including, one might add, any commitment to the reader—that at once renders them all the more unknowable and protects the autonomy they have achieved from assimilation into a disciplinary order.[41]

Fourth, this "denaturalization" of relationships—the product of both the unavoidable mobility and freedom of movement inherent in urban life—finds a textual correspondence in some of these fictions in a kind of denaturalization of linguistic relations, a severing of the assumed organic link between signifier

---

[41] The Foucauldian implications of this tension are notably present in "The Nightwatch" chapter of *Nightwood* (New York: New Directions, 1937), as Nora helplessly watches her lover Robin's forays into the anonymity of the night. Nora's furtive attempts at surveillance—hence the chapter title—only bring her visual confirmation of the betrayals she cannot afford to see: "In the years that they lived together, the departures of Robin became [a] slowly increasing rhythm.... Robin was an amputation that Nora could not renounce. As the wrist longs, so her heart longed, and dressing she would go out into the night that she might be 'beside herself,' skirting the café in which she could catch a glimpse of Robin.... Once out in the open Robin walked in a formless meditation, her hands thrust into the sleeves of her coat, directing her steps toward that night life that was a known measure between Nora and the cafés.... It was this exact distance that kept the two ends of her life—Nora and the cafés—from forming a monster with two heads" (59).

and signified that the performance and/or masking of one's "homosexual" identity and affiliation as a costume, as pure surface, has also already set into motion. In Barnes's *Nightwood*, for example, the radical dispossession that typifies its huge cast of social misfits and undesirables—including, among others, circus performers, mock aristocrats, charlatan doctors, wandering Jews, transvestite homosexuals, and butch lesbians—is mirrored in the tendency of all signifiers in the novel to divorce themselves from their signifieds and become (not unlike Robin Vote, "longing to be kept, knowing herself astray" [58]) linguistic "orphans" wandering in search of a never-to-be-attained home or meaning: one sign points to another without the guarantee of any stopping point or intervening "meaning." The result, Barnes's trademark surrealist dissociation of words from meaning and of objects from their "normal" contexts, yields a prose style that is deliberately artificial, ornamental, inorganic as opposed to natural—a style that, in a word, is perfectly "queer" in its refusal to allow for an unquestioned coupling of the label and labeled.

Likewise, the language play and stylistic indirection that characterize several of these texts contribute to this denaturalization of language by encoding and disclosing discourses specific to the gay enclaves growing within the interstitial spaces of the modern cityscape. The evolution of specialized argots or localized vernaculars that emerge as the signature of and password to these autonomous sexual (sub)cultures is a particularly *urban* phenomenon, their utility dependent on the geographical and spatial proximity of the community's disenfranchised members.[42] Such urban-specific vernaculars, in

---

[42] Evidence of the historical presence of specifically gay argot in use among urban homosexual subcultures reaches as far back as eighteenth-century London. In accounts of a series of raids on London's "molly houses" published in the 1726 *Select Trials*, informants testify not only to the suspicious sexual assignations going on in the back rooms of these sites of homosexual interaction but to the particular "dialect," or coded terms, that the men use to refer to their sexual activities. Cited in Ed Cohen, "Legislating the Norm: From Sodomy to Gross Indecency," in *Hidden from History* 183; for more on London's "molly house" subculture—which evocatively links urban sites, architectural space, and something close to twentieth-century "homosexual identity," see Alan Bray, *Homosexuality in Renaissance England* (London: Gay Men's Press, 1982) 81–114. Jeffrey Weeks, in *Sex, Politics, and Society: The*

"queering" expected or understood meanings, also help produce queer desires, queer subjects, and, not least, queer readers; for, integrated into the word play and deformation typical of modernist writing, such connotation-laden discourse initiates the reader unfamiliar with its ideolect into a new, because unexplored, linguistic/sexual order. The connotative force of such veiled gay argot, disseminating its content beyond the represented world of the text and into the world of the reader, thus performs a function similar to that of the gay enclave described in "Approach #3" above: the entire text, that is, becomes both a point of intersection and a traversable site, a space of transmission that is conducive to the spread of "gay" knowledge beyond its immediate boundaries.

Fifth, if the mobility of the autonomous gay urban subject as he or she navigates the geography of the metropolis shapes modes of characterization in these texts, it also marks their modernist formulations of narrative movement. The multiple yet intersecting paths or "stories" traced out by the individual human agents whose footsteps daily redefine localized spaces within the city grid constitute, as we have already seen, what de Certeau calls a pedestrian rhetoric. This description, intriguingly, evokes standard descriptions of the modernist text: splintered, disjunctive, paratactic, yet creating a multilayered "wholeness" from the intersections it renders among simultaneously unfolding scenes, actions, and thoughts. For, in fact, the reformulations of traditional narrative movement that often typify these queer examples of modernist practice spring from the same spatial redefinitions of temporality that the proliferation of these pedestrian rhetorics on the streets incites in the city dweller and the urban commentator. The textual desire that drives these texts does not simply flow but rather, like the

---

Regulation of Sexuality since 1800 (London and New York: Longman, 1981), also refers to the gay argot or "parlare," derived from theatrical and circus slang, that had become a part of late nineteenth-century communication and a mode of gossip among gay men, and he suggests that by this time there existed "a widespread and often international homosexual argot, suggesting a widely dispersed and organized subculture" (111). For a compendium of homosexual argot in America in the years before the gay liberation movement, see Gershon Legman, "The Language of Homosexuality: An American Glossary," in *Sex Variants*, vol. 2, ed. George W. Henry (New York: Paul B. Hoeber, 1941).

urban subject, moves in fits and starts, seeking points of intersection and/or crossing that serve as switch points from one
outpouring of energy to the next, tracing out a circuitry of
restlessly mobile desire that derails simple linearity in favor of
a dispersed temporality through a space that is multiple, simultaneous, and constantly changing. This description of narrative movement also calls to mind Deleuze and Guattari's
definition of non-Oedipal desire as a flow created by a prolif-
erating series of attachments and detachments among partial
objects: such a series of temporary couplings and blockages
provides an apt description of the erratic, nonlinear trajectories
that characterize both metropolitan space and the modernist
text, as well as the spaces of enunciation that both enclose.[43]
Hence the trajectories of several of these deviant modernist
texts not only serve a de-Oedipalizing function by defying the
contours of the Freudian masterplot (we find our end in our
beginnings) but also work against heterosexual presumptions
in their rejection of the structural dictates of the marriage plot
(where the cessation of the need to narrate is equated with the
perfect union of two—male and female—into one).[44] The literally and figuratively queer narrative trajectory of *The Young
and the Evil* offers a particularly vivid example of one way in
which the circuitry of the city grid becomes an analogue of the
desirous connections that the novel's sexually marginal characters map out in their shifting intersections with and departures from one another across the face of New York City in
general and the bohemian gay world of Greenwich Village in
particular. For Ford and Tyler's multiple characters roam the
Village's streets, speakeasies, cafes, and rooming houses in
order to attach to, detach from, and reattach to one another in
a chain of couplings and uncouplings that are mirrored in
their wildly fluctuating apartment and roommate arrangements and that provide the single thread linking together the
chapters of this otherwise nonlinear and highly experimental
fiction. These promiscuously shifting realignments, moreover,

---

[43] Gilles Deleuze and Felix Guattari, *Anti-Oedipus: Capitalism and
Schizophrenia*, trans. Robert Hurley, Mark Seem, and Helen R. Lane (1972;
rpt. Minneapolis: University of Minnesota Press, 1983) 1–16.

[44] See, respectively, Peter Brooks, *Reading for the Plot: Design and Intention in Narrative* (New York: Knopf, 1984); and Joseph A. Boone, *Tradition
Counter Tradition* (Chicago: University of Chicago Press, 1987).

are generally facilitated by some version of a sexual or fanta-
sized *menage à trois* that serves as a switch point, an intersection, allowing for the formation of a new (if equally temporary)
coupling: significantly, these triangulations, rather than serving simply as Girardian moments of mediation, instead help
create a radically de-Oedipalized, queer trajectory of desire that
ultimately devalues the "monogamous couple" as part of the
societal norm that the novel's rebels emphatically reject. Instead, the novel valorizes the constant stream of nonnormative, often anonymous, free-floating desire that the spatial positioning of its setting within New York's urban grid
helps encourage.

As a sixth and final point in pursuing these connections
between a theorization of urban gay space and experimental
writing, we need to consider the way in which the reconfigurations of narrative desire described above lead to a reconceptualization of narrative space, and hence of spatialized narrative itself. For these modernist fictions often "open up" non-
temporally organized textual spaces, veritable interstices
within the larger narrative grid, that in turn make room for the
representation of homoerotic content. These experiments with
narrative's spatial possibilities take any number of forms:
Nugent's extreme use of ellipses, which break the horizontal
flow of language with wordless gaps that, repeating from line to
line, visually create vertical "paths," literal openings, on the
page that evoke the ascending spirals of smoke of his title for
some readers and, for others, the protagonist's aimless footsteps as he wanders throughout the city; the desultory or di-
lated temporality that ensues from Ford and Tyler's near hal-
lucinatory, surreal stylization of the continually shifting sexual
alliances of their characters; Barnes's refraction of key actions
through Cubist-inspired verbal repetitions that create a sense
of suspended motion; Barnes's and Niles's similar use of non-
stop monologues that bring the forward momentum of their
plots to a near standstill, a technique that strategically clears
space for the emergence of Doctor O'Connor's and Mark's
counterhegemonic visions of the "Night" and the "shadow
world," respectively. In all these examples, there is a deliberate
perversion of narrative temporality that is at once a general
characteristic of modernist writing and, I would argue, a strategy specific to "queer" writing itself, making its narrative form
a material embodiment of the sexually dissident, queer com-

munities that these deliberately perverse texts struggle to usher into the field of representation.

So, what, finally, does my uncovering of such "queer sites" teach us, both about that sometimes polymorphous past that existed in the 1920s and 1930s and about our own wishfully queer present? As an indirect means of addressing this question, I would like to conclude by questioning some of the implications of what it means to clear a critical space, as I've just done, to do a "queer" reading, as I've also just done, of "modernism." What are the politics of relocating one kind of queerness to another period? Is "queer" still queer when grafted, even with the best of intentions, elsewhere? What, in particular, does it mean to take a mode of identification that is quintessentially postmodernist and show its "modernist" affinities? Is this a *useful* or appropriative move, and if so to whom and for what reasons? As I noted at the beginning of this essay, I'm not particularly interested in establishing an "origins" theory of queerness, for such an approach, it seems to me, inevitably vitiates what is potentially radical about today's queer movement—its resistance to assimilation into the mainstream—by revealing it to have been around all along. Such a sleight of hand assimilates contemporary queer theory and praxis not only into "history" but, perhaps more egregiously, into the literary/critical canon to boot. In comparing the modernist era to our queer moment, however, there is one major distinction that stands out: the ferment of protoqueer attitudes in urban spaces in the 1920s and 1930s, lacking an organized sexual politics, became, ironically, the prelude to a further reinforcement of the hetero/homo divide upon the onset of World War II, as the conclusion of Chauncey's *Gay New York* devastatingly illustrates, while the political advocacy of queerness in the 1990s self-consciously attempts to challenge and break down that binarism. Are we then to consider the former moment a failure? Or conversely, is the lesson that all queerness is destined to "fail," that is, destined to be assimilated or transformed into mainstream ways of thinking, and might this assimilability, perversely enough, turn out to be queerness' power, both then and now? I would like to end with Kristen Ross's thoughtful reply to those who would from hindsight judge any revolutionary eruption that never reaches maturity as a failure or a falling off: for those who lived such moments of rupture and transformation, she writes (she is specifically referring to the workers' takeover of Paris's urban spaces in the 1871 rebellion), "the fulfillment was *already there.*"[45] Perhaps the same might be said of those protoqueer lives that, however temporarily, began to transform urban space in the 1920s and 1930s; perhaps, in the next century, the same might be said of our queer moment: for us, the fulfillment is *already here.*

---

[45] Kristin Ross, *The Emergence of Social Space: Rimbaud and the Paris Commune* (Minneapolis: University of Minnesota Press, 1988) 45 (emphases are Ross's). As Ross also notes, "the lesson of the Commune can be found in its recognition that revolution consists not in changing the juridical form that allots space/time (for example, allowing a party to appropriate bureaucratic organization) but rather in completely transforming the nature of space/time ... citizens were no longer informed of their history after the fact but were actually occupying the moment of its realization" (41–42).

MEDIUMS, MESSAGES, AND LUCKY NUMBERS:
African-American Female Spiritualists
and Numbers Runners in Interwar Detroit

Victoria W. Wolcott

> Before I joined this church I used to play as big as fifty cents
> almost every day in policy and never hit. I went to visit the
> church, got a private reading. She told me to fast. I did three
> days and one day I played fifty cents and won. I then thought
> I ought to've played more so I put in fifty cents the next day
> and won. Nobody can tell me she's a fake. That woman
> knows what she's talking about.
>
> —African-American resident of Detroit in the 1930s[1]

"That woman" was a Spiritualist medium, an African-
American woman who was part of a thriving underground
economy of gamblers, bootleggers, and ironically, church leaders that shaped urban life in interwar Detroit. The Spiritualist
church led by this medium provided its parishioners with religious teaching and a space for ecstatic worship; less conventionally, it offered tips on what numbers to play in the immensely popular game of policy. African-American community
leaders scorned this coupling of sacred and secular space and
practice. They attempted to curtail the immorality and female
disorder associated with Spiritualist activity and gambling by
constructing a collective public identity based on bourgeois
values of respectability: thrift, sexual restraint, cleanliness,
and hard work.[2] For Spiritualist mediums, however, partici-

---

[1] Henry Allen Bullock, "The Urbanization of the Negro Church in Detroit," Second Semester Report to the Earhart Foundation for Community
Leadership per Dr. R. D. McKenzie, 30 May 1935, Extracts from the Experiences of Various Spiritual Leaders, appendix C-III, 50. Unidentified informant.

[2] My understanding of a "public identity" follows from James Scott's
definition of a "public transcript" as a "shorthand way of describing the open
interaction between subordinates and those who dominate." See James C.
Scott, *Domination and the Arts of Resistance: Hidden Transcripts* (New Haven:
Yale University Press, 1990) 2. For a discussion of the "politics of respectability" within the African-American community see Evelyn Brooks Higginbotham,
Righteous Discontent: The Women's Movement in the Black Baptist Church,

pation in the underground economy and religious sects led to cultural authority and economic independence. During the Great Migration of Southern African-Americans to Northern cities, and for the ensuing two decades, community leaders and female participants in the underground economy clashed over whether urban space would become primarily a site of "respectable" public performance or a site of leisure and labor. In this essay I want to explore this dispute over the use and abuse of social space.

African-American men and women employed two major spatial frameworks during the crucial transition decade of the 1920s. The first was constructed by African-American ministers, social workers, club women, and reformers who responded to a massive influx of new migrants into Detroit by labeling them Southern rural peasants who needed to be taught Northern values of urban citizenship. Contradictions inherent in this Southern/Northern dichotomy became evident as working-class African-American women developed new strategies of survival that transcended geographically based identities constructed by black elites. Thus urban spaces such as storefront churches became contested ground in 1920s Detroit: for some they represented a Southern primitive past; for others, a location of economic and cultural empowerment.

During the Great Migration African-American leaders attempted strategically to fix the geographic identity of working-class Southern migrants. In the late 1910s and early 1920s, for example, African-American migrants arriving in Detroit's central train station were likely to receive an Urban League pamphlet that included two juxtaposed photographs (fig. 1). The first depicted a woman sitting on trash-covered steps outside her home. She wears a housecoat, nightcap, and slippers and sits with her legs spread apart. Directly opposite is a second photo of the same woman; in this image the steps are clean and she is demurely dressed, her hair well groomed, and her legs pressed together.[3] These two images, distributed by

---

1880–1920 (Cambridge: Harvard University Press, 1993) 185–229; and Willard B. Gatewood, *Aristocrats of Color: The Black Elite, 1880–1920* (Bloomington: Indiana University Press, 1990) 23, 182–209.

[3] Brochure of the Detroit Urban League, 1918, box 1, folder 9, Detroit Urban League Papers, Michigan Historical Collections, Bentley Historical Library, University of Michigan, Ann Arbor, Michigan (hereafter cited as DULP-

the Dress Well Club, an organization of young, educated African-American men, reflected a dichotomy central to the discourse of urban migration and resettlement: on the one side disorder, dirt, licentiousness, and a disheveled appearance, on the other self-restraint, cleanliness, chastity, and respectability. Throughout the interwar period Detroit's elites viewed African-American female migrants as embodiments of the disorder and backwardness represented by the rural South. By policing the behavior and appearance of female migrants, these elites sought to instill "Northern" and "urban" characteristics into the community as a whole.

Within this new language of urban migration African-American women were viewed as the caretakers of neighborhoods and homes, responsible for the visual appearance of community, family, and private property. In the increasingly overcrowded city of Detroit this visual presentation of respectable public identity was of paramount importance to African-American elites as whites and blacks interacted in workplaces, public transportation, and city streets. The behavior and demeanor of individual African-Americans—their houses, churches, and stores—were on public display, actively fashioning a communal public identity. In 1917, at the founding meeting of the Dress Well Club, Forrester B. Washington, the first director of the Detroit Urban League, gave a speech asking, "Why is ... segregation increasing?" He attacks the individual behavior of female migrants: "Chiefly on account of the loud, noisy, almost nude women in 'Mother Hubbards' standing around in the public thoroughfares ... There are dirty white people of course, but white people are the judges and colored

---

MHC-BHL). This brochure was originally printed in 1918 and redistributed by John C. Dancy, the second director of the Detroit Urban League, in 1922. See David Allen Levine, *Internal Combustion: The Races in Detroit, 1915–1926* (Westport, CT: Greenwood Press, 1976) 117. Dancy wrote in his autobiography that 20,000 of these pamphlets were distributed after the second printing. He also remembered that the pamphlet was "very unpopular with some members of the community," indicating that some migrants may have been offended by the condescending tone of the Urban League literature. See John C. Dancy, *Sand against the Wind: The Memoirs of John C. Dancy* (Detroit: Wayne State University Press, 1966) 156.

HELPFUL HINTS

DON'T carry on loud conversations or use vulgar or obscene language on the street cars, streets, or in public places. Remember that this hurts us as a race.

DON'T go about the streets or on the street car in bungalow aprons, boudoir caps and house slippers. Wear regular street clothes when you go into the streets.

TRY to dress neatly at all times, but don't be a dude or wear flashy clothes. They are as undesirable and as harmful as unclean clothes.

General Disorderly Appearance

DON'T think you can hold your job unless you are on time, industrious, efficient and sober.

DON'T sit in front of your house or around Belle Isle or public places with your shoes off. Don't wear overalls on Sunday.

DON'T stay away from work every time someone gives a picnic or boat ride. Stay on your job. Others do.

DON'T spend all your money for pleasure. Save some of it for extra clothing and fuel for the winter and to take care of your family and yourself when sickness comes.

Figure 1. Between 1918 and 1922 Detroit Urban League workers handed out more than twenty thousand of these brochures to incoming migrants as part of an ongoing effort to reform the appearance and behavior of working-class.

DON'T forget that cleanliness and fresh air are necessary to good health. Keep your windows open.

DON'T do your children's hair up into alleys, canals and knots if you don't want other children to make fun of them. Keep them clean.

DON'T keep your children out of school. See that they attend the nearest school to you.

DON'T fail to start a savings account with some good bank or building loan association.

DON'T throw refuse and tin cans in your back or front yards. Keep your surroundings as clean as possible. This makes for good health.

Neatly Clothed and Orderly Appearance

DON'T fool with patent medicines in case of sickness. Send for a good doctor. In case you have no money, go to some of the Board of Health clinics.

DON'T be rude and ugly to people on the streets. Be courteous and polite and thereby keep out of trouble.

DON'T fail to meet the teachers of your children. Keep in touch with them. Every hateful thing that your child says about the teacher is not true.

DON'T fail to become connected with some church as soon as you get in the city.

DON'T make lots of unnecessary noise going to and from baseball games. If the parks are taken away from you it will be partly your own fault.

African-Americans. Brochure of the Detroit Urban League, 1918, box 1, folder 9, Detroit Urban League Papers, Michigan Historical Collections, Bentley Historical Library, University of Michigan, Ann Arbor, Michigan

people are being judged."[4] Similarly, the "helpful hints" listed on the Urban League brochure included prescriptions targeted specifically at African-American women's public appearance: "don't go about the streets or on the street car in bungalow aprons, boudoir caps and house slippers," and "don't do your children's hair up into alleys, canals and knots."[5] In the crowded streetscape of urban Detroit the visual presentation of "respectable" women would offset negative stereotyping of the race as a whole.

Detroit's African-American leaders were painfully aware that white employers and civic leaders were judging their community. Another Dress Well Club brochure advised, "don't allow your women folks to go about the streets ... if you want white people to respect them." The pamphlet concluded, "To do these things means to help yourself and 20,000 more of your own people in this city to make good in your jobs, to get better jobs and to keep down prejudice, race friction and discrimination."[6] To fight increasing segregation, ensure employment for the large numbers of incoming migrants during the period of the Great Migration, and aid in the "uplift" of the race, African-American leaders sought to create a cohesive identity that emphasized respectability, thrift, and cleanliness. This identity was also rooted in a geographic place—the urban North—that represented the polar opposite of the migrants' imagined origins.

During the interwar period this public community identity was gendered around attributes of female respectability such as morality, cleanliness, and religiosity. Female respectability had been a central theme in racial uplift ideology since the late nineteenth century in both the North and the South.[7] Like

---

[4] Forrester B. Washington, September 1917, box 1, folder 8, DULP-MHC-BHL. A "Mother Hubbard" is a long, loose housecoat or dress.

[5] Brochure of the Detroit Urban League, 1918.

[6] Dress Well Club brochure, n.d., Detroit Urban League Papers, box 1, folder 8, DULP-MHC-BHL.

[7] The strong emphasis placed on young African-American women's morality in the discourse of migration and urbanization stems partly from the increased visibility of female reformers during the late nineteenth century and the first decades of the twentieth century, known as the "woman's era." For examples of this rhetoric see Mattie Hurd Rutledge, "A Hint to Our Women," *Colored American Magazine* 5, 2 (June 1902): 141–42; "The Way of the World:

white female Progressive reformers, African-Americans placed ideologies of domesticity, morality, and sexual restraint at the center of their uplift work.[8] For African-American women, however, a discourse of female respectability was also a potent defense against white beliefs in their inherent immorality and lack of virtue. As African-American leaders faced the challenges of the Great Migration, they used the language of respectability and the protective programs of female reformers as a blueprint for socializing all migrants.

Although female migrants were portrayed as naive and in need of the message of racial uplift and urban assimilation, it was likely they had already encountered these prescriptions for self and community betterment in the South. Many of Detroit's female migrants had come from Southern cities where they had encountered an urban terrain similar to Detroit.[9] Hence I view their inaccurate characterization as rural peasants as a

---

Our Noble Womanhood," *Colored American Magazine* 7, 8 (August 1904): 530–31; and Addie Hunton, "Negro Womanhood Defended," *The Voice of the Negro* 1, 7 (July 1904): 280–82. See also Kevin K. Gaines, "Uplifting the Race: Black Middle-Class Ideology in the Era of the 'New Negro', 1890–1935" (Ph.D. dissertation, Brown University, 1991); Cynthia Neverdon-Morton, *Afro-American Women of the South and the Advancement of the Race, 1895–1925* (Knoxville: University of Tennessee Press, 1989); and Dorothy Salem, *To Better Our World: Black Women in Organized Reform, 1890–1920* (Brooklyn, NY: Carlson Publishing, 1990).

[8] For a comparison of African-American and white women's reform work during the Progressive era see Linda Gordon, "Black and White Visions of Welfare: Women's Welfare Activism, 1890–1945," *The Journal of American History* 78 (September 1991): 559–90; Anne Firor Scott, *Natural Allies: Women's Associations in American Histories* (Urbana: University of Illinois Press, 1991) 91–92, 146–49, 168–69; and Louise M. Newman, "Laying Claim to Difference: Ideologies of Race and Gender in the U.S. Woman's Movement" (Ph.D. dissertation, Brown University, 1992).

[9] Of the 250 families surveyed by Forrester B. Washington in 1920, 63 percent, or 158 heads of families, had come from Southern cities. See Forrester B. Washington, *The Negro in Detroit: A Survey of the Conditions of a Negro Group in a Northern Industrial Center during the War Prosperity Period*, vol. 2 (Detroit: Research Bureau of the Associated Charities of Detroit, 1920) 104. Carole Marks, in her book *Farewell—We're Good and Gone: The Great Black Migration* (Bloomington: Indiana University Press, 1989), stresses the number of Southern migrants who lived in cities prior to the Great Migration (34–35).

rhetorical strategy employed by community elites who wished to present migrants as not fully formed urban residents, potential "troublemakers" who needed to be taught the lessons of urban citizenship. This rhetorical strategy would counter biological notions of inherent African-American immorality and criminality, replacing them with a sociological model that stressed environmental factors. The image of the South as primarily rural and backward was a useful foil in this project. This public community identity, however, veiled a more heterogeneous set of categories that made up individual African-American identities. Some female migrants continued to cook Southern food or listen to Southern music; nevertheless, many of them could capably navigate the urban terrain.[10]

The social terrain of the city after the Great Migration also shaped the contours of a collective African-American identity in Detroit. Major cities were potential sites of integration in many forms: gender-, race-, and class-mixing were endemic in an overcrowded and dynamic urban center. By the early twentieth century Progressive reformers became concerned that a migration of black and white single women to cities would lead to the growth of vice, particularly prostitution.[11] Reformers saw these female migrants as both dangerous and endangered in the heterosocial city, and a multitude of settlement houses, employment offices, boarding houses, and other institutions were founded to contain migrants in sex-segregated and supervised spaces.[12] The urban influx of large numbers of Afri-

---

[10] For a similar analysis see Ann Ducille, "Blues Notes on Black Sexuality: Sex and the Texts of Jessie Fauset and Nella Larsen," *Journal of the History of Sexuality* 3 (1993): 418–44. As applied to African-American female authors and blues singers, Ducille criticizes the belief in an "authentic" African-American identity constructed as "southern, rural, and sexually uninhibited" (423). See also Hazel Carby, "Policing the Black Woman's Body in an Urban Context," *Critical Inquiry* 18 (Summer 1992): 738–55.

[11] For a history of single white women's influx into the city see Joanne J. Meyerowitz, *Women Adrift: Independent Wage Earners in Chicago, 1880–1930* (Chicago: University of Chicago Press, 1988). See also Carby, "Policing"; and Jacqueline Jones, *Labor of Love, Labor of Sorrow: Black Women, Work, and the Family from Slavery to the Present* (New York: Basic Books, 1985) 155–56.

[12] Mary Ryan, in *Women in Public: Between Banners and Ballots, 1825–1880* (Baltimore: Johns Hopkins University Press, 1990), argues that "the politics of the public streets divided women by race and class, and between

can-American migrants during and after World War I raised the specter of "race-mixing" in illicit spaces, such as "disorderly" houses[13] where African-American prostitutes worked.[14] White and African-American reformers used these threats to urban spatial order to justify the planning of public spaces (such as parks), the increase of a police presence, and the legal containment of vice. Community leaders policed those spaces of leisure where class-, gender-, and race-mixing were most likely to occur—saloons, houses of prostitution, even baseball parks—with particular zeal.[15]

In Detroit, as in most cities, the African-American community was largely segregated into one neighborhood, the East side.[16] It is no coincidence that this neighborhood was also

---

the dangerous and the endangered" (93–94). See also Judy Walkowitz, *City of Dreadful Delight: Narratives of Sexual Danger in Late-Victorian London* (Chicago: University of Chicago Press, 1992) 18–22; Elizabeth Wilson, *The Sphinx in the City: Urban Life, the Control of Disorder, and Women* (London: Virago Press, 1991); and Sarah Deutsch, "Learning to Talk More Like a Man: Boston Women's Class-Bridging Organizations, 1870–1940," *American Historical Review* 97 (April 1992): 379–404.

[13] *Disorderly houses, sporting houses,* and *buffet flats* were terms used for houses of prostitution during the early twentieth century. These establishments also offered gambling, music, illegal liquor, and other services.

[14] African-American community leaders and urban dwellers were vehemently opposed to racial segregation in Detroit. Elite African-Americans, however, were also wary of lower-class blacks having contact with white Detroiters in unregulated spaces because these contacts could undermine the project of constructing a respectable public identity, and the "criminal element" among the white working-class community might entice vulnerable migrants into disreputable occupations such as bootlegging.

[15] For theoretical discussions of space see Henri Lefebvre, *The Production of Space* (Cambridge: Blackwell, 1974); Shirley Ardener, ed., *Women and Space: Ground Rules and Social Maps* (New York: St. Martin's Press, 1981); Mark Gottdiener, *The Social Production of Urban Space* (Austin: University of Texas Press, 1985); E. Soja, *Postmodern Geographies* (London: Verso, 1989); and Michael Keith and Steve Pile, eds., *Place and the Politics of Identity* (New York: Routledge, 1993).

[16] The East side community was also referred to as the St. Antoine District, Black Bottom, and in the 1930s Paradise Valley. By the mid-1920s some middle-class African Americans began to settle in a small area of the West

identified as the city's primary vice district, home to numerous speakeasies, houses of prostitution, and gambling dens. The designation of the African-American community as a center of vice made it particularly difficult for community elites to create a public identity that emphasized respectability. Because racial segregation led to class integration, with elite and working-class blacks living in close proximity, public displays of bourgeois respectability were muted by the identification of the neighborhood as anything but respectable. A relative lack of gender segregation, with male boarders living in cramped apartments and few opportunities for reputable recreation, reflected negatively on the community because it suggested the possibility of illicit encounters between the sexes and thus racial immorality. The crowding of the African-American community also meant that there were few homosocial spaces available where African-American women could congregate.[17] In Detroit, African-American club women used available spaces—in churches, the Detroit Urban League's settlement house, and the YWCA—to offer female migrants classes and clubs that taught domestic skills, health, hygiene, and social mores. The physical neighborhood also became a target for reformers, who attempted to shut down "disorderly" houses, shame prostitutes working on the streets, and close the numerous "unsightly" storefront churches that occupied the abandoned stores of fleeing white merchants.

In the social mapping of early twentieth-century America clear divisions between classes, and different social roles for men and women, become evidence of a racial or ethnic group's social advancement. These class and gender divisions are

---

side, and a few African-American satellite communities were founded by migrants on the outskirts of the city.

[17] In her article "Learning to Talk More Like a Man," Sara Deutsch describes female urban reformers' efforts to "create space where working women could appear in public without having their virtue questioned by being 'on the streets'" (390). For African-American women whose virtue was always questioned by whites, the imperative to get off "the streets" was even stronger. See also Kathy Peiss, *Cheap Amusements: Working Women and Leisure in Turn-of-the-Century New York* (Philadelphia: Temple University Press, 1986), on the decline of homosocial space.

mapped in the built environment.[18] Therefore, advocates of racial uplift viewed the gender and class integration of the African-American community as an impediment to racial progress. For African-Americans attempting to counter negative stereotypes of their community, the endemic crowding of Detroit's East side was a barrier to further reform. By sanitizing public space through class and gender segregation, and hiding or removing evidence of vice, reformers hoped to "uplift" Southern migrants and decrease *racial* segregation within the city. In an effort to attain this goal, they linked the migrants with an imagined image of the South as backward and primitive. Through the imagined transformation of Southern rural disorder into Northern urban order, Detroit's African-American community would prove capable of earning the trust and respect of the white community.

The dichotomy Southern/Northern, however, was never a stable one. Threatening urban spaces like gambling parlors, pool rooms, and dance halls were labeled by community leaders as dangerous, unruly, and illicit: an incarnation of Southern cultural practices, which reformers identified as the epitome of social disorder. In reality, these spaces encapsulated Northern urban identities *and* Southern rural ones: one could observe "sophisticated," urbanized women wearing the latest fashions at a cabaret, eating Southern food, and dancing to jazz. The pervasive illegal activities of gambling and prostitution were not only sustained by the higher wages and larger population of the Northern city, but the music, dance styles, and way of life that accompanied such practices reflected complex combinations of Southern and Northern cultures.[19]

---

[18] Daphne Spain, in *Gendered Spaces* (Chapel Hill: University of North Carolina Press, 1992), argues that spatial segregation leads to greater social stratification (15–18). For a discussion of how gender inequality becomes part of the built environment see Dolores Hayden, *The Grand Domestic Revolution: A History of Feminist Designs for American Homes, Neighborhoods and Cities* (Cambridge, MA: MIT Press, 1981); and Leslie Kanes Weisman, *Discrimination by Design: A Feminist Critique of the Man-Made Environment* (Urbana: University of Illinois Press, 1992).

[19] For a discussion of the complexity of African-American culture and place see Barnor Hesse, "Black to Front and Black Again: Racialization through Contested Times and Spaces," in *Place and the Politics of Identity*

Similarly, the very definition of respectability was contested by the lives of many African-American women. A recent migrant may have attended a local church and belonged to a woman's club, both "respectable" activities by middle-class standards, and also played the numbers or danced at a cabaret. These seemingly contradictory practices were part of a multiregional and working-class notion of respectability that emphasized the education of children and support of family and downplayed public displays of "refined" behavior.

***

Two sets of cultural practices—the Spiritualist church and the numbers business—reflected an alternative set of values and urban identities that African-American leaders attempted to eradicate. These urban institutions and practices reflected a more mobile and complex matrix of identities and economic strategies that did not fit easily into a Northern/Southern dichotomy. Rather, in the segregated neighborhood of Detroit's East side African-American women ingeniously made use of the community's limited economic resources and took advantage of the crowded streetscapes to make better lives for themselves and their families. Thus a different spatial dynamic within Detroit facilitated the growth of alternative practices that were not bounded by bourgeois definitions of respectability.[20] Within the segregated African-American neighborhood

---

162–82; and Paul Gilroy, *The Black Atlantic: Modernity and Double Consciousness* (Cambridge: Harvard University Press, 1993).

[20] I prefer to use the term *alternative* rather than *oppositional* when discussing women's involvement in the underground economy because these women were not consciously opposing elite reform strategies, although their activities did at times clash with elite expectations of appropriate behavior. For a discussion of alternative versus oppositional practices see Raymond Williams, "Base and Superstructure in Marxist Cultural Theory," *Problems in Materialism and Culture: Selected Essays* (London: NLB, 1980). I am indebted to Robin Kelley for sharing his thoughts on this subject with me. See his essay, "'We Are Not What We Seem': The Politics and Pleasures of Community," *Race Rebels: Culture, Politics, and the Black Working Class* (New York: Free

black women made links among a variety of institutions such as the Spiritualist church and the numbers racket. As a result a new urban identity—that of the female medium who many believed had a unique power and authority—emerged and flourished.

African-American women engaged in gambling because Detroit's job market was limited by racism and sexism, offering them few options for legitimate employment. The segmentation of the work force compelled them to choose from a few varieties of personal service: laundry work, day work in private homes, and domestic service in hotels, department stores, or office buildings.[21] Some enterprising female entrepreneurs also owned and ran beauty salons, coffee shops, and clothing or millinery stores. But does this tidy listing of "occupations" (from the studies done by the Detroit Urban League and the Mayor's Interracial Committee) capture the ways in which female migrants were able to survive in such a hostile economic climate? What this list reflects are those occupations viewed as "respectable" for women in the African-American community, jobs that were available through employment offices and often filled at the discretion of community leaders. This "above-ground" economy had severe occupational limitations that prevented African-American women from adequately supporting themselves and their families.

In reality, another layer of occupations, ways to make money, ways to find a place to live, ways to provide care for children was located in Detroit's underground economy, a social space that was much more class-, race-, and gender-integrated than service work.[22] Unlike the factory floor or the

---

Press, 1994) 35–54, for a discussion of alternative leisure practices in working-class African-American communities.

[21] Thomas, *Life for Us* 32–34; Young Women's Christian Association, "The Employment of Women for Day Work," 1917, United Community Services Papers, box 5, Walter P. Reuther Library, Archives of Labor and Urban Affairs, Wayne State University, Detroit, Michigan; and Mayor's Interracial Committee, *The Negro in Detroit* (Detroit Bureau of Governmental Research, 1926), section 3, "Industry," 26.

[22] For a sample of the literature on the underground economy see Louis A. Ferman, Stuart Henry, and Michele Hoyman, eds., *The Annals of the American Academy of Political and Social Science: The Informal Economy* 493 (September 1987); Cyril Robinson, "Exploring the Informal Economy," *Social*

private white homes where many African-Americans labored, the workplace of the underground economy was the street and neighborhood, places where class- and gender-mixing were endemic.[23] Because of the integrated and illicit nature of the underground economy, reformers attempted to shut down the houses of prostitution and "blind pigs" located within the African-American community,[24] but the streetscape of the underground economy was also shared by respectable churches, community centers, and businesses. Indeed, gamblers and

Justice 15, 3–4 (1988): 3–16; Carl P. Simon and Ann D. Witte, *Beating the System: The Underground Economy* (New York: Auburn Publishing Co., 1982); and Philip Mattera, *Off the Books: The Rise of the Underground Economy* (London: Pluto Press, 1985). Most of the literature on the underground economy consists of sociological studies such as those listed above or ethnographic studies of inner-city communities. For examples of the latter see Carol B. Stack, *All Our Kin: Strategies for Survival in a Black Community* (New York: Harper & Row, 1974); Leslie M. Dow, "High Weeds in Detroit," *Urban Anthropology* 6 (1987): 111–28; and Mitchell Duneier, *Slim's Table: Race, Respectability, and Masculinity* (Chicago: University of Chicago Press, 1992). Discussions of the informal economy in African-American history have been largely restricted to the "ghetto school" of urban history, which views criminal activity as evidence of a growing pathological culture within ghettos. See, in particular, Allan Spear, *Black Chicago: The Making of a Negro Ghetto, 1890–1920* (Chicago: University of Chicago Press, 1967); and Gilbert Osofsky, *Harlem: The Making of a Ghetto* (New York: Harper & Row, 1966).

[23] Spain, in *Gendered Spaces*, has suggested that women who worked in gender-integrated workspaces had more access to knowledge and thus power (28, 171–72). If one views African-American women's employment as limited to "respectable" occupations, which were segregated by both race and gender, their access to the tools of power appear very limited. Women's involvement in the underground economy, however, opened up new options for employment and empowerment. Robin Kelley, in his article "'We Are Not What We Seem'," makes a similar point, arguing that African-American women's employment in the leisure industry was "potentially empowering since it turns labors not associated with wage work—dancing, sexual play, intercourse—into income" (49). For a discussion of class integration in African-American "places of amusement" see Henry J. McGuinn, "Recreation," in *Negro Problems in Cities*, ed. T. J. Woofter (1928; rpt. College Park, MD: McGrath Publishing Co., 1969) 227–82.

[24] A blind pig was an illegal saloon during Prohibition, where gambling routinely occurred.

madams often used a store façade or a reputable-looking boarding house to shield their activities. This complex mixing of "legitimate" and "illegitimate" businesses made the work of sanitizing public space within the community particularly difficult for Urban League officials, middle-class club women, and ministers. In order to construct a public identity of communal respectability, these elites attempted to map which churches, stores, and boarding houses conformed to their norms and which should be labeled as illegitimate products of the Great Migration.

Storefront churches became a primary target of reformers engaged in this project of mapping social space within the African-American community. In the decades following the Great Migration migrants who felt alienated in Detroit's larger congregations often founded small churches in empty storefronts. Women were the mainstay of these small churches, just as they were the mainstay of the African-American church generally; yet, unlike more established denominations, storefront churches allowed women leadership roles as ministers, elders, saints, and church founders.[25] These storefront churches became social locations where women could exercise power and establish a sense of self-esteem through religious worship, but storefront churches also incurred the wrath of community leaders, who viewed them as outward-facing symbols of Southern primitivism.[26] Often run and always attended by women,

---

[25] See Cheryl Townsend Gilkes, "'Together and in Harness': Women's Traditions in the Sanctified Church," *Signs* 10, 4 (Summer 1985): 678–99; Carol Lois Haywood, "The Authority and Empowerment of Women among Spiritualist Groups," *Journal for the Scientific Study of Religion* 22 (1983): 157–66; Hans A. Baer and Merrill Singer, *African-American Religion in the Twentieth Century: Varieties of Protest and Accommodation* (Knoxville: University of Tennessee Press, 1992) 165; St. Clair Drake and Horace R. Cayton, *Black Metropolis: A Study of Negro Life in a Northern City* (Chicago: University of Chicago Press, 1945) 632.

[26] In *Black Feminist Thought: Knowledge, Consciousness, and the Politics of Empowerment* (New York: Routledge, 1991), Patricia Hill Collins identifies churches as a "safe space" that provides African-American women "a prime location for resisting objectification as the Other" (95). See also Farah Josephine Griffin, "'Who Set You Flowin'?': Migration, Urbanization, and African-American Culture" (Ph.D. dissertation, Yale University, 1992) 12–13, 137. Although I find both Collins and Griffin's use of "safe space" a useful mapping

these churches were also linked to the underground economy through Spiritualist mediums who provided numbers that African-American men and women would gamble in hopes of "hitting big."

Although storefront churches had diverse theological stances, urban reformers tended to group them together as an unfortunate byproduct of the Great Migration.[27] A 1926 study of Detroit's African-American community reported,

> There are scattered in various sections of Detroit a group of churches whose services cannot be better described than as religious hysteria.... They are characterized by the clapping of hands, shouting, yelling, moaning, rolling, and the exhibition of general emotional instability. Many of the members work themselves to the point where they roll up and down the aisles, shake their bodies, jump, fall into trances.... The individuals who form the membership of these hysterical churches are extremely ignorant, which fact is exemplified in the noisy and irreligious manner in which they carry on their services. There seems to be a general impression among them that shouting, dancing hither and thither, groaning, howling, crying protracted prayers, frantic embracing, the waving of handkerchiefs, groveling on the floor, the throwing up of arms, and similar "hysterical" outbursts are the sole means of expressing devotion to God.... Often those who shout, cry and groan the most and pray the longest prayers are the most immoral and hypocritical people in the community, who are constantly getting into trouble for stealing and for com-

---

of urban geography, I believe they underplay the importance of power relations within these spaces, which are never totally "safe" or neutral. Within the category of churches, however, storefront churches provided relatively more autonomy and potential empowerment for African-American women than the larger congregations.

[27] See Ira De A. Reid, "Let Us Prey!" *Opportunity*, September 1926, 274–78. Reid argues of storefront churches that "Neither their appearance nor their character warrants the respect of the community" (275). See also William A. Clark, "Sanctification in Negro Religion," *Social Forces* 15 (1937): 544–51; and Benjamin E. Mays and Joseph William Nicholson, *The Negro's Church* (New York: Russell & Russell, 1933). For a more positive commentary on the growth of storefront churches see Miles Mark Fisher, "Organized Religion and the Cults," *The Crisis*, January 1937, 8–10, 29, 30.

mitting other crimes which are supposed to be contrary to their religion.[28]

This same report identified the members of storefront churches as being "made up entirely of the unskilled laboring classes" and "the masses of Negro migrants." Thus reformers considered storefront churches, with their ecstatic style of worship, as a direct result of Southern migration and cultural practices that went against a community identity of respectability, self-restraint, and sexual control.[29] Community elites saw those who belonged to the storefront churches as unable to adapt to Northern urban styles of worship, and migrants were chastised by community leaders for their immorality, licentiousness, and lack of discipline.

In this report African-American church leaders and members of the Detroit Urban League lumped all storefront churches together as a cohesive and equally reprehensible group. There were, in fact, at least two significant types of churches that tended to be housed in storefronts: Sanctified and Spiritualist.[30] The Sanctified church is a general label given to Holiness and Pentecostal churches in which "saints" distinguish themselves from other Christians. Historian Townsend Gilkes has suggested that the Sanctified church provided African American women with "an alternative model of power

---

[28] *The Negro in Detroit* (1926), section 10, "Religion," 17–20. This section was researched and written by the African-American members of the interracial committee because it was not believed to have affected "race relations" ("Introduction" 14). An earlier report on Detroit's African-American community came to similar conclusions about storefront churches. See Washington, *The Negro in Detroit* (1920), vol. 10, "The Religious Life of the Negro in Detroit." Washington wrote, "It is impossible to find in the Christian religion any justification for such barbaric practices as go on in these so-called churches."

[29] This view is reflected in more recent studies of African-American religion as well. See, for example, E. Franklin Frazier, *The Negro Church in America* (New York: Schocken Books, 1963) 53.

[30] The other significant denominations represented in the category of storefront churches were "primitive" Baptist or Methodist churches that had broken off from the larger denominations and so-called "cult" religions such as the black Jews.

and leadership" within Protestantism.[31] Women in Sanctified churches had access to leadership roles as elders, pastors, bishops, and teachers of the gospel. Their role in Sanctified churches was also an extension of the female community within the neighborhood. For example, Elder Lucy Smith, the founder of the Church of All Nations in Chicago, related how she was able to become a successful church leader:

> I started with giving advice to folks in my neighborhood. This made me realize how much a good talking does to many people. Very soon they started coming more and more, and so for the last seven years I've been preachin' to larger numbers.[32]

This female religious authority was possible in the alternative space of the storefront, where neighbors congregated in a more democratic and less hierarchical setting than established African Methodist Episcopalian (A.M.E.) and Baptist churches.

The rituals of shouting, spirit possession, speaking in tongues, and dancing had their roots in small Southern churches, and many of the women and men who made up the congregations and sometimes founded churches were reacting against what they viewed as "citified ritual."[33] As a study of storefront religions reported,

> A man in Detroit, deacon in a store-front church, told one of the workers that he could not pray in a big church. Further inquiry ... revealed that the deacon really meant that he could not pray in the big Detroit church as he was accustomed to praying in the rural church of the South. His long, loud prayer would not be in place in the semi-sophisticated

---

[31] Gilkes, "'Together and in Harness'" 680. See also Zora Neale Hurston, *Sanctified Church* (Berkeley: Turtle Island, 1983).

[32] Drake and Cayton, *Black Metropolis* 644.

[33] Drake and Cayton, *Black Metropolis* 634. Quote from "One woman who has been in Chicago for 17 years." It should be noted that Sanctified churches and emotional worship styles also came under attack in the South. See, for example, Rev. S. A. Peeler, "What Improvements Should Be Made in the Religious Worship of the Churches?" in *The United Negro: His Problems and His Progress*, ed. I. Garland Penn and J. W. E. Bowen (Atlanta: D.E. Luther Publishing, 1902) 146–51.

Detroit church. He therefore organized a church of his own.[34]

Because of its clear Southern origins, the Sanctified church did fit well into the Southern/Northern dichotomy. The worship styles of Sanctified migrants were therefore identified by elites as "primitive" and "irrational" because of their Southern roots.

The conflation of "Southern" and "primitive" with immorality, however, did not fit within the teachings of the Sanctified church, which emphasized adherence to a moral and "clean" life in order to reach a state of sainthood. Elites' mapping of storefront churches as inherently immoral and illegitimate, then, failed to capture the complexity of female religious practices and identities facilitated by the availability of storefront space. Bishop Ida Robinson's Mt. Sinai Holy Church in Philadelphia, a church known for its large number of female preachers and elders, had this list of prohibitions:

> fornication, adultery, lying, stealing, backbiting, straightening the hair, impure conversation, swearing, participation in athletic games, attendance at football, baseball games etc., drinking intoxicants, smoking, polishing the nails, wearing short dresses, attending motion pictures, chewing gum, gambling in any form.[35]

Sanctified church teachings hardly appear worthy of the charge of "demoralizing practices," nor were these teachings a "dangerous element in the community." Rather, the female members and founders of these churches *were* carrying out a commitment to religious beliefs, religious education, morality, and community strength. Why, then, did their style of worship cause such concern? The act of ecstatic worship was in itself a reclaiming of the body as a site of what the cultural critic Michael Dyson calls "the intersection of the sacred and the secu-

---

[34] Mays and Nicholson, *The Negro's Church* 98.

[35] Quoted in Arthur Huff Fauset, *Black Gods of the Metropolis: Negro Religious Cults in the Urban North* (Philadelphia: University of Pennsylvania Press, 1944) 16. Bishop Robinson founded her church in 1924, and it is still thriving today.

lar, the spiritual and the sensual."[36] An integral part of the teachings of bourgeois respectability was the exercise of physical self-restraint, an ideal that ecstatic worship openly rejected.

The constant references to "demoralizing" also linked the "hysteric" actions of church members to other actions that would demoralize women: prostitution, "immoral" dancing, and public entertainment. "These highly emotional services seem to produce an unbalanced state which robs the individual of inhibitions which would make him a reasoning being and capable of self-control in sudden uprushes of passion," wrote Washington in 1920, "He, or she, would steal, indulge in crimes of violence and not infrequently in sexual crime."[37] The loss of self-control in the churches, then, could lead to the unraveling of control elsewhere in the community, and the ubiquitous physical presence of the storefront churches was evidence of this potentiality. Furthermore, like other "disorderly" spaces the storefront churches were thought to lead to dangerous and unregulated race-mixing. Sanctified and Spiritualist churches often welcomed white parishioners, some of them also from the South, to join in their services. Thus a parallel between a relatively integrated church congregation and the "black and tan" saloons where white and black customers were admitted became a powerful image of the dangers of race-mixing. In both spaces white Detroiters would see African-Americans in an emotional state, diluting their respectable public identity.

The practice of dancing and playing secular music (the inclusion of tambourines, banjos, and guitars was often noted by observers) was viewed as additional evidence of the immorality of religious practices in storefront churches. A contemporary

---

[36] Michael Eric Dyson, *Reflecting Black: African-American Cultural Criticism* (Minneapolis: University of Minnesota Press, 1993) 20. In his comparative study of religion, *Ecstatic Religion: An Anthropological Study of Spirit Possession and Shamanism* (New York: Penguin Books, 1971), anthropologist I. M. Lewis provocatively argues that female-dominated cults that encourage spirit possession are "thinly disguised protest movements directed against the dominant sex" because "possession works to help the interests of the weak and downtrodden who have otherwise few effective means to press their claims for attention and respect" (31–32).

[37] Washington, *The Negro in Detroit* (1920), vol. 10.

social scientist reported, "When the praying is over, and everyone is 'in tune with the Infinite', a song is started ... the musicians ... pick it up, always in good jazz rhythm, usually to the tune of one of the classical blues songs." Dancers start to perform in response to the music,

> The worshiper who first began to speak in tongues is seized with an urge to dance. She dances with great vigor, a dance which she executes with a degree of gratefulness that indicates she has put in a great deal of time practicing it. Others join in the dancing until a large number are participating, and the building is creaking from rhythmic vibrations.[38]

This blending of spiritual and secular music, common in storefront churches, led to the development of gospel music, which blended secular blues and jazz styles with earlier spirituals and traditional music. "While many churches within the black community sought respectability by turning their backs on the past, banning the shout, discouraging enthusiastic religion," argues historian Lawrence Levine, "the Holiness churches constituted a revitalization movement with their emphasis upon healing, gifts of prophecy, speaking in tongues, spirit possession, and religious dance."[39]

African-American elites attacked this blending of sacred and secular practices as dangerous in part because of the contradictions it revealed in their public identity. Storefront churches encapsulated both the urban practices of commercialized leisure, dance, and music and the rural-based religious "primitivism" that more established denominations were

---

[38] Clark, "Sanctification in Negro Religion" 547. Clark describes this dancing as being very individual in style and fitting "into jazz counterpoint" (548).

[39] Lawrence Levine, *Black Culture and Black Consciousness* (Oxford: Oxford University Press, 1977) 179–80. Levine points out that gospel performers such as Mahalia Jackson got their start in storefront churches. "In those days the big colored churches didn't want me and they didn't let me in," reported Jackson, "I had to make it my business to pack the little basement-hall congregations and store-front churches and get their respect that way" (quoted in Levine, *Black Culture* 183). For a more recent ethnology of dance and music in Holiness churches see Beverly Boggs, "Some Aspects of Worship in a Holiness Church," *New York Folklore* 3 (1977): 29–44.

working to leave behind.[40] The dangers of the dance hall became linked with the dangers of ecstatic worship; both allowed individuals to express emotion and spirituality through physical enactments. Moreover, the integration of sacred and secular culture within the storefront churches was made possible by the urban setting itself. In the city, musicians, religious women and men, and entrepreneurs mingled, exchanging religious ideas, dance styles, and musical innovations. Their locations in storefronts reflected the crowding in the East side neighborhood, where larger buildings could not be found or built. Storefront churches, then, were quintessentially urban, products of the social integration that community leaders were trying to impede.

A target perhaps worthier of attack by social reformers was the Spiritualist church, the second type of storefront church and one whose popularity grew quickly in Detroit in the 1920s and 1930s. As in Sanctified churches women predominated in the leadership and membership of Spiritualist churches; one study of three such churches in Detroit notes that 88 percent of the members were women.[41] African-American Spiritualism continues to be a highly syncretic religion combining elements of Catholicism, Voodoo and Hoodoo, black Protestantism, and Islam as well as the messianic and nationalistic movements of the 1920s and 1930s, most notably Marcus Garvey's ideology of African-American self-determination. While the Sanctified church emerged from the Holiness revivals of the 1860s and 1870s, Spiritualist churches emerged

---

[40] The apparent "primitivism" of ecstatic worship attracted writers of the Harlem Renaissance, who both romanticized a rural Southern African-American past and were enthralled by the music and dances of the "jazz age." See in particular Claude McKay, *Harlem: Negro Metropolis* (New York: E. P. Dutton & Co., 1940) 73–85. Levine quotes Langston Hughes's memories of a Holiness church in Chicago, "I was entranced by their stepped-up rhythms, tambourines, hand clapping, and uninhibited dynamics, rivaled only by Ma Rainey singing the blues at the old Monogram Theater" (quoted in Levine, *Black Culture* 180).

[41] Henry Allen Bullock, "The Role of the Negro Church in the Negro Community of Detroit," Sociology paper prepared for the University of Michigan, 29.

in the 1920s in urban areas, primarily in the North.[42] In 1924 the National Colored Spiritualist Association, which had split from its white counterpart, was founded in Detroit, where by 1940 there were between two hundred and three hundred Spiritualist congregations.[43] Spiritualist churches were in no way Southern imports but were rather urban institutions founded by women and men who sought both to make sense of the uncertainty inherent in urban life and actively engage in the underground economy. Like the Sanctified churches Spiritualist congregations were located in storefronts in neighborhoods dotted with gambling dens and houses of prostitution; yet the congregants in Spiritualist churches did not set themselves apart from this world.

The largest Spiritualist church in Detroit during the interwar period was the Father Hurley sect, which provides a useful example of the syncretism of the churches and the inventiveness of its founders. After receiving religious training at the Tuskeegee Institute in Alabama, George Hurley arrived in Detroit in 1919 and joined a storefront Holiness church, Triumph the Church and Kingdom of God in Christ, originally founded in Georgia in 1906. After he rose in the ranks of this sect to become the presiding prince of Michigan, he began attending meetings in a white Spiritualist organization, the International Spiritual Church. He then became a Spiritualist preacher, leaving the Holiness church to teach that God was a spirit and that "Heaven and Hell are states of mind, existing in the here and now."[44] Soon after joining the Spiritualist movement, Hurley reported having seen a vision of a "brown-skinned damsel" who turned into an eagle. Interpreting this as a message to found his own church, Hurley opened the Universal Hagar's Spiritual Church in 1923 and a year later founded the School

---

[42] See Arthur E. Paris, *Black Pentecostalism: Southern Religion in an Urban World* (Amherst: University of Massachusetts Press, 1982); and Vinson Synan, *The Holiness-Pentecostal Movement in the United States* (Grand Rapids, MI: W. B. Eerdmans, 1971).

[43] Hans A. Baer, *The Black Spiritual Movement: A Religious Response to Racism* (Knoxville: University of Tennessee Press, 1984) 114.

[44] Baer, *Black Spiritual Movement* 137. See also Bullock, "Urbanization of the Negro Church" 12–14. For an exposition of his beliefs see "Arrest of Prophet Hurley Desired by So-Called Baptist Leaders," *Detroit Independent*, 14 October 1927.

of Mediumship and Psychology.[45] In his church Hurley combined aspects of Spiritualism, communication with the spirit world and the deceased, rituals of black Protestantism, magico-religious rituals such as the use of charms and incense, astrology, an altar similar to those used in Catholic services, and ideological aspects of the black nationalist movements.[46] Hurley's personal history—his study of traditional religion in the South, his conversion to the Sanctified church in Detroit, and his eventual decision to found his own Spiritualist church—provides an alternative mapping of respectable religion. His traditional "respectable" religious roots were Southern, while the urban North provided access to a variety of secular and sacred teachings that he drew upon to fashion his own church, which reformers viewed as "unrespectable."

Universal Hagar's Spiritual church quickly gained a following among Detroit's African-American women. Hurley, who conducted his services in the evening so members of other churches could attend, became particularly well known for two popular sermons: "The Purity of the Blessed Water," which he delivered while standing in a large tank of water up to his neck, and "Domestic Peace," a sermon in which he offered a "free reading to every woman who wished to know where her husband spent his spare time."[47] These sensationalist services rivaled other local neighborhood entertainment and attracted large crowds. Hurley also geared his services to attract women by advertising themes such as "domestic peace." A Spiritualist church would be a relatively innocuous space for an African-American woman to visit, despite the protestations of community leaders. It was not as suspect as a pool room or blind

---

[45] Baer, *Black Spiritual Movement* 83.

[46] Hurley was himself a member of the UNIA. Another significant nationalist religious movement in Detroit emerged in the early 1930s, the Nation of Islam. See Erdmann Doane Beynon, "The Voodoo Cult among Negro Migrants in Detroit," *The American Journal of Sociology* 15 (July 1934–May 1935): 894–907. Beynon calls the Nation of Islam a "voodoo" cult because he apparently believed reports that Detroit's black Muslims carried out human sacrifices.

[47] Gustav G. Carlson, "Number Gambling: A Study of a Culture Complex" (Ph.D. dissertation, University of Michigan, 1940) 102.

pig but could offer music, entertainment, and rituals that could bring luck.

By the late 1920s Hurley had competition from new Spiritualist churches in the city, most founded and run by African-American women. Many of these church founders and the mediums who assisted them learned their trade in the school Hurley founded. One female church founder, Dr. Johnson, remembered:

> When I first came to Detroit from Red Bank, Georgia, I never dreamed that I would be doing this kind of work. You see my husband was a Baptist preacher in Red Bank and after his death, I sold out and came to Detroit. That was in 1919, just after the war. I met a lady at Providence Baptist Church and she asked me to go into this type of work. While I was in Georgia people were always coming to me for advice. I was a midwife and traveled in all parties late at night.... Well, before I opened this church I studied Spiritualism under Rev. Hurley. He tried to keep me with him by telling me I wasn't ready to head out for myself, but I tried it. Many people from his church came over here with me.[48]

Dr. Johnson, like Rev. Hurley, left the traditional denomination behind when she migrated from the South, embracing Spiritualism after her arrival in Detroit. Her Southern identity as a midwife and confidant, however, translated into her authority in the new urban community as a preacher. Dr. Johnson's identity as a Spiritualist leader was based on both her Southern experiences and her willingness to strike out on her own in the North. She employed business skills and entrepreneurial know-how to build a congregation and keep her church running efficiently. These skills, and the potential payoff of running a storefront church, provided an alternative employment option for some African-American women. In contrast to domestic service, which many African-American women found demeaning, serving as a spiritual leader, even one vilified by some elites, provided income and self-respect. Thus the underground economy and the plethora of religious sects widened

---

[48] Quoted in Bullock, "Urbanization of the Negro Church," appendix B-1. Extracts from the Experiences of Various Spiritual Leaders, Case of Dr. Johnson, 46.

the number of choices that African-American women were able to make about their employment and way of life. Their own agency as migrants and as entrepreneurs in the urban North was the primary catalyst for this expansion, which worked against the limits set by social reformers and a severely restricted labor market.

By 1926 all but one Spiritualist church was located in an urban center, and all of these churches incorporated secular services and eclectic teachings.[49] Indeed, one contemporary scholar called the Spiritualist church the "most urbanized of the religious institutions."[50] Like the dance hall or the disorderly house, the Spiritualist church combined aspects of Northern/urban and Southern/rural culture. While its practice of ecstatic worship style and combination of secular and sacred music were pioneered by Southern Sanctified churches, it was only in the urban North that migrants such as Dr. Johnson would come across messianic movements like Garveyism, a thriving gambling racket, and the many religious practices embraced by Spiritualism. Racial segregation within the city was instrumental in this layering of cultural practices. Thus the rituals developed by the Spiritualists were products of the mixing of experiences in the overcrowded African-American community that escaped the discursive boundaries mapped by African-American elites.

The most urban, secular practice of the Spiritualist church was its involvement in the numbers business, which formed the economic base of the underground economy. Numbers, policy, and mutuels all refer to forms of gambling that became immensely popular during the interwar period in African-American urban communities. In numbers, a game that can be traced back to at least the eighteenth century in America, the winning number was determined by the last three digits of the daily close of the stock market average, or by using combinations of numbers determined by race track results (mutuels), giving the bettor a one in one thousand chance to win. Policy was a game in which numbers between 1 and 78 were randomly drawn twice a day. Detroiters believed that Casper Holstein, an immigrant from the Virgin Islands, first

---

[49] Bullock, "Urbanization of the Negro Church" 11.
[50] Bullock, "Urbanization of the Negro Church" 2.

introduced policy to Harlem in the early 1920s.[51] Like many other cities Detroit had banned gambling and lotteries through a city ordinance in the late nineteenth century; yet policy pools, dice games, and other kinds of gambling remained underground forms of entertainment for such institutions as the Waiters' and Bellmans' Club, an African-American gambling club dating from the early twentieth century.[52] In the early 1920s the numbers business began to expand as the Great Migration brought many more customers to urban centers.[53] Not surprisingly, this practice caused great consternation to those who wished to present a respectable public image because the business of numbers took place on the street or in semipublic bars, cigar stores, and even churches.

In 1925, Bill Mosley, who was to become the most important numbers baron in Detroit, opened his first large establishment, The Michigan. By 1935 there were thirty-five such houses in the city. It is particularly significant that Detroit's African-American numbers bankers, unlike those in New York or Chicago, were able to retain control over their businesses against the encroachment of white mobsters. They formed the Associated Numbers Bankers in 1928 in response to an attempt by a group of Cleveland mobsters to break into the business. This association regulated the payment of winnings, divided the city into districts, organized payoffs to law enforcement, and hired their own lawyer.[54] Each bank employed between three hundred and five hundred writers or runners who solicited bets on street corners, in barbershops and pool rooms, and even door to door. Charleszetta Waddles, who migrated to Detroit from St. Louis in the early 1930s, remem-

---

[51] For a discussion of Holstein, who became a major numbers banker and supporter of the Harlem Renaissance's literary prizes, see McKay, *Harlem* 102–5; and David Levering Lewis, *When Harlem Was in Vogue* (New York: Vintage Press, 1982) 129–30.

[52] Thomas, *Life for Us* 116. See also David M. Katzman, *Before the Ghetto: Black Detroit in the Nineteenth Century* (Urbana: University of Illinois Press, 1973) 172–74.

[53] See J. Saunders Redding, "Playing the Numbers," *North American Review*, 1934, 533–42; Drake and Cayton, Black Metropolis 478–94; McKay, *Harlem* 101–16; Thomas, *Life for Us* 116–18; and Carlson, "Number Gambling" 127–59.

[54] Carlson, "Number Gambling" 54.

bered walking "from house to house" picking up numbers to earn extra cash.[55] A runner would usually receive 25 percent of his or her overall take, as well as a percentage of a winner's earnings. The runner gave his or her bets to a pickup person, who brought them to the house or bank. In the bank itself a cashier, a number of clerks, and checkers collected and counted the money and checked the results when the numbers were chosen. According to one contemporary observer, "During the time of the drawing the policy house resembles somewhat the stock exchange during the trading period with men rushing back and forth, numbers being called, and the general loud talking and excitement."[56] Like other illicit spaces in the community, the numbers banks emanated energy, bustle, and excitement in contrast to the demure reading rooms of the Urban League or the well-regulated club meetings at the YWCA.

Numbers running was big business in Detroit, and many felt that the African-American community could not have survived the Depression without it. A long-time Detroit resident remembered,

> One of the largest businesses among Blacks is the numbers business ... everyone played either the numbers ... or policy or both.... It offered its players daily chances to pick up on a

[55] Charleszetta Waddles, interview by Marcia Greenlee, 29 March 1980, p.32, Schlesinger Library, Radcliffe College, Cambridge, Massachusetts. See also Charleszetta Waddles, unpublished autobiography, manuscript, chap. 6, p. 6, MHC-BHL.

[56] Carlson, "Number Gambling" 52. The numbers business had an intimate relationship with the stock exchange, because numbers were often picked from stock market reports. In appendix B of his dissertation, Carlson reproduces dozens of letters collected by the New York Stock Exchange from the "number playing public." These letters, many from women, requested either early knowledge of stock sales so those numbers could be played or, more directly, that stock market officials allow a particular number to come up. A typical letter from "a worried mother" reads, "I am writing you this letter for I am a widow with a family of six.... I am not trying to get rich quick all I want is this money to save years of hard work which we have spent to get as far as we have. This will carry us over untell [sic] my boy can go to work and pay the rest of the money. So please try and help me by putting out my numbers" (Carlson, "Number Gambling," appendix B, letter to New York Stock Exchange, 26 January 1935).

few quick bucks without any questions asked. It was very popular ... because it was inexpensive and convenient; and perhaps because as it grew, it employed many Blacks as runners and clerks who could not find more socially acceptable employment elsewhere."[57]

Another resident recalling the Depression stated,

One of the areas that is not talked about, and why our dollars turned over in the community, was the black numbers business. Our local people here developed it, and we controlled it. Of course, it was considered illegal, but that money was put to good use in the black community, with the dollar turning over in the community five or six times. The pickup man, the lady that wrote the number, pickup man, the other pickup man, to the owner. The owner had all blacks working for his area.[58]

Although many customers were women hoping to make ends meet by placing an average ten-cent bet per day, African-American men were the primary direct employees of the business.[59] As in so many aspects of the underground economy, however, African-American women found a way to get a piece of the action as more than just numbers players. The primary vehicle for women to gain income from numbers running was working as independent Spiritualists or as mediums in Spiritualist churches. Mediums were thought to have the power to foresee numbers or feel a person's "vibrations" that might indicate what number he or she should play. From their vantage point in the storefront churches mediums were able to take part in a lucrative entrepreneurial business. Thus the same mixing and crowding that had engendered storefront churches

---

[57] Ines Marie Bridges, "Paradise Valley—Detroit's Black Bottom," based on a number of interviews with long-time residents, 1975, 6. Folklore Archive, Wayne State University, Detroit, Michigan.

[58] Oral history transcript of William Hines, in Elaine Latzman Moon, *Untold Tales, Unsung Heroes: An Oral History of Detroit's African American Community, 1918–1967* (Detroit: Wayne State University Press, 1994) 78.

[59] I have run across one example of a female number banker in Harlem: Madame Stephanie St. Clair, who later married the cult founder and labor leader Sufi Abdul Hamid (McKay, *Harlem* 111).

also encouraged a complex circulation of money within the community, a containment of the wages earned and spent by African-American men and women.

Church members received numbers from mediums in several ways. One method, supposedly first developed by Rev. Hurley, was the hymn method. The hymn number called out would simply represent the number that parishioners should play that day.[60] More common in Spiritualist churches was a direct method usually run by the female medium. During part of the service members who wished to receive numbers were asked to stand and march in single file past the medium, who stood near the altar. She dipped her hands in holy water, sprinkled the person, and whispered a number in his or her ear. Generally, the recipient would then deposit a quarter with a waiting assistant. One variation on this method was to put the medium in a coffin and have people receive the numbers from the "deceased" as they filed past. Another common way to receive a number was through the "test message." Before the service, assistants circulated among the congregation and sold numbered cards for a quarter. At the appropriate moment during the service the medium called out a number, and the person holding that card either stood or raised his/her hand. The medium would then relay the message she had received from the Holy Spirit. Occasionally, the message would include an actual number; but usually it was coded as a "key word" message. The words that were most clearly stressed by the medium must then be looked up in a dream book, an "encyclopedia of symbols" that could be translated into numbers.[61] The following is a test message recorded verbatim from St. Ruth's Spiritualist Church in Detroit in 1935:

> When I come in touch with you, all right, a beautiful *cloud* is over you. The spirit brings *cotton* to you. Watch yourself very carefully and you will succeed, said the spirit. A *bridge* is

---

[60] This practice extended to other churches when members played hymn numbers because they felt they were lucky and likely to hit.

[61] Carlson, "Number Gambling" 107–9.

standing before you and you will be successful in crossing this condition.[62]

The parishioner would look up *cloud, cotton,* and *bridge* in a dream book and play those numbers. Mediums might also encourage members to come to them after a service to receive a "special" message and would expect an additional donation in return.

As well as giving lucky numbers during church services, mediums worked as independent entrepreneurs, holding individual consultations during which they would dispense numbers as well as personal advice.[63] Mediums also sold lucky products—incense, holy oil, candles, amulets, and charms—during Spiritualist services and private consultations. These products were thought to aid in choosing numbers that would hit, and contemporary newspapers were full of advertisements for them.[64] Thus African-American women were integral to what became known as the "confidence racket," a subeconomy that grew up around the numbers business by promising customers a better chance to win. Like prostitution, running disorderly houses, and other "illicit" occupations, mediumship was a form of service work that depended on the circulation of wages within the community and was part of the broader leisure industry. The consternation of community elites over the activities of Spiritualist churches also paralleled the attempts to discipline other forms of leisure work.

Although community elites viewed Spiritualism as emblematic of a rural, primitive, Southern past, the work of mediums in fact derived from a distinctively urban milieu. Mediums were trained in urban Spiritualist schools and combined their religious knowledge with business acumen to create a customer base among those who sought ecstatic worship without the condemnation of gambling or commercialized vice. When congregations became disillusioned with a medium who

---

[62] Verbatim report of St. Ruth's Spiritualist Church, Detroit Michigan, 18 January 1935, 8 P.M. This service is reproduced in Carlson, "Number Gambling," appendix C. The italicized words were stressed by the medium.

[63] Carlson, "Number Gambling" 111.

[64] See, for example, *Detroit Independent*, 30 September 1927 and 10 June 1927; *Detroit Tribune*, 27 November 1937; and undated clippings in the appendix of Bullock, "Urbanization of the Negro Church."

was not able to give them winning numbers consistently, the medium would often move to another location, and the process would start again. Thus the relative anonymity possible in the city was also conducive to the smooth running of a Spiritualist church.

Mediums actively engaged with the underground economy, seeking out potential customers through proselytizing. In the 1930s an African-American migrant, who had arrived in Detroit in 1916 with her husband and three children, reported that her family would have been destitute "if it weren't for that Spiritualist woman." The following is her description of her encounter with an African-American Spiritualist.

> One day I was riding on the trolley and a Spiritualist woman sat across from me. She kept watching me, and when I got off she got off behind me. She told me that I was a woman of great trouble. She said if I would come to her house she would tell me how to improve the condition that is around me. I went home and went to see her that night ... she called me and just gave me a box of incense and a candle and told me to burn the incense and look to the west each night before I go to bed. She told me to put the candle in the altar down stairs in the church and light it. It was supposed to bring me success. It seemed that my luck changed when I joined this church.[65]

Meeting on a streetcar, a "moving theater" of urban relations, and conducting their business in a storefront church, these two women engaged in a kind of commerce and religious practice that had their roots both in the North and the South but were quintessentially urban in flavor.[66]

The Spiritualist church could only engage actively with the underground economy if it did not condemn behavior that was considered reprehensible by the "saints," most notably gam-

---

[65] Quoted in Bullock, "Urbanization of the Negro Church," Extracts from the Experiences of Various Spiritual Leaders, appendix C-II, 49–50. Unidentified informant.

[66] In "'We Are Not What We Seem': Rethinking Black Working-Class Opposition in the Jim Crow South," *Journal of American History* 80 (June 1993): 75–112, Robin D. G. Kelley describes the "interior spaces" of public transportation such as streetcars as "moving theaters" (103).

bling. Father Hurley stated in the 1930s, "I play numbers because it helps the poor fellow. Gambling is a God-sent blessing to the poor."[67] Many Detroiters felt the Spiritualists' acceptance of gambling, and other forms of "vice," was a welcome respite from the moralizing of other churches. Detroiters became attached to Spiritualist leaders who were able to help them financially; in return they bought Spiritualist paraphernalia and urged others to attend the services. Thus Spiritualist churches, unlike Sanctified ones, encouraged ecstatic performance without the enforcement of strict codes of morality. African-American women made use of this liminal space to gain authority and power within the community, as well as bringing in cash to the family economy.

***

During the interwar period, Detroit's African-American community leaders used a variety of spatial and geographic metaphors to construct a public community identity that conformed to bourgeois norms of respectability. As Southern migrants arrived in Detroit, they were imaged as an undifferentiated group of rural, naive, and disorderly workers who had to be taught how to live in an urban community. Within the city itself these migrants were discouraged from engaging in activities or frequenting establishments where people of different classes, races, and genders could mix freely. An elite focus on public displays of respectability as a reform strategy, however, had unintended consequences for race relations in Detroit. Dichotomies of respectable/licentious reinforced reformers' emphasis on bourgeois norms of respectability, making that vocabulary accessible to the white community. African-Americans would continue to be segregated within the East side community and be identified with the physical space they inhabited. The effort to sanitize this space and the women who symbolized its potentialities and dangers was doomed to failure as long as racial segregation and workplace discrimination persisted. Thus the assertion of a model female urban identity

---

[67] Quoted in Carlson, "Number Gambling" 140. Hurley was answering the question, "Why do you play the numbers?"

reinforced and reproduced images of who was deviant, other, and eternally Southern.

African-American women, meanwhile, created in Detroit their own social spaces and economic opportunities that did not conform to a top-down notion of community identity. Spiritualism and numbers running, for example, were cultural practices that could not be easily encapsulated within a public identity of female respectability, thrift, and self-restraint. Women who worked as mediums, elders, and preachers in the Spiritualist church, however, did not consider themselves completely outside these norms of respectability. Rather, their codes of behavior incorporated aspects of African-American culture that they felt *were* compatible with a respectable life: communal expressions of religious ecstasy, participation in the underground economy to support families and neighborhoods, and participation in leisure activities not sanctioned by community elites. Ecstatic forms of worship flourished in Detroit not because such practices had Southern rural roots but rather because the urban geography brought together a diverse group of women who had the ability and acumen to create new entrepreneurial activity within the streetscape of the underground economy.

The particular nexus of practices and beliefs that was the Spiritualist church could only have arisen in an urban center, where lines of geographical identity and norms of respectability constantly shifted and crossed. Indeed, the syncretism of Spiritualist theology is an apt metaphor for the diverse cultural and political practices that the public discourse of respectability failed to capture. The contrasting portraits of women who stared back at incoming migrants from the photographs in the Urban League brochure were merely geographic icons that could never accurately reflect the complex lives of Detroit's African-American women.

MODERNISM AND THE SPECIFICS OF PLACE

Gwendolyn Wright

It is a commonplace that modern architecture, as it developed between the two world wars, represented a universalistic project. Looking back on his influential *Pioneers of the Modern Movement*, Nikolaus Pevsner mused that in the 1930s "the architecture of reason and functionalism was in full swing in many countries, while it had just started a hopeful course in others."[1] Two young Americans, Philip Johnson and Henry-Russell Hitchcock, announced the triumph of an "International Style" in the book that accompanied their influential exhibition of 1932 at New York's Museum of Modern Art (MoMA).[2] The curators insisted that "consciously or unconsciously a considerable number of architects throughout the world accept parallel technical and aesthetic disciplines."[3] Ever since, advocates of modernism have insisted upon this universality. So too, more recently, have postmodern critics, lamenting the dull, placeless uniformity the style came to assume in the postwar decades.

Despite such rhetoric, modernism was really understood as a European phenomenon, at least in the years before World War II. The MoMA catalogue canonized four "chief pioneers," all European, whose buildings dominated the exhibition: Miës van der Rohe, Le Corbusier, Walter Gropius, and J. J. P. Oud (fig. 1). Americans, including the few displayed in the MoMA show,

---

An earlier version of this paper appeared as "Inventions and Interventions: American Urban Design in the Twentieth Century" in *Urban Revisions: Current Projects for the Public Realm*, ed. Elizabeth Smith (Los Angeles: Museum of Contemporary Art, 1994) 26–37.

[1] First published in London by Faber & Faber in 1936, Pevsner's book was retitled *Pioneers of Modern Design* in later editions. The quotes are from the forewords to paperback editions (Harmondsworth: Penguin, 1960) 17.

[2] Henry-Russell Hitchcock and Philip Johnson, *The International Style* (1932; New York: W. W. Norton, 1966). Alfred H. Barr, Jr. also used the phrase in his foreword to Hitchcock and Johnson's official catalogue, *Modern Architecture: International Exhibition* (New York: Museum of Modern Art, 1932; rpt. ed. New York: Arno Press, 1969) 15.

[3] Hitchcock and Johnson, *Modern Architecture* 22.

were thought to lack "any real understanding and sympathy" for the rigorous tenets of the movement.[4]

Most architectural historians, then and now, have likewise disparaged American modernism as parochial and derivative. Many still contend that the style emerged in a cultural vacuum, imitating the European architecture shown in the 1932 catalogue; that it developed without formal principles or political imperatives, oblivious to the "true" meaning of the modern movement, as articulated in Europe.[5] Later, when the modernist canon came under attack for its hegemonic absolutism in the 1970s and 1980s, Americans were in turn criticized for "masking" modernism's complete homogenization of global cultural life with their naively romantic local idioms.[6]

---

[4] Hitchcock and Johnson, *Modern Architecture* 20, 23. Frank Lloyd Wright had "a place apart" in the exhibition and almost withdrew in protest. While the curators acknowledged his "undaunted genius," Wright's individualism and romantic attachment to nature meant that he did not fit into the ranks of the International Style canon (29, 30, 37). This attitude toward Wright and others as "new traditionalists" rather than "pioneers" had first been set forward in Hitchcock's *Modern Architecture: Romanticism and Reintegration* (New York: Payson and Clarke, 1929). Several other Americans were given lesser roles in the exhibition, including Raymond Hood and the émigrés Richard Neutra and William Lescaze. See Terence Riley, *The International Style: Exhibition 15 and the Museum of Modern Art* (New York: Rizzoli for Columbia Books of Architecture, 1992). Riley points out that the exhibition and catalogue assembled somewhat different collections of buildings, though the role of the "chief pioneers" and the overall emphasis on European examples remained constant.

[5] One characteristic example will suffice. "But the mass of American architecture continued in its old derivative course," wrote J. M. Richards in 1940, "and even when isolated buildings of modern design began to appear they were regarded by most people simply as a new fashion—the latest from Europe" (*An Introduction to Modern Architecture* [1940; rpt. ed. Harmondsworth: Penguin, 1970] 94).

[6] For example, Kenneth Frampton says of American architecture since 1934, "That this movement was hardly as self-conscious or as polemical as its European counterpart was due to the fact that a comparable ideological basis did not exist. The 'movement' had, in any event, to be more sensitive to the issue of popular acceptance and to this end its anti-monumentality stemmed directly from its use of native materials and from its response to the vagaries of topography and climate" (*Modern Architecture: A Critical History* [London:

Figure 1. Model of Le Corbusier's
Villa Savoie at the Museum of Modern Art's *Modern Architecture* exhibition, 1932. Museum of Modern Art,
New York

All of this is partly a product of long-standing hostilities
toward the commercialism and supposed lack of self-consciousness in the United States and upper-class Americans'
own fear of cultural parochialism. It has produced an incapac-
ity to understand American modernism in its own national,
regional, and local terms. Cultural disdain stems as well from
an insistence that meaningful form must derive from grand
theory, and the accompanying failure to recognize cultural
significance in the pragmatic intellectual thought and architectural styles (usually dismissed as facile "modernistic" design)
prevalent in the United States during these years.[7]

Thames and Hudson, 1980, 1985] 239). Another popular recent text, especially critical of the United States, is Fredric Jameson, *Postmodernism or, The
Cultural Logic of Late Capitalism* (Durham: Duke University Press, 1991).

[7] See, for example, Hitchcock and Johnson, *International Style* 14.

In fact, given such a template, historians have failed to notice the importance of variations within modernist thought and practice, not only in the United States but in Eastern Europe, the European colonies, Asia, Latin America, and throughout Western Europe as well. Each of these alternative modernisms favored certain elements in the dominant canon and dismissed or downplayed others. The variations should not be seen as deviations but as vital evidence of modernism's real complexity and adaptability.

The time has come to move beyond the oppositions of orthodoxy or parochialism, relentless critique or defensive boosterism. We need instead to explore the nature of local phenomena. What did American architects of this interwar generation see as the conditions and expressive goals of their modernism? Did these attitudes predate the orthodoxy of the 1932 exhibition? How were they distinct from post–World War II modernism, with its luxury redevelopment districts, corporate monoliths, and public housing towers? What were the strengths as well as the limits of their architecture? And can it be said to express a cohesive ideology?

The pattern that emerges can be described in terms of four related domains: the process of discussion and design; the social program; the formal motifs and themes; and the principles underlying the architecture's goals, forms, and effects. One need not fall into the ideology of American exceptionalism to notice and explore the implications of Americans' distinctive emphases on community planning, architectonic variety, and regionalism, especially in the 1930s. A distinctive cultural milieu was constructed upon such foundations.

Above all, American modernism emphasized the significance of "community." Individuals and buildings found their identity not as isolated entities but as part of cohesive groups. Even émigré modernists paid heed to the preferences and patterns of their new locales. And active collaboration—the opposite of the myth of individual genius—defined much of the best work of this period.

Such teamwork had characterized the civic centers and campus plans of the City Beautiful era at the turn of the century (fig. 2). It continued into the 1920s, when individuals and firms joined forces to produce large commercial, institutional,

Figure 2. *Skyscrapers* ballet set at
New York's Metropolitan Opera
House by Robert Edmond Jones,
1926, from *Modern Music*, 1926, New
York Public Library

and residential building groups, ranging from Rockefeller Center to Coral Gables. Governmental agencies played a major role during the next two decades, hiring teams and subsuming individual names into collective enterprises like the PWA, TVA, CCC, and FSA. Landscape architect Garrett Eckbo contended that the best ideas of the era could only be developed in a "completely collaborative group."[8]

The intellectual context for architectural debate developed new dimensions, too, as advocacy and study groups coalesced, sometimes around a school or a journal, most often around the cause of local environmental problems. Architects wrote for *T-Square* and *Twice a Year*, for *Fortune* and *The New Republic*, as

---

[8] Garrett Eckbo, "Site Planning," *Architectural Forum* 76 (May 1942): 267. These acronyms stood for the Public Works Administration, the Tennessee Valley Authority, the Civilian Conservation Corps, and the Farm Security Administration, all of which undertook extensive architectural projects in cities and the countryside.

well as the established professional magazines. They became members of the Regional Plan Association in New York, the Architectural Research Group in Philadelphia, or Telesis in San Francisco. Museums helped organize special committees, re sulting in exhibitions designed to situate problems and proposals for their own cities within a national and transnational vision of modern progress.[9]

The matrix of such associations remained loosely structured and highly decentralized. Yet the intensity and frequency of collaboration produced new forms of architectural "discourse"—in a Rortyian rather than Foucauldian sense of the term, based upon ongoing, wide-ranging conversations about modern definitions of beauty, functionalism, and appropriateness.[10]

Programmatically, too, communities represented the formal and ideological focus of many design projects, as architects tried to capture the forces that drew people together. They did this under the commercial auspices of the 1920s, creating a multitude of settings for business and entertainment that embodied the vitality of urban life. Designers carefully analyzed how to entice various crowds: the cosmopolitan elite at night clubs, bedazzled audiences at cinemas, cheering fans at baseball stadiums, eager consumers at urban department stores and neighborhood shopping centers. Public space radiated a pulsating modern vivacity (fig. 3).

By the 1930s architects focused on less commercialized kinds of public buildings: governmental institutions, neighbor-

---

[9] Among these exhibits are the Philadelphia venue for the Museum of Modern Art's *Modern Architecture* show of 1932; that museum's numerous other exhibitions—including *Architecture in Government Housing* (1938), *Regional Building in America* (1941), *Wartime Housing* (1942), and *Look at Your Neighborhood* (1944); the Dallas Museum of Art's *Architecture of the Southwest* (1940); and the San Francisco Museum of Art's *Space for Living* (1940) and *Domestic Architecture of the San Francisco Bay Area* (1949).

[10] On this sort of "discourse" see David Hollinger, "Historians and the Discourse of Intellectuals," in *New Directions in American Intellectual History*, ed. John Higham and Paul Conkin (Baltimore: Johns Hopkins University Press, 1979), rpt. in Hollinger, *In the American Province* (Bloomington: Indiana University Press, 1985), chap. 8; and Thomas Bender, "Recent Trends in the Historiography of Intellectuals in the United States," unpublished paper.

Figure 3. Installation sketch from the
Telesis group's *Space for Living* at
the San Francisco Museum of Art,
1940. *Arts and Architecture* magazine, 1940

hood community centers, and schools. Each type was conceived as a multipurpose facility, with general-purpose meeting
rooms as well as specialized services that operated twenty-four
hours a day. Under the economic and social duress of the Depression, architects sought to reinforce the bonds of public
participation while providing equal access to a variety of
amenities. Later, during World War II, this community ideal
infused the rhetoric about American designs for postwar cities
and suburbs. Closely knit clusters of dwellings, augmented by
social and recreational facilities, supposedly embodied the values for which the war was being fought: in theory, such ample,
pleasant collective spaces nurtured "freedom" and individualism.[11]

---

[11] See, for example, "New Buildings for 194x," *Architectural Forum* 78
(May 1943): 69–152.

Figure 4. View and site plan of the
Crow Island School, Winnetka, Illi-
nois, 1940, by Eliel and Eero
Saarinen with Perkins, Wheeler &
Will. From Elizabeth Mock, *Built in
the USA*, 1945, Museum of Modern
Art, New York

Architects' attention turned as well to the people who
constitute a community. The impact of homelessness during
the Depression oriented the profession toward the scale of the
residential enclave. Whether apartments for workers in the city
or single-family homes for the middle class in the suburbs,
housing emphasized a shared or collective identity rather than
personalized homes for each family. Describing a 1933 exhibi-

tion on housing sponsored by New York's AIA, Lewis Mumford proclaimed, "*the community rather than the individual dwelling is taken as the unit of design.*"[12]

Replication of dwelling units supposedly represented the cohesive quality of the social group. Yet Americans were never fully comfortable with the idea of uniformity so central to European tenets of modernism, disliking its associations with visual monotony and social homogeneity. Architects recognized that their clients wanted some variety in massing, roof lines, and detailing, feeling that this would counteract the threat of tedium and conformity. Soon after he began work on Broadacre City, Frank Lloyd Wright alluded to comparable dangers for the architect when he declared, "Standardization is a mere, but indispensable tool"; embraced without reserve, it risked becoming "a prison house for the creative soul and mind."[13]

Implicitly, the model for most American housing projects of this era remained the village: a small, homogeneous community in which individual autonomy and collective identity seemed to balance harmoniously (figs. 4 and 5). Indigenous historical precedents were often invoked, extending from eighteenth-century New England towns to the planned suburbs of the 1920s. But the most important model for residential design was undoubtedly Clarence Arthur Perry's concept of the "neighborhood unit": an archetypical social organism and planning unit comprising 750 to 1,000 families.[14] Perry assumed that the residents would share cultural values, as well as socioeconomic class, if the community's scale and design affirmed their commonalities. Necessary components included a common standard of decent housing, easy access to nature, and, above all, the representational and sociological force of

---

[12] Lewis Mumford, "The Planned Community," *Architectural Forum* 58 (April 1933): 253.

[13] Frank Lloyd Wright, "In the Cause of Architecture: What 'Styles' Mean to the Architect," *Architectural Record* 63 (February 1928): 145.

[14] Perry's neighborhood unit was developed in the 1910s under the auspices of the Russell Sage Foundation, then taken up by the Regional Plan Association as well as the architects of Forest Hills Gardens and Radburn. By the 1930s it had become familiar in Europe and a mainstay of all American discussion about residential design. See, in particular, Perry's *Housing for the Machine Age* (New York: Russell Sage Foundation, 1939).

SPECIAL BULLETIN OF
THE SAN FRANCISCO
HOUSING ASSOCIATION

Figure 5. Holly Courts, PWA housing
project in San Francisco, 1939–40,
by Arthur Brown, Jr. San Francisco
Housing Authority

the "social center" as a nucleus. In principle, as expounded in diagrams, the concept would extend to higher densities of population, with an appropriate scale and complexity for each constituency: a neighborhood elementary school, a district high school, and a centralized cultural center serving an entire city.

If urbanism was certainly a central tenet of modern architecture on both sides of the Atlantic, it took on various meanings in each locale.[15] In the United States the private sector as well as local, state, and federal governments undertook large-scale housing, usually for profit, though occasionally with limited dividends as reform efforts. Yet the greatest difference was that American architects did not seek to reinvent the city—in part because of the strong presence of the market. Instead, they set out to show improvements over existing American conditions, affirming the possibility of more equitable, orderly, and attractive cities, from their bustling downtowns to their frayed edges.

This modest approach circumvented the problems of size, diversity, and inequality in American metropolises. In the United States, when architects spoke of an urban scale during these years, they usually meant a fragment, carefully inserted into the surrounding context: a distinctive skyscraper complex or residential neighborhood in the 1920s, a cultural center or housing project in the 1930s or '40s. Those who designed whole entities usually restricted themselves to small communities: the Farm Security Administration (FSA) towns for migrant workers in California and the Southwest, the Tennessee Valley Authority (TVA) town of Norris, or the several Greenbelt towns for white-collar suburban families. While these designers did much to address the needs of an impoverished rural underclass, both governmental policy and cultural ideology by and large downplayed the more complex problems of urban poverty. Even public housing was intended for the "working poor" who had "temporarily" lost their jobs or for war workers who had been relocated.

---

[15] While modern architecture was not universal, it was transnational. This applies not only to Americans' growing interest in the European modern movement but to the equally strong allure of *américanisme* in Europe.

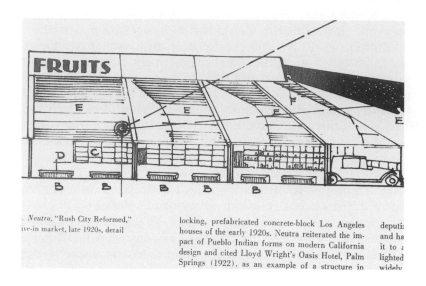

locking, prefabricated concrete-block Los Angeles
houses of the early 1920s. Neutra reiterated the impact of Pueblo Indian forms on modern California
design and cited Lloyd Wright's Oasis Hotel, Palm
Springs (1922), as an example of a structure in

deputi:
and ha
it to ;
lighted
widely

Figure 6. Drive-in market from Richard Neutra's "Rush City Reformed,"
begun in 1925 when the Viennese
architect moved to Los Angeles.
Shelter, 1938

This focus on urban elements that could be "improved"
led, in turn, to an open-minded ability to look at the reality of
cities. Unlike Le Corbusier or Ludwig Hilberseimer, even vi-
sionaries like Frank Lloyd Wright or Richard Neutra—both of
whom explored large, truly metropolitan dimensions of design—based designs on the emerging physical structure and
varied social patterns of existing cities and suburbs. Like other
American architects they accepted the physical and experien-
tial actuality of their time: embracing the awkward and fragmented quality of modern urban life, the fast-paced extension
outward toward suburbs, the rapid pace of change in culture
and fashion, and the heterogeneous nature of public taste.
They also recognized the limits of and resistance to the forces
of modernity, steering clear of ideal environments, such as
completely rational grids or dense groups of uniform towers.
The American notion of modern space was designed, as it was
experienced, in pieces that juxtaposed new and old, speed and

tranquillity, working class and middle class, without imposing a totalizing order on the whole.

By the 1930s many commentators characterized American modernism as an effort to "humanize" the austerity of the European modern movement, especially as it had been represented in Johnson and Hitchcock's exhibition of 1932. Thirteen years later, in 1945, the Museum of Modern Art produced a sequel and antidote, *Built in USA*. Elizabeth Mock, the curator, described a design philosophy for architecture that sought to be "'humanly satisfactory' in the broadest sense."[16] She asked whether architecture shouldn't "tell a story" and noted the figurative quality of recent buildings, which downplayed pure abstraction in favor of familiar vernacular forms.[17]

Here too, of course, the phenomenon was not unique or restricted to Americans. But "humanism" took on special significance in this country, where the political scientist Howard Woolston contended that a "humane" process of socialization had to emphasize individuality and idiosyncrasy.[18] Such goals encouraged a spirit of flexible compromise rather than authoritative exactitude.

Thus design and construction often involved a give-and-take process in which the architect had to take into account diverse constituencies. Oskar Stonorov's Carl Mackley Houses in Philadelphia, built in the mid-1930s under the auspices of the PWA, exemplify this evolution. The severe slabs of the original scheme represented an international manifesto on design, geared principally to the audience who admired the model when MoMA's "Modern Architecture" of 1932 traveled to Philadelphia. Later modifications addressed the future residents, members of the Full Fashioned Hosiery Workers Union. Stonorov now broke up the relentless straight lines typical of German social housing, which was usually set in uniform rows called *Zeilenbau*. A clubhouse and swimming pool, augmented

---

[16] Elizabeth Mock, ed., *Built in USA—Since 1932* (New York: Museum of Modern Art, 1945) 23.

[17] Mock, *Built in USA* 23.

[18] Howard Woolston, *Metropolis: A Study of Urban Communities* (New York: D. Appleton-Century, Co., 1938) 92–115.

by underground garages, responded to Americans' expectations of pleasure and convenience in their housing (fig. 6).[19]

The familiar precepts of the modern movement were thus encoded in a system that downplayed spatial discipline and abstract metaphor, while it emphasized environmental responsiveness and concreteness. In distinct contrast to their European counterparts, American architects highlighted comfort, variety, and legibility. The shift in emphasis extended to many of the basic tropes of modernism.

For example, while Americans assumed that new technology would help define their urban visions, it remained a practical toolbox of materials and techniques rather than an idealis tic metaphor of scientific rationality. Technological images were not abstract references to the machine's potential but tangible statements about modern corporate strength and American engineering skills. This imagery—intensely visual but essentially nonvisionary—reverberates in the majestic skyscrapers of the 1920s, symbols of the market's power. It propelled the abundance of ingenious prefabricated housing experiments in the 1930s and 1940s: evidence of innovative construction systems, but with façades often made to look like conventional wood-frame dwellings rather than flaunting evidence of advanced technology.

Urban infrastructure has always played a pivotal role in the American celebration of modern technology. Highways embodied an entirely positive public dimension during these decades, facilitating access to the countryside and to other urban areas; they promised to unify every region and to liberate every individual. Although no one yet recognized their destructive potential, few architects envisioned new highways that would demolish existing neighborhoods to speed transportation for

---

[19] Stonorov worked in association with Alfred Kastner as his draftsman/designer and (since neither of these two was registered) with an established Philadelphia architect, W. Pope Barney. See Richard Pommer, "The Architecture of Urban Housing in the United States during the Early 1930s," *Journal of the Society of Architectural Historians* 37 (December 1983): 235–42; Eric J. Sandeen, "The Design of Public Housing in the New Deal: Oskar Stonorov and the Carl Mackley Houses," *American Quarterly* 37 (Winter 1987): 645–67; and Gail D. Radford, "Modern Community Housing: New Responses to the Shelter Problem in the 1920s and 1930s" (Ph.D. dissertation, Columbia University, 1989).

commuters, as would happen in the aftermath of the Federal-Aid Highway Act of 1956. By and large this earlier generation simply magnified the scale of existing circulation routes or projected new connectors in previously unused spaces. Thus Raymond Hood in New York and William Christian Mullgardt in San Francisco drew up visions of colossal skyscraper bridges during the 1920s, stressing the metropolitan (rather than suburban) quality of thoroughfares that extended the urban region. Los Angeles in particular reconceptualized urban design and experience around a new system of "super" highways, overlaid upon rapid transit routes: continuous, high-speed corridors traversing and unifying the city's sprawl. Richard J. Neutra praised the "crisscross communicating in all directions," such as he had envisioned in his utopian proposal, "Rush City Reformed."[20]

Likewise the landscape continued to figure prominently at every level of American urban design. Europeans expressed their admiration for the East Coast parkway systems and the extraordinary strategies for rerouting water in the West and Appalachia. Nature was not simply passive and bucolic in the United States. Extensive undertakings by the New Deal in rural areas—shelter belts, dams, highways, electrification—modernized the landscape and radically changed the lives of Depression-era Americans, connecting them to distant neighbors and new leisure activities. Nature also represented a locus for recreation and other active, even commercialized, forms of public entertainment; every town and metropolis added parks, playgrounds, and public beaches, both within the city and

---

[20] Richard J. Neutra, "Homes and Housing," in *Los Angeles: A Preface to a Master Plan*, ed. George W. Robbins and L. Deming Tilton (Los Angeles: Pacific Southwest Academy, 1941) 191. Neutra began work on his remarkable "Rush City Reformed" in Berlin in the early 1920s; it continued to evolve in New York, Chicago, and Los Angeles throughout the 1930s. Drawings were first published in *Wie Baut Amerika?* in 1926. Looking back in the 1950s, the architect insisted that the proposal did "not base itself on an abstract and theoretically rigid scheme" but rather on "a belief in the wholesome flexibility of city planning" (Willy Boesiger, ed., *Richard Neutra 1923–1950: Buildings and Projects* [New York: Praeger, 1964] 195, cited in Thomas S. Hines, *Richard Neutra and the Search for Modern Architecture* [New York: Oxford University Press, 1982] 61).

Figure 7. Indented courts and public
swimming pool at the PWA's Carl
Mackley Houses, Philadelphia, 1935,
by Oscar Stonorov. *Urban Housing:
The Story of the PWA*,
Library of Congress

along its periphery. Formerly useless terrains and oppressive climates now became the very basis of design, less hidden behind picturesque landscape refinements. "The modern architect enjoys the challenge of these climactic difficulties ... and rugged land," explained Elizabeth Mock in her catalogue of 1945.[21]

A major consideration in American housing design, as with public settings, involved the open space around dwellings. Not simply a residue or a viewpoint for architecture, nor a calibrated source of light and air, as was often the case in Europe, these spaces were purposefully designed for a variety of activities. Site plans articulated specific areas for children's play, adult recreation, socializing, or pleasant vistas (fig. 7). Site planning became the very basis for many public housing designs, especially if the site was difficult and hilly, as at Chatham Village in Pittsburgh or at Channel Heights outside Los Angeles. Of course, such terrains had the value of being inexpensive, but they also reinforced Americans' need to modulate the regularity of building façades and tied buildings to their surroundings in an informal, seemingly organic manner.

This same spirit of modified adaptation extended to the surrounding built environment. Designers by and large avoided grand gestures in favor of a piecemeal or incremental approach that tried to reinforce what was already in place (fig. 8). Most new housing deferred to its context, replicating the prevailing pattern of principal streets, orientation, and scale, even as it organized units and blocks into more orderly groups. Row houses generally followed the street wall, often modulating it with regular setbacks and generous openings onto landscaped courtyards. Despite the use of modern systems of construction, most public housing remained low-rise—at most four stories high, except in New York City.[22] Commodious public spaces at junctures with major thoroughfares served as linkages, providing significant connections to the surrounding neighborhoods.

---

[21] Mock, *Built in USA* 21, 23.

[22] It was not until the 1950s that American public housing authorities turned toward high-rise towers as a visible expression of economic efficiency and the modern architectural prototype of Le Corbusier's "tower-in-the-park." See Gwendolyn Wright, *Building the Dream: A Social History of Housing in America* (Cambridge, MA: MIT Press, 1983) 236.

If the European avant-garde acclaimed the Spartan beauty of the *Existenzminimum* (a functional minimal standard for human dwellings), American architects considered that far too

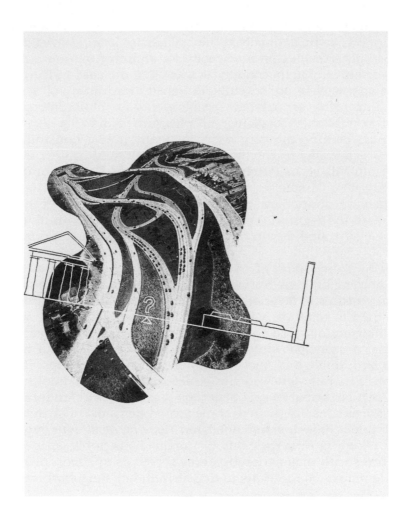

Figure 8. Highway montage from "Where is Modern Architecture Going?" *Architectural Forum*, 1938

severe and institutional, even for working-class housing. They acknowledged the desire for informal massing and ornamented façades, preferably with historicist references, characteristic of popular taste. Even the smallest project featured copper roofs, ceramic tiles, sculptural friezes, wide corner windows, and handsome brickwork. Designers often incorporated motifs drawn from historic dwellings in the area: Georgian doorways in Boston, wrought iron railings in New Orleans, stucco and arcades in the Southwest. Anticipating the pastiche of post-modernism, the heterogeneity of mass culture and local habits was thus assimilated into a modern aesthetic.[23]

In all of these senses, American architects responded to the physical and social actualities of cities and urban life, seeking to improve what was there. They believed in the reform impetus and analytic techniques of modernism but did not insist that these goals were inherent in any one stylistic formula. Most intercessions accepted both the pattern and the diversity of American life rather than trying to reformulate them into a single mold. In the words of *Architectural Forum* magazine, their visions were "more preventive than remedial, ... subject to a number of limitations."[24] Le Corbusier's urban visions were seldom emulated in the United States during these years, for they seemed conspicuously utopian, demanding a complete transformation rather than feasible interventions in the existing fabric and life of a city.[25] (After World War II—with its unprecedented investment in new technology, rational organization, and a centralized command over an extensive global cam-

---

[23] In any case, the PWA was in business to provide jobs during its early years, so its Housing Division imposed few restrictions on cost or design before 1934.

[24] Albert Mayer and Julian Whittlesey, "Horse Sense Planning, I," *Architectural Forum* 79 (November 1943): 62.

[25] Here, too, exceptions prove the validity of a basic, yet never absolute, trend. The most notable and exacting applications of Le Corbusier's Radiant City scheme were those of William Lescaze, sometimes called the "Le Corbusier of America." His PWA housing, known as Ten Eyck (later called the Williamsburg Houses) in Brooklyn (1935–38), rationalized the layout as a sequence of uniform geometric shapes. Interlocked along a vast superblock, the buildings stood purposefully aloof from the surrounding streets and houses; nature became a sea of blank greenery, a backdrop to the regularity of the built forms.

paign—American businessmen and political leaders, as well as architects, embraced Corbusien models for massive urban redevelopment projects across the country.)

American modernism during the interwar years entailed more than contextual sensibilities and collaborative compromise. It also involved an explicit stance against any absolute order. Most architects rejected the idea that universally beautiful forms could provide appropriate solutions in every circumstance or setting. In overall terms, the American goals and methods exemplify what Barbara Herrnstein Smith, in *Contingencies of Value*, has recently called "the local figuring/working out, as well as we, heterogeneously, can, of what seems to work better rather than worse."[26]

The earlier aversion to orthodoxy was less an avant-garde transgression against rules than a concerted rejection of any standardized solution. The U.S. Public Housing Authority issued specific warnings against "architectural fantasies," calling instead for designs that "begin with a frank recognition of the economic and social problems.... [The architect] must really become a 'functionalist' in the full sense of the word."[27] Organizing an exhibition on such housing in 1936, the Museum of Modern Art sought to "interrupt abstract arguments," replacing them with "concrete examples of new construction which may be of vast significance in the future, not only of our architecture, but of our entire environment."[28]

Given the broad range of such sentiments, what we might call a "pragmatic" attitude in architecture and urban design— so readily associated with American culture, so often dismissed as uncritical compromise of European ideals—merits closer attention (fig. 9).

This is not to say that architects studied pragmatists like William James or John Dewey, or even that they self- consciously tried to work out a distinctive theory of design. But

---

[26] Barbara Herrnstein Smith, *Contingencies of Value* (Cambridge: Harvard University Press, 1988) 179.

[27] National Housing Agency and Federal Public Housing Authority, *Public Housing Design: A Review of Experience in Low-Rent Housing* (Washington: Governmental Printing Office, 1946) 3.

[28] Museum of Modern Art Committee on Architecture and Industrial Art, "Architecture in Government Housing," bound typescript, 1936, n.p.

Figure 9. Aerial view of Harlem River
Houses, New York, by Archibald
Manning Brown with John Louis
Wilson et al., 1937, showing the
connection with Frederick Douglass
Boulevard. *Architectural Forum*, 1938

they did employ both a language and a method of resolving
problems that echoed those of philosophical pragmatism.
Writing in the *Architectural Forum* in 1943, Albert Mayer and
Julian Whittlesey called it "Horse Sense Planning."[29] More eloquently, Garrett Eckbo insisted, "Good site planning is largely

---

[29] Albert Mayer and Julian Whittlesey, "Horse Sense Planning," *Architectural Forum* (November 1943): 59–74; (December 1943): 77–82; (January
1944): 69–74.

a matter of real common sense, aided by a completely open mind, a lack of esthetic prejudice and an uninhibited sense of form."[30]

Giles Gunn speaks of the site of pragmatism as a ludic or liminal space, a border or transitional zone—in this case, between two other conceptions of space.[31] To one side is the shared, familiar environment of everyday events and experiences; to the other, a place of solitude and completely independent thought. A pragmatist does not simply replicate existing reality nor withdraw into a hermetic domain. In between the two extremes, the individual artist or thinker tries to look at the familiar environment in a different way, envisaging new possibilities. William James called pragmatism no more than "the habit of always seeking an alternative, of not taking the usual for granted, of making conventionalities fluid again, of imagining foreign states of mind."[32] One finds a similar outlook, together with the technique of continual adaptation, in much American urban design, especially during the interwar era.

Yet questions remain: How clear, strong, and consistent did those principles prove to be? How much were they merely rationalizations of an easy simplification? Did the principles turn into a tedious formula in the hands of less thoughtful designers and bureaucrats? How often did the focus on the commonplace turn into a celebration of the banal, whether in national parks or in urban neighborhoods?

We cannot take even the tentative theorizing of American architects too literally, no more so than the European appeals to functionalism and universal benefits. Common sense alone cannot produce good design, certainly not "good architecture." The problems fall into two categories. At a formal level the aesthetics were seldom inspiring. Much of the public housing is rather tedious, barracks-like in its austerity or sentimental in its historicism, despite the comfortable low-rise scale and the sensuous relief of the excellent site planning. Only a few

---

[30] Eckbo, "Site Planning" 265

[31] Giles Gunn, *Thinking across the American Grain: Ideology, Intellect, and the New Pragmatism* (Chicago: University of Chicago Press, 1992) 12–15.

[32] William James, "The Teaching of Philosophy in Our Colleges," *Nation* 23 (1876): 178, quoted in Gunn, *Thinking* 36.

public buildings command a truly monumental presence that can stir public emotions or visual delight.

Moreover, even when architects embraced difference and ambiguity, they did so without challenging the dominant order. Social diversity *was* sometimes acknowledged, in contrast to the normalized standards prevalent in Europe. Joseph Hudnut declared emphatically, "No four-family apartment is suitable for every family: Irish or Polish, Yankee or Middle West, Catholic or Puritan, tradesman or industrial worker."[33] Yet only one governmental agency, the FSA, took the matter seriously enough to explore the particular needs and cultural habits of its clients: migratory and permanent farmworkers, including families and single individuals coming from the Midwestern Dust Bowl and later from Mexico.[34]

Respect for difference usually translated into the separation of different groups instead of a heterogeneous urban mixture. The decision to follow existing living arrangements often meant replicating racial and class segregation without considering alternatives. A professor at Cornell, writing in the *Architectural Record*, declared emphatically that postwar neighborhoods would likewise "be homogeneous in character ... [following] the basic principle of democracy—respect for the wishes of the people ... [and] natural social trends."[35] Such restrictive homogeneity is, of course, an integral part of the

---

[33] Joseph Hudnut, "The Art in Housing," *Architectural Record* 93 (January 1943): 59.

[34] Despite severe budgetary restrictions and a fast-track schedule, architects with the Farm Security Administration (FSA) built temporary and permanent communities for farm laborers: primarily displaced Midwestern farm families and later, after 1942, itinerant Mexicans. Adapting the most rigorous modern design to highly specific circumstances, they explored a variety of forms. At Yuba City, Woodville, and other settlements, there were special areas for men and women to gather at their respective tasks, pleasant day care centers and schools, community centers for self-government, and familial privacy even in the smallest cabins or mobile trailers. Using photographs by Dorothea Lange and other FSA photographers as evidence, the *Architectural Forum* praised the "willingness to experiment," as well as the "quality and thoroughly American character" of the designs (74 [January 1941]: 3).

[35] Thomas W. Mackesey in collaboration with Gilmore D. Clarke, "Planning the Postwar Community," *Architectural Record* 93 (January 1943): 84.

legacy of those cherished New England Puritan towns. Modern architects sought to create a life of comfortable well-being and familiarity, providing natural amenities and technological benefits to people who were much like one another. In their opposition to a single, totalizing vision of reform, most American architects eschewed the possibility that either design or social experience should be radically transformative or unsettling.

All the same, they did address important modern issues about the social and formal implications of public dialogue and public space. Even if they did not clarify a fully articulate statement, the goal was that of a broad synthetic scope: professionally, among designer, clients, and the public; and formally, among new building, open spaces, and existing surroundings.

Such equilibrium did not necessarily mean either artistic or technological conformity. As in Europe, a spirit of experimentation often permeated the design process. Antonin Raymond, one of the first architects to build an American war housing community, cited the government's "liberal far-sighted program" for "'small laboratories of housing with the architects as chief scientists'."[36] Both William Wurster's prefabricated, demountable housing and schools for war workers, set in the hills of Vallejo, California, and Frank Lloyd Wright's majestic Fallingwater, spanning a waterfall at Bear Run, Pennsylvania, used inventive construction technology and highly tactile materials to achieve remarkable architecture. As Joseph Hudnut, dean of Harvard's Graduate School of Design, insisted, "Architecture ... develops, not by pure thought, but by experimentation and test."[37] Moreover, American designers recognized the centrality of experience, both perceptual and cultural, personal and collective, as fundamental to architecture. If they did not adequately take account of class, race, and gender differences, they did not assume that "modern man" had only one set of purely rational needs. Designers spoke openly of myths and fears, memories and opportunities, regional and

[36] Anton Raymond, "Working with U.S.H.A. Under the Lanham Act," *Pencil Points* 22 (November 1941): 694.

[37] Joseph Hudnut, "Architecture after the Peace," *Magazine of Art* 36 (April 1943): 126.

Figure 10. William W. Wurster's
prefabricated masonry housing at
Chabot Terrace, California, for primarily female war workers in the
Vallejo shipyards, 1942. *Arts and Architecture*, 1942

national identity. At its best, American modernist writing and
designs of this era sought to explore the multitudinous nature
of collective experience rather than dictate a rigid set of standards. The aim was that of a conversation among architects,clients, and various segments of the public, not an indoc-
trination.[38]

---

[38] Pamphlets and exhibition panels posed questions, asking "Would this
be anything like *your* idea of a pleasant community?" or "Do you like where
you work?" Such questions remained open-ended, awaiting a multiplicity of
responses. For example, see Elizabeth Mock, "Tomorrow's Small House," *Bulletin of the Museum of Modern Art* 12 (Summer 1945): 19; the Telesis catalogue, *Space for Living* (San Francisco: San Francisco Museum of Art, 1940);
and Louis I. Kahn and Oscar Stonorov, *Why City Planning Is Your Responsibility* (New York: Revere Copper and Brass Company, 1942).

The distinctive nature of places was perhaps the most fully articulated theme in this dialogue. Whether in Manhattan or Miami, Denver or Detroit, in one neighborhood or another, American modernists acknowledged and even nurtured the particularity of each setting (fig. 10). Their choice of materials, orientation, programmatic and spatial organization adapted to the surroundings. And those surroundings were understood as a complex amalgam of architectural, ecological, historical, and cultural conditions.

Such vernacular or place-specific divergences from the universalist orthodoxy of modernism often came under harsh attack as sentimental or backward.[39] Yet it is the specifics of place, like the specific nature of any other problem, that defines a pragmatic response. This approach can incorporate the possibilities of change as well as the desire for familiarity. Equally important, it shows a willingness, in the words of William James, to refuse to believe in perfect solutions but rather to press continually forward with "a program for more work."[40]

---

[39] The term *vernacular*, often associated with unselfconscious simplicity, actually refers to something or someone specifically tied to a particular locale. It derives from the Latin *verna*, a slave who was bound to the lands of his or her owner, and has since extended to mean local languages or architectural styles, usually in contrast to more universal formulations such as Latin or classicism. See Gwendolyn Wright, "Dilemmas of Diversity: Vernacular Style and High Style," *Precis* 5 (Fall 1984): 117–23.

[40] William James, *Pragmatism and Other Essays* (New York: Simon and Schuster, 1963) 26, cited in Richard Shusterman, *Pragmatic Aesthetics: Living Beauty, Rethinking Art* (Cambridge, MA: Basil Blackwell, 1992) 261.

PART FOUR: REMAPPING IDENTITY POLITICS

LANDSCAPES OF TERROR:
A Reading of Tuskegee's Historic Campus

Kenrick Ian Grandison

In 1966, Sammy Younge, a twenty-one-year-old black college student and civil rights worker, was shot in the head after demanding to use a "whites only" rest room at a gas station in Tuskegee, Alabama.[1] The murder served as a catalyst for the Black Liberation Movement nearly a century after the South had begun an unceasing campaign of domestic terrorism aimed at its black "citizens" in order to force their political, social, and economic subordination and to ensure white supremacy. What impact did this terrorism have on the way blacks selected, planned, and developed their landscapes?

The relationship between landscapes[2] and terrorism can be documented historically. The great walls surrounding me-

---

I wish to thank all who contributed in some way to this paper: 1) the 1995 African American Landscape Symposium organizers at North Carolina Agricultural and Technical State University, Greensboro, for inviting me yet again to present my work; 2) the University of Michigan Office of the Vice Provost for Academic and Multicultural Affairs and School of Natural Resources and Environment Research Development Office for funding this project; 3) my special friend, University of Michigan Associate Professor of English Marlon Ross and Associate Professor of Architecture Sharon Sutton who read and offered priceless critique of drafts of this manuscript; 4) David Barnes and Shalini Priyadarshini, who provided research assistance; 5) the scholarly work of Edward Pryce at Tuskegee, Richard Dozier at Florida A & M, James Chaffers, Kenneth Polakowski, Anne Herrmann, and Rachel Kaplan at the University of Michigan, and Darrel Morrison at the University of Georgia, who have all continued to inspire me; 6) Everett Fly for first suggesting the idea of investigating the landscape of Tuskegee.

[1] William Van DeBurg, *New Day in Babylon: The Black Power Movement and American Culture, 1965–1975* (Chicago: University of Chicago Press, 1992) 41.

[2] Landscape, as used here, refers to products of the whole range of choices and interventions that humans make to select and modify sites to meet their physical and psychological needs. It includes not only broader planning statements, such as the arrangement of buildings and circulation systems, but also site details, such as the design of planted areas (including

dieval cities, for example, served as fortification against attacks by rival feudal lords. The trench constructed on the Kuwait border to separate it from a hostile Iraq serves as a more contemporary example. So, too, do the barriers to access associated with segregated communities of many urban and suburban American landscapes, as well as the whole concept of defensible design championed by Oscar Newman.[3] These may all be considered "landscapes of terror" in that they were conceived and constructed largely in response to the real or imagined possibility that their inhabitants may become the victims of hostility.

Scholars of landscape architecture history, however, have not examined the impact of the hostile environment within which many African-American landscapes were (are) shaped. We have failed to explore, for instance, how Southern blacks, as they planned their spaces, responded to the state-sanctioned hostilities against them, to the more insidious extralegal wrath of secret orders like the Ku Klux Klan, and to the unpredictable violence of "average" citizens who felt blacks in some way violated the elaborate social dictates imposed by cultural norms and by the law.

In this essay, I will present ideas from my research in progress on how the planning and development of African-American landscapes at the turn of the century were affected by such domestic terrorism. I will focus on the historic campus of Tuskegee University as a case study. As a black school emerging in the heart of Alabama just after Southern Reconstruction, Tuskegee provides an ideal setting to explore this idea. Its location in the Black Belt of Alabama, just forty miles east of the birthplace of the Confederacy, Montgomery, placed it squarely within the infamous region of terror that arose during Reconstruction and continued at least until Sammy Younge's murder in 1966 (fig. 1). Du Bois, in commenting on President Harding's decision to locate a federal hospital for black veterans at Tuskegee in 1921, portrays this sentiment succinctly:

---

layout and choice of species) and the use of physical barriers like walls and fences.

   [3] *Defensible Space* (New York: Collier Books, 1973).

> The last place on God's green earth to put a segregated Negro
> hospital was in the lynching-belt of mob ridden Alabama ...
> [where] there is no protection ... for a decent Negro pig-pen,
> much less for an institution to restore ... life and health.[4]

Furthermore, the school's national prominence meant that it
was often the focus of attention, weathering both the positive
and negative consequences of this dubious status. Tuskegee's
administration, on a subliminal if not a conscious level, had to
have taken this reality into consideration as it planned and
developed its campus in the midst of this region of terror.

Below I use aspects of Tuskegee's past as a black educational institution to review the history of the tyranny of the
South against its black citizens at the turn of the century.
Then I show how some features of the location and physical
form of Tuskegee's campus were likely responses to this hostile
context.

Southern Tyranny

In 1881, after much resistance, the Alabama government
finally approved a bill to establish a "Normal School for coloured teachers at Tuskegee."[5] The South had always been
particularly intolerant of black education. The wealth of the
powerful "cotton barons," the white landed elite of the South,
hinged on the coercive control and allocation of labor. This
planter class, quite naturally, viewed the education of the laboring masses as a threat to the viability of the Southern
plantation economy. Thus, even before Emancipation, the
South had passed laws that explicitly banned the education of
slaves, imposing severe penalties on them and on owners who
were found to be in violation.[6]

---

[4] Raymond Wolters, *The New Negro on Campus: Black College Rebellions
in the 1920s* (Princeton: Princeton University Press, 1975) 151.

[5] Anson Phelps Stokes, *Tuskegee Institute. The First Fifty Years: Founder's Day Address. Fiftieth Anniversary Celebration* (Tuskegee, AL: Tuskegee
Institute Press, 1931) 7.

[6] W. E. B. Du Bois, *Black Reconstruction in America: An Essay toward a
History of the Part Which Black Folk Played in the Attempt to Reconstruct De-*

Even with these constraints, thousands of slaves had learned to read and write before Emancipation. When Lincoln proclaimed their freedom, therefore, ex-slaves moved decisively to attain literacy, averring that the one sin of slavery they could not forgive was that it robbed them of their education.[7] Through their own initiatives at first, then with the support of agencies such as Northern missionary societies and the Freedmen's Bureau, they developed numerous schools across the region. Young and old alike flocked to places of learning, turning the planters' ideology regarding their education on its head.[8] Indeed, history has credited the former slaves with instituting the concept of universal public schooling in the South.

Blacks saw their schools as the most viable means of lifting themselves up from their subordinate place in Southern society. James Anderson suggests several specific reasons for this conviction.[9] First, education enabled them to decipher the labor contracts they made with landowners, thus safeguarding their interests. Anderson cites an old black woman who was determined to read and write "so that the Rebs can't cheat me." Second, during the brief period of black male suffrage, literacy enabled black men to read the ballot and eventually became a means by which they could challenge the laws that sought to deprive them of the right to vote. Finally, education, the ex-slaves hoped, would enable them to compete more effectively with white workers for better-paying jobs in industry and the professions.

Within a relatively short period after Emancipation, therefore, blacks had achieved enormous success in their push to become literate. This was interpreted by Southern whites as nothing short of an "uprising" that seriously threatened planter rule.[10] The elite landowners feared a dwindling labor supply as blacks, equipped with the tools of education, left the plantation in search of the higher-paying jobs in the cities.

mocracy in America, 1860–1880 (New York: Russell & Russell, Inc., 1935, 1962) 638.

[7] James D. Anderson, The Education of Blacks in the South, 1860–1935 (Chapel Hill: University of North Carolina Press, 1988) 6.

[8] Anderson, Education of Blacks 4.

[9] Anderson, Education of Blacks 18.

[10] Anderson, Education of Blacks 5.

Booker T. Washington recalls this sentiment in describing how many whites in the Tuskegee area felt about his school in 1881:

> There were not a few white people in the vicinity of Tuskegee who looked with some disfavor upon the project. They questioned its value to the coloured people, and had a fear that it might result in bringing about trouble between the races. Some had the feeling that in proportion as the Negro received education, in the same proportion would his value decrease as an economic factor in the state. These people feared the result of education would be that the Negroes would leave the farms, and it would be difficult to secure them for domestic service.[11]

But white worries were more than just economic. They were also social, based on the reality of white privilege, as Washington's description indicates. The economics of the plantation would hardly have been affected by the unavailability of workers for "domestic service." Rather, the black domestic served as a symbol in a social order, assuring whites of their advantaged status and ensuring that blacks not forget their own subordinate place. By challenging this order, the educated Negro caused much apprehension among the privileged. As W. E. B. Du Bois comments, citing a Freedmen's Commission Report on this issue, the South's "intense and bitter hostilities" toward black education were provoked by the feeling that blacks desired education to "render themselves equal to whites."[12] In a similar vein, Washington describes the image whites in the Tuskegee area held of the "educated Negro":

> The white people who questioned the wisdom of starting this new school had in their minds pictures of what was called the educated Negro, with high hat, imitation gold eye-glasses, a showy walking-stick, kid gloves, fancy boots, and what

---

[11] *Up from Slavery: An Autobiography* (Garden City, NY: Doubleday, Page & Company, 1925) 119–20.

[12] *Black Reconstruction* 645.

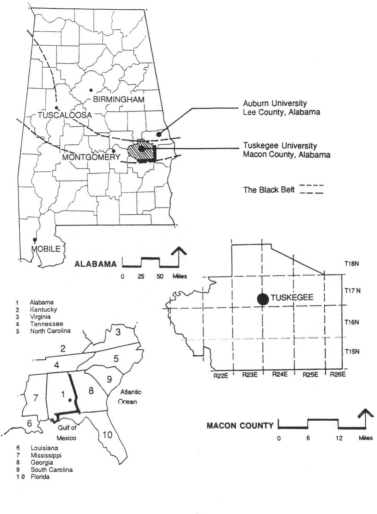

Figure 1. Tuskegee University's
location

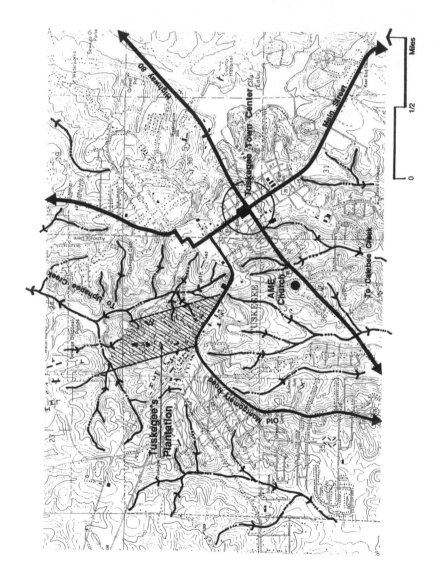

Figure 2. Tuskegee University's local context. By kind permission of Tuskegee University Archives

not—in a word, a man who was determined to live by his wits.[13]

The "uppity" educated Negro, who was neither in the fields nor in the kitchens of the white elite, was too threatening to the established social order of the South to be tolerated.

Yet another concern of whites can be linked to the ideology of white supremacy. Some white people in the South felt the notion of educating their former slaves was absurd. Du Bois records the response of a member of the Louisiana legislature upon encountering a school for blacks that was set up by the Freedmen's Bureau in New Orleans just after the Civil War:

> He stopped and looked intently, and then asked, "Is this a school?" "Yes," was the reply. "What, for niggers?" "Evidently." He threw up his hands. "Well, well," he said, "I have seen many an absurdity in my lifetime, but this the climax."[14]

Not surprisingly, then, Washington found that some whites "questioned" the "value" of education "to the coloured people," who, after all, as the sons and daughters of Ham, were meant to be laborers. Emancipation was not to erase deeply rooted racist beliefs.

Most important, however, propagandizing these beliefs, then as now, helped to fuel bitterness between the white and black working classes, which were pitted against each other in the job market, the voting booth, and other such institutions. Feuding masses could be easily distracted from the activities of the invisible few who held the reigns of Southern power. Out of this reality emerged the secret organizations of antiblack terrorism, such as the Ku Klux Klan and the Knights of the White Camellia, and a whole genre of American literature—racist propaganda such as Thomas Dixon's *The Clansman.*

Therefore, when federal troops retreated from the South, after radical Reconstruction had ended in failure by 1877, the landed class gradually instigated a full-scale legal and extralegal assault on black improvement in order to continue to exploit black labor and to maintain the social, political, and eco-

---

[13] *Up from Slavery* 119.

[14] *Black Reconstruction* 637.

nomic subordination of blacks. In the wake of this raging tyranny came an extraordinary trail of violence against blacks and against those institutions that were geared to their advancement in the South. This violence escalated throughout Tuskegee's early history and stretched well into the twentieth century.

In 1881, however, the correct mix of circumstances allowed the passage of the Alabama legislative bill establishing Tuskegee. Blacks in Macon County were not yet disfranchised; As in other counties that had belonged to the ante-bellum "Cotton Kingdom," they now held a voting majority. In that brief period, Macon County's blacks could use the power of their vote to negotiate bills in their interest.[15]

Moreover, the declining economic fortune of Tuskegee's once-prosperous Black Belt region also favored the establishment of the school. Louis R. Harlan points out that in post-bellum Alabama, the town of Tuskegee itself, once a wealthy cotton market center, now faced an uncertain economic future as a new industrial economy, centered in Birmingham, emerged to replace the once-preeminent agricultural economy of the Black Belt.[16] He argues that some whites, concerned about the very survival of the town, welcomed the idea of a new institution despite their apprehension. Harlan suggests that merchants, benefiting from the patronage of faculty and students from two white schools already located in the town— the Alabama Conference Female College and the Park High School—probably looked forward to the economic stimulus that yet another school would offer.

Alabamans also feared black emigration, which threatened labor shortages. Blacks accounted for at least 40 percent of the agricultural labor force in Alabama, and their migration worried the Southern landowners. As early as the 1860s promot-

---

[15] Louis Adams, a former slave and a man highly regarded in the Tuskegee community, was said to have bargained with the Democratic contender for Macon County's seat in the Alabama Senate in 1879, former Confederate army officer Wilber Foster. He apparently secured black political support for Foster in return for a promise that, if elected, the candidate would introduce and promote the passage of a state legislative bill to establish a normal school for blacks at Tuskegee (Stokes, *First Fifty Years* 7).

[16] *Booker T. Washington: The Making of a Black Leader, 1856–1901* (New York: Oxford University Press, 1972) 111–12.

ers began offering them the opportunity to migrate to states like Kansas and Oklahoma to enjoy new opportunities and freedom from the tyranny of the South. Louis Harlan points out that in Macon County itself, a wave of black emigration had already occurred in 1879, indicating that, according to a 1881 local newspaper editorial decrying the loss of population, "Negroes [had] again felt the restless urge to migrate.... Labor agents were said to be in town quietly enticing black men to break share-crop contracts and leave."[17] Harlan argues that whites, who were becoming increasingly alarmed by the situation, probably felt that satisfying the persistent desire of blacks to attain education would lessen their desire to leave the area.

Finally, the changing economy of Alabama also influenced the launching of Tuskegee in 1881. In Alabama, as in states across America, industrialization resulted in the emergence of a new elite that needed skilled labor and advocated training workers both black and white to meet this demand. Thus industrialists such as Carnegie and Rosenwald were willing to use the power of their wealth to support both black and white industrial schools.

The economic future of the town of Tuskegee, the fear of black labor shortages, and the labor demands of burgeoning industry coincided with the power of the black vote and the intense desire of blacks for education to will Tuskegee into existence. White attitudes toward the venture, however, were at best conflicted. Some elements, particularly the local merchants, though worried about the consequences of a black school, recognized and welcomed the potential benefits to business. Many whites, on the other hand, initially held the position of the *Tuskegee Daily*, which did not approve of establishing the school. Furthermore, despite the presence in the state legislature of Tuskegean Wilber Foster, the former Confederate officer who introduced the bill to establish Tuskegee, only $2,000 per annum was appropriated for the school. No provision was made for the procurement of physical plant and equipment.[18] These, the bill stipulated, were to be provided by the people who were to benefit from the school: Tuskegee's black people, upon whose desperate poverty Alabama thrived.

---

[17] *Making of a Black Leader* 112–13.

[18] Albert Scipio, *Pre-War Days at Tuskegee: Historical Essay on Tuskegee Institute (1881–1943)* (Silver Springs, MD: Roman Publications, 1987) 5.

It was in this complex moment, therefore, that Washington, who was teaching at his alma mater, Virginia's Hampton Institute, was asked to assume the leadership of Tuskegee. Aboard the colored car of the Louisville and Nashville Railroad, he made his way to the heart of Alabama.[19]

Campus Location

Playing School on the Spoils of White Men. Apparently, immediately upon arriving in Tuskegee, Washington began his search for the ideal spot for a permanent location of his new school. Richard Dozier points out that he had already selected a site when the school was first opened at temporary accommodations in the annex of the Butler Chapel A. M. E. Z. church on the edge of town.[20] But the school lacked the funds to pay for it.

The property was an unusual one as campus sites go. It was an abandoned hundred-acre cotton plantation located about one mile from the town itself (fig. 2).[21] It bore the scars of war and abandonment after years of abusive cotton cultivation. Its mansion had been burned during the war, and the only existing structures on the site were three ancillary build-

---

[19] Richard Dozier, "Tuskegee: Booker T. Washington's Contribution to the Education of Black Architects" (Doctor of Architecture dissertation, University of Michigan, 1990).

[20] Dozier, "Tuskegee" 102. It is significant that the first accommodation for the school was a church. Historically, the black church in the South was the only place where large numbers of blacks were permitted to meet. Furthermore, it was usually the only institution in black communities that was totally funded and controlled by them (see Benjamin E. Mays and Joseph W. Nicholson, *The Negro's Church* [New York: Russell & Russell, 1969]; and Edward F. Frazier, *The Negro Church in America* [New York: Schocken Books, 1964]). For this reason church buildings were often the logical sites for black schools. In this sense, then, even the temporary location of the fledgling school was in part a response to the hostility of the South toward its black citizens.

[21] Figure adapted from United States Department of the Interior Geological Survey, 7.5 minute series: Tuskegee Quadrangle, Macon Co., Alabama (Photorevised in 1983).

Figure 3. Tuskegee's original site. By
kind permission of Tuskegee
University archives

ings: a stable, a chicken coop, and a kitchen.[22] The site's
heavy, clay-rich soils, inherently not the best for cotton cultivation by Black Belt standards, were now severely eroded,
about 80 percent being classified by 1937 as "eroded phase."[23]
It contained little in the way of existing infrastructure to establish a college campus (fig. 3).[24] What, then, could have
made this place so attractive to the ever-pragmatic Washington?

---

[22] Booker T. Washington, *Life and Work in Harlan*, ed. Louis and Raymond Smock, vol. 1 of *The Booker T. Washington Papers* (Urbana: University of
Illinois Press, 1979) 36.

[23] United States Department of Agriculture and Alabama Department of
Agriculture and Industries, *Soil Survey: Macon County Alabama*, series 1937,
no. 11 (November 1944) 31.

[24] See Washington, *Up from Slavery* 130 for description of property.
Historic photograph reprinted with the permission of the Tuskegee University
archives.

Certainly, at $50 an acre, it was cheap land. Though still beyond the reach of the poorly funded institution, it may have been the best land the school could have dreamed of owning. In this and other instances when blacks were allowed to acquire real estate, their financial privation, the result of racial antipathy, was one of the factors that restricted them to the least expensive and most marginal land available.[25] It restricted them, for instance, to the "black bottoms" of the South and North or to the windswept, hurricane-vulnerable islands off the coast of South Carolina or to the declining, low-rent districts of uptown Manhattan. In this sense, therefore, racial hostility, from the stage of site selection early in the site planning process, would have left its mark on historical African-American landscapes.

But prohibitive cost was not the only factor that restricted African-Americans to marginal lands. Rather, like the reasons underlying Southern disapproval of black education, social concerns relating to white supremacy were also important. Thus, even when blacks could afford valued property, in the South as elsewhere, they were prevented from purchasing it because such an action, as Du Bois indicated, "provoked the feeling" that they "desired to render themselves equal to whites." Therefore, even though Lewis Adams, the black man who first negotiated to establish Tuskegee, was a very successful businessman, owning a substantial store on Tuskegee's town square, he lived in a small house located in the shady, secluded backyard of Thomas Dryer, the town's leading white merchant.[26] Adams, the powerful broker between black interests and white political ambitions in Macon County, had to be content with a home in another man's backyard. The humble abode of so successful a black man recalls a previous era. This tradition, prevalent throughout the South, was a vestige of the days of plantation slavery, recalling what Michael Vlach refers

---

[25] The marginality of property refers not to some inherent value but to that placed on it by the dominant group in society at a particular point in time. The Sea Islands, for instance, are now considered prime property for temporary homes and tourism. The value of the property has risen, driving out the very black people who had earlier settled. Gentrification of urban neighborhoods provides another example of the same phenomenon.

[26] Harlan, *Making of a Black Leader* 131.

to as the slave landscapes "back of the big house."[27] The pattern, which persisted well beyond Reconstruction, connoted the same social hierarchy as in the old days. Now, however, it also represented the necessary compromise made by a "free man" to permit the success of his store, which depended on white patronage in a racist Tuskegee.

As a native Southerner, Washington knew and intimately understood these social dictates. He must have considered, therefore, the social advantages of locating so bold an enterprise as his black school on abandoned land. His decision to house Tuskegee in the animal shelters of a deserted property would have served to calm the apprehensions of Southerners, assuring them that he understood the holy tenets of their social order and was willing not to transgress them. If his school was to succeed, he decided, as Adams probably had before him, that prevailing Southern attitudes toward black improvement had to be accommodated.

Beyond the site's abandonment is the issue of its previous function as a plantation. A cotton plantation, ironically the very symbol of generations of black oppression, was to be reconceived by its new black owners as a means of advancement. The relationship at first appears unlikely, but, again like Adams's seemingly odd compromise, it was probably a wise choice given the hostile circumstances the school faced. Washington wanted blacks to have a school, but the South, yearning for the good old ante-bellum days, would have preferred them to have a plantation on which to work. From his place of limited power, therefore, Washington, the "wizard of Tuskegee," selected a plantation for his school.

Indeed, the new campus was referred to not as "the College," as was the East Alabama Male College at Auburn[28] in adjacent Lee County, but strategically as "the Farm." White

---

[27] John Michael Vlach, *Back of the Big House: The Architecture of Plantation Slavery* (Chapel Hill: University of North Carolina Press, 1993).

[28] Auburn University, located in adjacent Lee County, developed during the same period as Tuskegee. However, while the school shared Tuskegee's central Alabama context, its privilege as the State's public (whites only), land-grant college, makes its campus ideal for comparison with that of Tuskegee's. For additional discussion on this issue, see forthcoming, Kenrick Ian Grandison, *From Plantation to Campus: Progress Community and the Lay of the Land in Shaping the Early Tuskegee. Landscape Journal* 15.1 (Spring 1996).

Southerners, and Northerners too, pleasantly surprised by Washington's emerging vision of the new "educated Negro," began to throw their support behind the fledgling "school." A friend from the North, for instance, gave $100, stipulating that it be used to purchase a horse to work the farm. Moses Pierce of Norwich, Connecticut, gave another $100 to buy "tools, seeds, and equipment to put the farm into operation."[29] The project was so unclear that historian Louis Harlan wonders whether the early Tuskegee was a "one horse school or a one horse farm."[30] It is not surprising, therefore, that one year into the school's life the once-skeptical *Tuskegee News* wrote: "The course of study seems to be good, expenses low, and advantages superior." The newspaper proceeded to acknowledge its error in not approving of the venture initially.[31]

Washington's instinctive response to the South was to mature over the decade, so that by 1895 his famous address to the Atlanta Exposition articulated his strategy as a full-fledged philosophy of compromise and accommodation, which was to become the mark of his controversial leadership. To the approving cheers of his Southern audience, he spoke with the air of humility for which he was much admired:

> Casting down your bucket among my people, helping and encouraging them as you are doing on these grounds, and to education of the head, hand, and heart, you will find that they will, buy your surplus land, and make blossom the waste places in your fields.[32]

The abandoned Bowen plantation provided the opportunity to demonstrate this principle, and so in yet another sense its selection was related to the hostile realities of Tuskegee's setting. The farm offered one hundred acres of cheap land. More important to the black school in "mob ridden Alabama," however, it offered the surprising advantages of being a place thrown away by white men—a waste place spent by years of cotton cultivation, destroyed by war, and abandoned by the "barons" who now deemed it unfit for their kind. It was ready for occupation

---

[29] Harlan, *Making of a Black Leader* 128.

[30] Harlan, *Making of a Black Leader* 128.

[31] Harlan, *Making of a Black Leader* 131.

[32] Washington, *Up from Slavery* 221.

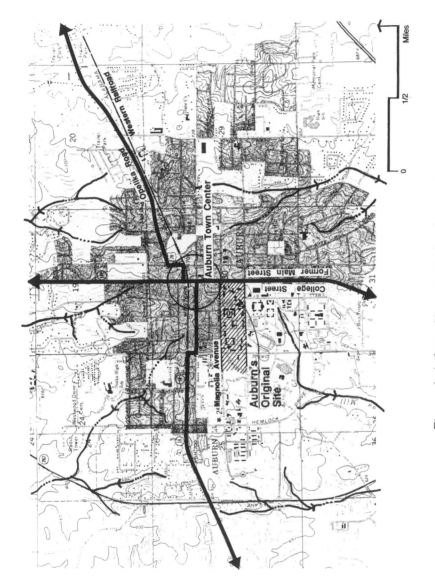

Figure 4. Auburn University's local context

by members of a grateful black mass who could play school on it to their hearts' content. This made a threatening institution more palatable.

On the Other Side of the Tracks. If locating the school on Macon County's finest land was unwise, locating it squarely within the town of Tuskegee would have been perilous. The one-mile distance between the plantation and the town of Tuskegee, though unusual for a college campus in America, may have been another attractive feature of the site. Many college campuses in America physically embraced the towns in which they were located. For instance, Auburn University, the former East Alabama Male College mentioned above, was located in the heart of the town of Auburn (fig. 4)[33]. So certain was this school of its right to belong there that it was sited on Main Street, which was eventually claimed by the institution and renamed College Street. This audacity is not surprising, for the East Alabama Male College was built for the sons of the "courageous and ambitious settlers ... who had risked the hazards and hardships of frontier life ... [and were] now reaping the reward of a bountiful nature."[34]

Not only was Tuskegee's site out of town, but vehicular access to it was limited. Montgomery Road was the only major thoroughfare between the site and the town at the time. Furthermore, a district of the piney ravines carved by branches of the Callebee and Uphapee creeks formed a distinct barrier between "town and gown." This barrier remains unviolated to this day (fig. 2). The institution, therefore, was sited away from public view where it would have been less likely to affront those who did not approve of it. Otherwise, some would surely have been troubled by the sight of several dozen Negro students and teachers traipsing around town with books rather than cotton sacks in their hands.

Even so, the school still established strict rules of conduct for students and faculty in relation to the distant town. One

---

[33] Figure adapted from United States Department of the Interior Geological Survey, 7.5 minute series: Waverly, Alabama Quadrangle, (1971), Loschpoka, Alabama Quadrangle (1971), and Oplika West, Alabama Quadrangle (1971).

[34] Centennial Committee, *Auburn's First 100 Years, 1856–1956*, prepared for Centennial Celebration (Auburn, AL: Alabama Polytechnic Institute, 1956) 5.

faculty member from the North, unused to Southern traditions, was admonished by the dean for carrying too many books. The dean feared that whites "would get the impression that Tuskegee was training the intellect rather than the heart and hands."[35] When a sociologist from the University of Chicago offered his resignation because he could not understand why the administration, in the old-fashioned style of Mr. Washington, was so anxious to keep the good will of the white community, principal Russa Morton's response hit the mark. He accepted the professor's resignation, adding that "most teachers from the North don't fit in. We have a peculiar situation down here, and I imagine you have to be born in it to really understand it."[36]

Separation from town would have also allowed Tuskegee a greater degree of freedom from unwelcome white proscriptions and thus greater autonomy. On his secluded plantation, Washington could set the rules. If he deemed it appropriate, his students and faculty could wear top hats as tall as the sky and strut around as they pleased on their plantation one mile away from town. Washington, allowing for the constraints of the time, was the boss of Tuskegee. Moving out of town would have been the best way to keep the peace and promote this relative autonomy.

Campus Layout

Alabama's hostility to black progress, therefore, would have influenced the selection of the Bowen plantation for a permanent home for Tuskegee. By embracing the hostile realities of the South, Washington was able to win many white Southerners over to his cause. Moreover, as an additional precaution, he tucked his school away from public view, placing some distance and difficult terrain between it and the town. Was it now possible to build the campus without concern for its physical security? Unlikely. The activities of the agents of terror could not have been expected to be restricted to "Main-Street" Tus-

---

[35] Wolters, *New Negro on Campus* 144.
[36] Wolters, *New Negro on Campus* 144.

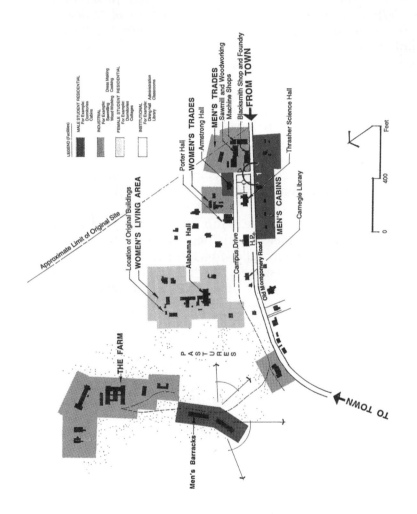

Figure 5. Tuskegee's campus plan (1897). By kind permission of Tuskegee University Archives

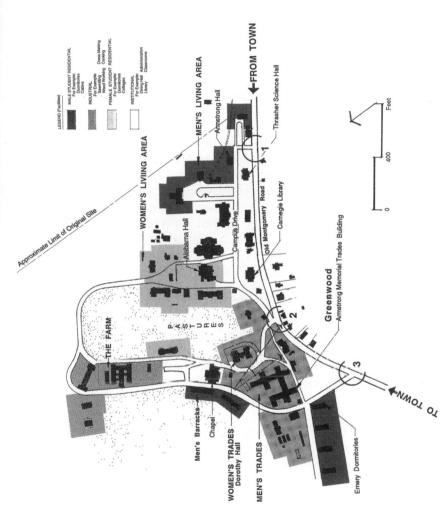

Figure 6. Tuskegee's campus plan (1909). By kind permission of Tuskegee University Archives

kegee. The Klan, for instance, if sufficiently agitated, could ride wherever it pleased in this "white man's country."

Numerous incidents in Tuskegee's history suggest that the people who built the institution could not possibly have ignored terror as a planning factor in laying out the campus. By 1900 the school had begun to enjoy some success. It was able to increase its land holdings from one hundred acres to twenty-five hundred acres. Furthermore, it was busy buying up additional property for Greenwood, its model Negro community located next to the campus. From its three original utility buildings, the school by 1900 had grown to forty-six buildings, many of which, due to Washington's special penchant for brick structures, were the finest in Macon County. Washington's well-oiled "Tuskegee machine" had increased the value of the school's physical plant from $500 to between $300,000 and $400,000.[37] Moreover, from its early days, the institution, in the interest of cost efficiency, had begun to produce food and industrial items for use in its day-to-day operation. By 1900 the considerable surplus of these products was being sold on the local market. This upset the same local merchants who, in the early days, were enthusiastic about the payroll the school brought to the declining town. To say the least, it was beginning to become clear that these Negroes hidden away on their plantation were not merely "playing school." This situation was to rekindle white jealousy and fear of the venture.

Thus, Black Belt conservative governor William Jelks, probably further agitated by the 1906 race riots in Atlanta, on the same platform as Washington on Negro day at the state fair, denounced black education, claiming that it was luring blacks away from the field. In a follow-up letter to Washington on the issue, he focused on Tuskegee itself, contending that "an education in your school educates the boy away from the farm."[38] Washington, like a medieval serf, lavished Jelks and other Alabama governors with gifts of turkeys, chickens, peaches, butter, and other products from his now-bountiful

---

[37] Max B. Thrasher, *Tuskegee: Its Story and Its Work* (New York: Negro Universities Press, a division of Greenwood Publishing Corp., 1969) 39.

[38] Louis R. Harlan, *Booker T. Washington: The Wizard of Tuskegee, 1901–1915* (New York: Oxford University Press, 1983) 241.

waste place. In return, he hoped for their mercy, upon which Tuskegee increasingly depended.[39]

But despite such measures the school remained vulnerable to white scare campaigns. Around 1907, the begrudging merchants of Tuskegee spearheaded attempts to have the state legislature strip the institution of its tax-exempt status. These attempts were validated by cries that Tuskegee was "trying to buy up the whole county" and drive whites away or that Washington was trying to subvert white supremacy.[40] One state representative, during a legislative debate on the issue, summarized the situation in one sentence: "I believe Booker T. Washington and his gang would prove to be a curse to the South, and if I had my way I would wipe his institute off the face of the earth."[41]

Washington's increasing prominence as "the leader of the Negro race" created its own problems. Though he was a supreme diplomat, his much-publicized activities and positions sometimes met with disapproval. When, for instance, as a black man he dared to dine with President Theodore Roosevelt at the White House in 1901, the Southern white reaction was intense outrage. Samuel Spencer documents some of the responses of the Southern press. The Macon *Telegraph* reminded its readership of the gospel according to the South: "God set up the barrier between the races. No president of this or any country can break it down."[42] Young Southerners sang a new popular song:

> Coon, coon, coon
> Booker T. Washington is his name;
> Coon, coon, coon
> Ain't that a measly shame?
> Coon, coon, coon
> Morning, night, and noon

---

[39] Harlan, *Wizard* 241.

[40] Harlan, *Wizard* 166.

[41] Harlan, *Wizard* 169.

[42] Samuel Spencer, Jr., *Booker T. Washington and the Negro's Place in American Life* (Boston: Little, Brown and Co., 1955) 134.

> I think I'd class Mr. Roosevelt
> with a Coon, coon, coon.[43]

By separating his black school from the town, Washington demonstrated his understanding of Southern realities. That, however, was not a sufficient condition for tolerance and goodwill on the part of his neighbors. It would have been surprising if the institution did not consider and prepare for the possibility of violent retribution for perceived indiscretion on the part of Washington, his faculty, or his students. Plans of the campus from 1897 and 1909 show what precautions planners may have taken (figs. 5 and 6).[44]

Campus Orientation and Vehicular Access. The 1897 plan indicates that the early campus was served by just one vehicular entry from Montgomery Road, which, as already mentioned, was the only major vehicular route to the site at the time. The road flanked the southern boundary of the property, and since it occupied the crest of the broad, flat-topped Tuskegee Ridge, topography would have posed no hindrance to the number of places where convenient and safe vehicular entries to the campus could have been located. Yet only one entrance was established at first, two more being added by 1909 (fig. 6). Indeed, rather than taking advantage of the existing Montgomery Road to orient adjacent campus buildings, the institution chose instead the more costly alternative of installing an internal campus drive leading from the entry and running parallel to the public road. Buildings such as Thrasher Science Hall and the Carnegie Library front this internal drive, turning their backs decisively to the public street. Thus today, as the campus has expanded across the public road, the road seems to be an intrusion snaking past the backs of these original buildings (figs. 6 and 7).

Again, this pattern is different from most American college campuses, which tend to embrace their surroundings more thoroughly. Consider, again, the campus of Auburn University. Its main academic building, sited on Auburn's Main Street, was oriented not to the rest of the college grounds, which ex-

---

[43] Spencer, *Booker T. Washington* 135.

[44] Figures adapted from Feb. 1897 and June 1909 Sanborn Fire Insurance Maps of Tuskegee, Macon Co. Alabama obtained from the collection in the Geography and Map Division of the Library of Congress.

Figure 7. Carnegie Library's orientation (1994), facing Montgomery Road
(top) and facing campus (bottom)

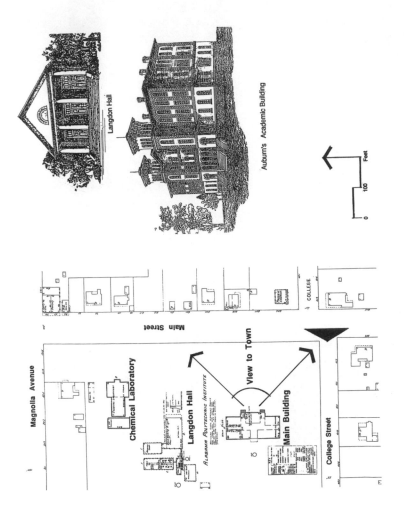

Figure 8. Auburn's main entrance and academic building (1897). By kind permission of University Archives, Auburn University

tended from Main Street westward, but to the town itself (fig. 8).[45] The same is true of Langdon Hall, the other major building on the campus at the time. When the campus jumped over Main Street, therefore, the public road, flanked by the fronts of campus buildings on either side, seemed to belong to the development. Auburn's academic buildings asserted themselves in their Southern setting. In contrast, their counterparts at Tuskegee turned their backs to this context, embracing instead the plantation, the revered symbol of hope and progress (fig. 9).[46]

The contrast is equally evident with regard to the number of vehicular entry points. There seemed to be no attempt to limit the number of vehicular entries to Auburn's campus. In fact, ease of access was apparently given primary consideration. A current plan of the campus indicates that entries are located frequently along Magnolia and College avenues and are interconnected by internal roads that thoroughly traverse the campus (fig. 10). Along Main Street alone, six entries lead to the original core of the campus extending westward. In contrast, at Tuskegee, three entries lead from Old Montgomery Road to the original core of the campus extending to the north (fig. 11). This despite the fact that Auburn's former Main Street was a primary highway connecting the town with adjacent counties. On the other hand, Tuskegee's Old Montgomery Road, as a secondary highway, served primarily to connect the vicinity with the town of Tuskegee itself. Clearly, it would have been easier and less expensive for Tuskegee to access its campus directly from the public road. But despite the limited funds available to it in the early days, the institution chose the costly option of building a parallel campus road. The difference raises the question: Could Auburn's privilege, as a white school in post-Reconstruction Alabama, have allowed it the flexibility of

---

[45] Figure adapted from Jan. 1897 Sanborn Fire Insurance Map of Auburn, Lee Co. Alabama obtained from the collection in the Geography and Map Division of the Library of Congress. Historic sketches reprinted with the permission of the Auburn University archives.

[46] Figure adapted from Feb. 1897 Sanborn Fire Insurance Map of Tuskegee, Macon Co. Alabama obtained from the collection in the Geography and Map Division of the Library of Congress. Historic photograph reprinted with the permission of the Tuskegee University archives.

accessing its campus wherever it pleased—a privilege that the black Tuskegee could not be so reckless as to enjoy?

Campus Surveillance, Entry Location, and Land Use Patterns. The location of the entries also raises some issues. The 1897 plan (fig. 5) shows that the single entry was located to the eastern extreme of the Montgomery road frontage of the property. One might have thought that an entrance would have been located nearer the center of the frontage where it would have coincided with the highest elevations along that section of the road and would have been nearer to the three original buildings that the school inherited with its plantation. But that was not to be. Instead, this first entrance was located closest to the town. In this way, from the point of view of surveillance, a traveler along Montgomery Road, coming from the direction of town, would have had to pass this entrance before proceeding past the rest of the institution's grounds. The same reasoning would have held for the western entrances, created later, for travelers coming from the other direction (fig. 6).

Curiously, too, both the 1897 and 1909 plans show that entry areas were associated with housing for male students. To the east, Armstrong Hall, the first men's dormitory built on the campus, immediately greeted the visitor entering the eastern gateway in 1897 (fig. 5). Then, in 1900, when the school had moved many of its industrial facilities into the new Armstrong Memorial Trades Complex on the western side of the campus, the building that had housed the foundry and blacksmith shop and, Cassedy Hall, the building that had housed men's trades, were also converted to men's dormitories, thus creating a distinct male domain (fig. 6). At the new western entries, the same pattern is evident. The Emery men's dormitories were constructed to the west of the westernmost entry. Additionally, two wooden barracks for male students, which once guarded the west edge of campus, probably now enjoyed a considerable view of the middle entry (fig. 6).

Young women, on the other hand, from the very beginning, were relegated to the interior of the campus. When the school's first building, Porter Hall, was constructed in 1882, women were housed in its attic. The building was placed about 1,000 feet from the eastern entrance (fig. 5). Later, in 1884, Alabama Hall, primarily a female dormitory, was located even

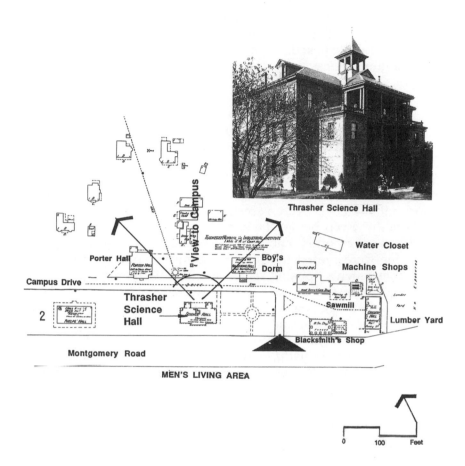

Figure 9. Tuskegee's main entrance
and academic building (1897). San-
ford Fire Insurance map. Photo by
kind permission of Tuskegee University archives

further to the interior of the campus, where the original plantation buildings were located (fig. 5). Eventually, a distinct female precinct was established behind Alabama Hall, occupying
the approximate center of the site and, removed from Montgomery Road as well as from the entrances to the campus (fig.
6).

The cultural dictates of the Victorian era prescribed not only the separation of the sexes but also that the "fairer" of the two not be "exposed," lest its "chastity" be compromised. Washington writes:

> The number of students, of both sexes; continued to increase. We could find rooms outside the school grounds for many of the young men but the girls we did not care to expose in this way.[47]

Does the decision to locate the more "exposure"-tolerant young men at the edges of the campus rather than the interior indicate that the edges were perceived as being in some way more vulnerable? Even before the school was able to house its male students on campus, cabins located just opposite the eastern entrance were rented to provide accommodation for them. So, even then, men's housing was associated with entrances or, as in the case of the barracks, with the edges of campus. Here they could survey passing traffic on Montgomery Road heading from or toward town, and they could potentially serve as a first line of defense in case of hostile intrusion.

Agriculture, Industry, and Church as Cover for School. The location of industries relative to the entry areas is another curious feature of the 1897 campus plan (fig. 5). Before the second and third entries were constructed, as already mentioned, in addition to men's residences in Armstrong Hall and in the cabins across the street, men's trade facilities were also located there. Later, with the opening of the western entries all of the trades, except the sawmill, were moved there. The Armstrong Memorial Complex was located in this area and, for the first time, violating the pattern of clustering women's facilities away from entrances, Dorothy Hall, the women's trade building in which young ladies were taught the skills of needlework, laundry, general housework, and "the art of scrubbing," was placed in this new industrial district in view of the entrance.[48] Also, the pastures of the school's farm, located in the Big Valley below, would have been clearly visible to anyone entering the

---

[47] *Up from Slavery* 177.
[48] Thrasher, *Tuskegee* x.

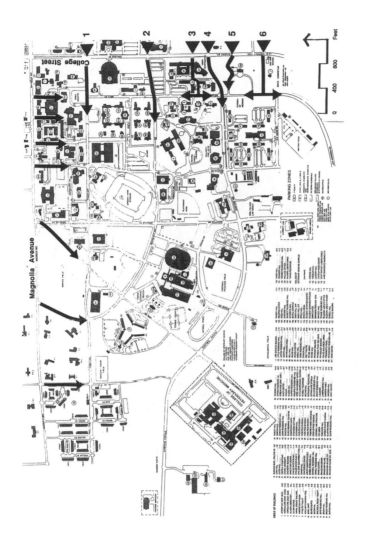

Figure 10. Access to Auburn's campus (1995). By kind permission of the Office of the University Architect, Auburn University

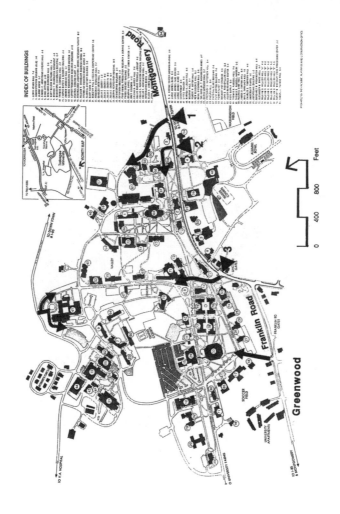

Figure 11. Access to Tuskegee's campus (1995). Base map illustrated by
T. Peters, Architect, Tuskegee University

campus via these west entrances. So, too, would the chapel, lest the "heart" of Washington's "carefully conceived hand and heart" equation for black education appear to be left out of the picture (fig. 6).

Not even official land-grant colleges such as Auburn University flaunted the evidence of their mission so boldly. For instance, Auburn's imposing academic building greeted the visitor entering the campus at the intersection of College and Main in 1897 (fig. 8). Its Chemical Laboratory and Langdon Hall which housed its woodworking and machine shops within remarkably imposing classical architecture, were located beyond this main building. Its farm operations were located a mile away. At Tuskegee, on the other hand (fig. 9), Max Thrasher, upon entering the campus in 1890, writes:

> At the right of the main entrance, as one enters the grounds, is Cassedy Hall, ... a dormitory for boys. Adjacent ... is another small brick building also used as a dormitory. Near these buildings the visitor may often see piles of logs—oak, pine, and poplar, ...They have been cut on one of the school's timberlots, and drawn in for lumber. The building in front of which they have been left is the sawmill, and the strident "buzz-z-z" of a stout circular saw which comes from the building, shows that the mill is in operation.[49]

Was it a school, or was it a lumber camp or a farm? Thrasher, it appears, was too preoccupied with the "buzz-z-z" of the sawmill to wonder about the oddity of Tuskegee's layout.

Washington had adopted the practical-education model of his alma mater, Hampton, with great enthusiasm. But was his enthusiasm so enormous that he could not resist the temptation to decorate the entries to his campus with such a remarkable display of working industry, no doubt complete with ancillary stockpiles of raw materials, smoke plumes, and industrial waste? Again, probably not. At least on a subliminal level, like the choice of his plantation, Washington must have considered that the high visibility of industry and agriculture on his campus would serve to allay the suspicions of those who questioned the work of the school and to make less threatening the sight of the imposing academic buildings that lay beyond this

---

[49] Thrasher, *Tuskegee* 39.

rough display. Thrasher's reaction, then, would have been exactly the effect the pattern was intended to have on visitors. The stereotypical "educated Negro," with "high hat ... kid gloves" and "what not," engendered fear among white Southerners who, Washington tells us, found it difficult to see "how education could produce any other kind of Negro."[50] Showcasing working industry, agriculture, and the church immediately at the school's entrances ensured that the South would not miss the fact that education could actually produce another kind of Negro. What better way to show the South that Tuskegee's work was consistent with the role it believed "Negroes" should play in its economy?

Conclusion

The tyranny blacks faced (and still face) in America has left its mark on the landscapes they have molded. Landscape architecture history, however, has made no record of this because it has generally focused on the places of the wealthy and powerful. From the Medici in 15th century Italy, to Louis XIV in 17th century France, to the Vanderbilts in 20th century America, our discourse has been centered on the experience of those who built landscapes with significant resources at their disposal and with powerful institutions under their control. Meanwhile we have ignored the stories of poor, marginalized, and oppressed people. The seemingly ordinary spaces hewed out of the land by "common folk," however, like great works of art and literature, are documents, not only the lives of those who created them but also of their interactions with the larger community. The landscapes of ordinary people, like those of the privileged, therefore, tell the story of the whole. Tuskegee's historic campus, as interpreted here, reflects the centrality of racism to the American ethos. From site selection to site development, antiblack terrorism has had physical consequences on the land. The resulting landscape is a critical artifact of Ameri-

---

[50] *Up from Slavery* 120.

can realities, which though painful and embarrassing to remember, should never be forgotten.

THE POLITICS OF TRUST

Bernard Williams

Two Images of Trust

Jean Starobinski recounts the effect on Rousseau of the incident in his childhood, narrated in the *Confessions*, when he was falsely accused of breaking a comb and found that his true denial was not believed: "From that moment, paradise was lost, since paradise was the reciprocal transparency of consciousnesses, a total and confident communication between them."[1] Starobinski sees all Rousseau's later efforts toward improvement as attempts to regain that lost transparency.

> It is enough to be sincere, to be oneself, and from then on natural man is no longer a remote archetype to whom I compare myself; he coincides, rather, with my own presence, with my existence itself. The old transparency came from the naive presence of men under the eyes of the gods; the new transparency is an interior closeness to myself, a relation of the self to the self. It comes about in the clarity of his view of himself, which allows Jean-Jacques to represent himself as he is. (32)

Granted a total clarity of view, and an impulse to total candor, it should have been simple for Rousseau to explain himself to others, but in fact his explanations were never a success, and his failures to explain himself informed his increasing paranoia:

> No one knows me except I myself. I see that people who live most intimately with me do not know me, and that they at-

---

[1] *Jean-Jacques Rousseau: La Transparence et l'obstacle* (Paris: Gallimard, 1971) 19; trans. by Arthur Goldhammer as *Jean-Jacques Rousseau: Transparency and Obstruction* (Chicago: University of Chicago Press, 1988). The translations from this work in the present text are my own. Subsequent page references appear parenthetically in the text.

tribute most of my actions, for good or ill, to motives quite different from those that have produced them.[2]

As Starobinski puts it, Rousseau's concern in the *Confessions*

> starts with this question: why the interior sentiment, which is immediately evident, does not receive an immediate recognition in which it can find an echo. Why is it so difficult to bring about a concord between what one is for oneself and what one is for others? (218)

It is easy to see the turns of thought in which Rousseau was trapped when he found it hard to achieve the transition from the personal to the social. If self-understanding were immediately at hand, only sheer deceit, a willful desire to mislead, would withhold it from others. Since he was not deceiving others, and only desired to reveal himself to them, their failure to understand him could only represent malice on their part. It might seem an argument against the idea of their malice that he could not understand why they should be so malicious; but if he could not, then that must be because they made it impossible for him to understand what they were doing, which proved they were malicious.

The ideal of transparent communication contains a political as well as a merely social conception. It represents the politics of trust as an attempt to recover a state of transparency, a kind of archetypal identity that might be realized in some state of high shared civic aspiration such as the condition of social immediacy that would make possible the expression of the general will. The hopes for a politics of trust, when expressed in such terms, rest on several assumptions. Such a politics requires, first, the authority of trustworthy self-declaration: the idea that sincere, spontaneous, nondeceitful declaration can guarantee a true understanding of motive. It implies, second, that what is so revealed and understood will be coherent: it will represent a steadiness of character or nature. Moreover, since trust is meant to yield a politics, it cannot only be the case that we trust what each of us declares.

---

[2] This passage, rejected from the *Confessions*, is preserved by Starobinski, *Jean-Jacques Rousseau* 218.

What each of us declares might merely be noncooperative self-interest. Rather, what we declare must itself form the basis of trusting one another, in the sense of providing the substance of living together. The motives that are honestly revealed must provide the basis of a shared life; they must be in some sense moral or self-transcending. Rousseau's work provides a complex dialectic: the self revealed in sincere and spontaneous declaration must be the real self, and the real self is that which expresses itself in the general will, transcending the divisive motivations of particular self-interest.

Rousseau's politics of trust stands in sharp contrast to the tradition associated with Hobbes and his intellectual successors. In this tradition trust is a hard-won achievement through which human beings can, with certain costs, secure the benefits—in the first place, the self-interested benefits—of a cooperative and regulated social life. Certainly, Hobbes's account makes the obstacles to the achievement of trust so high, and a society based on it so potentially unstable, that the solution has to be exceedingly drastic if it is to work at all. The solution—Hobbesian sovereign power—is so drastic in fact that many, such as Locke, have found it hard to distinguish from the problem.

We can realistically and helpfully relax several of Hobbes's conditions, as Hume did. We can accept that even "in a state of nature" people do not act simply as egoistic individuals—that politics must be understood as starting from the concerns of the family or other prepolitical groups that define shared interests. We can accept too (using game theory) that the game being played is the Assurance Game rather than the Prisoners' Dilemma—that is to say, individuals prefer outcomes in which they genuinely cooperate rather than those in which they get the benefits of cooperation without having to do their part.[3] Even with such benevolent changes, however, a theory in this style will preserve the spirit of Hobbes's account as contrasted with Rousseau's. Trust—and the institutions and dispositions

---

[3] Some writers who rightly criticize the assumptions of microeconomic egoism unfortunately tend to assume that any discussion that uses games theory or other types of rational decision theory must be committed to those assumptions. For additional discussion see "Formal Structures and Social Reality," reprinted in my *Making Sense of Humanity* (Cambridge: Cambridge University Press, 1995).

that express and support it—will be seen as constructed and justified in terms of cooperation, mutual support, and the benefits of the division of labor. But such an account stands opposed to the first and third assumptions of Rousseau's account. It is true that not all trust can be constructed in the manner of game theory: language would be unlearnable unless there were many primitive situations of mere openness in which the accuracy and sincerity of the speaker do not come into question. But in the kinds of interaction that demand a politics of trust, sincere and open utterance can be neither counted upon nor understood as a default position from which deceit and concealment must be seen, as they are under Rousseau's first assumption of trustworthy self-declaration, as a corrupt falling-away.

For similar reasons, the neo-Hobbesian account cannot share Rousseau's third assumption, that the self-transcending motivations of a moral will serve as the starting point for a politics of trust, which must address the question of how such a will may be fully and accurately expressed. For the neo-Hobbesian, the existence of such motivations must once again, at any political or social level, represent an achievement. It is true that such motivations, including the motivations to honest declaration itself, as well as to keeping one's word, fulfilling expectations, and so forth, cannot be understood simply in the blank instrumental terms proposed in the theories of Utilitarians or of Hobbesian contractualists such as David Gauthier. If sincerity is to carry the burden of securing trust and cooperation, many social arrangements will require it to be understood as something like an intrinsic value, and sincerity cannot be understood in those terms if it presents itself to reflection as merely an instrumental device for generating utility or serving the aims of long-term rational self-interest.

If it is to work as an intrinsic value, sincerity has to be intelligible from inside, to the agent, as an intrinsic value, which requires that it be intelligibly related to other values that are important to the agent.[4] Given these modifications, however, the spirit of the account is still different from Rousseau's

---

[4] The relations of sincerity to other values have taken different forms under different social circumstances, in ways that have involved much secondary elaboration. I hope to discuss the construction of such values in forthcoming work on the value of truth.

since it explains the value of sincerity in terms of other interests, some of them individual interests, even though its relation to them will not be blankly instrumental.

A Very Different View: Rameau's Nephew

The conflicts between even a modified neo-Hobbesian account and Rousseau's remain, and they are deep. Yet in other areas these two accounts can be seen as having too much in common. In particular, the neo-Hobbesian account appears to share Rousseau's second assumption: that the self that is plain to the subject and can be revealed to others (or, as Hobbes reminds us, concealed from them) will be of a coherent or steady nature.

An altogether different view of the self—and of the self's relations to sincerity and authenticity—emerges from the remarkable work by Rousseau's contemporary, friend, and hence—inevitably with Rousseau—enemy, Diderot's *Rameau's Nephew*.[5] This work perhaps remains less familiar, certainly to philosophers, than it should be. It presents a conversation between, we may suppose, Diderot, who is identified as Moi, and a character identified as Lui, who is Jean-François Rameau, the nephew of the famous composer. An extraordinary figure, he is, as the narrator puts it,

> one of the weirdest characters in this land of ours where God has not been sparing of them. He is a compound of the highest and the lowest, good sense and folly. The notions of good and evil must be strangely muddled in his head, for the good qualities nature has given him he displays without ostentation, and the bad ones without shame. (33–34)

---

[5] It was first published in a German translation by Goethe from a manuscript lent him by Schiller, a manuscript that then disappeared. Only an imperfect French manuscript remained until 1891, when a perfect copy in Diderot's hand was found by chance in a bookseller's box on the Quai Voltaire. The edition cited parenthetically in the text is *Rameau's Nephew and D'Alembert's Dream*, trans. Leonard Tancock (Harmondsworth: Penguin Books, 1966).

His appearance, his clothes, and his build vary greatly from time to time depending on his fortunes. He suffers wild swings of mood even in this one conversation. He has a deafening voice and amazing powers of mimicry, and in the course of the dialogue he goes into several turns, toward the end rendering all the parts of several pieces from French opera. Besides these set pieces, the dialogue moves with great ease and freedom over all sorts of topics: vice and virtue, sincerity and hypocrisy; philosophy and scientific materialism; French and Italian opera.

Rameau's Nephew has caused critics a lot of anxiety. There is a question of what the dialogue is supposed to be about; but it is not clear why it has to be about any one thing. Critics are worried, too, about the point of view we are supposed to adopt. If the preferred point of view is that of the shameless Rameau, even in part, are we heading for "the overthrow of all moral values," as a recent translator rather desperately asks?

As Wilda Anderson has said, this is a text that each reader has to process for himself or herself.[6] This point is itself related to its content. It is already clear from the surface of the conversational drama that neither Lui nor Moi is an authority figure. Moi, though he makes various interpretive and sometimes condemnatory remarks in asides, collaborates in some of Rameau's more outrageous opinions. It is with some help from Moi that Lui gets going on the psychology of virtue:

> you think that happiness is the same for all. What a strange illusion! Your own brand presupposes a certain fanciful [*romanesque*] turn of mind that we don't all possess, an unusual type of soul, a peculiar taste. You dignify this oddity with the name of virtue and you call it philosophy. But are [they] made for everyone? (64)

> why do we so often see the virtuous so hard, tiresome and unsociable? Because they have subjected themselves to a discipline that is not in their nature. They are miserable, and when you are miserable yourself you make others miserable

---

[6] *Diderot's Dream* (Baltimore: Johns Hopkins University Press, 1990).

as well. That's not my idea, nor that of my patrons. I have to be gay, adaptable, agreeable, amusing, odd. Virtue commands respect, and respect is a liability. (69)

A recurrent theme is that Rameau is not inconsistent:

Devil take me if I know what I am. As a rule, my mind is as true as a sphere and my character as honest as the day: never false if I have the slightest interest in being true, never true if I have the slightest interest in being false.... I have never reflected in my life, either before speaking, during speech or after. (79)

And Lui says of him in summary:

That indeed was the most obvious difference between this man and most of those that we meet. He owned up to the vices he had, and which others have—he was no hypocrite. He was no more abominable than they, and no less. He was simply more open, more consistent, and sometimes more profound in his depravity. (111)

As I have already said, this is a work that one has to make something of for oneself, and that this should be so is true to what it is about. It can be helpfully turned to the interests of philosophy, even though it may not be best served by extracting opinions from it, which is what I shall do for the most part. Even so, I hope to give it fairer treatment than it received in its most famous encounter with philosophy, when it turned up, though not explicitly by name, in Hegel's *Phenomenology*. Hegel has contempt for Moi, whom he takes to stand for simple, unreflective consciousness, while he sees in Lui the historically higher phenomenon of the unhappy consciousness, which separates itself in irony from accepted circumstances of social power. Besides its remorseless abstraction from most specific features of the dialogue (as, indeed, of anything else), Hegel's reading is, ironically, very undialectical in setting Lui in an entirely positive light against Moi. One might say that in representing Lui as the more reflective of the two, Hegel is untrue to the character as he appears in the dialogue, but this would exaggerate the extent to which Hegel is even interested in making such a discrimination. My objection to Hegel's handling of the work is rather that in using Lui simply to illustrate a stage in the history of consciousness, he loses the sense of what it might be for such a person to confront someone else, as Rameau confronts the narrator and conspires with him in generating this conversation. In neglecting this central conversational dimension of Diderot's writing, Hegel also loses sight of some of its major ideas.

Some of those major ideas are these. Rameau is authentic, true to himself: he is certainly and conspicuously not self-deceived. We might say that he *possesses* a lot of truth about himself. He is also to an unusual degree sincere. He certainly flatters and lies, but he is unusual in the degree to which he admits that he does so. He *reveals* a lot of truth about himself. In these qualities, he offers an exceptionally clear example of sincerity in its basic form of uninhibited expression or enactment, rather than in the secondary form of the reported findings of self-examination. He is unguardedly spontaneous even in his second-order or reflective comments. The model of sincerity as uninhibited spontaneity applies, perhaps rather paradoxically, even to his flattery and deceit. In those activities, as he makes clear, the expectations of his audience lead him actually to become, for a while, what they require; his availability to them takes the form not of a systematic misreporting of his states but rather of an instantaneous impersonation, an improvisation of another short-lived personality.

Rameau's qualities immediately raise a question the answer to which is taken for granted in Rousseau's account. How much is secured morally and socially by sincerity and authenticity? Rameau's nature certainly strikes down at once the simple association to which Rousseau was so attached—that such virtues can somehow guarantee a life or character that will serve the desired purposes of morality: cooperation, self-transcendence, social dignity.

Perhaps few, except Rousseau himself and some other enthusiasts of sincerity (some of them involved in the French Revolution), have supposed that the association might be so simple. But the situation darkens further with the thought that the true self, if there is such a thing—at the very least, the self revealed and understood in authenticity—may not be very well adjusted to morality, let alone guarantee an association with it. The relations of the self to others and their interests will be a matter, rather, of temperament, and in many temperamental circumstances this can be a strain, a question of rather desperate contingency.

It is not in any case merely a matter of the character of the revealed self. The self is anyway not revealed on the spot. Rameau, we have been constantly told, is consistent, always the same, but that is because he freely and unashamedly expresses very different things at different times. Diderot was always attracted to a picture of the self that he often expressed as constantly shifting, reacting, and altering: as a swarm of bees; as a clavichord or harp or other instrument, with the wind or other forces playing on the strings or keys. This image resembles Nietzsche's picture of our desires and needs groping around inside us and reaching out, as though they formed a kind of polyp. This means that any declaration of self at a given instant can only be a declaration of self at that instant.

It may well be a sincere declaration. But some things that can be declared, in particular beliefs, are such that a person will seem inconsistent, contradictory, or hopeless if they change too often. Indeed, if they change too often for purely psychological reasons, they will not be beliefs but something like moods. With some states that count as beliefs, such as memories of particular experiences or the retention of pieces of information, their relation to their subject matter, their mere semantics and epistemology, requires them to be steady if they are to count as such states at all. With other states that may be counted as beliefs or opinions—narrative understandings of the past, for instance, or estimates of people, or evaluative outlooks—we do not always find what philosophers often seem to demand, an unchanging dispositional state, steadily prepared to be activated in declaration or action. As Diderot says elsewhere, in *La Rêve de d'Alembert*, "our real opinion is not the one from which we have never wavered, but the one to which we have most regularly returned" (164).

Yet our declarations certainly need to be patterned in some ways and not others if they are to count as declarations of any sort of belief or opinion. When we leave those relatively straightforward cases, such as the retention of information, where the identification of belief is strongly controlled by the subject matter, we need some other assurance that sincerity in the form of spontaneous declaration will have some validity over time. For the most part, in characters more usual than Rameau, we have it, but we have it in a social form. The assurance rests in the practice that socializes people into having such beliefs. It is not given to the subject or his hearers in the instant of the declaration but is, rather, presupposed in the practice that enables us, most of the time, to read such declarations as coherent declarations of belief.

Sometimes, of course, we are unclear about what we think we believe or intend or want or need. Then we have to interpret ourselves much as we interpret others or others interpret us, using the small but real advantage (one of the many denied to us by behaviorism) of having a sense of what at that instant we may be disposed to express and what expressions at that instant we may be disposed to inhibit. So we must leave behind the assumption, common to Rousseau's model and to the neo-Hobbesian, that the move must be from a transparent self-understanding to giving other people either a sincere revelation of our beliefs from which they understand us (or, as Rousseau bitterly found, misunderstand us) or else a dissimulation that will mislead them. At a more basic level, we all contribute to the social activity of mutually stabilizing our declarations, moods, and impulses, thereby creating such things as beliefs and attitudes. Moreover, it may be the case, to degrees we have barely begun to think about, that we carry out this process very badly.

As Rameau, Lui, reminds us, feelings, needs, passions, identifications actually come and go: in some people less than in others and in most people less than in him. Those people are, as one might say, steadier. But what is it to be steadier? How is it done, for one thing, and what are its workings? Here we should consider the following thought. Sincerity as uninhibited self-expression, as opposed to a model of sincerity as self-directed accuracy, does not involve monitoring the truth about oneself, but it does involve truth: not as what is discovered but as what is expressed. Perhaps, in certain cases sincerity serves to create truth. I am bound to others in various ways, sharing life and affections with them and having need of them. Consequently, I can have reason to become, for a while at least, what I have sincerely declared to them; or perhaps I become my interpretation of their interpretation of what I have sincerely declared to them.

Authenticity and Social Identity

Steadiness, as *Rameau's Nephew* reminds us, has its costs, sometimes in hypocrisy, frustration, and bitterness. Yet some degree of steadiness is so important to human interaction and a manageable life that much effort is devoted to constructing relatively steady beliefs and outlooks out of the shifting sounds of Diderot's psychic musical instruments. In various historical and social circumstances, different structures may serve to build a self that will at once make sense of episodic feelings and beliefs—render the subject, as we have put it, steadier—and relate the person to others in a way that will serve the politics of trust. These structures may of course be intimately related to the workings of those values that, as I mentioned earlier in discussing the neo-Hobbesian account, help to make the shared conception of sincerity into something that is valued intrinsically, as more than a mere instrumental device.

Such a structure is related to two problems, which have taken a particularly acute and familiar form since the eighteenth century. One is the political problem of finding a basis for a shared life that will be neither too oppressively coercive (the requirement of freedom) nor too dependent on mythical legitimations (the requirement of enlightenment). The other problem is the personal problem of shaping the self into a form that will fit with these political and social ideas but will at the same time represent a life that is worth living. A typically modern invention, the politics of identity, tries to provide a structure that will solve both these problems at once. Rousseau foresaw the need but provided only a mere assertion to meet it, linking in one gesture sincere self-declaration, morality, and the politics of the general will. Both the political and the personal terms in the equation have come to require something richer than this, something more distinctive for each of us, and all of us, to be.

According to the politics of identity, an identity is something that each of us individually has, but it is also something that is essentially shared: it is a group identity, such as an ethnic, religious, or (in certain cultural surroundings) sexual identity. A man, for example, who thinks of himself in such terms thinks of his relations to the group as representing in some sense what he really is; indeed, he might say this affiliation is what he is in essence. Yet it is important to these thoughts that this idea of one's essence is not related in any very simple way to one's diachronic personal identity. An essential property in the standard metaphysical sense—the property of being a human being, for instance—is something that one cannot possibly lack and still exist. If I am around in the world at all, then I am in it as a human being. If an ethnic culture or way of life is destroyed, it is sometimes said the people who earlier lived under it will have lost their identity; as a people, they have ceased to exist. But this cannot mean that each of them has ceased to exist, and this is not a mere philosophical quibble, for an important part of the objection to the destruction of such a way of life implies that the individual people will exist. It concerns precisely the way in which those very people will then exist—culturally impoverished and robbed of the expression of their identity.

Social psychology understands an identity in this sense as a social category to which value is attached, but this is something of an understatement. Someone may set great store by his membership in a college or learned society, but he would be in a bad way if such a membership came to constitute his identity. To form an identity, the social category has to be rich enough to permeate many of the most important aspects of life, at the limit, to form the structure of a whole way of life. Just as "natural kind" is not an arbitrary classification but represents a significant and explanatory grouping of properties, so an identity can be seen as a social or cultural kind.

Thus an identity cannot be simply a matter of decision. If I could join a group merely at will, that in itself would not constitute an identity. As befits something that comes close to being my essence, it must be something that I can discover. Yet mere factual discovery will not be enough either. I might find out as a matter of fact that I do belong to an ethnic group but be quite indifferent to the idea that it contributes to my identity, and if in good faith and without evasion I can live with that idea, then this is indeed not my identity. The relevant notion here is acknowledgment. Someone may come to acknowledge a certain affiliation as an identity, this being neither a mere discovery nor a mere decision. It is as though the identification were forced upon the person in a way that recognizes

its authority to structure and focus that person's life and outlook. There are circumstances in which what was a mere recognition of fact may come to compel acknowledgment, as when
many assimilationist Jews in the 1930s came to acknowledge a
Jewish and perhaps a Zionist identity after realizing that there
was no way in which without evasion they could go on as
though it made no difference that they were Jewish people.

How are these recognitions or acknowledgments possible?
What truths am I discovering about myself? Must it not be a
myth to think that one might find a shared social essence that
is in some way inescapably one's own? The model of sincerity
as self-expression rather than as accurate self-discovery will
help answer these questions. The presence of the others who
share this identity is vital. Sincerity helps to construct or create truth: drawn to bind myself to the shared values of other
people, to make my own beliefs and feelings steadier (to make
them, at the limit, for the first time into beliefs), I become what
with increasing steadiness I can sincerely profess. The sense
that I am contributing to this project—that it is a project—fills
out the idea that acknowledgment is more than mere factual
discovery, while at the same time my sense that there is discovery involved is related to the need to resist fantasy in making sense of my beliefs and allegiances in this way. The resistance to fantasy, the consciousness that I cannot merely make
things as I would wish them to be, is a feature of all genuine
inquiry, and it lends a sense of objectivity to these acknowledgments. All the more so because there is an element of hope
or prediction involved; I should be able in fact to steady my
beliefs in this way and live under the social requirements of
this shared identity. What I have to ask myself, and resist
fantasy in doing so, is precisely whether I can live without
fantasy while accepting these understandings. How heavy this
commitment may be turns on several questions: How widely
and deeply do these understandings reach into one's life? How
long, even when they are acknowledged, are they expected to
last? Presumably, the original idea of such an identity was that
it lasted a lifetime, but in some places now, certainly, an
identity may itself represent only the shorter-term project of
stabilizing the self, and it may be possible to adopt a Rameau-
like attitude toward it.

If the politics and psychology of authenticity do turn toward identity politics, there will always be further questions at

hand: whether any social identity stands in an intelligible relation to my needs and self-understanding as they already are; whether the political, social, and institutional expressions of that identity operate in good faith, and so forth. The politics of identity is always questionable, and it is not a mystery that it can readily lead to ethical and social disaster.

Even when the climate is favorable for the politics of trust to take this particular form, there are warnings to be borne in mind from both Diderot and Hobbes. Diderot reminds us that it will be exceptional if the politics of identity can be lived wholeheartedly, without self-deception and without strain. The so-called essence of the self, particularly a virtuous essence, can usually, and often creatively, be subverted by spontaneity. The neo-Hobbesian reminds us that even when the politics of identity is functioning, it by no means solves all the problems of the politics of trust. For one thing, the problems of trust still need to be negotiated within the politics of identity. The sense of a shared social identity by no means guarantees openness between people, even if it creates channels for it.

A last reminder—and this is one in which Diderot and the Hobbesian can join—is simply that the politics of identity is not necessarily a friend of plain truthfulness. It breeds, almost inevitably, its own myths or, not to put too fine a point on it, lies. It may be very important to rescue from the authenticity of communal attachment the more elementary virtue of simply possessing and recognizing, as Rameau's nephew did, a lot of truths.

FRONTIERS, ISLANDS, FORESTS, STONES:
Mapping the Geography of a German Identity in the Habsburg Monarchy, 1848–1900

Pieter M. Judson

In July of 1885, the newly founded League for the Bohemian Woods (*Böhmerwaldbund*) advertised a special sale in its quarterly newsletter under the headline "Relief Maps of Southern Bohemia." Using the maps of the Imperial and Royal Military-Geographic Institute in Vienna, a retired infantry lieutenant had developed a technology for producing finely detailed three-dimensional reliefs, which the journal praised enthusiastically. The league had negotiated an agreement with the inventor to produce relief maps of the Bohemian Woods at a reduced price, depending on how many orders he received. "We therefore urge all municipal and county governments, school administrators, financial institutions, and associations of every kind," wrote the editors, "to consider ... whether they wish to order this extremely important product, which will contribute considerably to [the growth of] exact knowledge about our land."[1]

In the 1880s, "exact knowledge about our land" became a new and vital concern for German nationalist organizations like the League for the Bohemian Woods. As voluntary associations like this one labored to create a sense of national identity among German speakers in the multiethnic Habsburg Monarchy, they situated that identity in local geography and history rather than, as tradition dictated, in allegiance to certain abstract cultural ideals. Familiar local relationships were to be redefined in terms of nationalist struggle as a way of making German identity a more compelling part of local village

This paper is dedicated to Milan Hornak and Lars Larson, with whom I witnessed the return of several Sudeten Germans to southern Bohemia and Moravia and some of its rhetorical consequences. I would like to thank Laura L. Downs, Daniel A. Segal, and Douglas McKeown for their insightful comments on earlier drafts of this paper.

[1] *Mittheilungen des deutschen Böhmerwaldbundes* [*MDB*], no. 2 (1885): 35. The journal cited the expert opinion of the foremost geographic journal of Germany, that this new type of relief map constituted a potentially rich font of knowledge for schoolchildren and amateur geographers.

life. German speakers in the ethnically mixed Moravian town of Iglau (Jihlava),[2] for example, should no longer think of themselves as Iglauers or even as Moravians but above all as Germans. Their ties to other Germans in Central Europe must now outweigh the familiar social and commercial relationships they enjoyed with neighbors who spoke Czech.

This transformation of identity would be accomplished by locating national identity in the geographic spaces people occupied, by redefining those spaces according to their particular nationalist significance. To continue with the example of Iglau, the town became known in the 1880s primarily as an *island* of Germans surrounded by a sea of hostile Czechs. Provinces like Moravia, where many such islands were to be found, became known as *frontiers*, where Germans and Slavs met on imagined borders. New historical traditions were gradually developed to justify this reconceptualization of local identity in national terms. Activists claimed the *forests* of Southern Bohemia (the Bohemian Wood), for example, as the ancestral home of ancient Teutons, and they pointed out the ways in which architectural styles and town planning, the very *stones* themselves, confirmed the uniquely German character of the landscape. Using several of these related strategies, German nationalists hoped one day to supplant parochial village identities with more self-consciously nationalist ones.

In this paper I examine the way nationalist activists in the Austrian half of the Habsburg Monarchy transformed their rhetoric about the German nation, using spatial metaphors that attributed a national identity to the very landscape itself. In doing so these activists sought to establish a common and politically useful national identity for all German-speaking inhabitants of Austria's socially and geographically diverse regions.[3] German identity, formerly a desirable elite cultural

---

[2] Wherever possible I have tried to use English terms for place names in the ethnically mixed regions of the monarchy. Where such terms do not exist, I have relied on nineteenth-century German place names as they appeared in the newspapers, almanacs, and records of voluntary associations that I examined for this paper, and I have added the common Czech, Slovene, Polish, or Romanian name in parentheses. The choice should in no way imply a preference for the German names on my part.

[3] In 1867 the unitary Habsburg Empire had been divided into an Austrian and an Hungarian state, each with its own domestic government but

commodity, became more of a popular local identity in the
1880s, defined empirically according to language use and
rooted in physical landscapes. If earlier definitions of Germanness stressing culture and humanist conviction never died out
completely, the radically changing political and social conditions in the empire helped foster newer, more empirically
based forms of self-identification. These later nationalisms presumed a transhistorical concept of identity, a concept that required the maintenance of cultural purity. Activists anchored
the new German identity in identifiable spaces, conferring a
specifically German identity on the land itself and staking a
claim to any territory that was either currently or had been
historically occupied by German speakers.

All too often, historians analyze the emergence of nationalist differences in any society by assuming that people necessarily privilege one set of attributes (such as language use) over
others (such as common regional culture). Yet, contrary to
popular myths about the nature of politics in the multicultural
Habsburg Monarchy, differences in language use alone did not
magically produce nationalist politics. Those who believe that
class or regional politics inevitably crystallized around existing
and historic differences of language ignore at their peril the
situational specificity of national identities. Differences in language use may have been decisive for identity formation in
some, but certainly not all, cases, as Gary Cohen, Istvan Deak,
and Katherine Verdery have demonstrated in works on differ-

---

both sharing a common foreign and commercial policy. The Habsburg mon-
arch was both emperor of Austria and king of Hungary. This paper deals with
the Austrian half of the dual monarchy, a state whose territory included the
present-day states of Austria, the Czech Republic (Bohemia and Moravia), and
Slovenia as well as substantial pieces of Italy, Poland, and the Ukraine. For
convenience I refer to this state as "Austria" or simply as the "monarchy." The
following is a breakdown of how people identified their "language of daily use"
(*Umgangssprache*) according to the census of 1880, the first to record this
information: German: 36.75 percent; Czech: 23.77 percent; Polish: 14.86 percent; Ukrainian: 12.81 percent; Slovene: 5.23 percent; Serbo-Croatian: 2.6
percent; Italian: 3.07 percent; Romanian: 0.87 percent. See Adam Wan-
druszka and Peter Urbanitsch, eds., *Die Habsburgermonarchie 1848–1918*,
vol. 3/1 (Vienna: Verlag der Osterr, 1980) table 1.

ent regions and institutions of the monarchy.[4] Cohen's masterful work on Prague's German-speaking minority clearly shows that, over time, people of the urban lower classes often changed nationalities if no German nationalist community infrastructure (clubs, schools, theaters, etc.) adequately addressed their social needs in specifically German nationalist terms.

Furthermore, if we examine early forms of German nationalist rhetoric, we find that they were not even necessarily founded on language use. To mid-nineteenth-century Austrians who thought about it, German identity corresponded far more to the cultivation of middle-class, liberal cultural values like education, enlightenment, individual self-control, and economic independence. The very first German nationalist association founded during the Revolution of 1848 proclaimed a belief that Germanness was based "not simply on the soil of birth or language of culture but rather on ... nobility of action and the worthiness of conviction."[5] In theory at least, individuals from any background—Jews, Slavs, peasants, and workers—could eventually attain a German identity through education and acculturation. German nationalists in the Habsburg Monarchy viewed Germanness as a relatively open identity, one available to anyone who adopted its principles and lived according to its norms, even though few individuals outside the middle class might actually obtain the requisite income or education. For these German speakers, nationalism served as an ideology of public integration in Central and Eastern Europe, one that would eventually wipe away the backward and particularist attitudes held by uneducated peasants and Slavs, joining them all in a great German liberal nation.

These early German nationalists rarely justified their preeminent social position in terms of their numbers, even though

---

[4] See Gary B. Cohen, *The Politics of Ethnic Survival: Germans in Prague, 1861–1914* (Princeton: Princeton University Press, 1981); Istvan Deak, *Beyond Nationalism: A Political and Social History of the Habsburg Officer Corps 1848– 1918* (New York: Oxford University Press, 1990); Deak, "Comments," *Austrian History Yearbook*, no. 3 (1967); and Katherine Verdery, *Transylvanian Villagers: Three Centuries of Political, Economic and Ethnic Change* (Berkeley: University of California Press, 1983).

[5] *Schwarz-Roth-Gold*, a newspaper published by the Association of Germans in Austria, no. 1 (11 July 1848).

theirs was the language spoken by the largest number of people (ca. 36 percent) in the monarchy. Rather, they constantly
referred to their culture's historic mission as creator of a civilized public sphere in Central Europe. According to these liberal nationalists, neither geographic location nor the sheer
number of people who spoke a given language was as decisive
in determining a group's relative status or power in the monarchy as was quality, defined by the group's cultural and financial achievement. As one nationalist author pointed out, "With
the exception of Italian, German is the only one of all the languages spoken in the Austrian Monarchy that has an absolute
value; the others have only a relative, local value."[6]

The internal structure of the empire encouraged this kind
of cultural definition of German nationality. Proficiency in
German was a crucial prerequisite for any upwardly mobile
bourgeois seeking higher social status by entering government
or military service. In reply to Czech nationalist accusations of
government favoritism toward German candidates for the civil
service, for example, the Liberal minister of the interior could
state, "the primary consideration in bureaucratic appointments
is an official's ability to do his job. If a candidate is fluent in
German, then no matter what his ethnic background, he would
be considered qualified in this respect."[7] As the language of
much interregional commerce, German was also closely associated with financial and social achievement. Many German
liberals presumed that as upwardly mobile Czech or Slovene
Bürger became financially successful and better educated, they
would naturally identify themselves as Germans, as indeed
many did in the 1850s and 1860s.[8] Nor did early Austro-
German nationalists demand what we would call complete
ethnic assimilation from those who aspired to a German iden-

---

[6] Anonymous pamphlet, *Die Deutschen im Nationalitätenstaat Österreich*
(Meran, 1887) 21.

[7] Gustav Kolmer, *Parlament und Verfassung in Osterreich*, 8 vols.
(Vienna & Leipzig: C. Fromme, 1902–14) 1:89.

[8] See, for example, Peter Vodopivec' discussion of Slovene academic and
writer Dragotin Dezman in "Die sozialen und wirtschaftlichen Ansichten des
deutschen Bürgertums in Krain vom Ende der sechziger bis zum Beginn der
achtziger Jahre des 19. Jahrhunderts" in *Geschichte der Deutschen im Bereich
des heutigen Slowenien, 1848-1941*, ed. H. Rumpler and A. Suppan (Vienna:
Verlag für Geschichte und Politik, 1988) particularly 87–93.

tity. In theory, at least, German nationalists encouraged the local preservation of non-German languages and cultural traditions. After all, what language one spoke in the private sphere of the home or even at the local community level was hardly a matter of political concern. Nationalists did, however, expect strict assimilation to cosmopolitan German values in the context of one's public or institutional life.[9]

Since the very existence of the central state guaranteed the German language a functionally privileged status, German liberals thought of themselves proudly as the monarchy's *Staatsvolk*, or "state people," and not at all equivalent to the other competing ethnic groups. They connected their own special status to the very survival of the state. Not surprisingly, the sporadic attempts by a handful of German activists to develop a politics organized specifically around German nationalism before 1880 typically met with embarrassed silence or outright opposition from liberal leaders. German speakers needed no special nationalist movement; theirs was after all the language and culture of civilization. For the same reason German liberals interpreted early Slav nationalist demands for linguistic parity in the 1860s and 1870s more as a threat to the very state itself, and to the liberal ideas of civilization it embodied, than as a national threat to the Germans.

Neither this liberal vision of German identity nor the liberal understanding of community was completely transparent in its enthusiasm for the eventual inclusion of ethnic others in the nation. Most liberals believed that full membership in the civic community had to be earned. They considered the vote, that ultimate token of inclusion, to be a political function assigned to people who had reached a certain level of economic independence and educational achievement. In the 1870s, for example, German Liberal party leader Ernst von Plener challenged the Socialists' characterization of the vote as a natural or civic right, calling it instead a function "that the state can

---

[9] German Liberal party discussions of the proposed texts of a nationality clause for the 1867 constitution stressed the local rights of individual ethnic groups while retaining a privileged position for German in the administration. See especially Gerald Stourzh, "Die Gleichberechtigung der Nationalitäten und die österreichische Dezemberverfassung von 1867" in *Der österreichisch-ungarische Ausgleich von 1867. Vorgeschichte und Wirkungen*, ed. P. Berger (Vienna: Herold, 1967) 186–218.

confer on those who offer a guarantee that they will exercise it properly."[10] Laboring and petty-bourgeois males might gain the vote as they became more like the liberals themselves, that is, as they achieved sufficient property and education.

The same could be said of liberal ideas about the monarchy's various ethnic and religious groups. Neither geographic location nor sheer quantity (the number of people who spoke a given language) was as decisive in determining a group's relative status or power as was quality, defined by cultural and financial achievement. Liberals based this understanding of the world on a set of crucial (if unacknowledged) epistemological dualities that underlay their visions. They divided the universe into two theoretically separate and implicitly hierarchically arranged spheres, the worlds of active and passive citizenship. The boundaries separating these two worlds were often masked by a universalist rhetoric that stressed active participation and civic inclusion. Liberals insisted on political equality for the inhabitants of the public sphere. Nevertheless, the importance they assigned to financial independence and education enabled them to maintain hierarchically arranged relationships with the women and children, as well as racial and class inferiors, whose immaturity and dependent status kept them in the private sphere. One of liberalism's most powerful legacies to the new nationalism in Austria was to be the translation of this fundamental relationship between the public and private spheres into a new set of public hierarchies organized around national identities.

An 1861 pamphlet entitled "The Germans in Krain" illustrates the startling ways in which ideas about national identity were still developing along the lines of liberal hierarchic conceptions of active and passive citizenship rather than according to purely linguistic or ethnic concepts of identity.[11] The pamphlet replied to Slovene nationalist arguments that the identity of the province Krain (roughly comparable to present-day Slovenia) was primarily Slavic, a claim based purely on the

---

[10] See *Stenographische Protokolle des Hauses der Abgeordneten* (Vienna, 1867–1911) session of 17 December 1874; also quoted in Wilhelm Wadl, *Liberalismus und soziale Frage* (Vienna: Verlag der Österreichischen Akademie der Wissenschaften, 1987) 233.

[11] Anonymous, *Das Deutschtum in Krain. Ein Wort zur Aufklärung* (Graz, 1862).

evidence of how few people spoke German as opposed to Slovene. The German-speaking author attributed the misguided belief that linguistic use alone determined national identity to the bad influence of Napoleonic ideas about universal suffrage. ("Popular rule established by a revolution is always inimical to culture.") The author then proceeded to explain why the national identity of Krain should be considered German. To begin with, "the history of the region suffices to prove that Krain was always a part of the German Confederation." Thus political tradition (which also placed Bohemia and Moravia in the German confederation) pointed to a common identity with the rest of the German lands. But what political history tells us is of minor importance compared to what cultural history can reveal about national identity. "Whoever ... wanted to make any kind of career for himself, or to educate himself in any way, spoke and read German.... Over time," continued the writer, "things developed so that on one side stood a raw, ignorant mass opposed to a small number of Germans on the other side who enjoyed the civilized pleasures of life." Here the author admitted that German speakers constituted a minority of the population. Nevertheless, their mere presence gave the province a German national identity.

The author then reminded the reader that a German cultural identity is certainly available to other peoples. After all, the Slav "who strove for education and who sought out Germans in order to gain culture from them was only following a natural urge; he sought his advantage.... Humanity strives for knowledge and culture, which the Slavs can only seek from the Germans, not the other way around."[12] History was working inexorably, it seems, to create Germans of Slavs, once the latter had committed themselves to the general project of gaining enlightenment. In conclusion, this same author claimed that since "in every state intelligence, not numbers, has ruled," the "Germans in Krain have the mission, as history demonstrates, to raise the Slovene people to a higher level of education, and it must fulfill this mission, *without wanting simply to Germanize the people*." [emphasis added][13] The writer made clear that his intention was not "simply to germanize" the populace, for that would involve forcing an emancipation that only education and

---

[12] *Deutschtum in Krain* 9–11.

[13] *Deutschtum in Krain* 15.

self-knowledge could bring about. And yet a chasm separated those who achieved culture and education from the "raw ignorant mass." The occasional Slovene who wished "to make something of himself" could only do so if he bridged the gap and joined the Germans. The differences in levels of civilization between German and Slovene cultures would always remain so large that Slovenes could obtain enlightenment only by becoming Germans; there was no other possible alternate route to independence and active citizenship.

This pamphlet typified the views of German-speaking liberals on matters of citizenship in the 1860s and 1870s. It suggested both the idea of universal inclusion (anyone can become German and an active citizen) as well as the implicit notion of superiority and hierarchy (only Germans have a valid national identity). Given this set of beliefs, German liberals saw little need to respond to the nationalist challenges posed by Czechs and Slovenes using arguments involving numbers. They militated against any attempt to pin down Germanness and the German community by specific location or population statistics. Relief maps marking German territories were the furthest thing from their minds; after all, their understanding of national identity implied that any territory in Central Europe could become German and that Germanness could not be limited simply to places where German speakers constituted a numerical majority. German power in the monarchy, they believed, derived not from numbers but from an advanced civilization that guaranteed German its privileged position as the language of the bureaucracy and the language of instruction at all Austrian universities, from Graz to Prague, from Lemberg (Lvov) to Czernowitz (Cernauti).

Historians traditionally believed that this attitude changed abruptly in 1866 when Prussia defeated Austria militarily and ejected it from the German Confederation. In particular they claimed that this event launched a significant German nationalist movement that sought to join the primarily German-speaking regions of Austria to the new German Empire. Yet with the exception of a politically insignificant minority, most German-speaking Austrians did not adopt this view.[14] Modern

---

[14] In 1865 the emperor had suspended the constitution of 1861, and most Austrian German politicians interpreted the defeat of 1866 in moral terms as a result of this egregious form of government misrule. They used the

nationalist movements do not grow out of simple facts such as language use or objective appraisals of census results. And in Austria in the 1860s, the political power and cultural hegemony of the German middle classes was still very much on the rise. Only a year later in 1867 the German liberals in Austria celebrated their greatest political triumph as the emperor reluctantly conceded to their demands for a real constitution. The simultaneous division of the empire into self-administering Austrian and Hungarian halves in 1867 only reinforced the notion of a predominantly German cultural identity for the western half.

These political circumstances changed only in the 1880s when the German liberals unexpectedly lost their majority in the Austrian Parliament. Still, it was not the fall of the German Liberal cabinet that changed people's views on national identity so much as the aggressively anti-Liberal and explicitly anti-German tone adopted by the new government. This coalition of conservative, clerical, and Slavic nationalist parties under Count Eduard Taaffe, known as the Iron Ring, created an Austrian state that no longer explicitly endorsed the privileges of German culture and language.[15] The new government moved quickly to pass a series of laws designed to equalize Czech and German language use in provincial courts in Bohemia and Moravia, and it divided the Charles University in Prague into German and Czech-language sections. By themselves these measures did not necessarily constitute an attack on the interests of German nationalists. The second measure had in fact attracted some German liberal support in the 1870s when it was first debated. The new government, however, framed this legislation explicitly as a well-deserved concession to the Czech nationalist parties and thereby caused panic among German liberals in Bohemia and Moravia. The same thing occurred when the government decided to reduce suffrage requirements from ten to five gulden in annual taxes. Although some German liberals had proposed similar measures in the 1870s, they now saw the measure as a blatant at-

---

defeat as an opportunity to argue for a restoration of the constitution and an expansion of the civic rights that it had guaranteed.

[15] On the advent of the Iron Ring and its policies see W. Jenks, *Austria under the Iron Ring 1879–1893* (Charlottesville, VA: University of Virginia Press, 1965).

tempt to alter the balance of power in favor of the Slavic parties in Parliament. In ethnically mixed provinces, German speakers tended to belong to the wealthier urban commercial and industrial classes, while Czechs and Slovenes were primarily peasants or involved in rural industries. The government's lowering of the franchise tax requirements tended to increase the proportion of Slavic to German voters.

It was only at this point that German national identity became detached from its traditional association with the central state. With this detachment came a politicization of German nationality as a means of combating the hostile new order that had taken over the reins of government. Self-identified German liberal nationalists developed defensive strategies against the new government's policies, strategies modeled on successful Czech nationalist politics as well as on liberal organizational traditions. A network of regional and interregional voluntary associations based on the example of liberal political clubs, and organized around nationalist issues, spearheaded the new movement.

These associations published universalist appeals, inviting all Germans to join in a common venture that outweighed any possible social or political distinctions.[16] In doing so, they began subtly to transform the earlier liberal appeal to a culture of elite humanism into an ethnically limited vision of nation based on linguistic and cultural ties. Within that nation, relations would be egalitarian, since members of any class or degree of education would share a common right to Germanness. "The German national movement," wrote one activist in 1881,

---

[16] These organizations, like their liberal predecessors, tended to reward their wealthier or better educated members with higher status positions of leadership. In this sense they inherited the liberal principles that combined a rhetoric of universal participation with an implicit system of social deference that privileged the wealthier or better educated members of a community. Lower middle-class German nationalists, frustrated by their inability to gain much influence in this new nationalist movement, often turned to anti-Semitic German nationalism as a more democratic alternative. See Pieter M. Judson, "'Whether Race or Conviction Should Be the Standard': National Identity and Liberal Politics in 19th-century Austria," *Austrian History Yearbook* 22 (1991): 76–95.

knows no division of the community interest into individual
interests ... the movement detests political organizations that
try to invent and sharpen differences between city and countryside. We Austro-Germans desire the welfare of our united
people; every member of the race, whether in priest's or bureaucrat's dress, whether in *Bürger* or farmer's clothing, is
welcome in our national union.[17]

The appeal not only worked to erase potential class differences
within an imagined German community; it also began, however
subtly, to delineate the spatial dimensions of that national
community, clearly locating it in *both* the city and the countryside. Since, in fact, those in the countryside had expressed
very little interest in nationalist issues up until this moment, it
was important to locate national identity as much in the rural
areas as in urban ones.

The new nationalist associations emerged primarily, but
not exclusively, in ethnically mixed regions, often to combat
incursions by rival Czech nationalist organizations, which had
themselves been busy defining local politics in terms of nationalist identity for over a decade. As language use replaced
humanist ideals or financial accomplishment as the primary
standard for measuring an individual's identity, and as knowledge of German no longer guaranteed local supremacy, activists increasingly worried about numbers. They aimed to regain
political power by mobilizing superior numbers, to mobilize
new social groups into the public political sphere where they
could reinforce German nationalist claims to social privilege.
Still, liberal nationalists faced several dilemmas as they struggled to create a politics organized around national identity.
They sought to recruit new social forces to help strengthen
their movement *without unleashing the violence of a social
revolution.* The task was epic in proportions, for it required coordination among several ambitious projects. If all German
speakers had to be convinced of the primacy of their German
national identity—itself no small task—they also had to be
mobilized in a useful, controlled way, one that did not endan-
ger bourgeois leadership within this expanded German community.

---

[17] Hans Stingl, *Die Nationalvereine der deutschen Bürger und Bauern*
(Krems, 1881) 2–3.

I have dealt elsewhere with the specific ways in which liberals worked to control this mobilization by defining the external marks of Germanness in terms of bourgeois modes of behavior.[18] Here I am more concerned with examining the other half of the equation, namely with the question of national rhetoric: just how did activists generate enthusiasm for national identity at the local level? How did they manage the ideological transformation of the German community from an abstract but exclusive collective hovering over Central Europe to one more tangibly rooted in local situations and landscapes? How did nationalist activists embed new ideas about national identity in a context of local identities? How, for example, did activists create a belief that profound differences separated neighbors who had hitherto shared several elements of local identity in a multilingual society?

The activists who promulgated the new nationalist identities drew from a fairly limited repertoire derived from their political experiences in the old liberal-dominated polity of the 1860s and 1870s. At first, their liberalism shaped the nationalist identities they constructed. Like liberalism, which had theoretically transcended the boundaries of ethnicity, region, or religion, the new nation constituted a community whose members, of whatever class background, shared a fundamental identity, one that far outweighed their real-world social differences. Yet also like liberalism, the new nationalism was organized around a series of essential differences, hierarchically arranged, separating members of the German community from members of other nations. If language use was to serve as the primary measure of this national identity—rather than education or accomplishment—it would still be within a liberal conceptual framework. The strategies for locating this new national identity in local contexts were organized around a reconceptualization of the local landscape according to terms derived from history and geography.

The first and most critical of these strategies involved the idea of the *frontier*, the border, the geographic place where opposing nations met and confronted each other, the setting for

---

[18] See Judson, "'Whether Race or Conviction Should Be the Standard'" and "Inventing Germans: Class, Nationality and Colonial Fantasy at the Margins of the Hapsburg Monarchy," *Social Analysis* 33, special issue *Nations, Colonies and Metropoles*, ed. Daniel Segal and Richard Handler (1993): 47–67.

the colossal and daily struggle between nations.[19] Language use was the critical marker of identity that situated the individual in this newly nationalized geographic setting. Regions in Bohemia, Moravia, or Styria became known as *frontiers*, although not because of their relative geographic or economic marginality to the rest of the monarchy.[20] Rather, the term indicated that German speakers in these territories lived among peoples who spoke other languages.[21]

While people on this *frontier* fought daily battles to maintain their German identity, others in the centers of German culture mobilized to support them, like home-front volunteers during a war. The Vienna-based German School Association (*Deutscher Schulverein*), for example, worked to awaken Germans all over the monarchy to the plight of their brethren on the *frontier*. This organization, founded in 1880, raised money to fund schools in ethnically mixed regions where not enough German-speaking children lived to warrant state support for German-language schools.[22] Using an alarmist rhetoric which

---

[19] This struggle was conceptualized by some in terms borrowed from the colonial experiences of Britain, France, and Germany. Certainly, the reconceptualization of Germans as a people bringing civilization to the rugged, uncivilized East suggests this comparison, as did the Lockean notion that the Slavs, like other colonized peoples, forfeited ownership of the land because they could not cultivate it as productively as the Germans. The comparison, although powerful, is mainly a rhetorical one, since economic relations in the disputed territories do not resemble the colonizing experiences of Europeans in Africa, Asia, or the Americas.

[20] In the 1880s Bohemia and Moravia were in fact the most important centers of industrial production in the monarchy.

[21] The historian must be careful to avoid lending any credence to the notion that inhabitants of ethnically mixed regions somehow had a prior authentic national identity due to their language use, even if they remained technically unwilling to see themselves in such terms. In many regions of the monarchy individuals used several languages depending on the social context, whether domestic, public, or commercial. According to earlier definitions, a good knowledge of German might qualify an individual for a German identity, even though he might use a different language at home. By the 1880s, however, such an assumption no longer held true.

[22] For the state to support a primary school in a given language, there had to be at least forty school-age children in a single locality who spoke that language.

suggested that the German language was dying out "on the frontier" for lack of German-language schools, the association rapidly gained the highest membership—over 100,000—of any bourgeois organization in Central Europe. As they adopted a rhetoric of numbers and national competition, activists also broadened their concerns from schooling to creating economic opportunities for German speakers of the working classes who might otherwise emigrate. By claiming to address a variety of specifically local social problems, albeit in nationalist terms, these organizations quickly gained a significant following for themselves in the ethnically mixed regions.

The Union of the Bohemian Woods, for example, sponsored educational and apprenticeship programs for workers and employment bureaus and craft fairs to improve economic opportunities for artisans. It admonished its female members to hire only German-speaking domestics, and it also worked to lower the rate of illegitimate births and alcoholism among German-speaking working women. In an effort to lure tourists away from nearby Bavaria, the union even published guidebooks that touted the splendors of hiking the hills of southern Bohemia.

The *Südmark*, founded in 1889 to protect German interests from Slovene attack in South Styria, went so far as to promote immigration by poor farming families from South Germany. This organization hoped to buy up land that it could then make available to settlers at reduced rates and "gradually create bridges among the urban islands" of German speakers that dotted an imagined ocean of Slovenes.[23] The organization openly admitted its goal, "not simply to protect existing [German] property" but to "win new land." Another association, the Union of Germans in North Moravia, also promised to "win back ... territory that once belonged to us."[24]

Like the idea of the *frontier*, the new term *Sprachinsel* (literally, "language island") was another strategic innovation, coined to refer to towns inhabited by a majority of German speakers surrounded by a Slavic rural population. The changing self-identification of the German-speaking elite in the small

---

[23] See Friedrich Pock, *Grenzwacht im Südosten: ein halbes Jahrhundert Südmark* (Graz, 1940) 8.

[24] "Der Bund der Deutschen Nordmährens" in *Deutsche Volkskalender für das Jahr 1888* (Olmütz: Alpenland-Buchhandlung Südmark, 1888) 5.

Moravian city of Iglau mentioned at the outset again provides an instructive example. In the 1850s, a travel account written by a prominent Moravian casually mentioned that while "the language of the inhabitants [of Iglau] is predominantly German ... the domestic servants speak mostly Bohemian or Moravian." Like other German-speaking liberals of his time, the author unselfconsciously linked language use to class position and not to membership in separately defined cultural or national communities. He did not even refer to the language spoken by the servants as a single rival language, Czech, which would imply national competition, but simply as local dialects (Bohemian and Moravian). Thirty-five years later, however, when the city's political leaders created the German Association for Iglau, they dramatized their national isolation by invoking the spatial metaphor of the island. Their program vowed "to nurture and protect the Germanic basis of our language island, to keep it undiminished and unbowed."[25] Creating an image of an island under siege, they redefined local identity along national lines. They downplayed the attention to class position that had struck the earlier observer as the more significant form of difference while mapping their linguistic identity using a geographic metaphor.

As part of yet another strategy to make the national status of these *frontiers* and *islands* visible to their inhabitants, German activists pointed to an array of local physical markers as the repositories of German identity. These markers might be cultural repositories of Germanness, as in the case of architectural and farming styles, or what I refer to as *stones*. Yet the very physical landscape itself might also be claimed as a specifically German place, as with *forests* like the Bohemian Woods. In both cases these familiar markers helped to map national differences in the confusing world of cultural mixing. Not only did these signs embody the German spirit of a certain locality; they also served to negotiate between local community identities and the larger, transregional nation. These markers helped to distinguish what was authentically German from what was Slavic at the local level and to connect those local German elements to a larger, Central European German culture.

---

[25] See *Deutscher Volkskalender für die Iglauer Sprachinsel* (1887) 7–8.

Nationalist associations encouraged people to meditate on the specifically German elements in their personal identities by attributing civilized virtues like "rationality," "neatness," or "careful planning" to German farms and towns in ethnically mixed regions. These virtues had the advantage of making Germanness so vague in content that it was easily visible to the casual observer (or as one nationalist noted, "every human activity that raises itself above the lowest levels is German, and only in the lowest categories does German work share its tasks with Slavic work"). That said, "sloppiness" clearly became the most recognizable attribute of the Slavs.[26]

It was not only important to establish the visible superiority of Germanness; the German history of these places also had to be made visible. Activists often referred to a civilizing mission undertaken by German-speaking colonists of the Middle Ages who had established outposts in barbarous Slavic territories. Even the recent Slav migrations back into those territories could not erase signs of German civilization planted centuries before. Discussing urban landscapes on the frontier, the Moravian Armand von Dumreicher guided his readers' attention to the few physical remains of this bygone civilizing influence. "Even older neighborhoods in present-day Slavic municipalities show a German orientation. All of this eastern culture was planted by German burgher colonists."[27] "Today, a bustling Slavic folk life fills the mighty and worthy frames left over from a German past. If the German people have vanished, their creations can still be found. *The stones still speak there ...* they speak of that which was and is no more."[28] The *stones*, through their rational and distinctive placement, offer physical proof of the German identity of the place.

Taking this strategy to a new level, well beyond those who located the German identity of the region in the ostensibly civilizing ventures of medieval German colonizers, another writer claimed the entire Bohemian Woods region as the original (*ur*) home of ancient forest-dwelling Bavarians. He attrib-

---

[26] See discussion of this and further examples cited in Judson, "Inventing Germans" and Maria Lammich, *Das deutsche Osteuropabild in der Zeit der Reichsgründung* (Boppard am Rhein: H. Boltd, 1976) 37–40.

[27] Armand von Dumreicher, *Südostdeutsche Betrachtungen* (Leipzig: Duncker & Humblot, 1893) 33.

[28] Dumreicher 38.

uted the ethnically mixed character of much of the region to recent Czech nationalist attempts to infiltrate the region and discredit its history as a purely German place.[29] Like much of this genre, his argument cites historical example in its attempt to establish an authentic German identity for the natural landscape. Yet by giving the Bohemian Woods a German identity, the writer produced an ahistoric vision of that local landscape. The place is German because it was *originally* German, despite whatever developments the vagaries of history have brought. This epistemological confusion shows how these arguments merged the older concept of German national rights based on cultural achievement with a more essentialist concept of national rights based on timeless truths. Paradoxically, the popular liberal mania for an empiricist, positivist science seems to have worked equally well to support both kinds of arguments.

Creolization of language and particularly of place names in ethnically mixed areas presented scientific-minded nationalists with a fertile field for connecting national identity to physical landscape.[30] In an exhaustive article entitled "Plöckenstein or Blöckenstein—A Chapter from Our Motherlanguage" one activist warned against the various Czechified place names that had come into common usage in Southern Bohemia.[31] "Plöckenstein or Blöckenstein" referred to the local names for a prominent stone peak that dominated the southern region of the Bohemian Woods. One of the two, it turned out, was in fact a creolized version of the original, purely German name. This "speaking *stone*" communicated its own authentic national identity and confirms the national identity of the natural landscape to those whose scientific tools are capable of locating its original name.

The same article cited other examples of creolized place names in the Bohemian Woods region, suggesting that the na-

---

[29] Reiner von Reinöhl, "Der tschechische Schulverein," *Deutsche Worte* (Vienna, 1885).

[30] Here I am not referring to those groups that tried to purify the German language of foreign expressions and constructions (usually French and Latin), found in imperial Germany as well as in Austria, but rather to those groups that sought to replace local place names and usages with the authentic German originals.

[31] See *MDB*, no. 2 (1885): 26–28.

tives had lost touch with their German history and identity. It was bad enough, for example, that the castle town Krummau (from *krumme Au* "twisted Au") was regularly spelled with a single *m* according to the Czech fashion (a flurry of protests and petitions orchestrated by the same author actually restored Krummau's authentic German spelling to some maps of the region); even worse, whole Czech words often blended with German words to create completely new names. According to this author, the town Unter-Wuldau offered a particularly disastrous example of this kind of creolization. Situated on the Moldau River downstream from the town of Ober-Moldau, Unter-Wuldau derived its name from a mixing of the German *Moldau* with the Czech *Vltava*, both names for the same river (*Vltava + Moldau = Wulda*).

Such articles alerted Germans to reflect on the names they gave their local surroundings. Their deeper aim, however, was to redefine the natural landscape itself as national property. Having read such a detailed article on linguistic origins, village inhabitants could never again look upon the landscape, dominated by either the mountain peak or the river, without reflecting on their German identity.

The high point of activity for nationalists on the *frontier* came with the decennial censuses of 1880, 1890, and 1900. The publication of the first of these seemed to justify the new nationalist arguments, which no longer measured a nation's importance by its degree of civilization but by the numbers of people it could muster.[32] German liberals read the 1880 census as a confirmation of their community's decline. This was largely due to recent political events and not to any particular statistical result. Had they retained control of the political system, for example, or successfully blocked some of the Iron Ring's linguistic reforms, German nationalists might well have continued to justify their predominance solely in terms of cul-

---

[32] There are remarkably few good analyses of social and political issues surrounding the decennial censuses in the Habsburg Monarchy. One of these, which relies on examples from Italian- and Slovene-speaking regions, is Emil Brix, "Die Erhebung der Umgangssprache im zisleithanischen Österreich (1880–1910). Nationale und sozio-ökonomischen Ursachen der Sprachenkonflikte," *Mittheilungen des Instituts für österreichische Geschichte*, no. 87 (Vienna, 1979): 363–439. See also Cohen's excellent analysis of the censuses in Prague.

tural achievement. Under the new political circumstances, however, their permanent minority status in provinces like Bohemia and Moravia itself became a cause for concern. The census enabled German nationalists to express their losses through the use of statistics, to map them, to shade their regions, and to locate linguistic boundaries with some accuracy. German nationalists might not accept the results of the 1880 census, might accuse the Czechs of all manner of chicanery, but they nevertheless used the census as a standard against which to measure future gains and losses.

In 1890 the Union of Bohemian Woods provided its members with several detailed strategies for dealing with the next census. The association changed its goal from raising the general proportion of German speakers in Bohemia to establishing that, although a frontier area, the Bohemian Woods was itself purely German. This change followed a general reorientation of German political strategy in the 1880s. Recognizing that the Iron Ring's suffrage reforms had made it impossible ever to regain a political majority in the Bohemia Diet, German nationalists instead demanded that the government enact a complete administrative separation between Czech and German regions of Bohemia. If the census results categorized the Bohemian Woods as a mixed region rather than as a purely German one, administrative separation would be far more difficult to achieve. The Czechs might even gain part of the region, some German speakers might eventually find themselves trapped in a Czech district, or the government would conclude that separation on the basis of language was impossible to achieve. Nationalist activists accused their Czech counterparts of stopping at nothing to achieve the latter result from the census:

> The Czechs will not even concede to us national rights and peace *in our own regions* [emphasis added]; they claim, in fact, that no closed, German-speaking region in Bohemia exists at all. They want to prove that Czechs live in every part of Bohemia, while Germans do not, that there is no place where Czechs do not live alongside Germans.... One of our rival associations makes no secret of its policy to send agents into purely German regions ... in order to create a small Czech enclave there.... If a handful of Czech speakers ... is employed as servants in a German town, then it isn't long before some leading [Czech] personality arrives demanding Czech schools

... which create new burdens for the German municipalities and sow disunity among their inhabitants.[33]

The writer of this article echoed the class-based resentments of an educated German minority, angry that the presence of a handful of uneducated Czech servants might be enough to discredit the authentically German identity of a region. The bitter realization that arriving Czech workers no longer willing to convert to a German identity or to learn the German language might threaten their region's traditional identity also led activists to blame Czech nationalists for "creating" false Czech populations where they would not otherwise have existed. As one writer noted, "Until now numerous Czech immigrants, almost all members of the lowest classes, willingly renounced their nationality and attached themselves to the Germans." The growing presence of Czech voluntary associations in German communities encouraged those workers who might have learned German to adhere instead to a Czech national identity.[34]

So far I have concentrated on tracing the rhetorical strategies employed by German nationalists. But how did these rhetorical transformations shape Austrian political culture? How politically effective was this nationalization of local identities? The old German liberal political culture of the 1860s and 1870s had functioned primarily in parliamentary coalitions created by regional bourgeois elites, all interested in maintaining the power of the central state. By contrast, the new politics rested on its ability to frame popular local identities in universal German terms. These identities in turn demanded unified action from the nation against the anti-German efforts of the central state.

Using aids like the relief map of Southern Bohemia cited at the outset to produce knowledge about local landscapes and peoples across the monarchy created important political consequences. German-speaking people in mixed regions often

---

[33] See the article "Zur Volkszählung" in *MDB*, no. 23 (December 1890): 241–42. The article provided several "horror stories" from the 1880 census involving German speakers who had been mistakenly categorized as Czechs due to the ruthless efforts of pro-Czech bureaucrats.

[34] Michael Hainisch, *Die Zukunft der Deutsch-Österreicher. Eine statistische-volkswirtschaftliche Studie* (Vienna: F. Deuticke, 1892) 9.

came to see themselves primarily in nationalist terms, and German speakers in the "homogenous" regions did come to identify their interests with those of their brethren on the *frontier*. Together, they created a popular, interregional German politics whose success constituted nothing short of a revolution in political behavior. The story of the Cilli (Cilje) crisis of 1894–95 illustrates the ways in which this interregional German nationalist identity exerted political influence. In 1893 the German Liberal party had finally returned to power in coalition with two other parties. One of the legacies of the pro-Slav Iron Ring government (1879–93) had been an agreement to fund a Slovene-language secondary school in the Styrian town of Cilli. The new Liberal government had no say in the matter; it simply had to budget the funds to administer this decision. When the new cabinet took up this minor administrative matter, however, it was shocked by the intensity of public reaction.

As expected, local German nationalists in Styria complained that placing a Slovene school in a *Sprachinsel*, an embattled German town surrounded by a Slovene hinterland, constituted an act of national expropriation. What astonished most politicians, however, was the intensity of the response among German speakers in other parts of the monarchy. For the first time, Bohemian and Moravian public opinion looked beyond its regional political interests to identify with the plight of a German community in far-away southern Styria. Clearly, these German speakers had adopted a transregional and spatially oriented concept of national identity, one that staked a claim to those territories, wherever in the monarchy, that were and must remain German. The extraordinary public outcry convinced the reluctant German Liberal party leaders to withdraw support from their own cabinet or risk losing the next elections to the more radically nationalist anti-Semites.

The relatively mild Cilli crisis was followed by serious outbreaks of public violence at the publication of the Badeni Language Ordinances for Bohemia and Moravia in 1897. The willingness of German speakers of all classes in Reichenberg, Graz, Brünn, or Vienna to take to the streets to fight legislation for Bohemia and Moravia that they all claimed deprived them of their "national property" ended any hopes for resolving nationalist conflict through negotiation. After this incident bureaucratic rule by decree gradually replaced the liberal parliamentary process.

Both these examples point to the power and limits of the
nationalist revolution as well as to the far-reaching consequences of grounding national identity in spatial terms. While
the new nationalist movement effectively coordinated an interregional nationalist system of defense, it was ultimately incapable of fostering a positive and unified national program, one
organized around a single compelling understanding of German identity. If their new nationalist efforts had helped to
bring the Liberals back into power in 1893, it had also caused
their downfall. In 1895 the German liberals found themselves
once more in the ranks of the parliamentary opposition, this
time thanks to the very success of their populist nationalism
rather than because of their lack of committed supporters.
They now experienced with bitterness the fruit of their efforts
to construct a mass politics, victims, in a sense, of their own
success. They had devoted significant resources and plenty of
rhetoric in the 1880s to mobilizing the public around nationalist issues in order to regain control of the state. Yet once they
had accomplished this aim, the nationalist fervor they had
unleashed turned against the state itself.[35] In fact, many activists now regretted the breakdown of public order that accompanied interregional nationalist agitation, and some of them
began to question the more radically essentialist arguments
about national identity that their followers had deployed. In a
revealing article analyzing the results of the 1900 census, the
Union of the Bohemian Woods seems to have repudiated numbers and ethnic purity for an older and recognizably liberal
rhetoric of cultural supremacy, to justify German hegemony in
local relations in that ethnically mixed region:

> The absolute numbers of the census results are not the cor-
> rect standard for measuring the relative significance [status]
> of a national group in a particular district or region. Of far
> greater meaning is the tax contribution, the degree of educa-
> tion, and other cultural markers. In ethnically mixed regions

---

[35] For a general account of the Cilli crisis from the point of view of party
politics, see Lothar Höbelt, *Kornblume und Kaiseradler* (Vienna: Verlag für
Geschichte und Politik, 1993) 106–16.

the political influence of one or another nation cannot simply be measured by the statistical size of each nation.[36]

Here we see a belated attempt to bring order and hierarchy back into the German community from above by returning to the older liberal values of education and property and downplaying the newer nationalist arguments that relied on numbers and territories. If "cultural markers" justified assigning the Germans a greater influence than their numerical minority status would allow, then the same values act as implicit standards to determine hierarchies within the German community itself. At the same time, giving greater weight to those cultural markers diminished the importance of linguistic or ethnic identity.

The creation of a mass politics organized around German identities and rooted in local geography replaced several traditional forms of community hierarchy with one standard of absolute value: Germanness. Much social and political conflict at the turn of the century came to be expressed using the rhetoric of Germanness. If one defined it in terms of civilization, education, or property ownership, then traditional elite groups might use Germanness to maintain their influence within this ever-expanding political community. If, however, one defined Germanness in other ways, as for example in terms of racial authenticity, then Germanness might become a tool for social revolution, for replacing the leadership of traditional bourgeois elites with that of emerging populist activists. In both cases, the location of Germanness in regional geography and identities had replaced the vague abstract culture of values it had encompassed in the liberal era (1848–79). If this culture had formerly hovered tantalizingly over several kinds of geographic and cultural spaces in Central Europe, it was now firmly anchored in specific places identifiable on a map.

Superficially at least, the creation of the Austrian Republic solved the question of ethnically mixed regions for many German speakers after 1918, as did the expulsion of the Sudeten and Moravian Germans from Czechoslovakia after 1945. Austria became an ethnically German state, while Bohemia and Moravia became ethnically Czech. Yet the fact that most Austro-Germans no longer lived in close contact with neighbors

---

[36] *MDB*, no. 44 (1901): 5.

who spoke different languages seems to have made little difference in how they understood their community identities. For
many of them, their national identity continued to be shaped
by the nineteenth-century nationalist rhetoric about society
that had emerged from liberal traditions in the 1880s. This
rhetoric combined public community equality for Germans,
however defined, with veiled concepts of hierarchy meant to
distinguish Germans from those ethnic and racial others who
remained outside the imagined community of German citizens.
But this rhetoric also continued the ideological innovations of
the 1880s, which had located national identity spatially in
particularly *German* spaces. This helps to explain an apparent
paradox that recent travelers in the Czech Republic, including
this writer, have noted: the vociferous descendants of the
Sudeten Germans argue at every opportunity on their visits
there that the Bohemian Woods, although now inhabited only
by Czech speakers, is in fact German.[37]

----

[37] In the summer of 1989 I made the first of several research trips to the
Bohemian Woods. Before crossing into still-Communist Czechoslovakia I
climbed a tower that had been erected in Austria at the top of a hill to afford
tourists a view across the border. The place had been dubbed the *Moldaublick*,
and indeed, each of us binoculared tourists had a splendid view of the southern Bohemian Woods. At the *Moldaublick* I read an informative historical description of the view in a pamphlet printed by the nearby Gemeinde Ul-
richsberg, as well as a poem entitled "Verlorene Heimat" (Lost Homeland),
which was provided free of charge to all visitors. What struck me about this
poem was not so much the expected lament for a lost homeland but rather the
specificity with which the poem located this idealized *Heimat* village of Glöckelberg in the landscape itself. One could stand atop the tower armed only with
the poem and locate Glöckelberg's geographic situation, its placement in a
certain valley, and its relation to other natural and manmade landmarks. Yet
it was not so much the geographic content of the poetry that intrigued me but
rather the confident identification of the natural landscape itself with a German national identity. That former Bohemian Germans and their descendants
might harbor a sense of ownership about lost communities, houses, or views
is hardly remarkable. But what did require some explanation was the confident endowment of the very physical landscape itself with a transhistorical
German identity.

PART FIVE: PHANTASMATIC HOMELANDS

DINNSHEANCHAS:
The Naming of High or Holy Places

Nuala Ní Dhomhnaill

In what can only be described as paroxysms of frustration and self-vexation that must ultimately be pathological, I have changed the text of this paper more times than I care to remember since I originally agreed to write it, way back last summer, and faxed over the title. In retrospect, it seems very much the case of "fools rush in" that I said I would be speaking of *dinnsheanchas*, which I translated as "the naming of high or holy places." My subsequent problems with this have been threefold and may be symptomatic in themselves.

The first one arises out of a sense of personal inadequacy. I have very much the sense of being included here due to some fundamental misapprehension on somebody's part. A classic case of false pretenses. I am a poet, not a scholar, and feel very out of place masquerading as such. At first I tried to handle my basic unease by producing a quasi-scholarly text, listing lots of my contemporary poets in both Irish and English and quoting extensively from them, but increasingly the piece began to resemble a busy modern train station, with names and quotations shunting in and out of it like so many commuter trains. It seemed lacking in some fundamental critical perspective, some necessary inner laser that would open up the subject, as a book falls open round the spine of an often-used page. So I finally bunged it out.

My second problem arises from the word *dinnsheanchas* itself. *Dinnsheanchas* is a compound word, from the two elements *Dinn* and *seanchas*. *Dinn*, cognate with Old Norse *tindr*, may originally have meant "a spike or a point" but by the period of Old Irish had already acquired the meaning of "a mountain, hill, or hillock" and the extended meaning of a "landmark, eminent or notable place." It is very much involved with the numinosity of place, the values of blood and soil, which is one of the fundamental tenets of cultural nationalism. The second element of the word, *seanchas*, is usually translated as "lore," though that is really an inadequate translation. The real meaning of *seanchas* is wide enough to include all the work of the professional learned classes of early Gaelic society, which included the genealogies of the powerful families, the

408

tribal lore, the stories of conquest or migration, the traditional laws and customs of the tribe. This is all very well in itself, but that at the moment for me the whole question of *seanchas* is complicated by the fact that the idealization of the "lore" of the "people" or "folk"—"folklore"—has been another stable and basic tenet in a cultural nationalism, the rampant nature of which, since the break-up of the former Soviet Union, and more especially Yugoslavia, at the very least gives one pause. The bloodcurdling and bloody-handed specter of Greater Croatia, or Greater Serbia, not to mention what we may yet witness in the emergence of a Greater Albania or Greater Macedonia or the last twenty-five years in Northern Ireland, must prove to us that these terms are not to be bandied about lightly. It may be true, what Maurice Goldring says in the last chapter of *Pleasant the Scholar's Life: Irish Intellectuals and the Construction of the Nation State*, that the nation is not an essence but a social and historical construction and that most national history is a fairy tale invented for grown-up children in the nineteenth century. But the fact remains that the violence and bloodthirstiness that all children know to belong to the regions of fantasy in real fairy tales are right now at this moment being acted out in actual terms in a nightmare from which we have yet to awake.

My third problem with this paper is not unconnected with the second. It is that, affected no doubt by the appalling vistas of the now-empty landscapes of Bosnia, I have experienced, you might say, a change of mode. Psychologically, it might be termed depression, but whatever it is is a withdrawal from ordinary extroversion, a going inwards and downwards into a form of introversion that is a necessary prerequisite for the writing of poetry, especially for dealing with new material and inspirations that are as yet nebulous and free-floating. This is coal-face work, which must go on in darkness and silence, way down within the deeply black-veined recesses of the psyche. A part of the job description and a necessary adjunct with the territory, this *abaissement du niveau mentalé* has as a rather unfortunate corollary that it unfits me at the moment for most social transactions and definitely any intellectual one other than the writing of poetry. I cringed recently when I heard myself broadcast on radio a lecture that I had written in the last few weeks. It seemed self-serving, and self-indulgent, and it was obvious to me that I had been unable to haul myself up out of the depths of my own inward involvement to anything that might be termed an objective perspective. So rather than attempt to fight this tendency in this paper, I have decided to go with it and speak from a point of personal witness and as an act of *pietas* rather than attempt an objective analysis, which at the moment I am incapable of.

But first some general information and commentary on the most important word in my paper, which is the word *dinn-sheanchas*. Translated recently quite baldly in O'Dónaill's modern Irish/English dictionary as "topography," actually *dinnsheanchas* is very much more than that. As Charles Bowen has suggested:

> we must try to imagine a science of geography based on "senchas" in which there is no clear distinction between the general principles of topography or direction-finding and the intimate knowledge of particular places.[1]

Dinnsheanchas has been from time immemorial one of the great branches of knowledge of the Gaelic world. For countless millennia in the oral tradition and for the fifteen hundred years of the written Irish-language tradition, it has been central to the culture. Indeed, *dinnsheanchas* is so endemic in early Irish literature as to be quite annoying for the modern reader, as it is often woven into the fabric of the myths and sagas in ways that obscure the primary narrative almost entirely. Thus just when one of the great sagas of the Ruaraíocht, or Red-Branch Knight Cycle, the *Táin Bó Cuailnge*, or Cattle-raid of Cooley, is really about to get into its stride, the story is quite rudely and abruptly interrupted by what can be seen as gratuitous toponomical asides. Even such a late tale as the *Aoidhe Chlainne Lir*, from the Mythological Cycle, which is known to us only in a late redaction, has numerous similar interruptions, which seem to the modern reader quite pointless and serve only to hold up the pace of the story. One of the most famous and very justly loved tales is the twelfth-century "Acallamh na Senórach," or the "Colloquy of the Ancients," a frame tale in the Fenian Cycle, which is held together by the very frame of *dinnsheanchas*. In it two of the last remnants of

---

[1] "The Historical Inventory of the Dindshenchas,". *Studia Celtica* 10/11 (1975–76): 115.

Fionn Mac Cumhail's warrior band, Caoilte mac Rónán, and Fionn's own son, Oisín, tell a series of stories about the landscape of Ireland that they travel through with the newly arrived St. Patrick. While giving him and therefore the reader (or the audience because what the exact relation was between the written text of a medieval tale and the form in which it was transmitted we do not know) a lot of information useful to him in his missionary activity, the text still manages to mount a constant and fairly hefty critique of the religion that he preaches. The placelore within it is almost without fail a praising of the great deeds of the mighty Fianna, now no more, and a funerary ode to their talents, wisdom, and especially their generosity, compared to which the codes of conduct of the new faith and especially its obsession with ascetic practices like fasting and bodily denial are but paltry and niggardly excuses for existence. This is a very beautiful and ecologically informed text and a major exemplar of *dinnsheanchas* in Middle Irish. Its literary qualities are very much based on a certain haphazard charm that follows from an intimate knowledge of the landscape of Ireland. As Charles Bowen says:

> Seen from this point of view, a modern road map transmits knowledge of a kind that primitive Celts would have found inconceivably abstract. Places would have been known to them as people were: by face, name and history. The last two would have been closely linked, for, as the Dindshenchas illustrates again and again, the name of every place was assumed to be an expression of its history.[2]

Though *dinnsheanchas* is rampant though the whole of early Gaelic literature, still we must pay especial attention to a particular corpus of it, written in Middle Irish and called *Dinnsheanchas Érenn*, which comprises one collection of poems and two prose and verse units, about two hundred poems and two hundred prose pieces in all. These pieces are generally funerary and elegiac in tone, and extremely fertile in the field of folk etymology, but do not by any mean exhaust the repertoire of *dinnsheanchas* as such, or tell us much about the form it took in the oral tradition rather than the literary and manuscript activity of the time.

---

[2] "Historical Inventory" 115.

Now I will move on to the subject of *dinnsheanchas* in modern Irish and have chosen, in the interests of brevity, to restrict myself to the oral tradition, and in it to a particular informant, Thomas Murphy, of the townland of Cahiratrant in the parish of Ventry, just west of Dingle, County Kerry. And this is where I must ask you to bear with me for a moment, while I declare my own personal stake in this material. My parents were married in Irish in Lancashire, and a relation of my mother's, Noirín Keevane, lived in with us, for the pure and express purpose of speaking Irish to us children. Nevertheless, my knowledge of the language was only passive, and when a return to Ireland was in the offing, it was the horror of having a child who could not speak Irish that caused my parents to farm me out to my aunt May, my mother's only sister, in the village of Cahiratrant, in the Kerry Gaeltacht, at the tender age of five. In retrospect this does seem a rather drastic step, and I'm sure it musn't have been easy for me, but this particular accident of personal history left me with my deepest allegiance, which is to the Irish language, and also led to that language being fused for me with the landscape of Corcha Dhuibhne, the "Gaeltacht" area of the Dingle Peninsula, and most especially with the parish of Ventry. This is deeply limiting in ways, because it means I cannot make my home anywhere. I am spoiled for everywhere else because of being so deeply bonded with one particular place, so that wherever else I live, I am always hankering after it. What I experienced in Corcha Dhuibhne then can only be described as an atavistic reaction. I felt a great sense of relief, a sense of belonging, of being a link in a long family chain, which had definitely been missing until then in my existence on a Lancashire coal mine. Recently, I have come across a piece of writing in the book *My Golden Trades* by the Czech novelist Ivan Klima, which relates to my sense of a particular *genius loci* without the connotations of blood and bloodlust that I find so terrifying in many formulations of cultural nationalism. Ivan Klima took the to many seemingly mad decision of returning to his country from Ann Arbor, Michigan, less than two years after the Soviet occupation. As he said recently in a paper given at the International Writers Festival in Dublin:

> I returned from a free country to a country in bondage precisely because I did not want to lose my homeland and

something that is of paramount importance for a writer: conceitedness with my native language and contact with people whose mentality and problems were close to me.

My own sentiments exactly.

In *My Golden Trades* in the piece called "The Archeologist's Story" he has this to say:

> The voice through which the spirit of place speaks to those who listen is common to us all: to me and to those people who moved from the backwaters of my homeland more than two millennia ago. By calling it a voice I don't mean anything mystical, a voice of blood and soil. I'm surprised that most people don't hear it, don't feel the natural reasons for affinity with each other. I'm surprised that they invent other reasons, more artificial ones, for sticking together: race, faith or ideas. They are more eager to believe their lives were influenced by the positions of the planets than by the shape of the mountains that surround their birthplace, or the height of the heavens above them, or the direction of the winds that bring the clouds.
>
> Is it possible not to feel some affinity for people who have followed every day the meandering of the same river, climbed the same hills, seen the same flock of birds with each spring, and to whom darkness and light, the cold season and the fruitful season arrived at the same time?[3]

It is something like this that I felt in West Kerry, aged five, and that wedded me to Irish in a way that has proven, if not fatal, then at least decisive. But a further accident that involved me in the whole fascination with placelore was that whereby the household that I was quite literally farmed out to, that of my aunt, was also that of Thomas Murphy, her husband, whom I got to know intimately and at great length during the following thirty-five years until his death two years ago at the age of eighty-four. I will now try to give some information about him and his way of being in the world, which was primarily the "way of *dinnsheanchas.*" In doing so, I do not wish to idealize him in the way done at the turn of the century by the Cultural

---

[3] *My Golden Trades* (London: Penguin, 1993) 94.

Nationalists like Pearse and Hyde, or as George Thomson or Robin Flower did subsequently with the Blasket Islanders. Thomas was no oil painting, and least of all an idealistic Laverty one. He was also most unlike Yeats's vision of the Connemara fisherman, "a wise and simple man." He was in many ways typical of the extremely patriarchal head of household of Arensberg and Kimball's classic story of the Irish smallholding. His still-surviving sisters are scathing in the hair-raising stories of his youthful high-handedness. My aunt did not have an easy life with him and as a woman seventeen years his junior for a long time was at the wrong end of the stick. Nevertheless, a certain power balance was established between them, and the relationship was always one of mutual respect, albeit within the rigid role-differentiated pattern of the rural family model. In his youth quite high-handed, he could often be an irascible and cranky old so-and-so in his old age, especially in the years before his hip-replacement operation, when he was in considerable pain from arthritis. Still and all, we got on very well, on the whole, and I was always sure of a welcome in his house. One of the main things that brought us together was my all-consuming interest in placename lore. A certain level of banter and mutual leg-pulling was also part of our interaction, with him setting me up and mocking my "book-learning" and me playing the dunderhead in order to get him to tell a well-loved story or anecdote again for the umpteenth time. Much of this interaction was informal and like all oral performance characterized by its ephemerality and impermanence. Nevertheless, I do have at hand any amount of entries in the forty-odd folklore and general working notebooks that I possess, and it is on them that I rely to draw this quick sketch of an until recently living exponent of *dinnsheanchas*.

Thomas Murphy was born in Cahiratrant on the 28th of December 1906. There was a fall of snow that night, and hence he was often known as "Thomáisín an Sneachta" "Little Thomas of the Snows." Early next morning his father Peaits took the shortcut up through Mám na Gaoithe and over through the three villages of the Leataithe, over to Cathair Deargan in the parish of Cill Mhaolchéadair, to inform his wife's people of the birth. How we know this story at all is that my grandmother was a young girl of twelve years of age, throwing snowballs from on top of the frozen-over *buaile*, or dung heap, when Peaits went by. Her father hailed him. "Bhuel, a Phaits, an bhfuil aon scéal nua agat?" "Have you any news?" "Tá, arsa Peaits," "mac ó aréir. Abhar fathaigh, cnámha capaill óig faoi is ní bhfaighidh sé aon fhuacht go brách." "Yes," said Peaits, "a son since last night. The makings of a giant, the bones of a young horse under him, and he'll never get a cold." The last part of the prediction proved remarkably true, because Thomas was one of the hardiest men who ever lived; he didn't even catch the great flu of 1918, though the whole village went down with it, including four of his uncles who were still living in the house with them. The rest of the statement unfortunately was not true, and he never grew to a great height, never reaching more than five foot four inches and retaining a great respect for height all his life. "Níl aon teora leis an scrothaíocht," he used to say, "fine physique is a mighty thing."

Little did my grandmother think that the child who was born that snowy night would grow up and that she herself would also grow up and marry and have a daughter who would grow up to marry that child. If she had, she would have been horrified at the thought, and actually she was, and my Aunt May's wedding was, as a result, as subtle a bit of subterfuge as you could get away with in a rural area. She simply got the banns read out in Ventry rather than in Dingle, so her mother had no inkling of the event until it was landed on her the night before as a *fait accompli*. One of the reasons my granny was horrified is that she considered Thomas Murphy to be of her own generation rather than her daughter's. This is not quite true—in mind set he actually belonged to an even older generation than herself. My granny was upwardly mobile and valued education, primarily for its material advantages, to the extent that on her husband's death she mortgaged the farm to give most of her children a university education, something totally unheard of in the area. She herself always regretted bitterly that she had had only one year of formal education. Thomas Murphy also had had no more than one year in national school in all. Though officially enrolled for four years, he was the eldest son, fated to inherit the farm, and was dragged out of school on any old excuse at all, to help with cows calving, to dig potatoes, to bring in the hay, to do the plowing. He once admitted to me that any year that he was officially on the school roll books never meant more than four months schooling in reality. This did not effect his Irish, as only English was taught in the schools in those days anyway, and he could be scathing and disdainful of "Gaeilge na leabhar," or book Irish, as taught in the school system since Independence. Thomas had an enormous encyclopedic knowledge of the local environment, which he first of all continually sought out. His way of being in the world was based on an enormous capacity to learn, because there is no such thing as a totally natural tradition bearer. You only get to know an awful lot of stories, songs, etc., by first of all having an enormous thirst for them, a need to learn them at all cost. Thus the renowned storyteller, Peig Sayers, was reviled in her youth by her sister-in-law, Cáit Ní Bheoláin, as being a big lazy slob; she did nothing around the house all day but sit listening to stories. Thus also did Seán O Griffin of Cathair Boilg walk fourteen miles to Abhann an Scáil and back in one night (twenty-eight miles in all) because he dearly wanted to hear a certain story, and he had heard that a certain tailor was telling it in a house there that night.

Thomas Murphy's interest in placename lore was likewise of an enormous and encyclopedic capacity. Though the son of a renowned Fenian storyteller and notable wit, Peaits O Murchu, he was not a *seanchaí* or storyteller as such, mainly because he had a bad stammer. While there are countless stories from his father collected by Joe Daly in the manuscripts of the Department of Irish Folklore in University College, Dublin, I could actually find only three stories by Thomas himself. In the notes to these stories he is described as a *mac feirmeora*, a farmer's son, which is correct, as he had not yet been given the title to the land. I got photocopies of these stories out once and presented them to him, but he was totally uninterested. I was therefore intrigued to be told later by Joe Daly himself that he had deliberately set out to collect stories from Thomas, and in particular had gone to get from him the beginning of a story about the king of Ireland's son and the eagle, where a battle of the birds and beasts is described that nobody in the whole peninsula remembered correctly except Thomas. (This is a story that had been collected in English in the turn of the century and is actually the basis of the action in Patricia Lynch's wonderful book for children, *The Turfcutter's Donkey*.) Thomas's lack of interest in any of the formal *Fiannaíocht*, or hero stories, probably encouraged his specialization in *sheanchas* and especially in *dinnsheanchas*.

At this point I would like to draw on the methods and categories developed by Séamas O Catháin and Patrick Flanagan in their book *The Living Landscape*, a study of the Irish-speaking townland of Kilgalligan in County Mayo, as most of their methods and material are equally applicable to the world view of Thomas Murphy. O Catháin and Flanagan early in their book seek to differentiate between two categories of lore, namelore and placelore. They say that namelore embraces any explanation or comment on a name or name element, whether factual or fictitious. Thus I could categorize quite a lot of material given to me such as his comments on places like Drom a' chapaill, a narrow ridge of cliff shaped a bit like a horse's back, or names such as Leacacha na bhFaoileán or Ceann an Chloichir.

Placelore, O Catháin and Flanagan tell us,

> includes a broad range of comment ranging from cultural appraisals of land, seashore and sea, to the identification and location of hazards at sea in the form of reefs and hazards on land such as the haunts of otters. In addition, this kind of lore contains reference to events, real or imaginary, which are reputed to have taken place at specific locations. There is also frequent comment on the functional attributes of certain places, many of which still maintain their prominence in the context of life in Kilgalligan today.[4]

This is equally true of the placelore repertoire of Thomas Murphy and its relation to the townland of Cahiratrant. Thus he would rarely mention Lic Caoil, a large rock lying south off his own land, without telling me how it was the petrified body of a giant. He also always connected it with Tráig Chaoil, or Caol's Strand, a short beach about one mile away, saying that this is where Caol's body had first been found when it floated in on the tide after the Battle of Ventry. He seemed totally unfazed at any contradictions between the floating of the body onto the strand and its petrifaction back on the cliffs. These things were not to be scoffed at or questioned. At some very deep level they were gospel.

---

[4] Séamus O Catháin and Patrick Flanagan, *The Living Landscape* (Dublin: Cumann Béaloides Eireann) 28.

One of the main features of his lore was a certain telescoping of time and events. This is equally a characteristic of *dinnsheanchas* in Mayo, as O Catháin and Flanagan tell us:

> Events are often telescoped in a bewildering fashion and it seems almost as if Kilgalligan people, as can be seen from the lore, do not feel the heyday of the Vikings, for example, to extend much further back than the famine itself.[5]

This was brought home to me most strikingly on one particular occasion. I had noticed from the perusal of some map or other that the Townland of Cahiratrant completely surrounded another townland called Na Ráithíneacha, or Rawheens in English. This is something I had never seen before and I questioned Thomas as to its meaning, or did he know how such a thing could come about. In his typical mode of mock exasperation he shot back at me: "Ná fuil a fhios ag an saol go raibh an Treanntach ro-mhaith do Fhionn Mac Cumhail?" "Doesn't the whole world know that de Terraunt was too strong for Fionn Mac Cumhail?" This is the first inkling I had had that the singular of "Raweens" could be construed as "Ráth Fhinn" or "The Rath of Fionn." And so the whole historical drama of the Norman invasion and the erection of a manse by the conquering soldier knight De Terraunt, thereby displacing the former Gaelic order, is summed up in one sentence, "Ná fuil a fhios ag an saol go raibh an Treanntach ro-mhaith d'Fhionn Mac Cumhail!"

For all their attempts at categorization, O Catháin and Flanagan finally succumb to an umbrella title, "placename lore," "which is intended to cover placelore and namelore, both of which are frequently represented in the same item." What they say about it is all equally true of what I learned from Thomas Murphy:

> The placename lore has its own peculiar style and structure, ranging as it does from truism to gossip and from the mundane to the fantastic, each item having its own validity though it is often difficult to differentiate between the real and the unreal. This kind of material has a specific function in Kilgalligan and in Irish-speaking Ireland since it is recog-

---

[5] Catháin and Flanagan, *Living Landscape* 47.

nized and acknowledged as a vehicle for the explanation of the structure of the local world.[6]

For me this wonderful heterogeneity of material is one of its main attractions, speaking of a spontaneous eruption of un- conscious material, with very little input from the organizing, linear left brain. Though annoying from the point of view of having to get to grips with it for a scholarly paper, it is a mode of thought that lends itself very easily to the associative regis- ter of poetry. Thus a poem of mine, "An Bóithrín Caol," grew naturally from the stories that I had heard from Thomas since my childhood.

> An Bóithrín Caol
> (translated as "The Narrow Path" by Michael Coady)
>
> Behind my mother's house
> down Bóithrín Caol,
> over from Bóthar na Carraige,
> through the land of the Kavanaghs
> people of Fán would journey
> three miles to the strand
> with horses bearing panniers
> for sand to dress
>
> their kitchen floors and byres;
> sand trodden into dung
> and then laid out at last
> on thin potato fields
> to feed prodigious Champions
> conjured out of famished land
> too lean to bed such promise.
>
> With creels lashed
> to their backs
> women
> used to clamber
> down these cliffs
> for sustenance of mussels.
> Four young girls were lost

[6] Catháin and Flanagan, *Living Landscape* 74.

at Leacacha an Ré—
Three Marys and fair Margaret
who set my heart astray—
and people saw
a red-capped man
astride the wave
that took them under.

Sometimes from the strand
I seem to glimpse
that red cap
lustrous in the spume
flayed off the waves,
and then,
without a word
a piper from a rock
beneath the cliff
releases drone
and chanter.
When horses
turn at nightfall,
swaying under sand,
the men who lead them home
chatter no longer.

An Boithrin Caol

Laistiar de thigh mo mháthar
anuas an Bóithrín Caol,
i leith ó Bhóthar na Carraige,
trí thalamh chlann Uí Chíobháin,
do thagadh muintir Fhána
le húmacha ar chapaill,
glan trí mhíle ó bhaile
anuas ar an tráigh
ag triall ar ghaineamh.

Gaineamh le leathadh
ar urlár thithe
is i dtithe ba,
chun go meascfaí é

le haoileach
is go gcuirfí ina dhiaidh san
amach ar ghoirt é,
chun go bhfásfadh bleaist seaimpíní
ó thalamh bocht
nach raibh puinn críche air.

Do théadh na mná scafánta
anuas na failltreacha
ag dul ag baint iascán
is cliabh ar a ndroim acu.
Bádh ceathrar cailín óg
ar Leacacha an Ré,
—*triúr Máire agus Máiréad Bán*
a chráigh mo chroí —
is chonaic na daoine
fear an chaipín deirg
ina shuí sa tonn a bháigh iad.

Uaireanta ar an tráigh
chím i mboghaisín
na dtonntracha ag briseadh
i gcoinne na gaoithe aniar
fear an chaipín chéanna.
Go hobann
tá píobaire ar an gcarraig
faoi bhun na faille
ag seimint
is gan aon fhocal as,
is nuair a fhilleann na capaill istoíche
faoi na húmacha lán de ghainneamh
ní bhíonn fir a dtiomána
ag portaireacht a thuilleadh.

Thomas Murphy was possessed of what Sheamus Heaney has called a "genealogical imagination." Not only could he go back in his own bloodlines but in those of every other member of the townland and also most of the parish, and their connections with many people from other parishes as well, often at least to the seventh generation. Thus he himself was "Tomás mhic Phádraig mhic Thomáis mhic Sheáin mhic Mhuiris mhic Mhuiris Ui Mhurchú." "Thomas, son of Pádraig, son of Tho-

mas, son of Seán, son of Muiris, son of Muiris Murphy," and
his sons Pádraig and Seán were the seventh generation of
those that he knew about. He claimed that they were originally
from Fán but then had moved to Cill Fearnóg and had lived
there until the three villages of An Cuan Íoctarach, An Cuan
Uachtarach, and An Cúilín Bán were evicted by a Corkman
called Leahy in the 1860s. His grandfather was six-and-a-half
years old when they moved to their present land in Cahiratrant, which was lying idle after the Great Famine. Likewise he
could put in other people's relationships to each other to a remarkable degree, and I have endless pages of notes that I have
taken down from him about my own family tree, with all the
ins and outs of it over many generations. These were the basis
of an almost endless source of comment, where the simplest
action or physical characteristic could be put back to a certain
long-dead relation or bloodline. When my second daughter
Ayse was born with curling toes, Thomas took one look at her
and declared "Hm! Tá méireanna marcaigh aici. Furaist a
aithint gur de shliocht Chill Uraidh í." "She's got rider's toes.
Easily known that she's the progeny of Cill Uraidh." Now, my
child's father is Turkish, and his mother was Bosnian, and my
own people haven't lived in Cill Uraidh since my great-
grandmother Cáit Ní Shé, yet Thomas was unmoved. The toes
were the giveaway. Later I found out that, yes, this physical
feature is well-attested for Cill Uraidh people, though I dare
say it was more from holding on to the flanks of donkeys and
mules on the precipitous *boithríns* of their townland, halfway
up Mount Eagle, that they developed such "rider's toes" rather
than from any great acquaintance with pedigree bloodstock!

Placenames were a source of fascination to Thomas Murphy at all times. There were even some free-floating placenames that he didn't know where they really belonged any
more. This was a major source of distress to him. One of them
was a place called Slí Uislí, which seemingly was a gap in the
cliffs over near where Cuan Íochtarach used to be, which he
had heard of from his grandfather but had never been able to
identify for himself. Another was a place called Seamair
Bhuaile, which for reasons of his own, never really disclosed,
he made out was on the northeast flank of Mount Brandon.
Any time he went over the Connor Pass to that side of the
peninsula he would ask anyone he met had they ever heard of
this place Seamair Bhuaile and did they know where it was.

Years later in the Department of Irish Folklore in University College, Dublin, I came across a fleeting reference to it. It is the description of two Fairy Women—Mná Sí—who were glimpsed striding along the countryside on the north side of the Connor Pass in the dead of night. They were carrying *buarachs*—that is, lengths of rope for tethering cattle—and were obviously up to no good. One of them was overheard saying to the other one: "ní beech bó ar bith ná beidh bleáite againn as seo go Seamair Bhuaile," "that there will not be a single cow that we will not have stolen the milk of from here to Seamair Bhuaile." I told this story to Thomas, and he was satisfied that it rang true with his own intuitions about the place, but unfortunately the story does not mention the coordinates of the place, or anywhere that might be adjacent to it, so we were still as much in the dark about it as before.

Two short sections of video of Thomas Murphy in the act of informing me about placenames give a flavor of the man and his style of narration. The first one is taken over in the graveyard in Ventry, Reilig Chaitlíona, where he is now buried. It was taken on St. Catherine's Day, 25 November 1987, which is the Pattern Day in Ventry, and I had gone down to do "the pattern," which is the annual pilgrimage made in many parishes in Ireland on the feast day of the patron saint of the parish. The patron saint of the parish of Ventry is St. Catherine, who is originally from Alexandria. The local legend has it that her body floated in to the strand and that she is buried in the nearby graveyard, the possibility being most strong that this particular saint was brought back from the Crusades and eclipsed an older, more pagan, deity. In the video Thomas is telling me the exact location of the west wall of the original Church of St. Catherine. It is just at the side of the grave of Peaits Mhic O Cinnéide, from Cahiratrant. Thomas knows the grave well because he has opened it himself four times. Later on, he tells me about a village, Baile an Teampaill, which once lay below the graveyard. On a fierce night of storm and wind the people eventually had to abandon it. There was also a freshwater well in the village, called Tobar na Mac, the Well of the Sons, and this can still be seen on the strand at low tide, where the water gushes up continually from the underground freshwater source. Of course, the sea was much further out in those days, he says. Thus one short segment of conversation encompasses a huge arc of local history, geography, and mythology.

The second section was taken a short time later up in his own living room. In this short piece he is talking about the fish salting trade, which flourished in Ventry Bay at the turn of the century and in which his father was a packer, working to pack the fish in layers of salt in boxes in a hulk that was moored just offshore. There were three main fish buyers coming in those days, and he gives us the name of two of them, Company Larsen and Company Nightingale. He disremembers the name of the last company on this particular occasion, but later it came to him out in the field, and the next time I went to visit him he told me that he had remembered it: Company Stormcock.

The only category of story mentioned by O Catháin and Flanagan that Thomas did not tell on a regular basis was fairy lore, though like all countrymen he had an implicit belief in An saol eile, the Otherworld, peopled by the souls of the dead, the fairies, spirits, hags, pookas, and those most redoubtable figures of all, Aingil an Uabhair, the prideful fallen cohorts of Satan. When I was quite young, he once started to tell me how he had seen a spirit by the road in Cill Mhic a' Domhnaigh, a huge giant sitting by the wayside with long skinny legs stretching across the road, who pulled each leg up slowly to let him pass. At this point in the story he looked away in some distraction, and I often wondered why. Later on, I came across a very similar story told about a similar personage encountered by someone else at that very same spot. Was it some lack of credence in the tale that stopped him, or a genuine dislike for passing off someone else's story as his own? I never got to the end of it, and he could never be prevailed upon to tell that story again. Folklorists make a distinction between stories told in the first person, as having happened to the teller himself, and other stories told as happening to other people. Thomas Murphy also made this distinction and was careful never to cross over from one category to the other. A literalist in some ways, he was not one to indulge in tall tales.

But whether or not he ever saw that spirit, there is one spirit that he definitely saw. He was out plowing the field called An Garraí Nua with a white gelding one fine day in May 1927 when "the Spirit of St. Louis" passed directly over the village, flying quite low. It had sighted land over An Baile Uachtarach in the Parish of Ballyferriter, had flown down the gap of Mám na Gaoithe and straight over the village of Cahiratrant and down southeast over Dingle Bay and the Iveragh Peninsula on its way to landfall in Le Bourget airfield, Paris. The whole village saw it. Thomas's neighbor, Mike Long, was pulling up lobster pots just under the cliffs and nearly fell out of the boat with the fright it gave him when it passed directly above him, flying low. Another neighbor, John Shea, was herding yearling bullocks, and they turned and nearly trampled him. Thomas was out plowing, and the white gelding bolted on him, and it was with great difficulty that he managed to hold it back. "Is that the first aeroplane you ever saw?" I asked him. Yes, it was, he told me. "And what did you think it was?" I asked, thinking back perhaps of the old man in my granny's village who when he saw his first motor car had rushed in to her swearing it was the devil incarnate, with huge lamps for eyes, trailing clouds of steam and sulfur behind it. "What else would I think it was?" shot back Thomas in return. "Sure and hadn't we been reading about it in the paper for a solid three days beforehand?" So much for my misguided apprehensions of a primeval state of mind, uncomplicated by the clutter of modern conveniences. And as I actually write this now, I suddenly remember a similar occasion, an evening in October 1957 when Thomas rounded up the children of the village on his *buaile*, or dung heap, which had the best view of the whole village. He scanned the heavens for a while and then pointed to what seemed at first one small star amongst the myriad others. "Féach ansan agaibh é," he said, "an sputnik." "There you have it, that's the sputnik," and our eyes followed the proof of the glories of modern science with almost as much wonder and admiration as his own. Of course, the fate of the dog Laika later became a great topic of conversation in the village but no great source of regret to a generation adept at "clifting" stray animals and unwanted litters—in other words quite unceremoniously throwing them off the very high cliffs that abound in this area. Slowly but surely, Laika also was subsumed miraculously into the great ever-changing tapestry of *dinnsheanchas*.

From this you can perhaps get a necessarily cursory idea of the all-comprehensive and multidimensional qualities of just one man's repertoire of *dinnsheanchas*. It is a great cornucopia of practical knowledge of a particular area, known intimately and in minute detail. Knowing Thomas Murphy has added a

great deal to my life. His influence acts on my work at all levels, even where it is not ostensibly about *dinnsheanchas* or
West Kerry. Witness, for instance, this new poem, in which he
has metamorphosed into a stranded merman. This is actually
based on a real incident, a time when I was about sixteen and
asked him for the name of a type of dogfish that I had found
drying on the beach. For the first and only time in his life he
apprised me of his belief in merpeople. He was never to do so
again, as later in his life he became rather coy and wary in
speaking of mermaids or of fairy lore. The fact that I and my
generation scoffed at him unmercifully from the heights of our
newly acquired knowledge of biology and geology did not encourage him to pass on his knowledge to us. Twenty-five years
down along the line, much humbler and more dog-eared, I feel
in no position to laugh at him. Actually, I feel that his world
view has much to offer us as a middle ground between the
severities of scientific abstraction and the loneliness of the individual in contemplation of them.

> A Remarkable Admission
> ("crib" or rough translation of "Admhail Shuaithin-
> seach")
>
> Only one time ever in my life
> did I get as much as the slightest
> inkling from any one of them
> that they had gone through a sort of ethnic cleansing
> and that some other place altogether, far away beyond
> was where they really belonged.
>
> I was sixteen or so when this happened.
> Mad into biology and chemical equations.
> I was enthralled by physiology and hygiene,
> up to the gills
> with accountancy and computer skills.
>
> I came across the Náth one day on foot,
> my jeans-legs turned up way beyond the knees,
> trailing behind a bit of flotsam I had found.
> I was curious about it.
> "What class of a fish is this I've here,
> Thomas," I asked. "Is it a dogfish?"

The old man lay his spade down on the strand
where he had been digging for lugworms. I remember how
they sparkled yellow, blackish-green and brown
as they slithered and seethed in the jam jar.
"That's no dogfish you have there," he said
"but a specked catfish." He lowered his voice,
glanced quickly left and right
and, in a whisper,

"There is no single animal up on dry land
that doesn't have its equivalent beast in the sea.
The cat, the dog, the cow, the sow;—
they are all there.
Even to the human being himself, and he's there too.
The name they call him is the merman."

A dark cloud passed over his sea-green eyes
that made them look like marine trenches.
I will never know what strange creatures swam
around in their great depths
because, just when I was about to pester the head
off him with chemistry, physics and the results
of the latest underwater explorations,
he turned on his heel and headed off

and left me stranded,
like a body floating between two layers of water.

Admhail Shuaithinseach
(the original poem)

Aon uair amháin riamh im'shaol
a fuaireas oiread is an leide is lú ó bhéal
aon duine acu
go raibh saghas éigin cine-ghlanadh gafa tríd acu
is gur ó áit éigin eile ar fad, i bhfad i gcéin
a thángadar.

A sé déag nó mar sin a bhíos nuair tharla sé seo.
Mé ag foghlaim bitheolaíochta
is teoiricí ceimice.
Bhíos faoi dhraíocht ag fiseolaíocht agus sláinteachas
is mé lán suas
de théarmaí staidéir gnó is ríomhaireachta.

Thángas de shiúl cos lá treasna an Náth,
mo threabhsar fillte suas go dtí mo chromáin
is smut de bhruscar cladaigh á tharrach im' dhiaidh agam.
Bhíos fiosrach faoi.
"Cé'n sórt bric í seo agam, a Thomáis?
Gadhar, ab ea?"

Do leag an seanduine uaidh a rámhainn ar an dtráigh
mar a raibh na luganna á mbaint aige.
Buí, dubhghlas is crón is ea do ghlioscadar,
ag snámharnach de shíor sa chróca romhainn.
"Ní haon ghadhar é sin atá agat," ar sé,
"ach cat. Cat ceanainn."
Do stop sé, thug catshúil thapaidh deas
is clé is cuir cogar-i-leith chugham.

"Níl aon ainmhí dá bhfuil ar an míntír," ar sé
"nach bhfuil a chomh'mhaith d'ainmhí
sa bhfarraige. An cat, an madra, an bhó, an mhuc;-
tá siad go léir ann.
Go dtí an duine féin, agus tá sé sin ann leis.
Sé ainm atá air siúd ná an mhurúch."

Ghluais scamall dorcha thar a shúile ar dhath na dtonn
a dhein tiompáin mhara dhóibh.
N'fheadar cad a shnámhaigh anall is anonn
sna duibheagáin doimhne sin
mar sar a raibh am agam i gceart
é a bhodhradh lem' chuid cleatrála is lem' chaint
ar cheimic, fisic, is ar fhiosriúcháin muireolaíochta
do chas sé ar a shál is d'imigh uaim.

D'fhág sé ar snámh idir dhá uisce mé.

In her book *Strangers to Ourselves*, Julia Kristeva suggests
that one of the greatest problems of our time is an implosion of
psychic space: that Christianity has been disempowered as a
belief system, and other competing systems have also not successfully stayed the course. There is no longer a cultural container for fantasy, a kind of anteroom where the contents of
the subconscious can be transformed and mediated before they
enter the world outside. Therefore symbolic material, whether
utopian fantasies or even the gods themselves, is forced to be
acted out in a childish, literalistic manner, and so enter the
world in a way that it was never meant to be. I personally believe that there is a psychosexual emotio-imagistic level of human nature (maybe you could call it the soul) that we deny at
our peril. It is a mythopoeic function natural to the human
being, which always and everywhere needs to be expressed but
has particular difficulty in Western civilization, where it has
fallen foul of the dominant mind/spirit duality and disappeared into the chasm between them. This mythic dimension
needs to be expressed, but that does not necessarily mean that
it needs to be acted out literalistically. On the contrary, literalistic acting out is a wholly inappropriate and uncalled for response to this dimension. What we need to do is find some
room for it in our lives, so that it can play itself out and dance
its dance on its own terms, which are imaginative ones.

I think that *dinnsheanchas*, which though not peculiar to
Gaelic literature is a very prominent part of it, can be considered a useful cultural container for our deeply held heartfelt
need for a homeland, another compound word that puts together two of the most powerful words in the whole vocabulary
of human identity. During the medieval heyday of *dinnsheanchas* Ireland was by no manner of means a nation, in the
sense that we use the word today. It was a mixum-gatherum of
anything up to 160 *tuaths*, or petty kingdoms, divided on a
clan system, in many ways like a rural version of the early
stages of the Greek city-states. Most members of a particular
clan ventured outside their own territory very much at their
peril; even saints had to be quite circumspect about whose
water is was that they dipped any particular big toe in. Nevertheless, the poets, who were the guardians, originators, and
constantly entertaining purveyors of *dinnsheanchas*, were welcome everywhere, as theirs was an art that surpassed all petty
boundaries and cemented the whole society together in a sym-

bolic way, however much that might be belied by the mundane and almost gratuitous head-bashing that constituted the daily nitty-gritty of cattle raiding. Of course, they had strong ideo-logical functions as well, and much of the material can be read as fabrications of legitimacy for one or other ruling family or dynasty, yet this in itself is fascinating and extremely useful to historians of the period. In its modern sense, it is epitomized by me in Thomas Murphy, whom I have chosen to describe out of a large number of possible informants of his generation only because he was married to my aunt, and therefore I was par-ticularly fond of him and had a long and easy acquaintance with him over a period of thirty-five-odd years. I could as easily have chosen any of his neighbors, with slightly different results in emphasis: Mike Long, as much a seaman as Thomas was a landman, whose toponomical lore would have been speckled with the very sharply observed naturalistic details that were his particular speciality; Joein Shea, who to this day is inca-pable of mentioning a placename associated with Fionn Mac Cumhaill without launching into all sixty-seven verses of the Fenian Lay on which that particular placename is based; Mike Shea, my own first and third cousin (his mother was my great-grandaunt), whose period of emigration to the States before his return in 1929 as a result of the Great Depression gave him a detachment and a certain modern streetwise slant of mind that was the source of a sly and very cynical sense of humor. To these and many others like them I owe a practical knowledge and sensible appreciation of *dinnsheanchas* as a lived dimen-sion of life, which has been enormously rewarding and en-richening to me, personally. I find myself thinking a lot of what Wendell Berry says in a recent interview; "A Question a Day":

> It is not the written word that impairs memory, but depend-ence on the written word to the exclusion of the spoken. Some experience cannot be put wholly into writing. And so as dependence on writing grows, the communicated experience suffers a corresponding attenuation. The most complete speech is that of conversation in a settled community of some age, where what is said refers to and evokes things, people,

places and events that are commonly known. In such a community, to speak and hear is to remember.[7]

Particularly in the Irish-speaking communities of the western seaboard of Ireland, but really more or less throughout the whole countryside, the collective memory of the community is enshrined in the *dinnsheanchas*. Recently, also, I have come to see it in wider context, as an example of that necessary psychic container that Julia Kristeva considers to be particularly absent in our time. Through *dinnsheanchas* we can possess the land emotionally and imaginatively without any particular sense of, or actual need for, titular ownership. Not unlike, in a lesser way, the reading of the future from tea leaves or coffee lees, it gives us an "objective correlative" on which we can hang the powerful and ever-changing dimensions and personages of our *paysage interieure*. The anthropologist Henry Glassie, in his classic study of rural Fermanagh, *Passing the Time in Ballymenone*, tells of the difficulty that he had in finding the center or nucleus of the local community, which in many ways was divided along sectarian lines, until he discovered that the stories, the *dinnsheanchas*, were the material held in common, were the cement that kept the community together and distinct in itself. The geographer E. Estyn Evans in speaking about Irish culture in a 1984 pamphlet called *Ulster: The Common Ground* has this to say:

> I found that running through the whole there was a single theme with many variations—and this variety is in itself very appealing, although it is also a great source of dissension. I think we have somehow to live with that variety and exploit it rather than let it disturb our peace; because it is precious in that it stands in contrast to the almost universal monotony of modern culture, its dullness, its commercial exploitation and material values, its mass production.[8]

I think that a sense of this imaginative stewardship of the land is something that is increasing at the moment in leaps

---

[7] "A Question a Day: A Written Conversation with Wendell Berry," in *Wendell Berry*, ed. Paul Merchant (Lewiston, ID: Confluence, 1991) 27.

[8] *Ulster: The Common Ground* (Gigginstown, Co. Westmeath: Lilliput Press, 1984) 3.

and bounds in Ireland. President Mary Robinson's concept of "The Fifth Province" is an expression of this highly potent imaginative dimension. The Australian poet Maurice Scully, who came to Ireland in the early eighties, complained of Irish people being like somnambulists stumbling around blindly in what was actually a supremely coded environment. I think that this was more a failing on the part of Scully himself than of anyone else's. For starters, he was looking in the wrong place. He would have been well to start with the Irish-speaking communities, where the meaning of the placenemes is still so transparent as to be considered quite ordinary and functional. Or maybe he was just a man before his time. The flurry of interest in local history and the plethora of clubs and organizations that have grown up in the last five to ten years, particularly in Northern Ireland, to cater for this interest bears witness perhaps to the expression of a primary need. I believe that a renewed interest in *dinnsheanchas* may enable us to share our love and admiration and wonder of the land of Ireland and can cater in an imaginative way for the need of many for a place to belong to so that we may love and cherish it rather than merely killing each other over it.

TRANSPARENT VEILS:
Western Women Dis-Orient the East

Billie Melman

The Flaubertian Paradigm: Colonialism as Sexuality

It is appropriate to begin this essay with a rather hack-
neyed description of a dance, a colonial dance, loaded with
sexual and political meanings. This particular dance offers us
a frame for a discussion of the Western experience of colonialism, for a reconsideration of the Western colonial identity, and
for a reworking of some categories currently used in studies of
colonialism and decolonialism. Although the description is
from 1851, and represents French orientalism at its height, it
is often used as a metaphor for the colonial encounter and its
representations in Western European discourses throughout
the eighteenth and nineteenth centuries. "Colonialism" covers
the longer period of European expansion, under a multiplicity
of forms, direct and indirect, military, juridical, economic, and
"cultural." I use the description of the dance because it has
been employed by students of colonialism as a metaphor for
the colonial situation and because it exemplifies the model
most typically used to define and categorize cross-cultural ex
change throughout the colonial era. I wish to question the
utility of current categorization for our comprehension and
historicization of colonialism.

In the description of the dance, Kucuk Hanim, the Turk-
ish-Circassian 'alimah—that is, dancer and prostitute—
performs the dance of the veil before her master/lover, the
young Gustave Flaubert.[1] When the dance ends, she uncovers

Early versions of this paper were read at the conference on colonialism
and decolonialism at the Institute for the Humanities, University of Michigan,
in the fall of 1993 and at the 1994 Millercomm Lecture at the University of
Illinois at Urbana Champaign. An early version of the part on eighteenth-
century usages of the metaphor of the veil was read at the 1993 MLA in To-
ronto. I thank Arjun Appadurai, Rashid Khalidi, Fred Cooper, Dan Diner,
Fatma Müge Göçek, Raymond Grew, Thomas Trautman, Martha Vicinus, and
Patricia Yaeger, who have commented on my paper and other work on orien-

herself before the obviously aroused novelist, who can then unveil her, both literally and metaphorically. For Flaubert knows Kucuk Hanim sexually and as a text, to be stripped, reconstructed, and represented in myriad utterances and writings, always as a woman with a veil: as Salome, as Herodias, as the Queen of Sheba. In the Flaubertian text, unveiling signifies a sexual as well as an ontological knowledge of the other.

In the rapidly expanding field of study of colonialism and decolonialism, particularly in that division of it that is devoted to the Western vision and construction of the Orient, or Orientalism in Edward Said's seminal definition, the Flaubertian metaphor of the veiled oriental woman has been elevated to one of sexual and political domination. Indeed, this metaphor is now used as a paradigm of the colonial situation, as well as for the construction of a Western colonial identity based on a colonized subject perceived and represented as the West's other.[2] The development of colonial identities and of the colonial situation itself is evaluated by casting Occident and Orient as binary terms. Since the appearance of Said's epochal *Orientalism* (which cites Flaubert abundantly), it has been repeatedly argued that the development of Western subjecthood in the age of colonialism hinged upon a construction of the colonized as an alterity. Indeed, "otherness" has become the key to understanding how individuals and groups in Western Europe came to grips with difference: between genders, between cultures, between races.

The Flaubertian text exemplifies that binary paradigm of colonialism and cross-cultural exchanges at work. The veiled

---

talism. Kate Perry, archivist and Librarian at Girton College, Cambridge, and Kathleen Khan, Librarian at the University Library, Cambridge University, were most helpful with the Power records on India. I am most grateful to Lady Cynthia Postan for permission to read Eileen Power's travel journals.

[1] I draw on the version in Gustave Flaubert, *Voyage en Egypte*, ed. Pierre-Marc de Biasi (Paris: Bernard Grasset, 1991) 280–90.

[2] See, for example, Rana Kabbani, *Europe's Myth of Orient, Devise and Rule* (London: Macmillan, 1986); Edward Said, *Orientalism* (London: Routledge and Kegan Paul, 1978); and the approach represented in Francis Barker, ed., *Europe and Its Others* (Colchester: University of Essex, 1985); Nicholas Dirks, *Colonialism and Culture* (Ann Arbor: University of Michigan Press, 1992) 1–27.

dancer is female, her audience male: she is naked beneath the transparent gauze, he is covered; impressively sensual, she is wordless, while he is articulate, the authoritative interpreter of an other that cannot represent itself, therefore, in Marx's phrase, needs to be represented. And Kucuk Hanim is "nature" to Flaubert's culture: she is an essential Orient that is denied historicity and the dynamics of change.

Flaubert's contemporaries were familiar with the trope of the veiled colonized woman. She had been a powerful and long-lived *topos* in orientalist discourses, notably about the Muslim Eastern Mediterranean and South Asia.[3] As students of orientalism have noted, this *topos* of the oriental female as the embodiment of all that was considered essentially Eastern pre-dated modern colonialism and may be traced back to polemical anti-Muslim writing in the early Middle Ages. Yet, as Said has observed, the Orient became particularly essentialized and feminized after the rise of modern colonialism.[4] Scholars argued that in modern colonial discourse she came to be a figure of alterity, the non-European's ultimate other. The Eastern woman as metaphor for otherness has occupied a central place in scholarship on colonial cross-cultural representations. Indeed, her position is strategic: as an other that is not only ethnic and religious but sexual too, she fits well into the unified binary image of Europe and the East built by Europeans.

The Historiography of Colonialism and the Uses of Binary Models: A Critique

Recently, scholars have modified their perception of a unified Western notion of, and discourse on, the colonial subject. We have become aware that that discourse was never monolithic, that it was never systematically conducted (indeed that

---

[3] Billie Melman, *Women's Orients—Englishwomen and the Middle East, 1718–1918: Sexuality, Religion and Work* (London and Ann Arbor: University of Michigan Press, 1992) 59–61; "Colonialisms and Sexualities," Millercomm Lecture, University of Illinois, 1994.

[4] Norman Daniel, *Islam and the West, the Making of an Image* (Edinburgh: University Press, 1960), for the medieval origins of the stereotype.

colonial rule itself never was systematic and all-powerful), and that it changed with time and place. In Lisa Lowe's succinct phrase: "Orientalism is not a single developmental tradition but is profoundly heterogenous."[5]

Feminist historiography of colonialism, a rather new project of recovery and interpretation, has made us aware of the influence of gender and class on the experience of colonialism and its representations. The scholarship of Margaret Strobel, Nupur Chaudhuri, Catherine Hall, Sarah Suleri, and Antoinette Burton, to cite but a few, has transformed the traditional notion of Western women as either passive spectators of colonialism or its victims. This scholarship, heavily concentrating on the Indian Empire, and my own work on the Middle East, has established that women were colonial agents, whose experience of colonialism was quite heterogeneous and whose discourse on and attitude towards oriental sexuality evolved differently from the mainstream male discourse.[6] Yet feminist historiography reinstates the dominant binary model, often describing colonial discourses in terms of patriarchal rule, of "male gender dominance, or patriarchy, in metropolitan societies." Both literary studies and the very few historical monographs on Western women and imperialism draw on this binary model of the colonial situation to analyze the construction of the modern Western female (and feminist) subject.[7] The

---

[5] Lisa Lowe, *Critical Terrains: French and English Orientalisms* (Ithaca: Cornell University Press, 1991); Sara Suleri, *The Rhetoric of English India* (Chicago: University of Chicago Press, 1992). Said himself modified his initial interpretation of orientalism as monolithic and unified in *Culture and Imperialism* (New York: Knopf, 1993). See also Melman, *Women's Orients.*

[6] Nupur Chaudhuri and Margaret Strobel, eds., *Western Women and Imperialism: Complicity and Resistance* (Bloomington: Indiana University Press, 1992), particularly the essays by Barbara N. Ramusack, Antoinette Burton, and Nancy L. Paxton. See also Jenny Sharpe, "The Unspeakable Limits of Rape: Colonial Violence and Counter-Insurgency," *Genders*, no. 10 (Spring 1991); and *History Workshop* 36, special issue on colonialism (Autumn 1993), especially Catherine Hall, "White Visions, Black Lives: The Free Villages of Jamaica."

[7] The phrase cited is Said's in *Orientalism.* The binary model is used in earlier feminist studies such as Helen Callaway, *Gender, Culture and Empire: European Women in Colonial Nigeria* (Oxford: St. Antony's/Macmillan series, 1987), and in more recent studies like Browning's, Ramusack's, and Paxton's

Western female subject, it is argued, evolved by pitting itself against an oriental female object that was seen as the Western woman's other and was denied historicity and agency. Feminist scholars agree that Western women shared a sense of cultural superiority and cultural prejudices that often bordered on cultural narcissism. In other words, women's discourse on colonialism reproduced the patriarchal and orientalist notion of the other.

One irony of the historiography of colonialism and decolonialism is that feminist scholarship created a narrative that supplemented Said's history of orientalism, substituting women for men colonizers while retaining the dichotomy of self and other, as well as the idea that Western women essentialized the oriental female as the embodiment of the "natural" East.[8] More significant, feminist scholarship implies, or states outright, that modern gender identity could have developed only in a process of denial of historical identity to a female other.

It is time to rid ourselves of the Flaubertian model of cross-cultural relations that afflicts so much of what is written on the colonial identity. We may seek alternative narratives by asking whether the identity of the colonist was unified and whether it could contain similarities with, as well as differences from, the colonial subject. We may ask with S. P. Mohanty, "Just how other we need to force ourselves to indicate, is the Other?"[9] How different did the non-European veiled woman seem to the unveiled one? What alternative mechanisms of difference built the European sense of likeness and

---

and Joanna de Groot, "Sex and Race: The Construction of Language and Image in the Nineteenth Century," in *Sexuality and Subordination in the Nineteenth Century*, ed. Susan Mendus and Jane Rendall (London: Routledge, 1989).

[8] This view is most eloquently argued by Chandra Talpade Mohanty in "Under Western Eyes: Feminist Scholarship and Colonial Discourses," *Boundary* 2, 12 (Fall 1984): 333–58, and Gayatri Spivak, "Three Women's Texts and A Critique of Imperialism," *Critical Inquiry* 12, 1 (1985): 143–61, rpt. in C. T. Mohanty, *In Other Worlds* (New York: Methuen, 1987) 134–53. See also Rajeswari Sunder Rajan, *Real and Imagined Women: Gender, Culture and Postcolonialism* (New York and London: Routledge, 1993).

[9] S. P. Mohanty, "Us and Them: On the Philosophical Bases of Political Criticism," *Yale Journal of Criticism* 2, 2 (Spring 1989): 5.

unlikeness between colonizers and colonized, and how was this sense influenced by gender and class?

The Alternative Discourse and the Literature on Veils

Representations of the veil and the veiled woman show that not alterity but a sense of similarity was crucial to the development of the Western colonial identity. The very prevalence of the veil in Western and Eastern cultures makes it both an accessible metaphor and an analytical tool for an alternative interpretation of the colonial situation. By the early 1850s, the veil had acquired for Europeans many diverse meanings. It denoted physical covering of the face, or of the head, or of other parts of the body—sometimes of the female sexual organs (as in one of Flaubert's versions). More broadly, it denoted the seclusion of women and children in separate quarters (*haremlik* in the Ottoman Middle East or *zenana* in India). More broadly still, veiling signified the familial and socioeconomic system conventionally referred to as the *harem system*, which included, in addition to segregation, multiple marriage and concubinage. Even more broadly, and most significant here, the veil was an overdetermined psychosexual and political symbol of the ultimate other.[10] In the mainstream orientalist discourse, as represented in male descriptions of the harem, the veil served as a microcosmic East, apotheosizing the two ineradicable components of the oriental colonial identity: sensuality and violence. But, I would argue, the veil figured differ-

---

[10] For a checklist of works on the face veil and the harem system in the Middle East see Melman, *Women's Orients*; and Leslie Peirce, *The Imperial Harem: Women and Sovereignty in the Ottoman Empire* (Oxford: Oxford University Press, 1993). For India consult David G. Mandelbaum, *Women's Seclusion and Men's Honor: Sex Roles in North India, Bangladesh and Pakistan* (Tucson: University of Arizona Press, 1988); and Shahida Lateef, *Muslim Women in India: Political and Private Realities 1890s-1980s* (London and New Jersey: Zed Books, 1990). For the psychosexual meanings of the veil see Melman, *Women's Orients*. The most useful anthropological interpretation is by Lila Abu-Lughod, *Veiled Sentiments: Honor and Poetry in Bedouin Society* (Berkeley and London: University of California Press, 1986).

ently in an alternative female discourse on colonialism that evolved between the beginning of the eighteenth century and the period of decolonization after World War II. That discourse developed a geography of the Western (and Eastern) identity that was far more complex than the so-called orientalist geography. The main locus of the alternative discourse is the Western literature on veils, inaugurated by Lady Mary Wortley Montagu in her *Turkish Letters* (1763), the first secular discussion by a Western woman of oriental women and oriental female sexuality. In the Western women's rendition of the experience of the Orient, the veil is a central topic and metaphor. Their narrative is dialogical, and, rather than dichotomizing the Western and Eastern identity, colonial power and powerlessness, it historicizes and humanizes the colonial subject, articulating similarities between her and the colonizer that cut across race and culture.

My *Women's Orients* (1992) investigated the mammoth body of domestic colonial writing by Western women that has been, for the most part, ignored. Yet so far the veil as a metaphor for colonial relations has not been systematically studied. This essay draws on published travelogues and ethnographies, as well as on unpublished material on the Middle East and India produced after the early and unpublished version of Montagu's reference text began circulating in Britain and France, as well as nonpublished records.[11] This literature uncovered areas in the lives of women in the veiling zones that were *terrae incognita* to Westerners, since the *haremlik/zenana* were sealed to Western men, whose accounts on oriental women perpetuated the myth of the "essential" Eastern woman. These firsthand accounts by Western women drew on observation, which characteristically produced what James Clifford called "participant observation" and an "intersubjective

---

[11] The larger study on the Middle East is based on 345 published works, and this figure does not include publications in periodicals and unpublished records. The material on India draws on a smaller sample of slightly fewer than 100 selected printed works. Archival materials include the records of the following: Royal Geographical Society, Egypt Exploration Fund, Palestine Exploration Fund, Royal Asiatic Society. University archives consulted include the manuscript divisions at UCL, Cambridge University, and Girton College Archives.

relation" between the colonial ethnographer and her subject.[12] Of course, seeing is a preprogrammed activity, which in itself does not guarantee empathy with the other culture. And seeing did not preclude prejudice and a sense of the West's superiority. But actual contact between Western and Eastern women resulted in a decategorization of both the Eastern and Western female identities. This contact brought on comparison between cultures and a powerful critique of Western gender ideology and of the colonial situation. Looking at veils, through and beyond veils, was a gaze at the self, a sober exposure of the ambiguity and instability of the Western female colonial identity.

Here I extend my research from the Middle East to India, in order to gain a more nuanced notion of the gendered encounter with the colonial situation. The two foci of research present very different colonialisms: India, even before 1857, was under direct British rule, economically, politically, and juridically. The Great Mutiny of 1857 precipitated the change from mercantile imperialism to the bureaucratic and military colonialism of the Western nation-state, which increasingly drew on racist ideology and on the notion of responsible rule. Colonialism in the Middle East, on the other hand, had been, until after World War I, much less direct. With the exception of Egypt, rule was not military and juridical, and economic influence varied greatly over place and time. India and the Middle East also differed in their status in the empire, in evangelical Christianity and the evangelical project of overseas expansion, as well as in Western political cultures and aesthetics. Moreover, India and the Middle East present different forms of the relationship between colonialism and sexuality. Sexual and familial aspects of the lives of British women and men were more interwoven with the lives of Indian people, especially Indian women.[13] So far, there is no evidence of comparable contacts in the Middle East.

---

[12] James Clifford, "On Ethnographic Authority," *The Predicament of Culture* (Cambridge, MA: Harvard University Press, 1988) 20–25, esp. 22, n. 1.

[13] On the relative places of the different "orients" see Raymond Schwab's classic *La Renaissance orientale* (Paris: Payot, 1950). On India in Western evangelical and "scientific" thought see Ronald Inden, *Imagining India* (Oxford: Basil Blackwell, 1990). On interracial sexuality and its regulation see Kenneth Ballhatchet, *Race, Sex and Class under the Raj* (London: Weidenfeld and Nicolson, 1980); and Ann L. Stoler, "Making the Empire Respectable: The Poli-

I begin with a brief discussion of the eighteenth-century paradigm of similarity in difference in Mary Wortley Montagu's writing on veils, which generated the alternative and gender-specific debate on colonial women. I then look in detail at the changes from Montagu's Augustan paradigm to models of difference from the Victorian through the interwar period. Much of the essay is devoted to the era of "high colonialism" between the 1870s and the aftermath of World War I, when British imperialism became more direct than ever before, while at the same time colonial authority was contested, especially in India but also by some critics in Britain. Finally, I explain the significance of the veil and veiled women as readily available and potent metaphors for similarity, in both religious and secular debates on female sexuality in the West. It is precisely this debate that elevated the veil to an overdetermined metaphor of likeness rather than alterity.

The Eighteenth-Century Model of Difference: Liberty behind the Veil

It is easy to pinpoint the beginning of the preoccupation with veils as a metaphor for similarity in difference. This metaphor, as well as the distinctly female discourse on the Orient, was practically invented by Lady Mary Wortley Montagu in the *Turkish Letters*, written in 1717–18 to fifty-two correspondents, widely circulated in piratical editions during the first half of the eighteenth century, and published posthumously in 1763. The *Letters* were to become a canonical text in the nineteenth century, the model for hundreds of Western accounts of domestic life in the *haremlik/zenana.*[14] Yet scholarship on orien-

---

tics of Race and Sexual Morality in 20th-Century Colonial Cultures," *The American Ethnologist* 16, 4 (November 1989) 634–61.

[14] The complete title is: *Letters of the Right Honorable Lady Mary Wortley Montagu: Written during her Travels in Europe, Asia and Africa to Persons of Distinction.* On the letters and their production see Robert Halsband, *The Life of Lady Mary Wortley Montagu* (Oxford: Clarendon Press, 1960). Relevant recent publications include Joseph W. Lew, "Lady Mary's Portable Seraglio," *Eighteenth Century Studies* 24 (1991): 432–50; and Melman, *Women's Orients.*

talism ignores Montagu. She is omitted from Said's orientalist cannon in *Orientalism* and only briefly mentioned in his *Imperialism and Culture*. In eighteenth-century literary studies, "traditional" as well as historicist, she is discussed quite outside the colonial context. With notable exceptions, such as Cynthia J. Lowenthal, feminist scholars largely ignore Montagu's orientalist writings or regard them as the work of a proxy for the male voyeur of the exotic harem. It is symptomatic of the limits of feminist scholarship on colonialism and gender that it largely ignores the first text by a woman orientalist.[15]

Montagu's significance is in introducing into Western discourse the paradox of the freedom behind the veil, of degrees of public and private freedoms of Ottoman women. At the same time, she criticizes contemporary European notions of liberty from which women were excluded. Furthermore, in her consideration of the veil and segregation between genders Montagu dissolves the association, central to the dominant Whig-Liberal thought, between freedom and the distinction between private and public spaces. Liberal thought between the late seventeenth and late nineteenth centuries sharply distinguishes between the private, domestic space and the public, political one. Women, identified in this thought with the home and the patriarchal family, were denied public and political freedoms, which were limited to the heads of families. Montagu realized that the veil, indeed the harem system itself, defied the Western dichotomy of liberty and bondage. Segregation neither precluded freedoms for women nor denied them public liberties. Moreover, Montagu noted that the veil, which functioned as a kind of mobile harem, defied any clear-cut distinction

---

Quotations are from Lady Mary Wortley Montagu, *The Complete Letters*, ed. Robert Halsband (Oxford: Clarendon Press, 1965).

[15] Cynthia Lowenthal, *Lady Mary Wortley Montagu and the Eighteenth-Century Familiar Letter* (Athens, GA, and London: University of Georgia Press, 1994). On Montagu as a proxy or a voyeur see de Groot, "Sex and Race." Examples of the lack of interest in eighteenth-century feminist criticism are Laura Brown, *The Ends of Empire: Women and Ideology in Early Eighteenth-Century English Literature* (Ithaca: Cornell University Press, 1993), and Margo Hendricks and Patricia Parker, eds., *Women, Race and Writing in the Early Modern Period* (New York and London: Routledge, 1994).

between private spaces (identified with women and taken to signify powerlessness) and public ones.

Of course, Montagu drives the paradox of the public liberty of segregated women *ad absurdum*, sometimes quite rhetorically:

> Tis easy to see they have more liberty than we have, no Woman of what rank so ever being permitted to go in the streets without 2 muslins, one that covers the face all but her Eyes and another that hides the whole dress of her head.... You may guess how effectively this disguises them, that there is no distinguishing the great Lady from her Slave, and 'tis impossible for the most jealous husband to know his Wife when he meets her, and no *Man dare either touch or follow a Woman in the street. This perpetual masquerade gives them more Liberty of following their inclinations.* (emphasis added)[16]

The paradox of the liberty behind the veil serves to gender the Enlightenment notion of freedom and relativizes this notion by connecting it to the colonial context. "Liberty" for Ottoman women was not political. Rather it was a complex of juridical, customary, and economic freedoms. But above all "liberty" here signifies the sexual freedom of the married woman to carry on her "inclinations." The notion of sexual freedom and individual liberty, as virtually all students of Enlightenment gender ideology have argued, extended only to men. The married woman's liberty imperiled the conjugal family and subsequently the stability of the commonwealth.[17] Montagu extends the notion of sexual freedom to women. Furthermore, she not only positions the veil, a symbol of subjection, as a signifier of liberty. She also uses the veil to challenge the very distinction between Western and Eastern women and, by implication, the West/East dichotomy. She considers the *yashmak* as a transcultural symbol: it is, she points out, donned in the West,

---

[16] Lady Mary to Lady Mar, 1 April 1717, *Complete Letters* 1:326.

[17] See, for example, Susan Moller Okin, *Women in Western Political Thought* (Princeton: Princeton University Press, 1982); Paul-Gabriel Boucé, ed., *Sexuality in Eighteenth Century Britain* (Manchester: Manchester University Press, 1986).

for example, by nuns. Moreover, she observes the presence in British society of invisible veils of varying degrees of transparency, which confine the married woman of the upper classes more than the *yashmak* limits the *hanim* (the legally married Ottoman woman). The married British woman owned no property of her own and was, according to Montagu, the victim of the double sexual standard that denied her sexual liberty while condoning promiscuity in men. Her Ottoman counterpart enjoyed economic independence and sexual autonomy.[18] By drawing an analogy between Ottoman widows and nuns, Montagu likens veiling in the Muslim East (which did not originate in Islam) to seclusion in the Western Christian tradition. In a letter to the Venetian priest and cosmopolitan *savant* Abbe Conti, published in 1718 and 1719 as *A Genuine Copy of a Letter Written from Constantinople by an English Lady*, she opines:

> Here are maxims for you, prodigiously contrary to those of your Convents. What will become of your Saint Catherines, your Saint Theresas, your Saint Claras and the whole bead roll of your holly Virgins and Widows? who, if they are to be judged by this System of Virtue, will be found to have been infamous creatures, that past their whole Lives in a most abominable Libertinism.[19]

Even in the context of the later attack of Enlightenment philosophers on the Roman Catholic Church and Christianity, Montagu's reference to the three saints as libertines is audacious. For Montagu attacks the Pauline-Augustinian doctrine of sexuality, which prescribed chastity for women and remained the basis of post-Reformation attitudes to female sexuality. She deuniversalizes this doctrine: what it praises, another belief condemns as unnatural and sinful. In Islam the nun and the virgin are considered to be "infamous creatures."

As far as gender is concerned, Montagu's rejection of the religious framework is more complete than that of later thinkers (for example, Diderot and Voltaire). For in Western religious discourse the face cover of the nun, reminiscent of the bride's

---

[18] Lady Mary to Lady Mar, April 1717, *Complete Letters*, 1:329–30.
[19] Letter to Abbé Conti, 29 May 1717, *Complete Letters* 1:364.

veil, was a symbol of authority denied to unveiled and sexually active women. As Ludmilla Jordanova has noted, the veiled woman had been an empowered figure in Western religious culture.[20] Christ's bride, like the saint "dead to the world" and secluded, escaped imprisonment in the flesh, the *damnosa hereditas* of Eve. But virginity, Montagu argues, was "libertine" and inhuman in that it denied "women's nature," or sexuality. A this-worldly religion, Islam, far more than Christianity, recognized the sexual nature of women and legitimized it.

The significance of Montagu's paradox of the veil is in her argument that it is transcultural and not necessarily Eastern, or Muslim. Thus in regard to her views on female sexuality she is a relativist. By identifying forms of gender segregation in Western religious and secular culture, she is able to point at similarities between British and Ottoman women. Furthermore, as a relativist, she is particularly sensitive to universalist notions of gender developed in Britain during the early Enlightenment, as well as to her European contemporaries' sense of cultural superiority.

Nineteenth Century Models of Sexuality

Montagu's legacy to the Victorians was the veil as a signifier of freedoms and empowerment for women, as well as the notion that veiling was transcultural and could be used to dispute assumptions about otherness. The Victorians and Edwardians were obsessed with veiling, seclusion, and segregation in varied forms. Colonialism introduced them to a large variety of segregation: between genders, between classes, between races, and between age groups. The diverse modes of seclusion made it possible for nineteenth-century women writers to historicize the veil and develop an attitude toward it that was far more complex than Montagu's. Thus when in 1848 the political economist, feminist, and abolitionist Harriet Martineau compared the life of harem women in Egypt to the Afri-

---

[20] Ludmilla Jordanova, *Sexual Visions: Images of Gender in Science and Medicine between the Enlightenment and Twentieth Centuries* (Madison: University of Wisconsin Press, 1989) 87–111.

can-American female experience of slavery, she was criticized by writers who argued that seclusion was not exclusively Muslim, that it took many diverse forms, and that it did not preclude degrees of freedom.[21] Martineau is worth citing because she is atypical. The majority of women writers on the Middle East and India, regardless of their attitude toward polygamy and seclusion, pluralized the veil and approached it historically. These writers argued that veiling varied enormously geographically and according to social class or status: that it was limited to elites; that it was urban rather than rural; and that it marked respectability. Rather than presenting an unchanging condition of bondage, the real veil signified to Western women a diversity of freedoms and autonomies that Western culture denied them. As American writer Anna Bowman Dodd put it in 1903, the rights and privileges of the oriental secluded woman are "many, so numerous, indeed, that after a review of them it is the European rather than the Osmanli women who seem to be still in bondage."[22]

Nineteenth- and early twentieth-century women writers retained the Augustan notion of the freedom behind the veil, as well as a sense of the precariousness of liberty for the unveiled woman. What these writers objected to was the Augustan interpretation of "freedom" as sexual freedom. The shift in the gendered interpretation of freedom marks a transformation in class culture and identity. Throughout the nineteenth century, the culture of empire increasingly became a middle-class culture. This transformation, which scholars like Catherine Hall have begun to map, characterized the colonial experience of both men and women.[23] Yet the new "bourgeois" orientalism that developed in the nineteenth century was related to middle-class constructions of gender. As my quantitative studies of

---

[21] Harriet Martineau, *Eastern Life, Present and Past* (London: E. Moxon, 1848) 293, 299. Lucy Duff-Gordon, *Letters From Egypt* (London, 1865; rpt. London: Virago, 1983) 112. For the dominant view among women ethnographers and travelers my "Desexualizing the Orient: The Harem in English-women's Travel Writing, 1763–1914," *Mediterranean Historical Review* 4, 2 (December 1989): 301–39.

[22] Anna Bowman Dodd, *In the Palaces of the Sultan* (London: Heinemann, 1903) 435.

[23] Catherine Hall, "White Visions Black Lives," *White, Male and Middle Class: Explorations in Feminism and History* (Cambridge: Polity, 1992 ed.).

oriental travel and travel writing demonstrate, during the nineteenth century both became distinctly middle class. Middle-class women constructed an image of oriental domestic life that was compatible with Western gender ideology. Foremost in this image was the challenge to aristocratic values.[24] Hence the criticism of Montagu, who was accused by her disciples of a latitudinarian attitude toward "excess" and of "excessive" interest in women of the Ottoman elites. For instance, in 1830 Julia Sophia Pardoe commented on Montagu's famous description of the nude bathers in Sophia's public bath (hammam), and in 1861 Emmeline Lott remarked on the Augustan writer's unhealthy interest in the Ottoman elites, to the neglect of the middling classes. In middle-class language and mentalité, sexual excesses were related to aristocratic culture.[25]

Thus the single most important change in the rhetoric of the literature on veils was its desexualization. Veiling came to stand for purity rather than active sexuality. The haremlik and zenana were increasingly represented as homes. Writers drew on the culturally legitimate vocabulary of the "spheres," which stressed the separateness of the middle-class home from civic and public spaces. In writings on the Middle East the oriental household was commonly identified with female virtue and morality. It is, writes Katherine Elwood in the 1820s and 1830s, "a haven," a "woman's place." And Mary Lucy Garnett, author of a number of comparative ethnographies on Asia Minor, as late as 1909 describes the Ottoman home as a woman's "sanctum sanctorum."[26] What is striking about the rhetoric of the spheres is its resistance to changes in gender ideology in

---

[24] Melman, Women's Orients 25–59.

[25] Julia Sophia Pardoe, The City of the Sultan (London: Henry Colburn, 1837) 1:136–37; Emmeline Lott, "Preface," The English Governess in Egypt: Harem Life in Egypt and Constantinople (London: Chapman and Hall, 1866) 1:v.

[26] Anne Katherine Elwood, Narrative of a Journey Overland from England ... to India (London: H. Colburn and R. Bentley, 1830) 1:153–54; Pardoe, City of the Sultan 1:136–37, Mary Lucy Garnett, The Women of Turkey (London: D. Nutt, 1890–91) 441; Fanny Blunt, The People of Turkey (London: Murray, 1878) 261; Mary Eliza Rogers, Domestic Life in Palestine (London: Bell and Daldy, 1863) 372.

Britain itself during the last quarter of the nineteenth century. Domestic vocabulary in travelogues and ethnographies focusing on the lives of women and the family outlives its equivalent in adjacent genres like the domestic novel.

In some writings on India domestication and desexualization become particularly elaborate. Quite a few writers prefer to discard the secularized sensuality of the earlier discussion on veils and instead compare veiling to religious seclusion. Here the face veil, or *dupatta*, is analogous to the nun's veil, and the community of women within the extended Indian Muslim and Hindu household to a religious *sororitas*. A late example is from Margaret Noble (1867–1911), also known as Sister Nivedita (in Swami Vivekananda's Hindu monastic community), a popularizer of Indian culture and advocate of Indian nationalism who accepted the social discipline of an orthodox Hindu woman so that she might become an effective educator of women in India. Noble is far from representative of the colonial British woman in India, especially in her enthusiasm for traditional Hindu life. Yet her idealized renditions of domestic life in Bengal, especially in *The Web of Indian Life* (1904), were acclaimed as authoritative accounts of the lives of Indian women on platforms as different in their colonial politics as the *Gentlewoman*, the *Manchester Guardian*, and the *Sunday Sun*. What appealed to reviewers and readers like the imperialist novelist Flora Annie Steel, not particularly known for her appreciation of Hindu culture, was precisely the handling of the veiled woman, whom, Steel thought, Noble "unveiled" and demythicized.[27] Noble represents the veiled Hindu mother as a virgin mother empowered by her kinsmen: husband, sons, and siblings. The sacralization of the veil and the association between it and motherhood made it acceptable to Noble and her readership. The Bengali mother, the center of domestic life, is at once a self-sacrificing madonna with child (implying a lack of sexuality and an escape from biological

---

[27] On Noble see Barbara Ramusack, "Cultural Missionaries, Maternal Imperialists, Feminist Allies, British Women Activists in India," in *Western Women and Imperialism* 124–25. On the reception of *The Web of Indian Life* see Margaret Noble, "Publisher's Note," *The Web of Indian Life* (London: W. Heinemann, 1904).

destiny) and a powerful domestic figure with social and cultural roles.

> Of the ideal woman of the religious orders the West today has very little notion. Theresa and Catherine are now but high sounding names in history; …yet without some deeper sense of *kindred* with these it will be hard to understand Hindu marriage, for the Indian bride comes to her husband such as the Western woman might enter a church.

And elsewhere:

> Yet how frail is the mother so tenderly adored. No Madonna of the Sistine Chapel can give that lofty purity of brow or delicate *untouched virginity* of look of any one of these Hindu *mother-maidens*, whose veil half covers, half reveals, as he rests on her arm, her son (emphases added).[28]

The significant point about the sacralization of the veil is neither its sentimentality nor its bathos but the fact that seclusion without its sexual aspect was acceptable to British women and seemed to them comparable to, and even compatible with, Western systems of gender segregation, especially religious ones. Roman Catholic imagery was quite common in Anglican writing and art, even outside High Church circles. The trend toward the spiritualization of Indian women characterizes even writers who condemned *purdah* as a major cause of the subjection of Indian women. Among Noble's contemporaries Josephine Butler, Kate Bushnell, and Elizabeth Andrew may be cited as examples.[29] This trend exists in earlier ethnographies and histories of India such as Charlotte Speir's (Manning) *History of Ancient India* and her *History of Medieval India*.[30] Comparable analogues between Western religious and

---

[28] Noble, *Web of Indian Life* 34–35.

[29] Ramusack, "Cultural Missionaries, Maternal Imperialists."

[30] Charlotte Speir Manning, *Life in Ancient India* (London: Smith, Elder, 1856). For the historicization of the Indian and its association with spiritual power see also Uma Chakravarti, "Whatever Happened to the Vedic Dasi? Orientalism, Nationalism and a Script for the Past," in *Recasting Women: Essays*

local usages of the veil may be found in the Middle Eastern context, in writings such as Emmeline Lott on the viceregal harem of Khedive Ismail or Mary Eliza Rogers on Muslim households in the hinterland of Palestine.[31]

The significance of the association among veiling, spiritualization, and motherhood was that the notion of freedom shifted away from the eighteenth-century idea of "positive liberties" toward the modern liberal idea of "negative freedom." "Positive liberties" are what Isaiah Berlin has described as "freedom for," that is, specific and defined liberties, whereas "negative liberty" is the "freedom from" coercion.[32] Western women are not the only writers to move from the earlier idea of specific entitlement to a sense of autonomy, for which some cite the writings of John S. Mill. But the change in their interpretation of the "liberty behind the veil" has a gender-specific angle. Western women were not physically veiled, but they were not legally free from coercion within marriage. As students of discourses of sexuality in the late Victorian and Edwardian eras have noted, the autonomy of the female body, interpreted by nineteenth-century feminists as women's right to control sexuality, was a central issue to the general public. Feminists, in particular, realized that avoidance of sex and denial of female sexuality could empower women.[33] Observers of the regulation of sexuality in the Eastern household were impressed with the oriental woman's entitlement to degrees of privacy and "freedom from" sex. As much as veiling was used to control female sexuality, it also succeeded in regulating male sensuality. As much as the veil secluded women, observers noted that it excluded men. This exclusion applied not only to strangers and not only in public but could be extended to direct kin, who were not bound by the rule of segregation. Travelers and ethnographers observed with great interest the costumes, gestures, and body language of veiled women that signified their desire for privacy and abstention from physical

---

in *Colonial Indian History*, ed. Kumkum Sangari and Sudesh Vaid (New Brunswick, NJ: Rutgers University Press, 1990) 27–88.

[31] Lott, *English Government* 2:238; Rogers, *Domestic Life in Palestine* 46.

[32] Isaiah Berlin, *Four Essays on Liberty* (Oxford: Oxford University Press, 1969), esp. "Two Concepts of Liberty" 112ff.

[33] Susan Kingsley Kent, *Sex and Suffrage in Britain, 1860–1919* (Princeton: Princeton University Press, 1989) 15–16, 35–39.

contact with male kin. Writers on the Middle Eastern *haremlik* were particularly impressed with the Ottoman custom of leaving the slippers for indoor wear (*cedik pabuk*) outside the doorway separating the *haremlik* from the *selamlik* (the public and male part of the house) to signify the desire for privacy or abstention from sex. Virtually all Western female writers noted the custom and its strict observance by women and men. And they also noted that the British married woman was not protected by custom from "intrusion" on her space and body. The addition of the slippers to the veil and the fetishization of both items of dress signify the change in the interpretation of the notion of liberty. The oriental wife or concubine was, to Western female observers, *free from* unwanted sex.[34] There is no record in the sources on India of the slipper custom, not even in accounts of Muslim households. But there is abundant reference to the myriad ways in which Indian women utilized veiling to exclude men from their company. Examples include Fanny Parks, *Wanderings of a Pilgrim in Search of the Picturesque* (1850), Lady Login's *Recollections*, Steel's *The Garden of Fidelity*, and Rosamund Napier Lady Lawrence's *Indian Embers* (her memoir of India during World War I, published in 1949).[35]

The new desexualized notion of "negative liberty," interpreted as female autonomy from sex, signified privatization. This notion made it possible for writers to detach seclusion from patriarchy and from the sexual aspects of the harem system. The very emphasis on autonomy rather than active liberty also meant that the association, so central in eighteenth-century writing on the Orient, between domestic oppression and civic and political tyranny could be severed. Male

---

[34] Examples include Pardoe, *City of the Sultan* 1:306; Agnes Dick Ramsay, *Everyday Life in Turkey: Seventeen Years of Residence* (London: Hodder and Stoughton, 1897) 108.

[35] Fanny Parks, *Wanderings of a Pilgrim in Search of the Picturesque, during Four and Twenty Years in the East; with Revelations of Life in the Zenana* (London: Pelham Richardson, 1850) 1:59–60; E. Dalhousie Login, "The Court of Oude," *Lady Login's Recollections: Court Life and Camp Life* (London: Smith, Elder, 1916) 39–48; Flora Annie Steel, *The Garden of Fidelity, Being the Autobiography of Flora Annie Steel* (London: Macmillan, 1930). Notwithstanding her general distaste for Indian sexuality, Steel on occasion spiritualized *purdah* women and emphasized the body language of exclusion.

Enlightenment writing on oriental domestic economy and politics—indeed, on domestic politics in general—hinged on the
analogue between marital (or parental) despotism and political
despotism. Witness the orientalist writings of Montesquieu,
Voltaire, and Diderot.[36] Montagu, despite her emphasis on the
oriental women's freedoms, was aware that the domestic easily
spilled over into the civic and political. But to most nineteenth-
century women writers, including writers who advocate reforms in the education of segregated women, the harem is not
a diminutive model of the oriental polity. The oriental man is
not typically perceived as a petty lascivious ruler.[37] Indeed, the
haremlik or *zenana* is regarded as a place onto itself: a female
community within a community placed outside the larger society and polity. It is a *sororitas*: self-sufficient, autonomous,
and self-ruling. To argue now that the feminotopia described
by some Western women writers had politics would be to impose current interpretations of sexual politics on the Victorian
gendered notion of autonomy and privacy. The notion of female
autonomy behind the veil was reconcilable with the Western
ideology of separate spheres and the moral superiority of
women. The first of these notions made it possible for Western
writers to stress economic and social aspects in oriental
women's lives. Production and reproduction, represented as
women's work, are depicted as the hallmarks of the veiling
zones, not a purposeless sensuality. Oriental women, regardless of class, caste, place, or legal position, are workers. But
they are first and foremost mothers.

Veiled Mothers: Segregation, Motherhood, and Power

The identification of the veil with motherhood is crucial. It
touches the very nerve of colonial ideology and the female colonial identity. As numerous students of British and continen-

---

[36] Melman, *Women's Orients* 144–45.

[37] These include Emilia Bithynia Hornby and Mary Eliza Rogers on the
Ottoman Empire and Noble on India. Critics of segregation too noted the
autonomies it offered to oriental women and stressed the moral force of the
separate female community. One example is Flora Annie Steel.

tal colonialisms have demonstrated, motherhood defined not only femininity but whiteness. White British motherhood safeguarded the physical and political integrity of the British Empire, helping to fix the ever-shifting boundaries among whites, *metis* populations, and nonwhites, between colonizers and colonized.[38] Furthermore, a maternalist language and politics were widely employed by British feminists operating in the empire, especially within the Indian context studied by Antoinette Brown and Barbara Ramusack. But motherhood was not only the British woman's vocation but a burden and a disempowerment. To guarantee British identity, the colonial family, particularly the Anglo-Indian one, was physically deconstructed, with British children habitually sent to Britain for proper education and socialization, and with the state, or class education system (the public school), stepping in, *in loco parentis*. Numerous memoirs and journals of the High Raj era focus on the powerlessness of British women, who are denied their motherhood for the empire. Subsequently, the core of their identity disintegrates and along with it the British nuclear family, which loses its children after school age.[39] Compared with the organic household of the extended Indian family, the amputated nuclear bourgeois family seemed unstable and insecure. Even to the occasional tourist, one of the most striking features of the oriental harem, whether Indian or Middle Eastern, was desegregation between mothers and children within the veiling spaces of the *haremlik* or *zenana*. This sharply distinguished the Eastern from the Western household, where children were spatially separated from mothers and fathers and shared space with working-class servants. Travelers constantly refer to the intimate contact between women in harem or *purdah* and their offspring. And not only

---

[38] Anna Davin, "Imperialism and Motherhood," *History Workshop* 5 (1978): 9–57; Jane Mackay and Pat Thane, "The Englishwoman," in *Englishness: Politics and Culture* 1880–1920, ed. Robert Colls and Philip Dodd (London and Dover, NH: Croom Helm, 1986) 191–230; Ann Stoler, "Making the Empire Respectable"; Barbara N. Ramusack, "Cultural Missionaries, Maternal Imperialists."

[39] On motherhood in this aspect see Suleri, *Rhetoric of British India*; Maud Diver, "Mother," *The Englishwoman in India* (London and Edinburgh: W. Blackwell, 1909).

were the authority and power of the veiled Indian mother admired by observers; the bond between women and children and the empowerment of mothers are extended from individual biological mothers to all women of the harem. Writers note that women gain legal status and authority within the family as "mothers of children" (*ummuweled*, a legal status throughout the Ottoman Empire, for example). Yet within the harem women raised all children jointly. The association among maternal empowerment, what I call "communal motherhood," and veiling are foregrounded in representations of the nightly ritual of putting harem children to bed. One example is Mary Eliza Rogers's description of the women and children of Mahmud Bey' Abd al Hadi household near Nablus, in the hinterland of Palestine, in her 1863 classic *Domestic Life of Palestine*. Similarly, in *The English Governess in Egypt* (1866) Emmeline Lott shrewdly reverses Montagu's earlier sexual interpretation of the entitlement given to women by the veil. In Lott's rendition, a veil covers (both physically and metaphorically) all women and children of the viceregal house of Ibrahim Pasha as they sink into sleep:
Above the entire group hung suspended an

> enormous large coloured muslin mosquito-curtain, made in the form of canopy, similar to that which is carried in Catholic countries over the heads of the dignitary ... when the host is being carried to a dying person.[40]

Passages like this, as well as general remarks on the power of veiled mothers by writers as different in their views on colonialism as Emily Pfeiffer and Margaret Noble, should be read alongside these writers' numerous references to their own disempowered and sometimes mutilated motherhood.[41] One such rendition of mutilation is Harriet Tytler's Mutiny journal, *The Englishwoman in India*. The journal has been interpreted as a document of a belligerent female colonialism, which it may

---

[40] Lott, *English Governess* 1:95–97; Rogers, *Domestic Life* 231–32.

[41] Emily Pfeiffer, "Woman's Claim," *The Contemporary Review*, February 1881, quoted in Jane Lewis, ed., *Before the Vote* (London and New York: Routledge and Kegan Paul, 1987) 381.

well be.[42] The only British woman stranded in the citadel of Delhi during the siege of Delhi in 1857, Tytler gave birth to a son whom she named Stanley Delhi Force. In a manner of speaking, he is the harbinger of the white Raj and Tytler herself the Raj's mother. Yet Tytler underwrites the discourse of white colonial motherhood by constantly reversing the role of the mother. She herself was an "abandoned" child of the Raj, and she will abandon her own children. Furthermore, she depicts a bizarre bond between mother and child. During the siege she keeps her other child busy by "scratching holes in my feet and telling her [daughter] that she must ... stop their bleeding.... No sooner did my wounds heal than she used to make them bleed again."[43] The scene reverses the Christian passion and the veiled, sacred motherhood within the *zenana*. Instead of the sacralized, Christianized Indian mother nurturing her child (and quite often British children, for Indian wet nurses were common), we have the child, who herself will be a mother, mutilating her mother. The self-sacrifice of the Indian mother empowers, whereas the British mother who sacrifices herself is disempowered.

The identification of maternal power and entitlement with forms of veiling did not preclude authority outside the harem. Writers who mapped the colonial experience of the early twentieth century, between the 1900s and the aftermath of World War I, were aware of the public and political role of the veiled wife and mother. Colonial national movements mobilized the veiled woman as a symbol of political autonomy. At the same time, oriental women could exercise the power of the veil to claim a national and feminine identity. Thus the veil as symbol of difference became even more difficult to define. Indeed, during the period of high colonialism and indigent nationalism, the veiled woman came to be an "undecidable" figure. She is

---

[42] Suleri, *Rhetoric of British India* 77–103; Patrick Brantlinger, *Rule of Darkness: British Literature and Imperialism, 1830–1914* (Ithaca and London: Cornell University Press, 1988) for a broader discussion of British women and the siege mentality of the Mutiny and post-Mutiny years. See also Jenny Sharpe, "Unspeakable Limits."

[43] Harriet Tytler, *An Englishwoman in India: The Memoirs of Harriet Tytler, 1828–1858*, ed. Anthony Sattin (Oxford: Oxford University Press, 1986) 149.

identified with the harem but not contained by it. Her authority is associated with both interiority and exteriority. And she may claim public entitlement. The association between veiling and public action may be tracked back to the Augustan model discussed above. Montagu was quite aware that Ottoman systems of gender segregation defied the categories of interiority and exteriority, not least because the Ottomans identified political authority with interiority and concealment: the Sultans themselves were concealed from the public eye. The Victorians and Edwardians too, notwithstanding their privatized notion of freedom discussed earlier, understood that the Western bourgeois private/public dichotomy did not apply to oriental societies where segregation was practiced.[44] What is novel in writing of the high colonial era is the sense that the veil was a political symbol and the veiled woman a political agent active in the public sphere. The identification of the public specifically with politics should be underlined. As many a writer noted, power could easily spill from *purdah* to the streets and marketplace and even to the sites of British colonial authority or Ottoman rule. In 1915 Grace Ellison noted the public action of Ottoman suffragists; Elizabeth Goodnow Cooper predicted in 1914 that traditionalist Egyptian women would play a role in social and political changes. Margaret Noble also saw a role for women, based on their position in the *zenana*, in the propagation of Indian nationalism. The shrewdest observations on the high visibility of veiled women come from Eileen Edna Lepoer Power (1889–1940), a prominent medievalist, ethnographer, and one of the earliest feminist historians. Both in her India travel journal and in a semiofficial report on India in 1921, Power detaches veils from sexuality and historicizes veiled women. She is aware of the limits of contemporary European notions of freedom, especially in relation to women. In her writings the authority of the veil is extended even to nonmothers and women who are "public" by virtue of their occupation and caste—Nauch women, for example (professional dancers and prostitutes). Thus she considers Nauch girls and women to be "perfectly respectable middle class" family women. Her description of the Nauch, traditionally seen in the West as sexual, reverses Flaubert's notion of the oriental prostitute's

---

[44] Melman, *Women's Orients* 148–59.

dance. Furthermore, her disruption of the Western association between veiling and subjection enables Power to appreciate the political potential of the veil:

> For inside the home the power of the mother over her sons and daughters in law is very great; the particularly deep affection of the Indian sons for the mother hidden behind the purdah and the respect with which the little family world treats her word are unguessed at by Europeans, who regard seclusion as synonymous with contempt.... But the point is that a force that is so potent while women are secluded can easily be exercised in the open.... Everyone knows how in Cairo [during the uprising of 1919] they picketed government offices during political strikes, rode up and down the town in tramcars shouting "Down with the English."[45]

Power is referring to the part played by veiled upper-class Egyptian women during the national uprising in the wake of World War I.[46]

Dialogue and Identity in the Literature on Veils

The power and appeal of the veil were not only in the challenge it presented to common Western dichotomies (subjection/freedom, private/public). Acquiring information about veiling destabilized some assumptions concerning the gathering, organization, and reconstruction of knowledge about the oriental subject. The literature on veils redefines orientalist authority, and indeed ethnographic authority, and its relation to the colonial subject. This redefinition was necessitated by the undecidability of veils. They were, as virtually all travelers

---

[45] Albert Khan Travelling Fellowships, Eileen Power, *Report to the Albert Khan Trustees* (September 1920 to September 1921) 28–29. On her cultural relativism see Billie Melman, "Gender, History and Memory: The Invention of Women's Past in the Nineteenth and Early Twentieth Centuries," *History and Memory* 5, 1 (Spring 1993): 32–33.

[46] Beth Baron, " Nationalism, War and the Egyptian Female Notables," in *Borderlines: Genders and Identities in Peace and War: 1870–1930*, ed. Billie Melman (New York and London: Routledge, 1996).

noted, never opaque but rather represented different degrees of transparency. Seeing through and beyond veils was a two-sided activity. The Western gaze was met by the veiled woman and often challenged. For the veils did not prevent those who donned them from looking "outside," discerning and criticizing the unveiled observer. Western women discovered that *purdah* allowed seeing without being seen, a position that they recognized as empowering. This sense of power is transmitted in conventional descriptions of harem or *zenana* women and Western women watching public men or public ceremonies from behind the *purdah.*

The colonial subject staring back is by no means an invention of Western women writers. As Judy Mabro has shown, Western men too were obsessed with the gaze of the veiled oriental woman.[47] In male orientalist discourse, however, this gaze has a sexual meaning and is sometimes interpreted as an invitation to sex, albeit typically vicarious . Suffice it to mention here Aziyade's eyes in Pierre Loti's novel of that name, or the look of Hejazi women in Richard Francis Burton's *Pilgrimage to Mecca and Al-Madina,* or again the ogle of prostitutes described in James Silk Buckingham's *Travels in Mesopotamia.* In most narratives by women the gaze from behind the veil is neither exclusively sensual nor dangerous but instead. inquisitive. Curiosity about cultural difference exists on both sides of the *purdah.* The veil, rather than separating the cultures, mediates a transcultural exchange that travels in three directions: the Western woman looks at the colonial subject, who returns her gaze, often with queries and comments upon the difference of Western women's morals and manners and their very strangeness. Then follows a self-scrutiny by the Westerner, who often consciously exoticizes herself. Moreover, the gaze back at Western culture and society may result in a critique on Western gender ideology and the colonization of women in the West.

The typical narrative describing the exchange of gazes and information is dialogical. Its most common literary convention is what I call "the reverse interview." Here the boundaries between the roles of the interviewer (the Western observer/eth-

---

[47] See Judy Mabro, *Veiled Half Truths: Western Travellers' Perceptions of Middle Eastern Women* (London and New York: Tauris, 1991) 42–43, 50.

nographer) and her interviewee, the veiled woman, become blurred. Their identities become difficult to define. Moreover, in the reverse interview it is not at all clear where cultural difference is located and who generates knowledge about this difference. The origins of the device as well as the role-reversal of the Western and non-Western subject may be traced back to the philosophical literature of the Enlightenment, for example Giovanni Marana and Montesquieu's "Persian" writings. Lady Montagu, too, used role-reversal in her famous description of the naked female bathers in the *hammam* at Sophia, a description that became a canonical orientalist text. The fully dressed Montagu is politely gazed at by the naked *odaliks*, who tolerate her strangeness.[48]

It was, however, only in the nineteenth century that the rhetoric of role-reversal in the colonial dialogue became conventionalized. Conventionally, the East-West conversation begins with remarks on dress, then moves to the issue of the condition of women. One example is the exchange from Fanny Parks's *Wanderings of a Pilgrim in Search of the Picturesque with Revelations on the Zenana* (1850). The peripatetic Parks is interviewed by the exiled queen of Gwalior in the queen's *zenana* at Frathighar. The topic of the exchange is the condition of Hindu and English widows, a highly politicized issue in Western discourses on Indian culture and society.

> She asked me how the English widows fare?
>
> I told her, An English lady enjoys all the luxury of her husband's house during his life; but, on his death, she was turned out of the family mansion, to make room for the heir, and pensioned off; while the old horse was allowed the run of the park, and permitted to finish his days amidst the pasture.... We spoke of the severity of the laws of England with respect to married women, how completely by law they are the slaves of their husbands, and how little hope there is of redress.

---

[48] Giovanni Paolo Marana, *Letters Writ by a Turkish Spy, who 'Liv'd Five and Forty Years Undiscovered at Paris* (London: J. Leake, 1687–99); Montesquieu, Charles-Louis de Secondat, *The Persian Letters* (1721; rpt. Harmondsworth: Penguin, 1987); Montagu, *Complete Letter* 1:314–15.

> "Who makes the law?" asked her highness. I looked at
> her with knowing she was not ignorant on the subject. "The
> men," I said. "I doubt it," said the Ba'i with an arch smile,
> "since they allow themselves only one wife." "England is so
> small," I replied, "in comparison with your ... Gwalior; if every
> man were allowed four wives, and obliged to keep them sepa-
> rate, the little island could never contain them; they would be
> obliged to keep women in vessels off the shore."[49]

It may well be argued that the dialogue was contrived by
Parks and that the queen of Gwalior is Parks's orientalist representation; that in Western colonial writing Indian women are
"spoken for" and do not speak for themselves. The point, however, is neither whether interviews like Parks's actually took
place nor whether (epistemologically) the colonial female subject "can speak." My point is that Parks and her contemporaries resort to the written in dialogue to relativize Western gender ideology. These set pieces do not reflect the cultural superiority attributed to "Western women in colonialism." Parks, for
example, argues that "The laws of England ... and the state of
slavery to which those laws degrade them, renders their lives
[the lives of Englishwomen] one perpetual sati ... from which
they have no refuge but the grave."[50] The reference to *sati*, the
self-immolation of Hindu widows by burning (a custom officially abolished by the British in 1829) is revealing. Dialogical
narratives are not limited to descriptions of encounters with
royal women (as in Parks's *Pilgrimage*, or in Lady Login's
Memoirs, or in Ann Blunt's *Pilgrimage to Nejd* and travel journal) but also appear in accounts of women of the lower classes
and castes. True, some British feminists do construct an image
of lower-caste Indian women as mute victims who cannot
speak for themselves. Josephine Butler's placing of Indian
prostitutes "somewhere between the Martyr Saints and the
tortured 'friend of man', the noble dog," is an example of such
objectification.[51] But as illustrated by Eileen Power's descrip-

---

[49] Parks, *Wanderings of a Pilgrim* 2:8–9.

[50] Parks, *Wanderings of a Pilgrim* 2:420.

[51] Quoted in Antoinette Burton, "The White Women's Burden: British
Feminists and the Indian Woman's Question," in *Western Women and Imperialism* 144.

tion of Nauch women, discussed above, nonabolitionist writing on lower-caste women and even on Nauch reads quite differently from the Victorian feminist literature. Overall, the use of dialogue and cross-cultural comparison serves to challenge dominant Western cultural assumptions about women and female sexuality. Above all, the dialogue destabilizes the privileged position of the Western interviewer, both as a source of ethnographic knowledge and as an unveiled, apparently free and mobile woman. As Mary Eliza Rogers remarks after describing an interview in which the women of the Hadi clan, near Nablus in Palestine, query her about the implications of Britain's having a "sultana"—Queen Victoria—for the position of British women: she might have "unwittingly given them the idea that women in England rule."[52]

The "Double Potential" of Veils:
Veiling and Female Sexuality in Western Discourses

The veil was such a prevalent and forceful metaphor for the similarities between the East and the West because it was a widely available figure in Western discourse on women and sexuality. The veiling and concealment of the female body had been tropes in this discourse before the advent of modern colonialism and had meanings that stretched beyond the colonial situation. These meanings touched on the indefinite status of femininity and female sexuality in Western culture.

Rather than providing a genealogy of veil metaphors used in the West, I will discuss the main attributes of these metaphors and examine them in the colonial and orientalist context. It is, however, important to stress at the outset the religious origin of the veil as an ambivalent symbol of female power. As argued above, this symbol is central to Christian representations of femininity, as well as to the Pauline ideology of gender that remained dominant after the Reformation even in Protestant cultures. According to Saint Paul, a woman can prophesy only when her head is veiled, because man's head represents the spirit in Christ whereas woman's is associated

---

[52] Mary Eliza Rogers, *Domestic Life in Palestine* 223.

with flesh and the body—that is, with sexuality.[53] And, indeed, in religious discourse the veil symbolized both sexuality and sexual purity, along with the authority this purity generates. The nun, Christ's bride, donned the bride's veil but was not sexual. Interwoven with the symbolism of sex and chastity is that of death: Christ's bride is dead to the world. And veils were donned in, and signified, mourning. The nun's veil remained a powerful metaphor after secularization. I use this last term in its commonly accepted sense, denoting the breaking of the grip of institutional religion over the life of individuals and the privatization of religion and its "takeover" by groups outside the Church.

Beginning with the Enlightenment, the veil underwent processes of desacralization. It still retained its associations with purity and virginity, and the authority invested in both, but, as Eve Sedgwick, Sandra Gilbert, and Susan Gubar have remarked, the veil became suffused with sexuality and was increasingly eroticized. At the same time veiling and the ability to unveil, or see through translucent cloths, covers, and surfaces, was increasingly associated with the uncovering of identity or truth.[54] This association particularly characterized the Gothic novel, where the veil is quite central, and Romantic literature. As Gilbert and Gubar have pointed out, in both traditions the veil held out "the mystery of imminent revelation, the promise or the threat that one might see, hear or even feel through [it]."[55]

Yet, as virtually all students of the veil and unveiling in late eighteenth- and nineteenth-century literary traditions have remarked, the ambiguity and fluidity of the veil as an emblem of a mystery, or an obscure potential, was also identified with women as the "repository of mysterious otherness." In

---

[53] 11 Corinthians 11.

[54] Eve Kosofsky Sedgwick, "The Character of the Veil: Imagery of the Surface in the Gothic Novel," *The Coherence of Gothic Conventions* (New York and London: Methuen, 1986) 140–75; Sandra Gilbert and Susan Gubar, "Made Keen by Loss: George Eliot's Veiled Vision," *The Mad Woman in the Attic: The Woman Writer and the Nineteenth-Century Literary Imagination* (New Haven and London: Yale University Press, 1979) 443–78; Elaine Showalter, *Sexual Anarchy: Gender and Culture at the Fin-de Siecle* (Harmondsworth: Penguin, 1990) 144–69. See also Jordanova, *Sexual Vision* 87–111.

[55] Gilbert and Gubar, *Madwoman in the Attic* 468–69.

literary and pictorial representations, as well as in scientific discourses examined by Ludmilla Jordanova, the veiled female became a site of alterity. Characteristically, the sexual powers of this figure were perceived to be lethal to men.[56] The linkage of veiling with a sexuality that controls reproduction and death—hence the danger of the veiled female—penetrated the domestic novel as well as popular adventure literature. One example is Rider Haggard's description, in his immensely influential 1883 novel *She*, of the draped statue surrounded by mummified, embalmed bodies at the entrance to Kor. The inscription on the statue reads: "Behold! there is no man born of a woman who may draw the veil and live."[57]

Thus in secular discourse beginning with the Enlightenment, the figure of the veiled woman was gradually transformed from an ambiguous symbol of female empowerment to a site of alterity. This figure increasingly came to be the "other" of the artist, writer, or male voyeur. The colonial female literature on veils reverses this cultural trend toward "othering." And it is precisely this reversal of a culturally available image that makes the colonial literature on veils crucial for our comprehension of identity formation during the colonial era. Women writers drew on the ambiguity of the veil in Western traditions, on its double potential: as a signifier of sexuality and purity, powerlessness and authority, of (feminine) nature and the social sphere. They developed this ambiguity and the undecidability of veils into a symbol of similarities between Western and Eastern gender systems and sexualities. Moreover, these writers fell back on the religious paradigm. For during the colonial era, when interest in gender segregation increased, the Christian origins of Eastern veiling were widely acknowledged. The better informed travelers were aware that oriental veiling and the harem originated not in Islam but in the Christian East, particularly in the Byzantine system of *gynecea* (or separation between genders).[58] As the many ana-

---

[56] Gilbert and Gubar, *Madwoman in the Attic* 471; Jordanova, *Sexual Visions* 88–111.

[57] Quoted in Showalter, *Sexual Anarchy* 144.

[58] Barnette Miller, *Beyond the Sublime Porte* (New Haven: Yale University Press, 1931) 91–92; Ellen Chennells, *Recollections of an Egyptian Princess, by Her English Governess* (Edinburgh: W. Blackwood, 1893) 1:72–73.

logues with religious sorority cited above suggest, women travelers anglicized and evangelicized the metaphor of the veil to fit it to middle-class practical religion.

To conclude, Western women represented veils and the harem system as they saw them. In that sense their geography of the East is as imaginary as the geography of the male orientalists. The little written evidence that we now have—from Middle Eastern women like Huda Sh'rawi, Malek Hifni Nasif, Nabawiya Musa, Zaynab Fawaz, and Seniha Sultan; autobiographies of Westernized women like Sayyida Salme/Emily Reute; as well as the writings of Indian (mostly Bengali) women—suggests these women's experience of veiling to be quite different.[59] But this essay is about Western women seeing veils, about the ways in which they represented the colonial situation and constructed a colonialist female identity.

This colonial seeing was a dynamic activity. It involved actual seeing—that is, participant observation of the life of Eastern women—cross-cultural comparison, and a critical self-examination of Western gender systems and ideologies of inequality. Often Western women developed a sense of gender solidarity that cut across religion, culture, and race.

Yet we should be wary of perceiving this dynamics as a linear change. As the evidence I have gathered suggests, there are breaks between the eighteenth-century model as instanced by Lady Montagu and the Victorian model, as well as between the Victorian and early twentieth century ones. Most significant is the move, in the nineteenth century, from a sexualized to a desexualized interpretation of the veil. This move reverses dominant literary, scientific, and orientalist discourses on the veiled woman. Another change concerns the politicization of veils in the era of high colonialism, especially manifest in writings on India. Common to all the writings discussed here, regardless of when they were produced or what part of the British Empire they describe, is the sense of likeness between women of different cultures. It is important to note, however,

---

[59] For theses and other sources see: Mervat Hatem, "Through Each Other's Eyes: Egyptian, Levantine-Egyptian and European Women's Images of Themselves and of Each Other (1862–1900)," *Women's Studies International Forum* 12, 2 (1989): 183–98; Dipesh Chakrabarty, "Who Speaks the Indian Pasts?" in *The New Historicism Reader*, ed. Aram Veeser (New York and London: Routledge, 1994) 342–70.

that despite the Western writers' emphasis on a cross-cultural experience of gendered inequality, they historicize the veiled woman and transform her from the West's other into a historical and changing subject. The central feature of the literature on veils is the dissolution of the essentialized, feminine Orient. Moreover, by looking at, through, and beyond veils, Western women writers destabilize the binary model of the colonial situation represented by Flaubert's dance of the veil, which was my starting point. In the women's renditions discussed here, the veil is not the emblem of a sharply categorized other. Veiling and segregation defy categorization. As undecidables, they undercut the West/East dichotomy. They hold the potential of power, public action, and autonomy from sex. Here the veil is perceived not as a divide between veiled and unveiled women but as a moving contact zone between spaces: interior and exterior, personal and political, Eastern and Western. It may not be identified as "oriental" because it is also prevalent in the West. The veil is transcultural in the sense of this prevalence in most cultures but also because it mediates across cultures. Furthermore, Western women's responsiveness to this transcultural aspect makes it difficult for them to construct their identity as colonists by simply pitting it against the identity of a nonwhite female colonial subject. As the sections on representations of female sorority and motherhood show, cross-cultural comparison dissolves two components in the identity of the colonial British woman: motherhood as the source of Western female authority and the notion of the white woman's freedom. In the domestic colonial ideology there are no clear notions of discrete geographical and cultural identities that are distinctly "Western" or "Eastern." The literature on veils reveals that the very notion of the other, or fixation on alterity as the basis for the construction of a discrete Western identity, is unworkable and probably unhistorical. "t'is with the Turkish Ladies as t'is with us," wrote Mary Wortley Montagu on 17 April 1717. "Mankind do not differ so widely as the voyage writers would make them believe."[60]

---

[60] Montagu, *Complete Letters* 1:329.

AUTOCARTOGRAPHY:
The Case of Palestine, Michigan

Anton Shammas

> A common experience, resulting in a common confusion. A.
> has to transact important business with B. in H.
> —Kafka, "A Common Confusion"

I

It all started when A. wanted to leave Michigan and go
home to Palestine. And it was painfully clear to her: this was
not about going back *somewhere* but, rather, about going
home. The difference being as simple as this: you go back to
some place that you have lived in in the past, but you go home
to a place that even though you may have never seen in your
life, still, it is as if you had; a place that is the other, deep end
of that pool of your created, acquired, and invented memories.
Most people—especially American writers of fiction—would tell
you that going home is virtually impossible. And you know
perfectly well that we don't ever leave home—we simply drag it
behind us wherever we go, walls, roof, and all. Home—it is
probably the one single thing we don't leave home without; and
that would explain the rumbling in our wake.

So A. wanted to go home to Palestine. The problem was—
outside her imagined memories and imagined space, as created
by her Palestinian father in the postnostalgic world of Dearborn, Michigan—there was, there is, no Palestine to go to. The
father belonged to those eight hundred thousand Palestinians
who had been deterritorialized with the establishment of the
state of Israel. Simply put, this meant that he'd become a Palestinian refugee after the Big Bang of 1948 and the scattering
of the Palestinians upon the face of all the earth, as a biblical
writer would have it. And after a decade in one of the refugee
camps in Lebanon, he made it to Dearborn, Michigan, joining
some distant cousins of Lebanese descent. And whenever he

would reminisce about his Galilean home village in front of his new in-laws, those cousins would ruthlessly remind him of what other Palestinians, commenting on their tragedy, would usually say: namely *rahat Falasteen*, meaning "Palestine is gone." True, the territory did not vanish in 1948, but theirs did, and it was renamed, thus cut from under their feet, hence gone. So there was no home to go to in the first place.

But A. wanted to go home to Palestine. And besides the geographical problem, or the absence thereof, there was the classic American problem of PR—how would one attractively package for the benefit of one's American friends the following twofold problem of pure common sense? First, there's no place to go to, there's no Palestine. Of course, there is the Palestine of Sunday schools, the land endearingly called the Holy Land. So *that* was there all right, in the geography of the biblical mind, but the Palestine of the father was gone, and gone was its holy spirit for him and for his American-born daughter. Second, up till now, everyone has had every reason to believe that home was here, in Motown, Michigan, U.S.A.; so what's the deal with this Palestine? That said, is a woman *supposed* to go home? Women, certainly according to the father's codes of decorum, are supposed to create their own homes, within the male domain; they are not supposed to *go* anywhere. Men do that. Men do that in fiction (American or otherwise); men do that in reality. Women are simply those who follow those men who want to go home.

A. had answers to none of the above. Moreover, she was soon to find out that the most difficult part of all was to explain to an American friend, whose geography, from coast to coast, is a five-hour flight, that this ten-minute Palestine of the mind, from the Jordan to the sea, if looked up on the map, would fall short even of filling up Lake Michigan.

II

Size *does* matter; and it is a question of bread and butter, literally.

If you are an American, and you think of yourself as such, then take a slice of bread, the size of your standard AAA map of the U.S.A., and spread over it a small lump of butter, the

size of what you would think of as your identity. You will see
that the spread is embarrassingly thin and that certain parts
of certain states are not buttered at all. (Incidentally, *butter*
could sometimes mean "to apply a liquefied bonding material
to a piece or area, as mortar to a course of bricks."[1] Mortar
would remind one, of course, of the biblical writer of the Babel
story.) Now, apply the same amount of butter just to Lake
Michigan, and you will see how *thick*, in comparison, is the
Palestinian identity or—for that matter—the identity of those
who come from even a smaller place than the Palestine that is
gone.

The postcolonial, postcommunist, post-nation-state, postmodern world has shown us, quite recently, that the smaller
the territory, the more passionate and consuming, or more fanatic and lethal, the nationalism that comes with it, or works
against it, depending on which side you are on. The tiny little
state of Lebanon is a perfect example for that.

When I think of a state, I think that what I have in mind,
first of all, is the geographic shape of that state as it was
drawn by the cartographers. I see brown mountains getting
darker toward the top, green for meadows, blue for water,
black tiny circles for towns and cities, and *broken* lines for
borders. But for the Muslim Bosnian soldier, I imagine, his is
not the map of Bosnia, or even that of his hometown, or even
his street; rather, it's the floor plan of his house in Sarajevo.
And if pushed to a corner, he'd admit that it's even smaller
than that: it's the map of a favorite room in that house. And
now that the house is gone, it's probably the remembered room
that he is fighting for, the room whose lingering space defines
that fragile presence that we call identity, forever humming in
our internal ear, like the sound that film editors add to the
special-effects track in order to give a touch of reality to a
scene—the noise that is referred to in the cutting room as
"room tone."

In a certain way, identity, then, is a noise (forget about
butter, and think of William Paulson's book on the *Noise of
Culture*), a noise that interferes with the messages that we
transmit and receive. It's hardly audible to the others, but we
hear it loud and clear. Yet it's not the kind of noise that both-
ers us; on the contrary, it gives us a sense of reality, a meas-

---

[1] *Random House Dictionary of the English Language*, 2nd ed.

ure of empowerment; it adds "room tone" to the otherwise hy-per-real world around us. Some may enjoy listening to it more than others; some may tune in to it more than the others would care to. And some play it so loudly just for the fun of it or in order to make the others listen; but the others usually do not and would not listen.

The Palestinian noise of identity has been muffled for nearly a century. It's only recently that it has become audible enough for the Palestinian case to be listened to, to be ad-dressed. From a Palestinian point of view, this has been a century of major disasters. First, it was the noise of absence, in the famous Zionist slogan, "Land without a people to a peo-ple without a land." Or the noise of Caliban in Herzl's *Juden-staat* : "We shall form part of Europe's fortified wall against Asia, and fulfill the role of cultural vanguard facing the bar-barians." (Traveling in Palestine, with "the innocents abroad," in September of 1867, Mark Twain wrote to the *Daily Alta Cali-fornia* about "dismal, desolate, smileless Palestine, ... the most hopeless, dreary, heartbroken piece of territory out of Ari-zona.") Then Lord Balfour, in 1917, told the Zionist Federation that "His Majesty's government view with favor the establish-ment in Palestine of a national home for the Jewish people." The displacement bomb started ticking then, and the worst was yet to come. And it did, in different colors and shades, some of which were self-inflicted. But above all, since World War II, the Palestinian voice was muffled because it always had to pass through that manmade black hole of the Holocaust, and so it was almost never heard; till 1987.

And that's when A. first thought of going home to Pales-tine.

III

For A.'s grandmother, an old refugee in Lebanon, Palestine is no more than a lemon tree in the backyard of the house she left in Jafa, or Yafa, as she would call it. Not even a room, not even the façade of a house, but just a tree in the backyard, hidden away from the bustle of main street politics; the tree under whose shadow she always imagines herself sitting, dreaming away her days. Say Palestine to her, and all she sees is herself, as she is now, not the young woman she was, sitting under that tree, breathing in the scent of its leaves and its early flowers.

Yafa was renamed as Yafo, and the lemon tree is gone from that backyard, but it's so deep-rooted in her mind, its fragrance so overwhelming, that it's hard to imagine what that famous handshake on the South Lawn of the White House could have meant to her. It is hard to imagine any connection between these two images that were mutually superimposed: the lemon tree of memories and the CNN-made image of the two political leaders, representing Yafa and Yafo, respectively, hoping, with a semi-nudged handshake, to draw some defining lines between the one homeland and the two states, totally leaving out the sweet 'n sour question of lemon trees.

The grandmother, then, thinks lemon—a very particular tree, totally outside the language of politics, or the language of history, and certainly outside the language of historiography that attempts to deal with her plight. And that tree is part of her plight—the impossibility of forgetting that tree, of letting it slip away, because if she did—as she believes—her whole life would slip away, her whole self, what she has been, what she is, and what she will ever be.

Her Dearbornian son, on the other hand, remembers that tree pretty well, but he has always mocked his mother's idea of a homeland: "*Rahat Falasteen*, Palestine is gone," he would say, "the whole country is gone, and she mourns her lemon tree!"

A. first heard about that tree when she was twelve, during her only visit with her grandmother in Lebanon. Her Arabic was better then, and she tried hard to imagine a backyard in Yafa, a place she had never been to, and a lemon tree in the middle of that backyard, just to make her grandmother happy and proud of her. Then, later, the image faded away with the Michigan years, but the Arabic word, *lamoon*, seemed to have found refuge inside A.'s personal diction, thus letting the distant past of her grandmother permeate her own present, the present that seemingly had nothing to do with that past. And like the persistent grains in a giant, one-way sandglass, ever flowing through the narrow opening, Palestine of the past kept invading the Dearborn present, grain by grain, through the narrow opening of a single word: *lamoon*.

It was an imagined geography, created by personal, oral histories and images that were conjured up while looking at the Michigan landscape. The narrow alleys of Yafa, as the grandmother imagined them, became long, two-lane streets and avenues in A.'s dreams, and she would walk down the street of her grandmother's house, under the falling, colorful leaves of the Indian summer, and could almost see the lemon tree in the backyard and could almost fill her lungs with its fragrance. But deep down she knew that something was wrong, that these images belonged to her immediate present, that the language she spoke was not the language of that tree, and that this language of hers would never be able to contain, let alone transmit, her grandmother's memories. And that's when she would realize, for a brief moment of countergrace, that—as the Lebanese novelist Elias Khoury once wrote—"one does not *return* to Palestine, one should simply *go*," and if that is impossible, one should, maybe, create one's own Palestine.

IV

K. called that night from Ann Arbor, Michigan. She asked if A. had seen the current issue of *Harper's Magazine*. "No," she said. "Well," K. said, "I think I have an ingenious solution for your problem." (K., who was very much in love with her initial, was also very partial to words like "ingenious.") She had read in the *Harper's Index* (November 1993) that the number of Palestinians worldwide, per square mile in the West Bank and the Gaza Strip, is 2,503, while the number of Japanese per square mile of Japan is 817. "That's thick," K. added, "that's very thick." Then there was a dramatic pause.

"But what's your ingenious solution?" A. finally asked.

K. told her that she had been browsing through the Gopher server of MTS that day, looking for a particular bit of information, when, by sheer chance, she hit the General Reference Resources and wandered into the U.S. Geographic Database; at the prompt "words to search for" she remembered A. and decided to look for Palestine for her, a Plan-B Palestine of sorts. And much to her amazement she found more than fifteen different Palestines, scattered all over the U.S. Palestines in Illinois, Ohio, Arizona, Tennessee, Mississippi, Pennsylvania,

Alabama, Oregon, Connecticut, North Carolina, Texas, West Virginia, Indiana, and, yes, Michigan! "Now," K. said, "since you have been telling us that you intend to go home to Palestine, and since we hate to see you go, I found an ingenious way for you to go to Palestine without even crossing the state border. Isn't that cool?"

There was another pause, and then A. laughed, though she didn't know why. She had always admired K.'s practical mind, K.'s tight-rope walking between the dead-serious and the hilarious, K.'s American way of finding an instant American solution for every possible non-American problem. It's a remarkable goof, A. thought, but the frightening thing about it is that it is far too practical to be plausible; the frightening thing about it is that it brings up a solid point to reflect upon.

V

In his essay, "The Work of Art in the Age of Mechanical Reproduction," Walter Benjamin wrote:

> The whole sphere of authenticity is outside technical—and of course not only technical—reproducibility.... The authenticity of a thing is the essence of all that is transmissible from its beginning, ranging from its substantive duration to its testimony to the history which it has experienced.... [T]hat which withers in the age of mechanical reproduction is the aura of the work of art. This is a symptomatic process whose significance points beyond the realm of art. One might generalize by saying: the technique of reproduction detaches the reproduced object from the domain of tradition. By making many reproductions it substitutes a plurality of copies for a unique existence.[2]

Has Palestine lost its "aura" then, its unique existence, its authenticity?

This question assumes that the American Palestines are exact replicas of the original, a Disney life-size imitation of

---

[2] Walter Benjamin, *Illuminations: Essays and Reflections*, ed. Hannah Arendt, trans. Harry Zohn (New York: Schocken Books, 1969) 220–21.

sorts, floating, say, in Lake Michigan. But, alas, this is not the case. Yet, A. thought, imagine this: a Palestinian refugee who makes Palestine, Michigan, her home—hasn't she, in a way, "returned" to Palestine? Hasn't she, in a way, blown the whole concept of displacement from within? Hasn't she, by this simple twist of fate, actually won the case in the most unexpected manner?

Benjamin would argue that "[t]he whole sphere of authenticity is outside technical—and of course not only technical—reproducibility." But America has solved more complicated problems than this one. Imagine, then, A. drawing her own internal map of return and going *home* to Palestine but this time in Michigan, the Palestine that is on 45° latitude by 87° longitude, in the most southwestern tip of the Upper Peninsula, in a county called Menominee. And imagine her planting a lemon tree in her backyard, a unique, single reproduction of that authentic, irreproducible tree in Yafa, with an aura of its own. And imagine other members of her extended family, driving all the way to the Upper Peninsula, in a caravan of pickup trucks that are loaded with their worldly Palestinian goods, among which are some of the same things they took with them forty-six years ago, when they were driven out of Yafa. They will settle in Palestine, Michigan, buy lands, build houses, plant trees, raise children, have dreams, write letters and send them out to their relatives who are scattered upon the face of all the earth, with a return address that reads, say:

46 Yafa Street
Palestine, MI 26109

Just imagine; because now that A. has found her own Palestine, she can take her time—there's no rush to go home anymore.

Postscript

Late in the summer of 1994, almost a year after writing the story of A., a friend who teaches Middle Eastern studies at Dartmouth College, and had read the story, told me in an e-mail message that she had just come across a book entitled

Jewish Agricultural Utopias in America, 1880–1910, in which there was a chapter dedicated to "Palestine, Michigan." She said she would mail me a photocopy and that I'd get a kick out of it.

I was struck dumb: could it be that I had sent away A.'s extended family all the way up north to the Upper Peninsula only to find out that—as the cliché goes—history repeats itself? Could it be that Palestine—the name, the geography, the space—is forever bound to be in a bitter, bloody dispute between consecutive generations of Jews and Palestinians, no matter where they go? Could it be that I have, inadvertently, trapped my A. within a Borgesian self-referential loop?

I looked for the book in the Graduate Library, but it was checked out. ("There's somebody out there," I thought to myself, "who knows about my own subject more than I do!") Then, long, impatient days later, the photocopy arrived, and I was dying to find out where I had gone wrong:

> The period of the 1880s saw two streams of emigration from Eastern Europe: one to North America; the other, much more modest in size, to Ottoman Palestine.... One minuscule group in America tried to combine its religious love for Zion with a desire to root itself in American soil. Its members aspired to create a "new Zion in Free America." Appropriately their venture was termed "Palestine." It took place in Michigan in the last decade of the nineteenth century.[3]

I stopped after the first paragraph, returned the photocopy back into the envelope, and put it away. My mistake—I started blaming myself—was that I'd never done any further research on my Palestine, Michigan, beyond what my modem had offered me. This was, apparently, the same mistake that the modemless founders of Zionism had made one hundred years ago: "A land without a people to a people without a land," as their slogan went.

Then I decided to break the spell and went back to read the whole story. Little by little the geographic mystery began to unravel, and it became clearer—as I became slightly disappointed because, let's face it, it would have made a better story

---

[3] Uri D. Herscher, *Jewish Agricultural Utopias in America, 1880–1910* (Detroit: Wayne State University Press, 1981) 61.

if we were talking about the same Palestine—that "my" Palestine was saved: the Palestine established by the East European Jewish settlers in the mid 1880s was near the hamlet known by the picturesque name of Bad Axe, some fifty miles east of Bay City. But unlike the other settlements in the "original," far-away Palestine, this one hardly lasted for a decade, because of agricultural inexperience, harsh conditions, and impatient creditors.

Much as I was relieved to find out that the journey to the Upper Peninsula was nonetheless worth the trouble, still, imagined images of the Bad Axe Palestinians kept haunting me. And I think their shattered geography will become a part of A.'s identity, their splintered dreams a part of her past.

I *know* they are a part of mine.

Notes on Contributors

Arjun Appadurai is Director of the Chicago Humanities Institute at the University of Chicago. He is the Barbara E. and Richard J. Franke Professor in the Humanities and teaches in the departments of Anthropology and South Asian Languages and Civilizations. His major publications include *Worship and Conflict under Colonial Rule* (1981), *The Social Life of Things* (edited 1986), *Gender, Genre and Power* (coedited 1991), and *Modernity at Large: Cultural Dimensions of Globalization* (forthcoming 1996). He is currently working on a book about territorial ideologies.

Joseph A. Boone is Associate Professor of English at the University of Southern California, where he teaches courses in the novel and in gay and gender studies. He is the author of *Tradition Counter Tradition: Love and the Form of Fiction* (1987) and the coeditor of *Engendering Men: The Question of Male Feminist Criticism* (1990). Currently completing a book on issues of sexuality and narrative in modernist fiction, from which this essay is excerpted, he is the recipient of a 1995–96 Guggenheim Fellowship for a new project on the homoerotics of orientalism.

Kenrick Ian Grandison is Assistant Professor of Landscape Architecture at the University of Michigan, Ann Arbor. He has been studying the African-American experience of and contribution to the American landscape. He is currently documenting the landscape history of the campus of Tuskegee University, Alabama. His forthcoming article, "From Plantation to Campus: Progress, Community, and the Lay of the Land in Shaping the Early Tuskegee," is scheduled to appear in the Spring 1996 issue of *Landscape Journal.*

Pieter M. Judson joined the history faculty of Swarthmore College in 1992. He is the author of a study of European liberalism and nationalism entitled *Exclusive Revolutionaries: Liberal Politics and National Identity in the Habsburg Monarchy, 1848–1914*, to be published by the University of Michigan Press. In addition he has authored several articles that explore the racial, gender, and sexual dimensions of ethnic identities in the Habsburg Monarchy. He is currently completing a book that examines the reproduction of colonial and metropolitan social relations in nineteenth- and twentieth-century Central Europe.

Rashid I. Khalidi teaches Middle Eastern history at the University of Chicago, where he is Director of the Center for Middle Eastern Studies. He is past President of the Middle East Studies Association, author of *British Policy towards Syria and Palestine, 1905–1914* (1980) and *Under Siege: PLO Decision-Making during the 1982 War* (1986), and coeditor of *Palestine and the Gulf* (1982) and *The Origins of Arab Nationalism* (1991). He was an advisor to the Palestinian delegation to the Madrid and Washington negotiations from October 1991 until June 1993. He is currently finishing a book on the emergence of Palestinian national identity.

Herman Lebovics is Professor of History at the State University of New York at Stony Brook. He chairs the New York Area French History Seminar. He is author most recently of *True France: The Wars over Cultural Identity, 1900–1945* (1992). The essay in this volume draws from a new study in progress on the beginnings of France's first ministry of culture. He will work on the book in 1995–96 as a Fellow of the Woodrow Wilson Center in Washington, D.C.

Mark Liechty is Assistant Professor in the Department of Anthropology at the University of California, Santa Barbara. He is working on a book on mass media and consumer culture in Nepal.

Billie Melman is Associate Professor of History at Tel-Aviv University. She is author of *Women and the Popular Imagination in the Twenties* (1988) and *Women's Orients: English Women and the Middle East, 1718–1914: Sexuality, Religion and Work* (1992; second, enlarged edition, forthcoming 1995). She is currently editing an anthology on gender and the First World War, *Borderlines: Genders and Identities in Peace and War (1880–1930)*, forthcoming from Routledge (1996). She has written on colonialism and gender, nationalism and feminist historiography.

Achille Mbembe teaches history at the University of Pennsylvania. He has written on democracy and the postcolonial state in Africa. He is the author, among other books, of *Afriques indociles. Christianisme, pouvoir et Etat en société postcoloniale* (1988).

Nuala Ní Dhomhnaill, born of Irish-speaking parents in Lancashire in 1952, was brought up in the Dingle Gaeltacht and in Nenagh, Co. Tipperary. Author of six volumes of poetry, most recently *The Astrakhan Cloak* (1992), she is working now on a new volume, *Cead Aighnis*. Ní Dhomhnaill also writes in Irish and has written two screenplays and four plays for children. Winner of many awards, including the American Ireland Fund Literature Prize in 1991, she has traveled extensively to lecture and give poetry readings in Ireland, England, Turkey, Canada, and the United States.

Janet Roitman is currently a Ph.D. candidate at the University of Pennsylvania. She recently returned from a two-year stay in Northern Cameroon, where she conducted research on representations of economic organization and paradigms of social order. Her study, "Objects of the Economy and the Language of Politics," was completed under the auspices of the Social Sciences Research Council, MacArthur Foundation Program on Peace and Security. Her articles have appeared in the *Journal of Modern African Studies, Critique of Anthropology*, and *Cahiers d'Etudes Africaines*.

Saskia Sassen is Professor of Urban Planning and also serves on the faculty of the School of Public and International Affairs at Columbia University. Her books are *The Mobility of Labor and Capital* (1988), *The Global City: New York, London, Tokyo* (1991), and the just-published *Cities in a World Economy* (1994). A new book, *Immigrants and Refugees: A European Dilemma?*, will be published in 1996 with Fischer Verlag in Frankfurt, and she is currently completing a book for Twentieth Century Fund, *Immigration Policy in a World Economy*. She has begun a new five-year project, the first phase of which will be the 1995 Leonard Hastings Schoff Memorial Lectures at Columbia University, to be published by Columbia University Press in 1996 as *On Governance in the Global Economy*.

Anton Shammas is a Palestinian novelist and essayist who writes in Hebrew and English. His first novel, *Arabesques*, was chosen by the editors of the *New York Times Book Review* as one of the best seven fiction books of 1988. A winner of a Whiting Writer's Award and a Lila Wallace–Reader's Digest Writers' Award, he has published essays in *Harper's*, *The New York Review of Books*, and *The New York Times Magazine*. He has been affiliated with the University of Michigan since 1987.

Michael Watts lives in San Francisco and teaches at the University of California, Berkeley, where he is Director of the Institute of International Studies and Professor of Geography and Development Studies. Trained as a geographer at the University of London and the University of Michigan, he has written widely on the political economy of West Africa and on agrarian transitions to capitalism. He is currently working with Allen Pred on a sequel to his book *Reworking Modernity* (1992) and on a piece on the Brazilian photographer Sebastiano Salgado for the journal *Transition*.

Bernard Williams is White's Professor of Moral Philosophy at Oxford and Deutsch Professor of Philosophy at the University of California, Berkeley. His principal contributions to philosophy have been in ethics, but he has also written on personal identity, the theory of knowledge, and the history of philosophy. He was chairman of a British government Committee on Obscenity and Film Censorship, which reported in 1979. He is also a Fellow of the British Academy. His publications include *Problems of the Self* (1973), *Moral Luck* (1981), *Ethics and the Limits of Philosophy* (1985), *Shame and Necessity* (1993), and *Making Sense of Humanity* (1995).

Victoria W. Wolcott recently completed her Ph.D. in history at the University of Michigan. Her dissertation, "Discourses of Respectability: African-American Women and the Politics of Identity in Inter-War Detroit," is a study of the lives and labor of the African-American women who migrated to Detroit in the first decades of the twentieth century.

Gwendolyn Wright is Professor in Columbia's Graduate School of Architecture, Planning, and Preservation, with joint appointments in the departments of History and Art History.

From 1988 to 1992 she directed the Buell Center for the Study of American Architecture at Columbia. Her books include *Moralism and the Model Home* (1985); *Domestic Architecture and Cultural Conflict in Chicago, 1873–1913* (1980), *Building the Dream: A Social History of Housing in America* (1981), and most recently, *The Politics of Design in French Colonial Urbanism* (1991).